the Unofficial Guide to PCs

T. J. Lee
Lee Hudspeth
Dan Butler

que

201 West 103r[illegible] [illegible]290

Unofficial Guide to PCs

International Standard Book Number: 0-7897-1797-2

Library of Congress Catalog Card Number: 98-86230

Printed in the United States of America

First Printing: June 1999

01 00 99 4 3 2 1

Trademarks

Warning and Disclaimer

Executive Editor
Angela Wethington

Acquisitions Editor
Stephanie McComb

Development Editor
Nicholas J. Goetz

Managing Editor
Thomas F. Hayes

Project Editor
Sossity Smith

Copy Editor
Barbara Hacha

Indexer
Mary Gammons

Proofreader
Tricia Sterling

Technical Editor
Kent Easley

Copy Writer
Eric Borgert

Layout Technician
Eric S. Miller

Contents at a Glance

Contents

Lee Hudspeth and T.J. Lee

Together Lee and T. J. are founders of PRIME Consulting Group, Inc. (`www.primeconsulting.com`), a computer consulting firm based in Los Angeles. Their background in computer publications is extensive. They are authors of seven books (this being the seventh), among them the *Office Annoyances* book series covering Microsoft Office 97, Excel 97, Outlook, and Word 97. They are Publishers of the free electronic newsletter *The Naked PC* ("what you need to know about all things PC" at `www.thenakedpc.com`), regular contributors to *PC Computing* magazine, and Senior Contributing editors at *Office Computing* magazine. Lee and T.J. were inaugural members of Microsoft's Consultant Relations Program that evolved into Microsoft's Solution Provider program, of which PRIME Consulting Group was an original member.

Both fellows are outstanding lecturers and trainers (available for company picnics, weddings, and smokers), having written countless courseware packages and manuals, co-authored the Microsoft Education Services course on Developing Applications in Word, and taught and lectured for thousands of developers and end users from Maine to Australia. Their company has been publishing a series of Microsoft Office add-ins (PRIME for Excel and PRIME for Word) since before Office was Office, and is a Microsoft Office Update Vendor Program Partner.

Lee's background is in operations research, programming, financial analysis, and marketing analysis (formerly with Unocal Corporation). He's been involved in systems development and consulting since 1981, and is a graduate of the University of Southern California's Business School. He's been a Microsoft Most Valuable Professional, is a certified Microsoft trainer, and surfs.

T.J. has a background as a Certified Public Accountant, and has done computer and management consulting for over a decade. He's a Microsoft Certified Product Specialist, a certified Microsoft trainer, and long rumored to be Tom Hanks' stunt double.

Dan Butler

Dan Butler is the Webmaster for Union Pacific Resources Group, Inc. (Fort Worth, Texas). He is also the founder of PlanB Group (`www.dbutler.com`) that develops Web sites and other forms of hypermedia for clients across the nation. Dan's background is in software solutions, data analysis, and documentation.

Dan has provided solutions using Perl, JavaScript, VB, VBA, WordBasic, and Lotus 1-2-3 that range from simple work enhancements to full replacements for complex processes. These systems run the gamut from mainframe, VMS, Unix, and PCs.

Dan is the Editor-in-Chief and marketing guru of *The Naked PC* newsletter, and has authored articles for *WUON* and *PC Computing's Undocumented Office* newsletters. Dan has also authored two technical books that are non-computer related.

Acknowledgments

Our heartfelt thanks to Stephanie McComb and Nick Goetz at Macmillan Computer Publishing for their editorial support and guidance, to Kent Easley for an outstanding technical edit, and Claudette Moore and Debbie McKenna for their agency representation. Thanks much to Bill Bradley, Mike Craven, Al Gordon, Christian Schock, Peter Simmons, and M. David Stone for their superb technical expertise.

Dan Butler extends his gratitude to his lovely wife Kelley and their children for putting up with him while writing this book. Special thanks also to my dad Scott, and to Dan Brown who allowed us access to their computers while we were away from home.

Lee Hudspeth thanks his endearing wife Liz, his sons Tate and Aaron, his parents Eloise and George, Gloria (his second mom), and Scott Fraser, a steadfast friend.

T.J. Lee not only thanks Loretta (who as a Daisy Troop leader, Cub Scout Den leader, wife, and mother who works much harder than he does), but also is extremely grateful she married him in the first place. Thanks also to his four kids, Andreana, Jason, Vicky, and Lillian, who are pretty much perfect, ah, most of the time. And thanks to M. David Stone for his help and counsel over the years.

Tell Us What You Think!

As the reader of this book, *you* are our most important critic and commentator. We value your opinion and want to know what we're doing right, what we could do better, what areas you'd like to see us publish in, and any other words of wisdom you're willing to pass our way.

As an Executive Editor for Que, I welcome your comments. You can fax, email, or write me directly to let me know what you did or didn't like about this book—as well as what we can do to make our books stronger.

Please note that I cannot help you with technical problems related to the topic of this book, and that due to the high volume of mail I receive, I might not be able to reply to every message.

When you write, please be sure to include this book's title and author as well as your name and phone or fax number. I will carefully review your comments and share them with the author and editors who worked on the book.

Fax: 317.581.4666

Email: `pcs@mcp.com`

Mail: Executive Editor
Que
201 West 103rd Street
Indianapolis, IN 46290 USA

PART I

Acquiring Your New PC

Chapter 1

Deciding on the Basic System Components

WHEN IT COMES TIME to buy your first PC or upgrade your old one, you need a literal shopping list. You must prepare yourself the same way you would if you were buying a car or home: Write down the features you want, talk at length with everyone who will use the computer (if the PC isn't solely for your enjoyment), study the latest offerings, refine your list, pick several places to go window shopping, kick the tires in the showroom, narrow down the candidates away from the pressure of the store, pick the winner, and then negotiate the price.

Because it pays to proceed carefully and diligently, this is not a short checklist. Even if you ultimately decide to buy a sub-$1,000 PC, you're buying something that will soon pervade your life and the lives of those around you. PCs have a way of doing that—sometimes in a good way ("Hey, I learned something new and useful today!") and sometimes in a bad way ("Doggone it, I'm gonna toss this thing right out the window if it crashes one more time!").

But rest assured that your PC won't just sit there and integrate perfectly into your life—unless you work with it, on it, under it, and around it. And that's where this book comes in.

Most computer manufacturers today have failed miserably at one common task: documentation. You take your brand-new PC

> "A sufficiently advanced technology is indistinguishable from magic.
> —Arthur C. Clarke"

> "Certainly the PC is not easy enough to use.
> —Bill Gates, at Microsoft Professional Developers Conference"

back to your home or office, and you open the big cardboard box the PC came in. You carefully pull out all the components, and you are amazed to discover that the only documentation included is a small fold-up diagram with all of eight steps on it. Not only that, but the documentation—all rendered in a cartoon-like style—looks more like a diagram for a piece of self-assembly furniture than a PC user's guide. This little diagram effectively tells you to plug the orange-tipped cable into the orange socket on the back of the PC, the yellow-tipped cable into its matching socket, and so on, until you're told to turn on the power switch. That's it.

We all know that this is by no means the end of your need for information and guidance—especially when the very next thing that happens is that Windows starts up and goes into an unfriendly, highly technical, esoteric process called the Hardware Detection Wizard. And this occurs because the unit in the factory wasn't configured for the specific monitor, printer, scanner, modem, and other peripherals you added or upgraded when you bought the PC. You'll be able to use this book to fill in these considerable, often insurmountable, gaps. We'll be right beside you every step of the way, providing checklists, tips, tricks, workarounds, definitions, and resources, and we'll tell you precisely what you need to know about and do with your new PC. But we won't overwhelm you with everything you can possibly know and do.

This is the definitive checklist to use when preparing to buy a new PC. The list of considerations breaks down across several dimensions. The PC and all its components and peripherals compose the physical hardware on which most buyers focus. But you also need to consider issues such as what operating system best suits your needs, whether software is included with the system you are considering or whether you should budget that separately, what the options are for upgrading, what kind of warranty is offered, and so on. These issues often get short shrift when compared to the sizzle of the hardware. By considering *all* the options, you'll be much happier with your system in the long run.

Many people buy a prebuilt, ready-to-go system from a retail store or via mail order and never give much thought to the individual components that make up that system. They look at the price and assume that they'll get everything they want and will need. Unfortunately, this is not always the case. You have to consider all the things you'll want to do with your system, where it will be physically located, the types of goodies you'll want included with the purchased system or will want to add to the system right away, and other concerns.

Often, even the prebuilt systems have options. Maybe you can choose between a tower and a desktop chassis, pick one bundle of software over another, upgrade to a larger monitor or a different video card, and so on. The way to start developing your shopping list is to assume that you can get everything you want a la carte. This way, if you go for a tailor-made system, you have your list of wants ready to go. And even if you opt for a prebuilt system, you can evaluate and compare the various package deals against your list and see which system starts off giving you *most* of the things on your list. From there you can investigate options and upgrades offered by the manufacturer.

Bright Idea
Heat is your PC's biggest enemy. If you get a PC with a cheap case, it may provide only the "snap out" type of expansion slot covers that can't be screwed back in place, in which case you'll have to buy the real thing at an electronics supply store. Not putting covers over unused expansion slots can disrupt air flow inside the case and overheat your system.

Chassis

You might not think that the chassis could be an important part of your future affair with your PC, but it is probably one of the most important parts. That's because the chassis—also called the case—dictates where you put the PC. No matter what shape you choose, make sure that the chassis is tool-free, which means that it can be opened easily without any tools. A quick-release or on-rails motherboard makes future upgrades easier as well.

Desktop Versus Tower

A PC is quieter when it's on the floor underneath or beside a desk rather than on top of one, because any disk, power supply, or fan noise will have farther to travel, and possibly, the noise will be absorbed by carpeting. A desktop PC will be literally throwing any sound it makes directly at you. So if quiet is an issue, you want a tower, and you want to position it below a desk. The catch with the "tower under the desk" scenario is that you must position it in an area where your feet won't inadvertently touch it, even slightly, yet you still need easy access to any drive doors, such as a Zip, a CD-ROM, or a floppy drive. Before shopping, be sure to measure how much vertical space you have below your desk. With a low desk, you might have to get a minitower instead of a tower. Towers generally have more drive bays (great for adding another hard disk or internal Zip drive) and sometimes more available slots for peripheral cards. If you are a hands-on, do-it-yourself type and plan on upgrading by yourself, you'll find that the towers are easier to work on because there's more room inside the chassis.

Watch Out!
Repetitive strain injury (RSI) is common to people who spend long periods in front of a PC (or do any specific task over and over again—thus the term "repetitive strain"). Be sure that your component- and furniture-placement decisions conform to known ergonomic standards. Visit sites such as Paul Marxhausen's Computer Related RSI site (`http://engr-www.unl.edu/ee/eeshop/rsi.html`), RSI Help (`www.rsihelp.org`), Possibility Outpost RSI Jump Station (`http://gateway.possibility.com/RsiJump.html`), and Stretching Inc. Online (`www.stretching.com/html/stretches.htm`).

A desktop PC takes up less space (has a smaller footprint, in ergonomic lingo) than its tower counterpart because it sits on your desk, usually right underneath your monitor. The funny part about this arrangement is that you end up with a monitor sitting so high above your desk that you're constantly craning your neck to see the screen. What you gain in more free space below your desk, you lose to sore neck, back, and eye muscles, and possibly a repetitive strain injury. So unless you simply don't have any below-desk space, stick with a tower chassis.

If you do go with an under-the-desk tower arrangement, make sure the cables you'll need are of adequate length to connect things such as the monitor, the keyboard, and the mouse.

RECOMMENDATION:

If you have the space to spare, get a tower or minitower unit and place it on a carpeted surface below a desk, out of the way of wandering feet.

Footprint

Along with considering the tower- versus desktop-chassis issue mentioned earlier, be sure to measure how much space you have available in all dimensions: height, width, and depth, depending on where you position the PC. Include an extra four inches or so at the back of the PC to accommodate cable connectors. Most, but not all, tower cases come with a flanged "stabilizer" on which the chassis sits. If you don't have one, get one; otherwise, your PC might be too easy to tip over. This stabilizer will stick out at least one to two inches on each side, so add that to your measurements. Keep in mind the type of ventilation near the spot where the chassis will sit. As already mentioned, heat is the enemy, so you'll want to ensure that you have as much air flow around the chassis as possible.

Busses, Slots, and Accessibility

When your shopping-list PC is configured the way you want it, if you have no more than one free peripheral slot, this isn't the right PC for you. You should assume that you'll be using this PC for the next three years and that you'll be upgrading some of its components (modem, hard disk, RAM, and video card are the most likely candidates). Always be sure that you have room to grow. If you buy a PC today that can't accommodate additional peripheral cards or memory, you'll soon regret that purchase.

Bright Idea
When shopping for or upgrading a PC or a motherboard, carefully compare the available slots. On a piece of paper write down "Slot 1," "Slot 2," and so forth down the rows. Set up one column in your table for each PC. Fill in each cell with the slot type and what card (if any) is already installed. When you're done, you'll see at a glance how much room each system has for expansion.

Having enough room isn't quite enough, though. Accessibility involves numerous factors, ones you'd think would be attended to by every PC manufacturer, but that's not the case. You want an easy-open, no-tool case, and it should be just as easy to remove as to replace. The motherboard should be easily accessible inside the case. It should be either rail-mounted or have a separate riser card with expansion slots; this segregates peripheral cards from the motherboard itself. Ideally, you should be able to access the CPU and system memory areas without entangling yourself in a Gordian knot of peripheral cards, the power supply, drive bays, ribbon cables, and so on. Believe it or not, clear labeling of interior components is only recently becoming commonplace.

The almost archaic ISA (Industry Standard Architecture) peripheral bus harks back to the days of DOS as the standard operating system. It is still in use, but fading fast. ISA is a 16-bit bus today (it originated as an 8-bit bus) with a transfer rate of

Unofficially... The capitalization of one letter makes a very significant difference here. MBps, or *megabytes* per second, uses millions of bytes in the numerator, whereas Mbps, or *megabits* per second, uses millions of bits in the numerator. Remember that a byte is 8 bits, so 8Mbps (megabits per second) is equivalent to 1MBps (megabytes per second).

between 2 and 8.33 megabytes per second (abbreviated MBps).

PCI (Peripheral Component Interconnect) is the current replacement for ISA. It's a 32-bit peripheral bus with a maximum transfer rate of 133MBps, and a newer 64-bit implementation of PCI provides a breathtaking 266MBps maximum transfer rate.

Beginning with the Pentium II processor, a special, new peripheral port called AGP (Accelerated Graphics Port) made the scene. Dedicated solely to handling graphics, AGP offers transfer rates up to 528MBps.

ATA (Advanced Technology Attachment) and IDE (Integrated Drive Electronics) are effectively synonymous terms for a peripheral bus used to support hard disks, CD-ROM drives, and certain tape drives. The outer limit today for ATA/IDE hard disk performance is called Ultra ATA (also Ultra DMA and ATA-4), which boasts a transfer rate up to 33MBps (disk to RAM); however, this is only in cooperation with new circuitry on the motherboards of the latest Pentium and all Pentium II systems. (For clarity, throughout this book we always use "ATA/IDE" instead of just "ATA" or "IDE.")

SCSI (Small Computer Systems Interface) peripheral bus began its career as SCSI-1 (also known as "regular" SCSI, similar to the way an original Pentium CPU is called a "classic" Pentium). SCSI-1 features an 8-bit bus and a maximum 5MBps transfer rate (at a 5MHz bus speed), and supports up to eight devices (one of which is the SCSI interface card, so that would be seven actual drive-type devices). Newer SCSI standards are in place, however. SCSI-2 comes in three variations: Fast SCSI, Wide SCSI, and Ultra SCSI.

Fast SCSI doubles the bus speed to 10MHz, so for an 8-bit bus you would get 10MBps throughput. Wide SCSI ups the ante to a 16-bit bus width to further improve transfer rates up to 20MBps depending on the bus speed, and it supports up to 16 devices (again, one is the interface card). A 32-bit version of Wide SCSI is available, but because of the thickness of the cables, it's rarely seen on typical computer systems. Ultra SCSI, the latest standard, comes in both 8-bit and 16-bit variations. The 16-bit variant doubles the bus speed from Fast SCSI's 10MHz to 20MHz for a maximum 20MBps transfer rate, and the 16-bit version has a top transfer rate of 40Mbps.

The newest peripheral bus you're likely to hear about is USB (Universal Serial Bus). USB has a maximum throughput of 12Mbps (mega*bits* per second), and one port can theoretically connect up to 127 devices. We have yet to see a 127-port USB hub, however; 2 to 4 is a more common configuration. USB will most likely replace the stodgy serial and parallel ports often used for external devices such as keyboards, modems, mice, and printers. With bus speeds, as with so many things in the PC industry, faster is better, and the more bandwidth and the greater the number of peripherals that will connect to it, the more you'll like it. We'll talk more about USB in Chapter 16, "Managing Devices and Device Drivers."

RECOMMENDATION:

We suggest that you look for one AGP slot (it may come shared with a PCI slot) and two or three free PCI slots, as well as two free slots for memory expansion. Also make sure that you get a PC with USB ports, an important consideration now that Windows 98 natively supports USB. With this dual corporate/home-consumer-market operating system in place, peripheral manufacturers have ramped up production on USB devices. Using a USB device instead of its non-USB counterpart frees up one IRQ, a common source of system constraints and configuration problems, as we discuss later in this chapter. Finally, never buy a system that has no free IRQs; you'll spend too much time tearing your hair out while adding new devices.

Microprocessor

A microprocessor, also referred to as a CPU (central processing unit), is your PC's engine. You've probably also heard it described as a PC's "heart," "brains," "core," and so on. In a nutshell, a microprocessor is a collection of very small transistors crammed together into a very small integrated circuit package that's no more than a few inches square. For example, the Pentium II chip contains 7.5 million transistors in the

Watch Out!
Trying to keep all the speed/types of available Intel CPUs straight is virtually impossible without a road map. The best one around is Thomas Pabst's Intel Roadmap at `http://www2.tomshardware.com/irm298.html`. It's a very nicely done, thorough, text-and-graphics time chart of the Intel Pentium processor family.

space of a chip that measures 5.5 by 2.5 inches. By adding power and external memory to the microprocessor, you have all the makings of a PC—just add a dash of peripherals and you're all set.

You've probably seen the ubiquitous "Intel Inside" ads on television and the logos stamped on PC boxes. Regardless of our opinion of the ad campaign itself, when it comes to the brain of your PC—the microprocessor—there's only one way to go: Intel. Yes, Intel's chip manufacturing operation has competitors (primarily AMD and Cyrix). In fact, several prominent manufacturers feature non-Intel microprocessors. Compaq Presario, Hewlett-Packard Pavilion, and IBM Aptiva models include an AMD processor. Compaq Presario and Packard Bell NEC's Multimedia models, among others, include a Cyrix processor. However, Intel is by far the market leader and is your best bet for performance, reliability, and compatibility.

Trying to get a bearing on Intel's Pentium family of processors isn't easy. Bewildering names exist, such as Celeron, Deschutes, Klamath, P54C, and Xeon, ad nauseam. Some names represent code names (before the products ship), and some don't—it's quite a confounding mess. So we've prepared a table showing the "Intel Pentium-Processor Family Tree" that you'll find in Appendix E, "Important Statistics," in the back of the book. This table shows the most important major Pentium-processor releases. These processor names and specifications should very closely match what you see in PC manufacturer spec sheets and in the data cards and newspaper ads for most retail computer stores. This way, you'll be able to compare apples to apples.

"In high tech, things move a bit faster than in other businesses. Our business has a way of bringing surprises as the year unfolds.
—Andy Grove, CEO of Intel Corporation"

Next we'll cover the most important factors to consider when choosing a microprocessor. Clock speed refers to how many cycles the system's clock generates per second. Clock speed is measured for today's PCs on a scale of millions of cycles per second (one million cycles per second is one megahertz, abbreviated MHz). So, for example, a Pentium II processor with a clock speed of 400MHz has a clock that pulses 400,000,000 times per second. The higher this value, the higher the PC's overall processing speed.

The system bus connects the CPU to system memory. The term *bus* is used by electrical engineers to refer to an electronic connection between two places—just think of a bus as a highway for electrons. The system bus speed, like clock speed, is measured in MHz. Early Pentium (classic) microprocessors have a system bus speed of either 60 or 66MHz; the system bus speed increased to 100MHz beginning with the Pentium II 350MHz processor, whereas a Celeron's system bus operates at 66MHz. A higher system bus speed enables the system to move more data and to move it faster, thereby increasing overall performance. As a historical note, the system bus speed for the 486 microprocessor family was 33MHz, half that of classic Pentiums and the Celeron.

Moneysaver
To save some bucks, stay one step *behind* the point the PC trade journals tout as "the latest and greatest." Staying below the "latest and greatest trend" is a sweet spot where you can easily save those hard-earned dollars.

The term *Level 1 cache* (often called L1 cache or primary cache) describes a small, very fast cache of memory that is inside the CPU chip itself. This is the first cache the CPU looks to for recently used data and instructions, thus the term *primary*. The term *Level 2 cache* (often called L2 cache or secondary cache) refers to a storage area that sits between the CPU itself and system memory, thus the term *secondary*. It is larger but slower than the Level 1 cache. If the CPU needs some information that isn't in the L1 cache, it checks the L2 cache, where it can get the information faster than if it has to go out to system memory, which is slower still. Having a Level 2 cache improves overall performance, and the larger the cache the greater the performance gain.

Watch Out!
These references to "slower" are all relative. For example, in a Pentium II 400MHz system, the primary cache runs at the processor's speed of 400MHz; the secondary cache runs at half that speed (200MHz); and system RAM runs at the speed of the system bus, which is 100MHz. (See the Intel Pentium-Processor Family Tree in Appendix E, "Important Statistics," for more information about these operating speeds.)

Many published metrics are available for evaluating (benchmarking) processor performance. The one we're using for the purposes of this chapter is the iCOMP 2.0 Index. Intel's full specifications for this index are available to the public at `http://www.intel.com/procs/perf/icomp/index.htm` and `http://www.intel.com/procs/perf/icomp/icomp_paper/`. Here's what Intel has to say about the index:

> Intel introduced the original iCOMP index in 1992 in response to the widespread misperception among non-technical PC purchasers that a processor's megahertz rating is a linear measure of its performance. Although the

> megahertz rating has important consequences for the design of a PC system…it is not necessarily a good measure of processor performance, especially when comparing one family of processors to the next. The solution that Intel developed to address this problem was a simple, single number (embodying a weighted average of several processor benchmarks) that would measure the overall performance of each processor and that would allow PC buyers to compare the relative performance of one Intel microprocessor to another…. Additionally, the iCOMP rating is an index of processor performance for any Intel architecture processor regardless of the family. Thus, it can be used to compare the relative performance of a Pentium processor at 200MHz and a Pentium Pro processor at 200MHz.

Table 1.1 shows the iCOMP 2.0 Index values for all the processors in the Pentium family by processor model and clock speed. Interestingly, a Pentium II 400MHz is almost 10 times more "powerful" than the classic Pentium 60MHz.

TABLE 1.1: ICOMP 2.0 INDEX VALUES

Processor and Clock Speed (MHz)	iCOMP 2.0 Index
Pentium 60	51
Pentium 66	57
Pentium 75	67
Pentium 90	81
Pentium 100	90
Pentium 120	100
Pentium 133	111
Pentium 150	114
Pentium 166	127
Pentium 200	142
Pentium Pro 150	168
Pentium Pro 166	186
Pentium Pro 180	197
Pentium Pro 200 (256KB)	220
Pentium Pro 200 (512KB)	240
Pentium Pro 200 (1MB)	unknown

Processor and Clock Speed (MHz)	iCOMP 2.0 Index
Pentium with MMX 166	160
Pentium with MMX 200	182
Pentium with MMX 233	203
Pentium II 233	267
Pentium II 266	303
Pentium II 300	332
Pentium II 333	366
Pentium II 350	386
Pentium II 400	440
Celeron 266	213
Celeron 300	226
Pentium II Xeon 400	unknown

Table 1.2 shows the processors that we recommend you consider in your search for a PC. At the low end is the Celeron 266MHz, and at the high end is the Pentium II Xeon 450MHz. Note that the Pentium II 400MHz system has 2.1 times the performance capacity of the Celeron 266MHz!

TABLE 1.2: RECOMMENDED INTEL PROCESSORS

Processor and Clock Speed (MHz)	iCOMP 2.0 Index	Bus Speed (MHz)	L1 Cache	L2 Cache
Celeron 266	213	66	32KB	—
Celeron 300	226	66	32KB	—
Pentium II 333	366	66	32KB	512KB
Pentium II 350	386	100	32KB	512KB
Pentium II 400	440	100	32KB	512KB
Pentium II Xeon 400	unknown	100	32KB	2MB
Pentium II Xeon 450	unknown	100	32KB	2MB

Comparing non-Intel processors such as the AMD and the Cyrix with the Intel chips is difficult. Not many sources of independent testing data are available (and the manufacturers either don't compare, or they test in a manner that gives their chip the advantage).

If you are trying to compare Intel with AMD and Cyrix microprocessors, keep in mind that you want to first group your candidates by bus speed, then by cache sizes. This at least enables you to compare apples to apples. A good site for comparison information is the Anand Tech CPU Reviews (`http://www.anandtech.com/html/reviews.cfm?types=yes&TopicTypes=101`).

RECOMMENDATION:

This is an easy item in the checklist. Go with an Intel microprocessor. If we were buying a system today—as we write this—we would use the following specific guidelines. If you plan on purchasing a low-budget system, get a Pentium II 233 or 266MHz processor. If you plan on getting a moderate- to high-performance system, get an Intel Pentium II 333MHz or higher. If you really need a kick in the computing pants, grab a Pentium II Xeon 400MHz or higher with the largest L2 cache available. With that said, things change in the CPU arena as quickly as the ink dries on this paragraph. So consider that as new and faster chips become available, you'll have to research the various chips (as we've done here) and weigh the latest performance data against cost in the low-, moderate-, and high-performance system categories. Keep in mind our earlier recommendation to stay one step *behind* the "latest and greatest" trend.

BIOS

BIOS stands for Basic Input/Output System. The BIOS is a little bootstrap program that jump-starts your PC into being able to deal with the peripherals attached to it, such as a hard disk, keyboard, and mouse. After a PC has run its BIOS program, it can then read in the rest of its operating system from the boot floppy or hard disk. The BIOS your system comes with from the factory is non-negotiable. You can, however, ask several intelligent questions about it (or test it yourself) before buying a system. A PC's BIOS should be Year 2000 compliant, should be able to recognize IDE hard drives larger than 2GB without additional software, should support a power management scheme, and should support Plug and Play (PnP) operating systems. You should also make sure that it's the most current BIOS available for your motherboard.

RECOMMENDATION:

Take the BIOS you get from the factory—you have no choice, anyway—and then use our guidelines in Chapter 4, "When and When Not to Assemble Your PC," to optimize your CMOS settings.

System Memory (RAM)

System memory, like disk space, is prone to the "you can never have enough" phenomenon. The absolute minimum you need to run Windows 98 is 16MB, but as Microsoft says on the box, "more memory improves performance." Microsoft's installation manual for Windows NT (now Windows 2000) indicates 12MB minimum, 16MB recommended. In reality, NT really needs at least 32MB, and 96–128MB is your best bet for the average system. Because performance does indeed improve dramatically with additional memory, we recommend a minimum of 64MB no matter what processor you select (and if you're running Windows NT/2000, a minimum of 96MB). Even if your PC is intended only for occasional use, you'll find that any process you throw at it runs better with more memory. For those of you who anticipate running lots of large, complex applications simultaneously (such as having all the Microsoft Office applications churning at once), go with 128MB or more. If you're using only one or two applications at a time but frequently load large documents (for instance, word processing documents with a hundred or more pages, large spreadsheet models, or even smaller documents with lots of graphics), you also need to be in the 128MB range.

Moneysaver
Go to Crucial Technology's Web site `http://www.crucial.com` and use its "Memory Upgrade Configurator" to search for your particular system. Then you'll see its factory default configuration. Next you can place an order for memory direct from the factory. Check out more RAM for your printer too.

Additional memory is the fastest way to improve system performance, and considering the amazingly low cost of memory per megabyte, you should get as much as you can. Dynamic RAM (DRAM) prices have fallen drastically over the past seven years. In 1991, 1MB of DRAM cost $41.24 (according to Dataquest Inc.), whereas the cost was $1.25 in January 1999. That's a significant drop in price! So the incremental cost to upgrade a system from 64MB to 128MB would be approximately $80. This incremental cost is such a small fraction of a system's total cost, even for a sub-$1,000 system, that the long-term performance benefits far outweigh the cost. In other words, max out on RAM.

Adding to the acronym soup are two terms used to describe the physical design of memory boards. You should be aware of two configurations: SIMMs (single inline memory modules) and DIMMs (double inline memory modules). SIMMs have either 30 or 72 pins, and DIMMs have 168 pins. Because more connectors provide more pathways for electrons to move around on, DIMMs are faster than SIMMs.

Not all memory is created equal; some types are faster than others, and you have to have the proper microprocessor if you want to use some of the faster memory types. Extended Data Out (EDO) is a technology that shortens the time needed to read data from the system's memory—by some estimates making EDO as much as 10% to 15% faster. Most Pentium motherboards can take advantage of EDO modules, whereas earlier processors can't.

Synchronous DRAM (SDRAM) is an improvement on Dynamic RAM (DRAM) and runs at speeds up to 100MHz, much faster than plain vanilla DRAM; as with EDO DRAM, only Pentium II processors with 100MHz bus speeds support this type of memory (see Table 1.3).

Watch Out!
When upgrading system memory, be sure to ground yourself. Don't shuffle your feet on a carpet while you work; be sure you have dry hands; and be very careful not to handle the modules roughly or force them into any slots. Careless handling of a memory module can destroy it immediately or cause damage that will manifest itself as erratic performance down the road.

If you are going to upgrade system memory yourself, set aside plenty of time and a clear, uncluttered workspace. Carefully and exactingly follow the instructions that came with your PC or those that came with the new modules. Careless handling of a memory module can destroy it immediately or cause damage that will manifest itself as erratic performance down the road.

RECOMMENDATION:

Get at least 64MB of memory; if you know you'll be running lots of large, complex applications or frequently loading large documents, get 128MB or more. Always get as much of the fastest type of RAM available when you purchase your system, and in a configuration that occupies the fewest possible number of memory slots (get one 32MB module instead of four 8MB modules, for example).

Hard Disk

When choosing a hard disk, you need to concern yourself with a number of operating characteristics. The most important choice is what type of hard drive to get (the *type* in this context often refers to the interface). The storage capacity or *size* of the drive needs to be adequate for the programs and data you intend to keep on the drive; and finally, the performance of the drive needs to be considered.

The two most common interface choices today are IDE and SCSI (Small Computer System Interface), pronounced "scuzzie." These interfaces both continue to be popular, and a detailed examination of the engineering behind each one is beyond the scope of this book.

Suffice it to say that you should use SCSI if you plan on connecting two or more storage devices to your PC; otherwise, use IDE, which is a considerably cheaper technology. IDE is commonly the interface that ships from the factory. However, as with most decisions, it's not quite that simple. When you're shopping around, you may also see references to EIDE (Enhanced IDE), which has faster data rates (4–16.6MBps), 32-bit transactions, and DMA (in some drives). EIDE is also known as Fast ATA, Fast ATA-2, and Fast IDE.

A very compelling benefit of SCSI is that a SCSI adapter card uses just one IRQ resource, whereas in an IDE configuration, each device needs its own IRQ. Because only 16 IRQs (numbered 0 through 15) are available on any PC, they quickly become precious commodities. (In fact, as we warned earlier, watch out for systems that come with no free IRQs.) So with SCSI, the adapter grabs the one IRQ, after which you can run up to seven other devices (15 with wide SCSI) on that same IRQ. Some people choose a SCSI hard disk interface simply to avoid wasting precious IRQs. Imagine the heartache of trying to run four IDE devices (the theoretical maximum) on the same system.

The SCSI interface supports more device types than IDE supports. SCSI supports hard disks, CD-ROM drives, tape drives, removable cartridge drives, scanners, and CD-R (CD recordable) drives, whereas IDE supports only hard disks, CD-ROM drives, and certain tape drives.

The next most important choice is size. You might think we're joking when we say, "Take whatever size you think is far-fetched, multiply it by two, and then go out and buy one." But it's only partly a joke. Hard drive storage capacities are steadily increasing, along with a commensurate decrease in the size (form factor) required to house this increasing storage. So by our rule, you might think that 4GB is a relatively far-fetched size for a hard disk—after all, Windows 98 itself takes up only 300MB (about 8%) of such a drive's total capacity—but in this situation you should go out and get an 8GB drive. And six months from now (as we write this), people will probably be laughing at drives smaller than 8GB. Believe it or not, terabyte drives (1,000GB) for consumer and office PCs are not too far away.

Unofficially... Fixed magnetic disks may be old technology in a few years, thanks to upstart TeraStor Corporation (San Jose, California). TeraStor has developed a technology called Near Field Recording (NFR) that holds the promise of dramatically increasing storage capacity (up to 40GB) while maintaining the same form factor and access speeds we're accustomed to today.

The next most important choice involves selecting manufacturers on the basis of overall performance. You should consider several metrics here: seek time, spindle speed, internal data transfer rate, and interface transfer rate. Here's a closer look at these factors:

- Seek time measures how long it takes the drive's heads to move between tracks. This metric is expressed in milliseconds (abbreviated ms), and you should look for a seek time of 9–11ms.
- Spindle speed tells you how fast the drive's spindle is rotating, and it is expressed in revolutions per minute (RPMs). Modern drives have spindle speeds ranging from 5,400RPM to 7,200RPM and beyond (although today's units operating at 10,000RPM and higher are very noisy). This number is fixed for any specific drive. But because a drive with a faster spindle speed has to wait less time for a random sector to appear below the heads after the heads are positioned at a specific track (so that a specific sector in that track can be read), a faster spindle speed is a good thing.

- Internal data transfer rate measures the rate at which data can be transferred from the physical disk platters into the next staging area (the drive's internal cache or a read buffer). This metric is expressed in MBps, and not surprisingly—more is better. This transfer rate is useful when you are comparing comparable drives.
- External data transfer rate (also known as the interface transfer rate and the buffer-to-host transfer rate) looks at the rate at which data can be transferred from the drive's internal cache or a read buffer to the system. In other words, it measures how quickly data can be carried from the drive's interface to the PC's memory. Practically speaking, this metric is more important than the internal data transfer rate because it measures what's happening as data is transferred to the system. A drive can have a very fast internal data transfer rate, but that performance will be constrained by the inherent maximum transfer rate of the type of bus being used (IDE, SCSI) to connect the drive to the system.

RECOMMENDATION:

Get yourself an 8GB hard disk at a minimum. If you plan on expanding to a second drive, start with a SCSI interface instead of IDE. Look for a seek time of 9–11ms, a spindle speed of at least 5,400RPM, and an external data transfer rate of 5–10MBps.

CD-ROM, CD-R, and DVD Drives

CD drives fall into one of three categories: the traditional read-only media, a version that lets you burn or record your own CD-ROMs, and the latest incarnation—Digital Versatile Disk, or DVD.

You're probably most familiar with the traditional CD-ROM (read-only memory) drive whose silvery disks hold up to 650MB of data (CD disks can be recorded only on one side). These are still the most widely used drives. They're fast, reliable, and cheap.

Recordable CDs (CD-R) are slower than the read-only version, they cost more, and they require special software. But as a long-term storage solution, they make an excellent backup media (as discussed in Chapter 11, "Backing Up." A *rewritable* version (CD-RW)is also available; it enables you to record multiple times on the same disk surface. A CD-RW drive costs more than a CD-R drive, and one drawback is that not all CD-ROM drives can read the disks created with a CD-RW drive.

DVD stands for Digital Versatile Disk; it is the upcoming successor to the traditional CD-ROM. DVDs hold approximately 4 *gigabytes per side,* giving them an 8GB capacity (although different specifications allow for DVDs with capacities from 4.7GB to 17GB). That's a huge increase, and their capacity makes it practical to play theatrical release movies on them (as you might expect, these drives are becoming popular in home entertainment devices). As in all breakthrough technologies, problems exist with DVDs. Standards are still in a state of flux and driver problems are common. Still, this type of drive will eventually replace the traditional CD-ROM.

Moneysaver
Before you spend a dime servicing what you think is a misbehaving CD drive or upgrading because you think you need better performance, check out the myriad informative links at the CD-ROM and Audio Help Links site (`http://mptbbs.simplenet.com/ctech4.htm`).

Like hard disks, CD drives (and we're including the DVDs here) plug into either an IDE or SCSI bus. If you've decided to use a SCSI controller card for your hard disks, the decision about your CD drive's interface is easy: SCSI. The other option is IDE, which is typically the case for a factory-installed CD drive, although IDE CD drives do require special ATAPI (AT Attachment Packet Interface) drivers in order to use the IDE interface.

The two most useful performance metrics for CD drives are access time and transfer rate.

Access time measures how long it takes the drive to begin reading data from the disk; this "how long" is officially defined from the time when the system tells the drive it wants data to the time when that data is in position to be read.

Transfer rate measures how much data can be transferred from the physical disk to the drive's internal controller in a fixed unit of time—for example, 1.2MB/second for an 8X drive. To really understand CD drive transfer rate metrics, a brief discussion of CD drive physics is required. The transfer rate you get depends on which spin technology a drive uses, constant linear velocity (CLV) or constant angular velocity (CAV). About 2.5 times more data is packed into the outermost track of a CD than on the innermost track (the outer tracks have larger circumferences). A CLV drive has the same minimum and maximum transfer rates because the drive adjusts its spin rate so that transfer rates from the inner and outer tracks are identical. So when evaluating a CLV drive, keep in mind that the transfer rate is the transfer rate under all conditions. Simple. A CAV drive, however, always spins the disk at the same speed. Manufacturers of CAV drives put their best foot forward by quoting a transfer rate based on reading from the outside track (very high), not the inside track (very low); but when a CD is produced, the data is written from the inside out. When you see a transfer rate for a CAV drive, remember that it is a maximum value—not an average—and that reading from the innermost track would yield a transfer rate about 2.5 times lower. For example, a 20X CAV drive has a maximum transfer rate of 3.0MBps and a minimum transfer rate of 3.0MBps divided by 2.5, or about 1.2MBps, the same as an 8X CLV-type drive! Also remember that in the case of a CAV drive, if you buy a CD that's only half full, you'll never even achieve half the manufacturer's quoted transfer rate.

Interestingly, the "X" speed you often see trumpeted by drive manufacturers and sales people is inconsequential. You should use access time and transfer rate to differentiate between the tortoises and the hares among CD drives. A drive rated at 1X spins at the speed of an audio CD (between 210 and 539RPM depending on whether you measure RPMs from the inside or the outside of the disk), whereas a 12X drive spins 12 times faster. But that doesn't guarantee that the 12X drive's transfer rate is 12 times greater than that of the 1X drive. Also keep in mind the use you intend for your CD-ROM or DVD drive. If it's to be for light business use, a relative slow drive won't noticeably degrade your system's performance, so you could save some dollars there. On the other hand, if you're a heavy gamer and prefer to keep game files off your hard disk, you'll want a screamer of a CD-ROM drive. (Even the fastest CD-ROM drive is much slower than a hard disk. For example, a 24X (CAV) CD-ROM drive has a maximum transfer rate of 3.6MBps, whereas a modern SCSI hard disk (a Quantum Fireball ST) using an Ultra SCSI-3 interface has an external transfer rate of 20MBps. One solution to the heavy-gamer's dilemma is to transfer gaming files to the hard disk; naturally this is a viable option only if you have lots of free hard disk space.)

RECOMMENDATION:

Both the CD-R and CD-RW types of CD drives are special-purpose drives. Unless you have a good reason to own one, stick with a traditional CD-ROM or the next generation DVD drive. Keep in mind that a fast CD-ROM drive can be purchased for less than $50, whereas a DVD drive can set you back several hundred. Given the price difference and the problems associated with a technology that is just beginning to be adopted, don't decide you have to have a DVD drive on your computer unless you have a real need for one.

In our opinion, a perfect CD-ROM supports a SCSI interface and has an access time at or below 100ms (one millisecond is one-thousandth of a second). If you're buying a preassembled system, you may not have a choice because most of these systems come with an IDE CD drive.

The transfer rate you get with your drive depends on which spin technology it uses—constant linear velocity (CLV) or constant angular velocity (CAV)—but a good compromise between these vying technologies, performance, and price is a 12X unit (for a CLV drive, that's 1.8MBps).

Watch Out!
If you fall on catastrophic times, can you recover your machine? Make a full backup of your system and keep it in an offsite location, such as your office or bank safe-deposit box. Then it will be there when you need it.

Backup Drive

One thing many people overlook when purchasing a new PC is the topic of backing up your data. We'll discuss a couple of backup strategies, and you'll need to factor this information into your total purchase. You might also want to review Chapter 11, "Backing Up," where we discuss the topic of system backup in more detail.

You need to decide whether you are going to keep full backups, meaning every file on your computer, or keep backups of only the data files you create. With today's large hard drives, full backups can be quite time-consuming—so much so that unless you are really dedicated, you may be tempted to skip them! It's better to choose a method of backup you will practice regularly so that you'll be able to recover in the event of a system disaster. Your first step, then, is to decide what exactly you want to back up. Certainly, any files dealing with your personal finances, documents you create, possibly your email, and any pointers to nifty Web sites are nice to recover, and don't forget about your address books or other Personal Information Manager files.

How often should you back up? No easy answer exists because everyone uses computers differently, and "precious data" to one person might be junk to another. The rule of thumb that we use is this: back up when you've done more work than you would care to do again.

You should consider two backup recovery scenarios. First, what do you do if you lose data through carelessness or through a system failure, and second, what do you do in the event of a catastrophe? In the second case, we're talking about a fire, flood, tornado, or similar event. Many of the records on your computer will be difficult, if not impossible, to restore in an event such as this. So we suggest two backup strategies: an online backup and an offsite backup.

For online backup our recommendation is to duplicate your files directly from your hard drive. Buy another hard drive that is a duplicate of your current drive and back up your files to that drive. We'll show you how to do this in Chapter 11, "Backing Up." The best time to buy the backup drive is when you purchase your new PC. This way, you can be assured of having an exact duplicate of your current drive. This approach will take care of the case in which you inadvertently delete some files or suffer a hard drive crash. Our experience shows that it is highly unlikely that two hard drives will fail at the same time.

For catastrophic backups, you have to have a removable media so that your backups can be physically removed and stored away from your system. Basically, you have three choices: tape drives, removable disks, or writable CD-R disks. Generally, we do not recommend tape drives for backup unless you need a full and complete copy of the contents of your hard drive. Tape is one of the few options for full backups—unless you want to spend a lot of money. When you look into tape drives, you'll want to get a drive that can hold your entire hard drive in one operation. So if you have a 6GB hard drive, you'll want at least a 6GB tape drive. Cost for a backup tape here is about $25 for an 8GB tape.

Bright Idea
If you decide to go with a tape drive, stay with a name brand such as Hewlett-Packard or Iomega. If you go with an off brand, you run the risk of not being able to locate a physical drive or the software to restore your files to a new computer in the event of a catastrophe, such as a fire.

The next option is a large-capacity, removable disk drive. The most popular in this category are the Iomega Jaz and the Zip drives. Jaz drives can hold up to 2GB of data per disk. Zip drives hold up to 100MB of data per disk. Both of these are good choices. Choose the drive that best matches the collective size of the files you'll be needing to back up.

The third option is to use a recordable CD-R drive. Each CD-R holds approximately 650MB of data, and the blank CDs are relatively inexpensive. Another advantage of recordable CD-Rs is that you can access the data on any machine without special hardware or software; all the machine needs is a CD-ROM drive.

No matter what you pick, consider an external device, if possible. If you've backed up your system and now you can't access it at all, you'll be glad you can quickly unplug your storage device and take it to another location. The only exception to this rule would be a Zip disk. The internal Zip disk runs very fast, and Zip drives are plentiful and cheap. Many of the systems you'll be looking at will come with a Zip drive built in.

The bottom line on backup is to just do it. The most important part is to actually do the backup; whichever device gets you to that point is the best one.

RECOMMENDATION:

We favor a two-fold backup strategy: a backup hard disk installed on the system, combined with a removable media drive for keeping backups of critical data. The backup hard disk gives you quick backups of your entire primary disk, and in the event of a disk crash, you can access everything from the backup disk. The removable media gives you a way to keep critical information stored offsite, away from the computer, to protect you from a disaster that destroys the physical computer.

Operating System

Most PCs today come from the factory with Microsoft Windows 98 installed. The exceptions are PCs marketed as high-end workstations intended for a corporate networked environment, or even for a smaller office where security is of paramount importance, in which case the PC would come with Microsoft Windows NT Workstation 4.0. Although WinNT 4 sports the Windows 95 interface, it doesn't support Plug and Play, so you'll find yourself in the unenviable position of having to fiddle awkwardly to set up devices, unless you have Information Technology support staff at your company to help you. Nor does WinNT 4 support Advanced Power Management, so no way exists to reduce the power used by your system. However, WinNT 4 does beat Windows 95 and 98 hands-down in the reliability, security, and networking arenas. Hopefully, Windows 2000 (the renamed WinNT 5) won't have these drawbacks.

RECOMMENDATION:

Unless you have very specific security concerns, network requirements, or desktop administration requirements, stick with Windows 98 for now. In mid-to-late 1999, Microsoft will release Windows 2000 (the renamed NT Workstation 5.0), which will include Plug and Play and APM, along with many other compelling features, and the Windows 9x product line will fade into the sunset.

> “Windows 98 is quite different than its predecessor. Windows 95 required you to change your drivers, required you to learn a new Internet, and to get real advantage of it, you had to buy new applications. Windows 98 doesn't have those speed bumps in the way. In 30 minutes, you put it in. It's up on your machine, and you'll start to see the extra speed and reliability without the new applications.
> —Bill Gates, at the Windows 98 launch”

Software Included

Many PC retail and direct purchase vendors offer software bundled with their PCs. Don't be hoodwinked by any vendor claims about what the bundled packages are worth. Do the math yourself by looking at what you would have to pay at a local software shop (or through a mail-order software catalog) for the same packages. Next, figure out which programs you're really interested in and which you aren't, and eliminate the latter group from your calculations.

Also bear in mind that just because a particular package has already been installed at the factory, that doesn't mean it is anywhere near ready for prime time. You'll probably have to fine-tune it after you've assembled your PC. Furthermore, the factory may not have used the setup style that best suits you (for example, having used a "Typical" install instead of a "Custom" install of Microsoft Office), so you end up reinstalling anyway.

RECOMMENDATION:

Bundled software is nice when it happens to match precisely what your needs are—which is rarely, if ever. Be sure that the operating system—the single most important piece of software included with your PC—is the very latest Microsoft release (synonyms are *upgrade, service pack, service release,* and *patch*). If not, you'll have to go to the trouble of ordering another CD from Microsoft, then waiting for it to arrive, and then installing it.

Chapter Ending

- Know what components you want for your system.
- Decide on the appropriate operating system.
- Don't be swayed by bundled software that you don't really need or want.

Chapter 2

Choosing System Peripherals

Now that you have an idea of what the core of your system will include, you must consider which peripherals to add to your system. This chapter focuses on the peripheral components that you need, such as a monitor and video card, sound, a connectivity device such as a modem, and a printer.

Modems

Modems are great. You definitely need one because they enable your computer to talk to other computers. Your modem is the artery for your home PC to reach the world outside, whether that world is a dial-up connection to your office, the Internet, a direct connection to someone else's PC, or faxing. In the past, a computer could get by without a modem, but now it's hard to imagine a PC without this peripheral interface to the world at large.

Choose your modem with care. Our first and foremost recommendation about modems is to always get an external model. If we had a dollar for every time we had saved ourselves having to reboot the system by simply turning our external modem's power off and back on, we'd be filthy rich. So get an external modem—that's the easy call. Unfortunately, from here on things get more complicated.

Watch Out!
Connecting to the Internet with a 56Kbps modem is not all it claims to be. With a traditional modem over copper-wire phone lines, the top physical limit you can hope to reach is 52Kbps. Taking general line noise into account, you can consider yourself extremely lucky to get a connection in the low- to mid-40Kbps range.

Traditional Modems

Modems used to be fairly straightforward. They all worked in the same basic manner, and you bought as fast a modem as you could afford. Speed is still, of course, the most desired feature, but how you come by that speed is by no means straightforward.

High-speed modems are available, with professed speeds up to 56Kbps. Initially, two competing (and mutually exclusive) high-speed modem technologies were available: K56flex and x2 technology. Early adopters were burned in some cases, buying a modem that supported the K56flex protocol and then finding out that their ISP (Internet service provider) went the x2 route and they could not take advantage of their modem's higher speeds.

The V.90 standard was issued to end the standard wars for high-speed modems. As long as you get a modem compliant with V.90, you should not have a problem (by mid 1999, most ISPs should have adopted the V.90 standard). It's important that you stay compatible with what's ultimately on the other end of your connection, so you might want to check with your ISP before you decide on a modem.

You can even find modems that combine two 56K modems (you hook up to two phone lines) and that claim speeds of up to 112K. We've never gotten this technology to work as advertised in our shop, although several of the computer-trade pundits have and seem very pleased with the results.

ISDN

A faster way to go is ISDN (Integrated Services Digital Network). ISDN requires your phone company to wire a special line that carries not only voice but also data in the form of a network connection or even video. ISDN gets you 64Kbps (on one channel), which is faster than what you'll get from traditional modems. ISDN (with two channels) gives you 128Kbps; compare that to the 44–48Kbps you get with a traditional phone line and a high speed modem.

In addition, because the connection is digital, you don't have to convert back and forth between digital and analog (don't let the techno-speak throw you; having to convert from this to that always slows down the throughput, which is the important thing to remember). Connecting to your ISP is nearly instantaneous (no more waiting for the modem to connect). Having your connection dropped due to line noise is unheard of as well.

Bright Idea
Open Channel BISDN allows multiple digital channels over a single phone line—an A channel and a B channel. By aggregating channels you can get an effective rate of 128Kbps. Alternately, you can use the second channel, which has its own phone number, for a voice line.

The downside is that your local telephone company may or may not offer ISDN connections in your area—you have to check. And you usually have to pay the telephone company monthly for your ISDN connection; then on top of that, you pay your ISP for your Internet connection (and you may pay a premium to the ISP on top of that just to connect via ISDN). Finally, ISDN modems (technically, they're not modems at all, but "terminal adapters") are more costly than the everyday type of modem. Still, ISDN is an attractive way to go if it's available in your area and you can afford it.

Watch Out!
Cable modems may be fast downstream, but upstream (uploading email, files, and the like from your computer to your ISP or Web site) is a lot slower compared to the downstream speed. Some cable providers provide downstream-only connections via the cable, and you have to dial out on a telephone line with a traditional modem for upstream activity. But some cable companies handle both upstream and downstream, with the upstream in the 700Kbps range.

Cable Modems

Cable modems are getting some very favorable reviews in the computer press. With a cable modem, you plug your computer into your existing cable TV hookup, provided that your cable company offers Internet access. What you get is incredibly fast "downstream" throughput. Downstream means downloading stuff from the Internet (email, Web pages, files, and so on) to your computer. How fast is incredibly fast? In the 10Mbps range. That's fast.

With a cable modem configuration, your Internet connection is always hot. If your computer is turned on, you're connected and ready to surf the Internet. The cable company acts as your ISP, so you don't have to pay twice as you do with ISDN. So are there problems? You bet.

Again, cable access to the Internet is not available everywhere, and if it is available, it's usually pricey (anywhere from 50 to several hundred dollars per month). Of course, you need a special cable modem that can't be used for anything else; you won't be faxing with it. The other issues revolve around cable companies being able to maintain their bandwidth. The reports we've seen on cable modems all talk in glowing terms about how fast the connection is. But how will that bandwidth hold up when everyone subscribing to a given cable company decides to go on the Net? Everyone on the cable shares the bandwidth, so things could bog down dramatically as subscriber count—and traffic—increases.

Cable modems are blazingly fast, but consider this a new, unproven technology and be suitably skeptical.

DSL

What may very well be the "next big thing" for connecting your computer to the Internet is Digital Subscriber Line, or DSL. This is the technology to watch. Very few standards exist yet, and many varieties of DSL are available—high-bit-rate (HDSL), single-line (SDSL), asymmetric (ADSL), very high-bit-rate (VDSL)—each providing different services. We've seen connections with 1.5Mbps speeds downstream and 384Kbps for upstream traffic. We've also seen balanced connections offered with 1.5Mbps throughput going both ways. With DSL you need a special modem/router instead of a traditional modem. DSL also requires a special phone hookup and exotic equipment, along with a hefty price tag, but it's the coming rage. You should talk to your local phone company to see what it has to offer.

RECOMMENDATION:

The key is to get the most speed for the buck while taking into account what technologies are available in your location and within your budget. You won't be unhappy with a faster connection, but for things such as ISDN, cable, and DSL, you'll be saddled with higher, fixed monthly costs. However, we've seen some extraordinary deals offered by various telephone companies across the nation, so you should definitely talk to your phone company before you decide on a modem solution.

If you go with a traditional modem, be sure to get one that supports the V.90 standard.

Monitors

Monitors fall into roughly two categories: CRT (cathode ray tube) and LCD (liquid crystal display). You've no doubt seen LCDs on notebook computers; LCDs have the advantage of being flat and not very deep (from several inches for standalone LCD displays to less than a half-inch for the screens on some notebooks).

LCDs as replacements for desktop CRTs is something we'll see at some point in the near future. Right now a big price premium exists for the LCDs, making the CRT a cheaper way to go. But the cost of LCD monitors will drop fast (some units are already within striking distance of CRT prices). When LCDs and CRTs are on a comparable price base, the LCD will be the way to go for business applications. For multimedia and graphics work, the CRT will still be the best choice because it has an edge in presenting sharper colors. If you're not sure what you need in this regard, you'll have to go out and kick some tires. Check out CRTs and LCDs with your own eyes to see which you're more comfortable with, given the type of work you'll be doing.

The real trick with monitors is to get one the right size, given the resolution you prefer. Remember, your monitor is going to sit all of about two feet from your face for hours at a stretch, so you must think about your personal comfort as much as possible when making this decision.

Unofficially... Most people go about choosing a monitor a bit backward. They buy a monitor and then try different resolutions in the hopes of finding one that looks right on that particular monitor. What you want to do is find a resolution you can live with day in and day out and then be sure to get a monitor that looks best at that resolution.

Resolutions Supported

Before we discuss monitor resolutions, a brief primer on how a monitor works explains some of the basic mechanics of screen resolutions. Tiny things called phosphor dots make up the inside of the CRT, and when a stream of electrons hits them, they glow. Three colors of phosphor dots (red, green, and blue) are used in color monitors, and they usually are arranged in triangular formations. A number of phosphor dots make up each pixel. Pixels are what we are referring to when we talk about screen resolutions, such as 640×480 (VGA resolution) or 800×600 (SuperVGA resolution). By changing the number of phosphor dots making up a pixel, the monitor allows you to choose from different resolutions. More than one trio of dot phosphors per pixel is better; some experts say that 1.2 trios to 1 pixel is ideal, whereas others feel that 1.5 to 1 is best.

Bright Idea
You don't hear much about monitor phosphor burn these days, but that does not mean that the problem has gone away entirely. Use Advanced Power Management features, run a screen saver, or manually switch the monitor off if the system is going to be on but unused for extended periods.

Because different size monitors have a fixed number of phosphor dots, however, you can run into situations in which not enough physical phosphor dots are present to create enough pixels to support a given resolution. That's why you won't be running 1,280×1,024 on a 14-inch monitor. Not that you'd want to, though—if you could get 1,280×1,024 on a 14-inch monitor, the resulting image would show things so small that it wouldn't be practical.

Table 2.1 is a good starting point to help you decide what monitors you want to look at.

TABLE 2.1: RECOMMENDED CRT SIZES AND RESOLUTIONS

CRT Size	Resolution	Comments
15-inch	800×600	Approximately 25% more viewable area than with a 14-inch CRT.
17-inch	1,024×768	Approximately 30% more viewable area than with a 15-inch CRT.
19-inch	1,280×1,024	Approximately 35% more viewable area than with a 17-inch CRT. Make sure that you are getting a "flat square" CRT and not an older spherical 19-inch CRT model.
21-inch	1,280×1,024 or 1,600×1,200	Approximately 60% more viewable area than with a 17-inch CRT.

Keep in mind that not all monitors support all resolutions, so you'll definitely need to check the capabilities if, for instance, you want to run a 17-inch monitor at 1,280×1,024. A monitor's specifications should list the minimum and maximum resolutions possible for that unit. The video card you choose can also impact the resolutions available to you, as well as the size of the fonts displayed at any given resolution. Video cards are discussed in a later section.

Dot Pitch

Shopping for monitors will bring you smack up against such terms as "mask" and "dot pitch." The mask focuses the electrons from the back of the CRT onto the phosphor pixels on the inner surface of the screen itself. Three types of masks are available: the shadow mask, which comes in classic and asymmetrical flavors; the aperture grille or stripe mask; and the slot mask.

The dot pitch is the distance (in millimeters) between a phosphor of one color and the next phosphor of the same color. This is measured diagonally for shadow masks (also referred to as dot masks) and horizontally for aperture grille/stripe masks or slot masks.

Generally speaking, the smaller the dot pitch the better. For the shadow mask (either classic or asymmetrical), you don't need anything higher than .28mm. For aperture grill/stripe mask and slot mask CRTs, you don't want anything more than a .25mm dot pitch.

Moneysaver
Comparing the dot pitch on different monitors is not as easy as it might seem. You have to be sure that both monitors are measuring the pitch the same way. For shadow masks (both classic and asymmetrical) the measure should be on the diagonal, whereas for the aperture grille/stripe and slot masks, the measure should be made horizontally. If a given model's dot pitch seems too good to be true, the manufacturer might be taking some liberties with how it measures the pitch. Buyer beware!

Displayable Screen Size

Figuring out the displayable screen size is confusing until you understand what the manufacturers are doing. CRTs come in different sizes and are spherically shaped, flat square, or flat tube. The trend is toward the flat tube, and you can expect to find a growing number of models with this type of tube.

For example, 14-inch, 16-inch, older 19-inch models, and 20-inch CRTs are usually spherical shaped. But 15-inch, 17-inch, the newer 19-inch, and 21-inch CRTs generally use flat square technology. Although both tubes are curved, the flat squares are much less curved than the sphericals, so you get less distortion in the image as you approach the edges of the screen. The flat tube CRTs are not curved at all and even appear to be concave at first. Flat square is a good price/performance tube, with flat tube being the best way to go if you find one you like and can afford.

Unofficially...
Bargain CRTs often use the older spherical tube technology. We recommend that you avoid spherical tubes at all costs because of the distortion you get around the edges of these screens. You'll be much happier with the flat square CRTs; or if you find a flat tube that fits your budget, get that.

You don't get the full CRT size (no matter what type of CRT it is) as your displayable screen size, and this has caused many customers to feel that they were being taken advantage of by monitor manufacturers. You don't get the full tube display because the plastic bezel of the monitor case covers a portion of the physical tube itself. This eats up an inch or more of viewable area.

Watch Out!
Comparing the viewable area measurement makes sense only if you are comparing the same size CRTs. Some manufacturers have built monitors using cheaper 20-inch spherical tube CRTs but advertise them as 19-inch monitors so that they show a larger viewable area than actual 19-inch flat square CRTs.

Manufacturers have had their arms twisted to list the viewable area of the screens along with the CRT size. You have to be careful with "viewable" area measurements. Depending on the monitor, the video card, and the resolution you want, you may not like the looks of the screen if you spread the image out to the extreme edges of the viewable area. An image so expanded may appear curved and distorted.

Footprint

It may seem obvious to say that a monitor has to sit on your desk, but don't forget that a CRT monitor takes up physical space not only in the diagonal screen measurement (will that 21-inch monitor fit under the shelf over your desk?) but also in the depth of the monitor chassis itself. A good deal of physical space is needed back there.

A 15-inch monitor is typically 15 inches deep (the diagonal screen measurement is the rule of thumb for the depth of the chassis). If your desk is placed against a wall or another obstacle, every inch you add to the depth of the monitor chassis moves the screen one inch closer to your face. This means that a 21-inch monitor is not something you can plop down just anywhere. Another factor that is commonly overlooked is how much these things weigh. A big monitor is heavy, so you'll want a sturdy surface to set it on and some help when moving it.

Bright Idea
If you have a shallow space that won't fit the depth of the monitor you want, consider that the flat LCD standalone monitors do not have this depth problem. And they are much lighter than their CRT cousins. Also, a growing number of "short-neck" CRTs are coming on the market; these give you a 17- or even a 19-inch monitor with a chassis only 15 inches deep.

Refresh and Scan Rates

The refresh rate is a measure of how often the phosphor dots are made to glow by the electron gun that's in the back end of the CRT. The scan rate is a measure of how many times per second the electron beam starts on the next line of phosphor dots.

Faster is better for both rates. A monitor with a slower refresh rate is more susceptible to screen flicker. For resolutions below 1,280×1,024, you really should have an 85 Hertz refresh rate (Hertz being the designation for cycles per second), and you'd want a rate in the low 70s for resolutions of 1,280×1,024 and higher.

The key to avoiding screen flicker is to actually see the monitor hooked up to a machine running the same graphics card you have in mind for your system. This is not always possible before you get your system set up on your desk, so check on the monitor's return policy. Let us stress again that the monitor is the part of your computer you stare at day in and day out, and if you're unhappy with how the screen looks, you'll be very unhappy indeed, to say nothing of eye strain, headaches, and the like.

Watch Out!
Older monitors used a trick in which they refreshed every other line each time. These interlaced monitors were much more susceptible to flickering. That technology has fallen by the wayside, with most of today's monitors being hawked as non-interlaced. Be aware of the term and don't let anyone sell you an interlaced monitor.

Ease of Use (Controls)

Monitor ease of use is an often-overlooked feature. You may find a monitor that's satisfactory on all other dimensions, but when you get it home, you're probably going to have to adjust its brightness, contrast, color settings, horizontal and vertical alignment, side curvature (geometry), and so forth. Sure, you might have to do this only once, but if the controls aren't up to the task, it could take hours instead of minutes.

If you're buying a monitor from a retail outlet, make sure that you've got a grasp on how the controls work by trying them out in the store. We've found that dedicated buttons on the monitor that do things such as move the image slightly to the right, or widen the image, are preferable to complex onscreen menus that involve multiple selections. But this matter is very subjective, and we know others in our field who think that the menus are easier.

Unofficially...
You won't be adjusting your monitor very often, but when you need to, you'd better be able to remember how. Monitors vary quite a bit in how their controls work, so you might want to jot down some notes on the process unless your monitor manual has very good instructions or the controls are very intuitive. After your initial system setup, you probably won't mess with your monitor controls until you upgrade your operating system or install some new software and suddenly your picture is shifted drastically.

Power Management

Monitors that support the EPA's Energy Star requirements (a similar European standard is called TCO NUTEK) are also called "green monitors." The adjective *green* refers to their being environmentally friendly by lowering their power requirements after a specified period of inactivity. These specifications state how much electricity—in watts—a monitor should draw in its suspend and off modes. Your operating system, monitor, and video card all must cooperate for this feature to work. Specifically, they must comply with the Video Electronics Standard Association (VESA) standard method

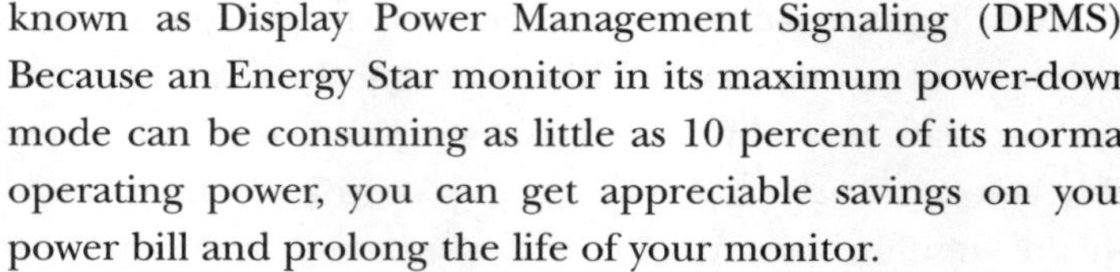

known as Display Power Management Signaling (DPMS). Because an Energy Star monitor in its maximum power-down mode can be consuming as little as 10 percent of its normal operating power, you can get appreciable savings on your power bill and prolong the life of your monitor.

Moneysaver
Most people don't take advantage of the power management features available on the newer systems. This is usually just a case of those features not having been turned on at the factory (in the CMOS); they're disabled by default. We recommend that you turn on these features when you first set up your system.

Bells and Whistles

We're starting to see monitors with Universal Serial Bus (USB) connections on the back. These let you connect USB mice, keyboards, trackballs, scanners, and so on to them under the assumption that connecting something to the base of your monitor is easier than getting to the back of your computer. This is a nifty deal when you're running a USB-compliant operating system such as Windows 98.

You'll also see monitors with other goodies such as built-in speakers, which is handy if you are constrained for space, but the tradeoff is poorer sound quality. We've also seen built-in microphones, and it's only a matter of time before someone offers a built-in camera for video conferencing. As with speakers, though, you'll get a better peripheral if you purchase it separately.

RECOMMENDATION:

First and foremost, nothing beats sitting down in front of the monitor you are considering and staring at it awhile to see whether you like the way it looks. Take into account the type of ambient lighting you have where you'll be using the monitor. If you work in a brighter environment, you'll want a higher quality monitor that cranks out a brighter image. If you work in a darker environment, a cheaper monitor will do because it won't have to be as bright. Get up close and personal with the screen; remember that it will be about 20 inches from the tip of your nose for hours on end. Screen flicker is to be avoided at all costs.

Watch Out!
Speakers, serial bus connectors, microphones, and the like might sound like a good deal at first, but keep in mind that if your monitor goes out, you'll lose these peripherals as well. The same holds true if you later upgrade your monitor to a model that does not have these extra features.

Key to monitor nirvana is to get a monitor that supports the resolution you want and that does not cause you any discomfort or eyestrain. If you think you might want to switch between different resolutions, get a monitor that can deal with the highest resolution you want and that supports the lower settings as well. And don't forget the physical-dimension limitations of your workspace where the monitor has to sit. Be careful you don't end up with a 21-inch screen three inches from your nose.

Bright Idea
If you are visually impaired, consider a larger monitor running at a lower resolution, which makes the onscreen image quite large.

We think that a 17-inch monitor is the smallest you should consider, and you want one that works well at either 800×600 or 1,024×768 resolution. If space and budget allow, you might want to take a look at the new 19-inch and 21-inch units. But don't just assume that bigger is better—you need to get in front of one of these monsters and make sure that it works for you.

Video Card

Between your computer and your monitor sits the video card, also known as the graphics adapter. This piece of hardware, along with the software drivers that make it work, goes a long way toward making your computer experience enjoyable or a living nightmare.

Unofficially...
Despite advancements in technology, video driver problems still seem to cause nearly 50 percent of computer problems. It is a good idea to check your video card manufacturer's Web site frequently to download any new or updated drivers for your card. (An alarming tendency is for manufacturers to release video drivers early and then fix the bugs with later updates.)

Two pieces to the graphics puzzle are key to understanding video cards and to getting a card (or cards) that meets your specific needs. First is the 2D element. If your computing life revolves around Windows and creating spreadsheets, creating word processing documents, managing your email, and the like, a 2D graphics card will do everything you want quite nicely.

3D Capabilities

On the other hand, if you want to play the current generation of computer games, you need a 3D card (and for more and more games, a 3D card is becoming a requirement). You can add a 3D card to your computer. That's right, you wind up with two separate video cards in your system: the 2D card plugs into the 3D card, and your monitor plugs into the 3D card. When you do the everyday stuff, the 2D card handles things, and when you fire up a graphics-intensive game, the 3D card takes over.

Also available are combo cards that have both 2D and 3D capability. They have the advantage of using only a single slot. As we write this, the quality of these combo cards is fair on the 2D side but poor on the 3D side. The good news is that we expect this condition to improve to the point where a combo card will be the way to go.

Unofficially...
Right now, you need 3D only if you play games, and only the high-end games at that. But as business software gets more sophisticated, it's only a matter of time before you'll need 3D graphics to run your spreadsheet or word processor.

Onboard Memory

Video cards come with their own onboard memory, and the general rule is that more is better. How much memory the card has controls what resolution you can achieve at a given color level.

Combo cards usually make the entire onboard RAM available for both 2D and 3D operations.

Bus Type

New Pentiums come with the PCI bus, but the Pentium IIs come with an AGP (Accelerated Graphics Port) slot that takes the graphics processing off the PCI bus and acts as a dedicated graphics pipeline, speeding up your graphics. If you want to take full advantage of the AGP slot, be sure to get a video adapter card that supports it.

The AGP is supported in Windows 98, but if you run Windows 95 on a Pentium II, you should be aware that you may see a conflict warning in the Device Manager dialog box when using an AGP video adapter (right-click My Computer, select Properties from the pop-up menu, and then click the Device Manager tab).

Bright Idea
If you use a combo card in addition to a dedicated 3D card, you'll find you get the best results if you place the combo card in the AGP slot and the 3D card in a PCI slot.

The conflict flag (a red X through a device's icon) or a warning flag (an exclamation point in a yellow circle) may appear next to the display adapter's icon even if everything is working properly. Don't be alarmed by this; it simply means that Windows 95 doesn't know what to make of the AGP device. Assuming that your monitor/video card is working properly, you can ignore these warnings. If you are having problems, you should see Chapter 16, "Managing Devices and Device Drivers," or Chapter 19, "Recovering from a PC Disaster," for help on troubleshooting hardware problems.

Flotsam and Jetsam

A growing number of gizmos and gimcracks seem to get added onto the basic video card every year. You can now get video cards that have TV tuners built into them so that you can see a small window of very bad-looking television on your computer monitor. The same goes for DVD decoder add-ons that let you use your computer monitor to watch a DVD recorded movie.

You can also get "video out" connections on the back of the card that enable you to hook up your computer to your television. We'll admit that it can be a hoot to play DOOM on a 42-inch home entertainment system, but again, unless you really need this type of functionality, there's no point in paying for glitzy features you don't need.

At best, a computer monitor is a poor substitute for a television set, and unless you have some compelling reason for these fluff features, we suggest that you stay away from them.

RECOMMENDATION:

Video cards are one of the fastest changing technologies in the already fast-paced computer field. We expect the early, poor 2D/3D combo cards to improve tremendously, so if you want 3D capability for gaming, you'll want to look at the combo cards. This method eliminates the added expense of purchasing a dedicated card and avoids sacrificing a second slot for your video infrastructure.

Chip sets made by 3Dfx (`www.3dfx.com`) are the current market leader, and we expect them to be a strong contender for some time to come. The key is to get enough onboard memory to drive your monitor at the resolutions you want.

Your 2D card at 16 million colors should have 4MB of video RAM for resolutions up to 1,024×768, 8MB for 1,280×1,024, and 16MB for 1,600×1,200.

If you have a dedicated 3D card in your system, you want at least 4MB of onboard RAM, but more is better. Think of 4MB as a minimum, with joy at 8MB and nirvana at 12MB.

Printer

Despite the promise, decades ago, that computers would bring us a paperless office, printer sales are still going strong, and it's the rare user who doesn't need a printer. The good news is that prices continue to edge downward for both inkjet and laser printers (the ancient dot-matrix printers have faded into techno-obscurity or are relegated to special-purpose use only).

At the low end, you can get color inkjet printers for as little as a few hundred dollars and a good black-and-white laser printer for about twice what an inexpensive color inkjet printer costs. At the high end, you can easily spend several thousand dollars for either type of printer, depending on the features and extras you want. The less-expensive printers do very nicely for the home office or if you need a printer for personal use at your desk at work. These printers run in the $200 to $600 range.

Basic Considerations for Printers

Moneysaver
PC Magazine publishes an annual printer issue that lists the leading printers in every category and provides in-depth reviews. Check your local library for the most recent printer roundup for a wealth of printer information. Use the recommendations in that issue to cherry-pick the various models you'll want to review.

Printers fall into two general categories: laser printers and inkjet printers. Although a third category exists—thermal wax printers—as the cost of color lasers continues to drop, we don't think these printers are a good long-term choice. Inkjet printers spray small jets of ink on paper and run much slower than laser printers. The laser printer bonds powdered ink to a page using heat. Both technologies have been around for a long time and work very well.

If you need to print typical business documents in which a clean, sharp text image is required, a laser printer is the way to go. If you want a printer for home that the kids can use to print in color, an inexpensive color inkjet might be a better decision. It all depends on what, and how much material you intend to print. Keep in mind that color printers are more expensive per page due to the amortized cost of the colored toner/inks.

Look for speeds in the 8 to 12 pages per minute (PPM) range for the less-expensive laser printers. The inkjets run at 4 to 6 PPM when printing straight black text and half that (2 to

3 PPM) for color. These are generalities, and individual printers might be a bit faster or slower.

Print quality is a function of the dots per inch (DPI) a given printer is capable of putting on a page. The more dots per inch your printer can squeeze out, the better the printed text and images will look. You can find low-end laser printers that print 600DPI.

Color inkjet printers usually have two DPI ratings: one DPI for printing black only (many at the same DPI as the laser at 600), and a second DPI for printing in color. Keep in mind, though, that a 600DPI laser will give you a sharper image than an inkjet at the same DPI. The inkjet sprays wet ink onto a page; because that ink spreads and is absorbed by the paper, you don't get the same crisp edges that a laser produces.

The color ratings vary quite a bit, ranging from 600×300DPI up to 1,440×720DPI (again, when doing comparisons, remember to multiply the two values to see dots per square inch). The importance of this feature depends on the type of color printing you'll be doing. Color pie charts with relatively large solid-color areas don't need the higher DPI you would want for printing color photos.

What kind of printing speed you need depends on the type of printing you'll do and how much time you want to spend waiting for your pages to pop out of the printer. The print quality also depends on the type of printing you'll be doing—text, graphics, a mixture of both—and the quality you'll need. If you're planning on printing color brochures and you want them to look as though you had them done at a commercial print shop, you'd better plan on taking your business to Kinko's or some other professional offset print shop.

The key is to test for yourself and find a printer you can run some sample pages through to see just how things will look. Go by a computer store and do this, even if you wind up turning around and buying the printer through a mail-order outlet.

Unofficially...
In "600 DPI" the 600 means 600 dots across one inch and 600 down one inch, so that's actually 600×600, or 360,000 dots per square inch. 300DPI gives you 90,000 dots per square inch. Keep in mind that most service bureaus print paper for commercial use at 1,200DPI (1.4 million dots per square inch), which is 4 times—not 2 times—crisper than 600DPI.

Bright Idea
You'll get a much better color result if you use special paper designed for color inkjet printing. The paper is coated and the ink is not as readily absorbed into the paper, thereby giving you a slightly sharper image. The catch is that this paper is up to four times more expensive than traditional laser paper.

Printer Upgrades and Add-Ons

Make sure your printer has the memory it needs to meet your printing requirements. When it comes to memory for your printer, the same rule applies as for computer systems: more is better. A laser printer builds an entire page in its local RAM from information sent to it from the system before it prints the page. The more memory available, the faster it can get to the actual printing. Most lasers come with 2MB standard, and you should be able to upgrade the RAM by adding more if you need it.

Inkjet printers don't have the same appetite for memory as lasers and usually come with 512KB, although we've seen inkjets in the $500 range with 2MB standard for printing photographs.

Moneysaver
The only difference between "laser" paper and "copier" paper is that the laser paper costs more and is a tad whiter. Using a whiter paper makes the printing that comes out of the laser printer look darker and sharper—very much like an optical illusion. If you're printing documents for your own use and don't need this quality trick, you can save a bit on paper by printing on cheaper copier paper.

Look for a paper tray that is easily accessible and that holds a good amount of paper (adding paper every time you turn around gets old very quickly), depending on the type of printing you'll be doing. If you print only the occasional memo, 25 or 50 sheets is a huge amount. But if your printer is cranking out pages all day long, you'll want a tray that holds 100 sheets or more.

Some printers have a built-in small-capacity feed tray, and you have to purchase an additional paper tray if you want more capacity. Add-on trays can be quite pricey for some printers, so if you think you might need additional capacity (beyond the printer's built-in tray), find out what the added cost is for the different models you are considering.

Give some thought as well to the type of paper on which you'll want to print. If your printing needs involve heavy paper stocks, be sure to check the printer's specs to make sure that it will handle the thicker paper. Some printers have a straight-through paper path and allow for a heavier paper, but many do not. If you run too heavy a paper stock, you are likely to damage the printer.

Most printers support printing the occasional envelope but may not easily accommodate the printing of 15 or 20 envelopes at a time. If you anticipate printing large quantities of envelopes, you'd better make sure that the printer can handle the job. This usually involves purchasing a special tray or an attachment.

As with the computer chassis and the monitor, you need to think about where you'll place the printer and how much room you have available. Some printers have fold-out trays (in front and in back), so make sure that the model you choose—with all its trays and add-ons fully extended—will fit in the space where you plan to put it.

RECOMMENDATION:

When you price printers, don't overlook the consumables. A cheap laser model may use toner cartridges that cost two or three times as much as a more expensive printer model. If you print enough pages, the higher-priced model might be the better buy. That applies to inkjet printers as well. Some color printers quote a cost per page for ink/toner and paper. If you want to compare the cost of consumables between two printers, make sure that they use the same assumed page coverage in their calculations (the amount of a page that is covered with ink).

Think through how you'll use your printer and how fast a printer you'll need (waiting for a page to pop out of a printer can be a real test of your patience). Inkjet color is very affordable if you can live with the quality (it won't look like offset printing despite what the sales clerk will tell you); it's so affordable that you might consider getting an inkjet to go along with the laser, provided that you have enough space and electrical outlets for both.

Color printers print using either three colors or five colors (four and six if you count black). Don't think that five-color printers are automatically better than three-color models. Five-color printers do photos very well but sacrifice some quality on graphics, and the current crop of three-color printers are beginning to rival five-color models on photo quality.

If text quality is your main concern and you still need color, a color laser printer is the way to go, but you'll spend in the range of $2,000 for a good printer.

If price is not a problem, you should consider a color laser, which gives you the best text quality and still provides very good color output. But for most systems where you primarily print business documents with only an occasional need for color, a low-end laser printer *and* an inexpensive inkjet is the way to go. For home use where text quality is not a paramount concern, an inexpensive inkjet gives you acceptable text and very nice color output at a great price.

Sound Card

Almost all new PCs come with a sound card of some sort. Depending on where you buy your new computer, you may or may not have choices as to which card is installed in the box. If you are an ordinary user who isn't going to be creating music with your machine, the sound card that comes with the machine is probably sufficient. On the other hand, if you are a heavy game player or intend to do some serious music composing on the machine, you may want to look at upgrading the sound card and getting more functionality. The key thing to look out for is a built-in sound card in which the components are integral to the motherboard. You need to know whether you can upgrade the sound card without changing the whole motherboard.

The de facto standard in the sound card category is Sound Blaster by Creative Labs. Almost all models offer some degree of Sound Blaster compatibility. And many games *require* Sound Blaster compatibility. Based on these facts, no matter which card your machine comes with, you'll want to make sure that it's Sound Blaster compatible.

One thing is sure: No matter what sound card you get, it will be outdated within just a few weeks. The multimedia market is the fastest-growing segment of PCs today. Because of this, you'll want to fully investigate your upgrade options before you buy. If you want to research up-to-the-minute information on sound cards, a number of newsgroups that you might want to check out on the Internet are listed in the Resource Guide located in the back of this book.

RECOMMENDATION:

Stick with the sound card that comes with your machine unless you know you'll need something more. Be careful with built-in sound cards that can't be upgraded. And make sure that the sound card is Sound Blaster compatible.

Speakers

You can buy the snazziest sound card on the market, but without speakers it isn't going to amount to much. Speakers run the gamut from simple plug-ins to full systems manufactured by Altech Lansing complete with external subwoofers. In fact, a good multimedia system may rival some stereo systems of just a few years past. A number of systems have monitors with built-in speakers. Before you start evaluating sound quality, you need to determine whether built-in speakers are an acceptable alternative to free-standing speakers.

Bright Idea
When you are out shopping for speakers, a good tip is to take your favorite music CD with you and play that through the system you are considering. You'll have a good idea what the music should sound like, letting you quickly size up a given set of speakers.

The main problem with built-in speakers isn't the quality but the ease with which you can replace them when a problem arises. Suppose that your speakers are built into your monitor. What happens when one of the speakers goes out? Do you have to replace the monitor? What if the monitor goes out—do you lose your speakers? These kinds of questions should be in your mind whenever you look at a system with built-in speakers.

On the other hand, standalone speakers require desk space. How much space depends on the speakers. Be sure you know how much desk space you have and how much of it you're willing to give up to your computer speakers. If you play a lot of games, it probably doesn't matter; you'll want the best you can get. For straight business use, it's a different story altogether—you need just enough to hear the computer beep (unless you have a yen to play audio CDs while crunching that spreadsheet). If you opt for a system that comes with a subwoofer (a bass enhancer), it will probably need to sit on the floor under your desk and will take up a good amount of floor space.

Naturally, you want to hear whichever speakers you are purchasing to make sure that they are producing all the sound they should. On a demo system in a store, open Windows Explorer, navigate to the `C:\Windows\Media folder`, and double-click a sound file of your choosing.

RECOMMENDATION:

Go with standalone speakers unless desk space is really at a premium. You can mount some standalone speakers on the sides of your monitor and later remove them if you change speakers or monitors. The "speakers built into the monitor" idea saves a lot of space (and an electrical outlet), but we think that the drawbacks make this an unwise choice.

We favor models that give you an easily reachable volume knob; bass and treble controls are also nice. As any audiophile can attest, no correlation exists between size and quality when it comes to speakers, so don't assume that bigger is better. The key is to get a set of speakers that sound good to you.

Bright Idea
An emergency backup power system, known as an uninterruptible power supply, or UPS, is something you should consider if a sudden loss of power while your computer is running would be catastrophic. When a power loss occurs, the UPS kicks in instantly and supplies backup power from powerful batteries while sounding an alarm that the main power is out. This enables you to save and exit your programs and perform an orderly shutdown of your system.

Other Peripherals

You can add a multitude of other peripherals onto your system: scanners to digitally translate printed documents into text and pictures on your system; digital cameras for taking snapshots that can be transferred directly to your system's hard disk; Web cams that let you post live pictures to your Web pages or have videoconferences with friends and coworkers on the Internet; emergency backup power supplies; network interface cards; joysticks, trackballs, and other mouse-alternative pointing devices—the list goes on and on.

RECOMMENDATION:

Much of what we've covered in this chapter on how to evaluate and choose a system's basic components applies to all the other peripherals you may need or want to add to your system. Focus on what you need to accomplish and on any special considerations you may have. Whenever possible, actually operate the peripheral under circumstances as close as possible to those under which you'll be using it. A given joystick may look great but have 20-pound springs, giving it a tactile feel that you find tiring and not at all what you want.

Think about what you'll be doing and try out each peripheral as much as you can before you spend any hard-earned cash.

Chapter Ending

- To decide on a modem may involve first choosing an Internet connection option other than a traditional phone line.
- To pick the right monitor involves a number of factors made more complicated by the different standards in use.
- Your video card has to work hand in hand with your monitor and support the features necessary for the applications (business and gaming) you run on your system.
- The printer you need is based on your need for color output, the sharpness you want for the text, and your budget.
- For sound cards, you must stick with the industry standard.
- Speakers can be attached or standalone but the sound quality, as you hear it, is the key.
- The best advice when purchasing peripherals for your system is, whenever possible, to try before you buy.

Chapter 3

Pricing Issues

IN THIS CHAPTER, we'll show you the different options that can affect the price of your system and how some "freebies" can make comparison shopping difficult. We'll talk about doing research and the various ways to purchase a computer, and we'll try to help you decide which venue is the right one for you.

Bells and Whistles That Affect Price

In the first two chapters, we discussed the system components and peripherals that make up the computer system. It's easy to see how these physical items can affect the price of the computer.

But a number of additional, intangible items can have a bearing on the final price of your system—and on our feelings about how much weight you should give them in your considerations.

Training

Some retail chains have started including "free" training when you purchase a system. "Free" is a misnomer here because you can be sure that the chains offering such training have included those costs in the retail price you pay for your system. One of the big computer superstores offers a training voucher with several of its packaged computer systems that, if purchased separately, would cost $175 dollars. Therefore, if you find training included with your system and you don't want to

Watch Out!
Be careful when signing up for training offered through a computer outlet because the class may not be held in the store where you bought your system. You may have to travel to another store location for the class you want.

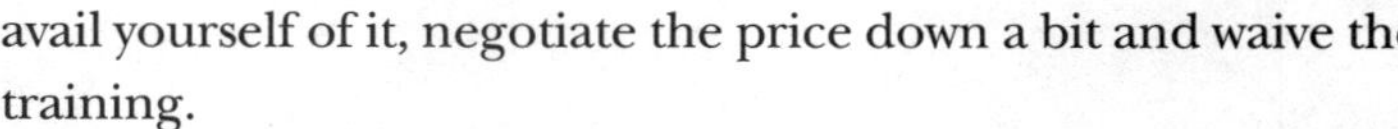

avail yourself of it, negotiate the price down a bit and waive the training.

RECOMMENDATION:

If the training is included whether you take it or not, take it; you've essentially paid for it, and it might prove useful. For example, CompUSA offers six half-hour classes on most of the more popular software packages and operating systems.

If you think that you want to purchase a computer class, first check with your local community college, which may offer extension courses in the areas you are interested. These classes are often cheaper than those offered by computer retailers.

Reliability

Computers have very few moving parts (storage media excepted), which makes them very reliable overall. If a circuit board works, it tends to keep on working (as long as it is not exposed to extremes in temperature). When you purchase a new system or component, you'll want to get it installed and running as soon as you can to see whether your purchase actually works and how the various pieces work together. If you're not happy with your system, you should get the issue resolved with the vendor right away. The longer you wait, it seems the more hassles you'll have with the vendor. So get your system up and running, and test all the components to see whether they're functioning as expected. We cover this process at length in Chapter 4.

Unofficially...
Just a few years ago, mean time between failure (MTBF) was a common metric for hard-drive reliability. Today it's largely irrelevant because even the most lowly of drives have a rated MTBF of 400,000 hours. That's 46 years!

RECOMMENDATION:

The good news is that most components outlive their technological obsolescence—that is, you'll want something newer long before they quit working. To check the reliability of a given component, you can't beat firsthand comments from people who have blazed the trail before you.

Various industry publications poll readers annually about reliability and publish the results. Take a look at *PC Magazine*'s ratings at `http://www.zdnet.com/pcmag/special/reliability98/index.html`.

See whether the manufacturer has a bulletin board on its Web site where you can ask questions about a given product and where your questions will be seen by other customers. Newsgroups also are a good source for customer-satisfaction (or lack thereof) information. (See the Warranty section in this chapter because many of our recommendations apply in determining how reliable a component or a company is.)

Warranty

Any system you purchase will come with a warranty. The question is, how good is the warranty? Use the following steps to research a company's warranty before you buy.

Start by visiting the company's Web site. See how easy it is to locate technical support information in general and warranty information in particular. See whether the company has online support via newsgroups or discussion boards, and then read through the current messages. Keep in mind that the satisfied customers aren't usually the ones posting messages, so you'll likely find a lopsided percentage of negative posts. What you want to pay attention to is how timely and how detailed the tech support staff is in answering the questions. Next, determine the phone numbers and try calling to see how easily you can get through to the support lines. Don't do this just in the middle of the day, but try just before the offices are closing and at other odd times. Then do an Internet search for Web sites and news messages discussing the company. Try going to `http://www.dejanews.com` to search for Usenet postings mentioning the brand name to see what kinds of discussions people are having.

You should look for several things in the warranty. First, see who pays the shipping when bad components must be returned. Some companies make you pick up the shipping, which, in the case of a whole system, can add up. Find out whether you pay both ways or only one way. Some companies match the shipping method, meaning whatever method you use to ship to them is the method they use to ship back. Some companies require Federal Express Overnight paid by you!

Find out whether the warranty covers the whole system or whether some components must be sent back to their individual component manufacturers. If, for example, your sound card fails, you'll want to know whether the company you purchased from handles the warranty or whether you need to deal directly with the manufacturer of the sound card. Basically, you're trying to determine the "hassle factor" of using your warranty. When things go wrong, you don't want to be doing all the work on deciding who to call, who to send what to, and how.

The other option you'll be offered by most stores or businesses is an extended warranty. Generally, these warranties are a bad idea and are designed to make money for the salesman and the company. Look at these if you want, but unless you have some extenuating circumstances, you should avoid extended warranties. One exception to this might be if you live in a remote area and the extended warranty offers you some onsite service you wouldn't be able to get otherwise.

RECOMMENDATION:

If you're happy with the manufacturer, take the standard warranty and pass on extended warranties. Also find out whether individual components are covered by warranties issued by the component manufacturer. If you have a one-year warranty on your system but the hard disk comes with a two-year warranty from the drive manufacturer, you need to make a note of that in case you have trouble downstream.

Service Options and Plans

When you purchase a PC, you get a service plan of some kind; sometimes it's included in the system base price, sometimes for a separate fee. Often a base service plan is included, and extended service plans are available as an upgrade for an extra charge. They usually have terms and conditions spelled out separately from the warranty on the system. For example, technical support is something not covered under a warranty that you'd get under a service plan.

If a system failure occurs within the first year, and you have to repackage and ship the entire system—all at your own expense—to a factory somewhere in the Midwest, that's a service option, albeit a suboptimal one. Or a qualified service technician might appear at your door the very next business day with a friendly smile and a very well-stocked tool kit, even though you're well into the third year of ownership. A wide array of meaningful service options are available from PC manufacturers.

RECOMMENDATION:

You usually have various service plans to choose from. You should make sure that your service plan contains the following:

- 24x7 toll-free telephone technical support.
- A special "getting started" telephone hot line, accessible for the first 30–45 days following the system's purchase.
- Web support—FAQs, troubleshooting forms and wizards, a file library, self-diagnosing tools, system component specifications (down to your specific system, identified by a special ID number), ownership transfer, parts ordering, and order tracking.
- Extended service options—you may elect, for an incremental fee, to receive onsite service from third-party service providers, either during the initial warranty period (usually one year) or for up to five years. If you think you'll benefit from such an extended option, be sure to do it at the time of purchase (or within 30 days of the purchase date; check with your manufacturer to be sure) to avoid any additional fee on top of the extended plan fee, and to avoid having to get the PC recertified. However, most PC components fail early in their life if they're going to fail, so you can save some dollars by avoiding extended-service options.
- Communication with service personnel via email.
- A toll-free "fax back" service through which you can get product specifications (and answers to some common technical support questions).

- For folks without Internet access, access to a bulletin board system (BBS) for various common file library activities.

Be sure to read the fine print of whatever service plan comes with your system and of any service-plan extensions you get. Not all manufacturers cover all of a PC's parts, and not all cover all of a PC's parts with onsite servicing (for example, you may have to wait for a box to arrive, remove the offending component, install the new component, and ship the flawed item back to avoid a charge on your credit card). These documents should all be readily available on the manufacturer's Web site; if not, quickly move on to another manufacturer.

Upgrades

The development cycle of PCs today is astounding. Every few months, components are getting faster and less expensive. You don't want to get stuck with a system that is difficult or impossible to upgrade. Even if you think you're buying all the system you need for the next few years, check out your upgrade options. You might decide you need more memory, a larger hard drive, a new sound card, or any of myriad other things. If you've purchased a system that has the sound card built into your motherboard, it might be difficult to switch it out yourself. Likewise, if you need a new CD-ROM drive but your old one is specially built to match the fancy case, you may be hard-pressed to find a replacement, or you may have very limited choices.

Ask whether you will be able to do upgrades yourself or whether you will need to take the machine to a special service center. Find out where you need to obtain upgrade items. Some companies with proprietary hardware will require you to buy your parts from them. Other companies, such as Gateway, offer special upgrade pricing for their customers.

RECOMMENDATION:

Look for an easily upgradable system that doesn't require special parts or service. Watch out for fancy cases that will be hard to match components to later. Make sure that you can buy standard components and install them yourself when you want to upgrade.

Setting a Budget

Before making your final decision, you'll need to set a budget. If you are on a tight budget and expect to be so in the future, you may be tempted to go with the lowest-cost machine you can find. Be careful; you'll probably do better with a medium-priced machine that won't be obsolete so fast. The three things you don't want to skimp on if you're on a tight budget are RAM, hard drive space, and your monitor. Other things can be upgraded fairly inexpensively over time, but you'll live with your monitor for quite some time. The amount of RAM you choose will have the biggest impact on system performance that you'll be able to detect. And no matter what size hard drive you purchase, you'll fill it up sooner than you think.

Moneysaver
The company you work for may have a group discount worked out with some computer manufacturers. Call your purchasing department and find out. The discount may be only one percent, but that adds up on a $3,000+ system. It could even cover your shipping costs or another upgrade!

Take your shopping list and start perusing newspaper ads, magazine ads, and Internet sites of the various vendors. Ask your friends where they purchased their machines, and find out what problems they did or didn't have. Keep in mind that magazine ads are several months old by the time you get them, and prices are almost assuredly lower by now than those that are printed.

You may notice that prices are seldom printed throughout this book. It would be impossible to quote an exact price for nearly any computer component because prices seem to drop almost daily. Instead, we've focused on how to make an intelligent, informed decision about component selection so that you'll get the best value.

Where can you get the best price overall? Mail order is your best bet for the lowest price (especially if you avoid any local and state sales taxes). Otherwise, it's a matter of being a smart shopper and doing the legwork to see which of the various outlets available to you has the best system or component price.

RECOMMENDATION:

Going with the latest and greatest technology is always a more expensive proposition than buying something that was considered hot stuff perhaps only three months ago. You can save quite a bit if you don't try to ride the technology wave and to always be the first to get the newest—and higher-priced—system or component (to say nothing of avoiding most of the early release bugs). This is what we call "staying one point behind the latest and greatest."

This strategy also can help you avoid the worst of the bugs that invariably infect the latest release of most technologies, and it could save you from adopting what turns out to be the wrong standard. If you must have the best and the latest, expect to pay accordingly.

Shop carefully, and then decide how much you're willing to spend on a new system at this time. You'll want to allow an extra couple of hundred dollars for upgrades or software that you've overlooked. After you have your price in mind, it's time to choose a purchase channel.

Choosing a Purchase Channel

You've made your shopping list, you have a budget, and now it's time to purchase that PC! But where are you going to do this? We'll look at the three major ways you can buy a PC, and the pros and cons of each, and then you'll be on your way.

Mail Order

The first choice is to go with one of the big-three mail-order houses: Dell, Gateway, or Micron. Certainly there are more than three, but Dell, Micron, and Gateway take the lion's share of mail-order sales. Each company also has online ordering with interactive forms for trying all your options before you order. With these companies, you either call in your order or submit it via the Internet. You won't see the product before purchasing, and delays in shipping often occur. We've known of machines that arrive "dead in the box," although this is the exception and not the rule. To offset these issues, you get very aggressive pricing and top-notch components from companies that have been around for some time. Even if you aren't considering mail order, swing by these Web sites and use their interactive forms to test configurations:

- Micron Electronics—`http://store.micronpc.com/`
- Dell Computers—`http://www.dell.com/`
- Gateway—`http://www.gateway.com/`

Mail order has the advantage of letting you buy your system with a minimum of shopping hassles, and you might be able to avoid some sales taxes. One of the biggest advantages to this channel is, in our opinion, the capability to customize a system by selecting particular components and upgrades to a base configuration. Still, mail order is not for everyone.

Little, if any, personal interaction occurs with a real, live human being. You need to research purchases thoroughly, know about the components you want on your system, and be willing to exchange a higher risk for a lower price. You can't be adverse to waiting days and/or weeks for your PC to arrive after you've ordered it; you can't panic if it arrives dead in the box and you have to ship it back; and overall, you must be willing to buy "sight unseen." If this is you, then mail order is the way to go.

If you don't have Internet access, you can review the base models in trade journals and magazines and then call the mail-order company. Keep in mind that publications have long lead times, and the information you see in an ad in a magazine that just hit the newsstands may already be out of date. You can get the latest information on systems and options by calling the mail order company and having them fax you the latest information.

Name Brand

Another option is to shop in retail outlets; however, even though you can see what you're buying, often the sales staff don't know their elbow from a hot rock. You can take advantage of seasonal or inventory sales, and you have the satisfaction of getting in someone's face in person if something goes wrong. Of course, just because you can get in someone's face doesn't mean that it will help. Find out whether warranty work (or work under a service option if one is part of your purchase) is done onsite or whether you need to take care of it on your own. Check the store's financing options as well. Sometimes you can get excellent financing with no interest and no payments for up to a year. This can be a good deal for you if you are disciplined enough to pay the bill before the interest starts.

If you have one of the electronic super-centers nearby (or any retail outlet that has a computer selection that interests you), and if you don't get intimidated by high-pressure, fast-talking sales staff who like to toss around a lot of acronyms (which they may or may not understand themselves), then the retail channel is for you. Usually you won't be able to pick your components on prepackaged systems, but if you watch the local ads and bide your time, you can get some great deals by going retail.

Moneysaver
Are you wondering whether that new component you're looking at is a good deal? Surf on over to Pricewatch at `http://www.pricewatch.com` and find out what the going prices are around the country.

Clone

You can flip through your local yellow pages and find mom-and-pop assembly houses (sometimes in a shop just down the street) that will build you a PC from scratch. The prices can't be beat, and if you're careful about whom you deal with, you can get a reliable system with quick access to the local repair staff. But when things go south, you may be left holding the PC in parts in a bag. We recommend this tactic only if you're a high-flying risk taker, really know your electronics and hardware, or are in a remote area and must have local service.

This channel requires you to know your components, but it gives you the capability to have your system delivered outfitted with exactly what you want on it, often at a really good price. This is the way to go for those not afraid to tinker with their systems and who can deal with owner's manuals that are in three languages. You won't be getting a service plan, and the warranty will usually consist only of what the individual component manufacturers provide.

RECOMMENDATION:

Don't limit yourself to one channel. Shop all three of our scenarios before making up your mind. Take your shopping list and see what will fit your budget. Above all, make sure that you are comfortable with the company you purchase from.

If you're new to computers and feel overwhelmed by the whole process of acquiring your first system, follow the steps we've outlined for first-time shoppers in the next section.

First-Time Buyer's Checklist

If you're a computer technology neophyte and are feeling a bit overwhelmed by all the information we've covered in the first two chapters, take heart. With a little study, you too can be tossing around terms such as bit, byte, and pixels in no time.

A good way to start is to do a trial run or two at your local computer store. Go on a fact-finding expedition so that you can get acclimated to the technology decisions you'll have to weigh when you start deciding on a system to buy. This exercise has value—even if you plan to purchase via the mail-order or clone-shop channels—because you can be hands-on with a variety of systems and look over different configurations. Here's a checklist of what to do on your first trial run:

1. Take a trip to your local computer store.

   Here you'll have an opportunity to see firsthand the various components at work. Every computer store has an array of PCs already set up and waiting for you, the customer, to explore. The number and variety of these floor-model PCs will vary from store to store. Don't expect these floor-model PCs to be spotless in physical appearance or to be completely normal in performance, though. The reason is simple: traffic. So many people come around and bang on these systems that they quickly develop quirks, missing files, disconnected wires, broken CD-ROM trays, and so forth. In fact, every time we visit a floor-model display area, we see at least one PC that's completely unable to boot up. On busy days, we've even seen people—presumably for fun; go figure—intentionally trying to cripple or crash these PCs. The point is, don't let floor-model idiosyncrasies scare you away from a specific brand of PC or peripheral. On the other hand, when you get your own PC, don't tolerate any such idiosyncrasies or misbehaviors, which we call warts. *Warts* is an affectionate term used in

Watch Out!
When it comes to the fine art of buying high-cost goods, there's plenty of psychology to consider. To many salespeople, someone with a "tangible object" in tow (such as a clipboard, notes, or this book) may appear to be easily compartmentalizable, and perhaps be taken advantage of. We're not here to espouse any particular consumer tactics because plenty of books are devoted entirely to the topic of how to be a smart consumer. Our main position is that you are buying a complex piece of equipment, so keep your thoughts organized and your notes handy, and, when it comes time to bargain, have someone along with you for backup. Don't fool yourself into thinking that you are outwitting the salespeople, because you're not. They've seen every trick 100 times over, so just go into the store with your own objectives in mind and get yourself the PC you want at a fair price.

The Naked PC, our electronic newsletter, to describe system defects (`www.TheNakedPC.com`).

2. Take along your notes, a pad of paper, and a pen or pencil.

   When you're evaluating systems, take your notes, a pad of paper, and a pen or pencil into the store with you. Don't fool yourself by thinking that you can remember all the various components, their specifications, and their prices. You'll have plenty to write down, so be prepared. This level of preparedness will come in handy later when you're ready to make a final buying decision.

3. Ask any questions you like because no purchase pressure exists on this trip.

   If a salesperson approaches you, this is a great opportunity to accomplish two things. (We say "if" because in some computer stores—due to either lazy sales staff or crowded conditions—you may have to grab a salesperson by the hair to get any attention.) First, you can get an early assessment of this store's demeanor toward customers. Second, you can ask any questions you have without worrying about the pressure of a purchase decision because you know you're not going to buy. *Just don't let the salesperson know that.* Ask your questions, be polite, and keep your purchase intentions to yourself.

   Speaking of sales pressure, don't get frazzled when the salesperson tells you about the incredible-today-only-giant-clearance-sale. Sales of computer equipment are like street cars, another one will be coming along shortly. In the next section, we'll talk about the best time to buy new hardware.

4. If you like the salesperson you talk to, make that person feel good.

   Because you might be buying your PC at the store you're visiting, if you get along with the salesperson you're talking to, make a point of getting his or her name and business card. This way, they're more likely to remember you when you come back, and you won't have to start from scratch explaining any special needs you might have to another salesperson. Also, if the salesperson offers to provide a quote for a system you're especially interested in, that's fine—go ahead and let them, but don't buy yet. Be sure to ask the salesperson whether he or she is on commission. If so, be sure to ask for that person when you come back as a little thank-you for taking the time with you the first go-round.

Selecting and Buying the Final Candidate

So far so good. By now you should have a clear idea of the class of system you want to buy and the components, peripherals, and specifications you want on it. Now it's time to reach deep into your pocket, yank out your wallet, and part with some hard-earned greenbacks.

The Best Time to Buy

A question we get all the time from friends and clients is, "When is the best time to buy a computer?" Know this: whenever it is that you buy your computer, you'll find it going for less a week later. It's impossible to get a system at its absolute lowest cost because of the nature of today's personal computer technology. It works like this: A great new computer system debuts, but because it's the latest and greatest, it's very pricey. So you wait—and sure enough—a few weeks or months later, the price comes down. You wait longer and the price drops further. You're tempted to buy, but if you wait longer still, you think the price will drop even more. And when you finally think the price has hit a ridiculous low and you're ready to buy, you realize the system is technically obsolete. You don't really want a slow, limited machine such as this one; you want a snazzy system with the latest, must-have features. You're back where you started.

Although the absolute lowest price will always elude you, prices are lower at some times than at others. Bargains can be found on systems and components whenever a new technology debuts and dealers want to move inventory so they don't get stuck with hard-to-sell items when the new technology becomes commonplace. This requires you to read industry trade magazines such as those published by Ziff Davis (`www.zdnet.com`), which include *PC Magazine*, *PC Week*, and *PC Computing*, or *InfoWorld* (`www.infoworld.com`) and similar publications so that you can stay abreast of what latest-and-greatest technology is coming.

Retail Computer Store

Retail computer stores aren't quite yet on their last legs, but more and more of us are buying PCs online, in many cases without ever speaking to a human being (unless an order snafu occurs or a dead component is shipped). Still, from the statistics, it's clear that retail stores are still where most of us shop, so let's cover that option first.

The following steps explain what can be a very chaotic process (depending on the store at which you're shopping, the expertise of the sales staff, and so on).

1. Before you make the "final purchase" visit, do your homework.

   By now, you've prepared your own system-and-components wish list. Study the ads in current computer magazines such as *PC Computing* or *PC Magazine*. See what kinds of price, terms and conditions, and component specification information you can glean from these ads. This gives you a feel for the going street prices. Fine-tune your ideal system to preferably one itemized list. If you absolutely must, go ahead and have a "Plan B" system list. But the more variations you have, the more difficult it will be to nail down exactly what your final system will cost. Naturally, if you have open questions about the capabilities or appropriateness of one or more components—for example, whether to use ATA/IDE or SCSI hard drives—then having two system lists makes good sense.

   Don't be rushed into a particular system because it's on sale the day you walk into the store. The computer hardware industry moves so fast that any inventory in a retail store is either already a clearance sale item or it will shortly become one. Be patient and stay focused on getting the system you really want and not one that happens to be "on sale."

2. As you did on your trial run, take along your notes, a pad of paper, and a pen or pencil. If you got a quote on a specific system and a salesperson's business card when you last visited, bring those, too.

   Less is more here— keep all your notes, ad clippings, spec sheets, and so on in a file folder or somehow out of sight but within easy reach. You want to be looking at only one sheet of paper—your final system list.

3. Find your salesperson.

   If you liked the salesperson you spoke with during your previous visit, find her or him. In fact, it will pay off to call ahead and be sure that the person is not on a break. Tell the salesperson that you're coming in, and schedule an appointment.

4. Focus on no more than two systems.

   As we mentioned earlier, if you're juggling too many systems, not only will you be confused, but you also may not get the salesperson's cooperation. If you have questions that need to be answered to finalize your list, ask them now. Be sure to get them answered to your satisfaction; don't accept "I think so" or "probably" as answers.

5. Now that you've got your final system list ready, it's time to deal. Negotiate the best price.

   Use your best negotiation skills to get the best price. Everyone has preferred negotiation tactics, so use whatever techniques and style suit you.

6. Carefully review the final quote.

   Ask the salesperson for a final printed quote; then look it over to be sure that everything you want is included, and at the right price.

Bright Idea
Many books on negotiating are readily available. Our personal favorites are Herb Cohen's venerable *You Can Negotiate Anything* and *Friendly Persuasion: How to Negotiate and Win*, by Bob Woolf.

7. Pay with a credit card.

   The foremost benefit is that in the event of a dispute over a "lemon" system, you can refuse to make payment for the system 30 days later when your credit-card statement arrives. Sure, you'll have a mess of paperwork to file with your credit-card provider, but this may be easier (and cheaper) than dealing with small claims court, arbitration, or civil court.

8. Unpack and set up your system as soon as possible.

   We get into the details of assembling and configuring your system in subsequent chapters. But you should do the actual assembly and configuration as soon as possible after the purchase, just in case you do have a "dead-out-of-the-box" component. It will be much easier to swap a dead monitor one day after the purchase date than after 31 days.

Watch Out!
Earlier, we discussed the issue of offered or bundled "training" packages. Be wary of these deal add-ons and carefully analyze any service plans or extended warranties. You might wind up paying for something you're already getting under the manufacturer's warranty.

If you're going to buy from a retail store, and particularly if this is your first purchase, take someone with you. That way, you have a friend with whom you can consult and who will be able to rescue you if you seem to be on the verge of making a decision you might regret later. After all, because $1,000, $2,000, $3,000, or more is at stake, you need all the backup you can muster. Your friend doesn't need to be a computer consultant (although that helps, naturally), just someone whose judgment you trust in case you aren't sure what to do about a purchase of this magnitude. Before you waltz in to make a final purchase, coach your buddy to drag you out of the store for a cooling-off period if you appear ready to buy and the situation doesn't seem appropriate to your companion.

Mail Order

Ordering a system over the phone or over the Internet is the way more and more computers are being purchased. The big three mail-order firms, Dell, Gateway, and Micron, have Web sites that are designed to make buying a computer outfitted to your specifications easy. The capability to customize a system that is built to your order is a major advantage to buying via mail order.

In this section, we'll focus on using the Internet, but the basic concepts apply to buying by phone as well.

What's nice about the order systems available on the Internet is that you can put together different systems based on different processors, chassis types, and with various combinations of system components and peripherals, and then you can compare prices between different systems and between vendors—all before you actually buy.

The Web forms for the individual vendors we've worked with (Dell, Gateway, and Micron) each work a bit differently, but the process we describe here works for all of them, with minor variations. You may have to choose a category first, such as Large Business, Small Business, Education, or Home, or you might pick a particular base system right from the main page. The last time we built a system on Micron's Web site, we first selected Computers, then we selected from Desktop, Laptop, and Server options.

You start off by choosing a base system, which gives you a particular microprocessor and chassis type (desktop, minitower, or full tower). From there you can add or remove components and see the effect your choices have on the system price. Be sure to review the service options available and get a service package that you feel comfortable with.

Bright Idea
As you configure systems using the online mail order forms, don't forget to print out each configuration so you can review the components and prices. It's easy to start changing things, and soon you forget which configuration cost how much.

As well as this process works, you still need to watch out for some things. You usually don't get an option to select a SCSI card and drives on the less-expensive base models. Neither can you get these models in full-size tower cases, so instead, you must go for a minitower.

Sometimes you cannot eliminate an option. Although you can elect to forgo a monitor on a system, you may not be able to remove the video card from the system.

When in doubt, call the toll-free number you'll find prominently displayed and ask questions about what you can and cannot do regarding the components on a given system. Take

Unofficially...
A growing market exists for refurbished equipment—that is, used computers. Dell, Gateway, and Micron sell refurbished systems with warranties and often with 24-hour technical support included. Gateway even has a trade-in program that lets you trade in your Gateway system after two years.

notes of any conversations you have and get the service representative's name.

After you've decided on the configuration and have a price you find acceptable, you're ready to order. Using the same Web site on which you order your system, you can usually track your order as it's manufactured. This is a great feature, which lets you keep tabs on when your system will actually ship from the vendor to you.

After your system arrives, be sure to assemble and test it as soon as possible. If a problem exists, you want to know about it as soon as possible and contact the vendor. We'll discuss this process in detail in Chapter 5, "Configuring Your New PC."

Neighborhood Clone Shop

If you decide to buy a new PC from your neighborhood clone shop, apply the same rules you would when buying retail. Many clone shops are owned and staffed by computer enthusiasts. They can be great sources of information on the actual performance of individual components. A good shop will discuss your component choices with you and give you advice on the relative merits of different drives, monitors, cards, and the like. Be wary of a shop that recommends very cheap components that you've never heard of, because you may wind up with a cheap but inferior system.

Bright Idea
When you're buying a clone system, it's very important to determine how long the clone shop has been in business. If it has been operating less than two years, it will have no track record on honoring warranties, so be cautious. Also, talk to at least one customer (not just the owner's brother-in-law). And carefully check out the shop with your local Better Business Bureau office (see `www.betterbusinessbureau.com`).

Chapter Ending

- Evaluate the extras that can affect the price.
- Set a realistic budget based on your needs and available funds.
- Choose the purchase channel best suited to you.
- Gain hands-on experience for first-time buyers.
- Select and purchase your system.

Chapter 4

When and When Not to Assemble Your PC

THERE IT IS—YOUR NEW PC. If the IT (Information Technology) professionals on staff have unboxed, assembled, and installed your new system for you, all you have to do is sit down at the keyboard and start enjoying your new computer. In that case, you can safely skip this chapter.

But for all the rest of you, who, like us, have to roll up your sleeves and assemble your own PC, pour a cup of coffee and read this chapter from start to finish. We've traversed the no-man's land you are about to enter more than once, and you'll definitely benefit from our experience.

Whether you ordered your system through the Web or mail order, or purchased it from the electronics or computer superstore down the block, most likely what you see at this point are two or more very large cardboard boxes: a squirt one containing the monitor and a rectangular one with the system chassis in it. "Some assembly required" just does not do the situation justice.

> "We fear what we do not understand, and so ordinary people fear computers more than they fear filing cabinets....
> —F. J. M. Laver"

The Best Day and Time to Assemble a New PC

Folk wisdom says that when you buy a new car, you don't want one that was assembled on a Monday or a Friday. The theory is that on those days the car assembly-line workers may not have their mind on the job to the extent that they do on the other three days of the week. For assembling your PC, a different rationale applies, but the underlying reality is the same: some times are better to assemble your PC than others.

Allow Enough Time for Assembly

Don't start assembling your PC unless you are reasonably sure that you'll be able to work uninterrupted from start to finish. Figure on spending between one and two hours for the physical assembly of the main system components (the monitor and CPU). It may take longer if you're installing additional peripherals such as a printer or a scanner, or if anything happens that requires you to call the manufacturer and troubleshoot a problem. The rest of your time will be spent dealing with getting your system software installed and configured (discussed in Chapter 5, "Configuring Your New PC").

When you begin, have roughly half a day set aside for the project, with a high probability that you won't be interrupted. If you're setting up your system at home, pick a time when the kids, spouse, and house pets are otherwise occupied.

Try not to let yourself be disturbed or interrupted while you're setting up your system, especially if you have never put one together before. Boxes, styrofoam, plastic bags, and assorted packaging are going to be strewn everywhere; the system unit will be sitting in the middle of the floor; things will be blocking the walkways; you'll have the monitor sitting on a desk or table with cables trailing across the floor; and you won't want anyone (including you) tripping over something or knocking things over while distracted.

"Butler's Law—The chance of running into a missing-parts problem when assembling a PC increases in direct proportion to the likelihood of the nearest computer supply store being closed."

Finally you'll want to do this job during a day and time when your local computer store is open. Why would you need a computer store when your PC comes with everything you need to assemble it? That would be due to Butler's Law of Assembly.

Make Sure Supplies Are Available

An open computer store can solve a number of problems, all of which we have experienced at one time or another. For example, suppose the monitor power cable is inexplicably missing; the system power cable is too short for where you need to place the CPU; or you need a power cable with a right-angle plug to go into the outlet behind the bookcase. The modem phone cord might be missing or it's too short, or you need a second cord so that you can run the phone line through your surge suppressor. If you're installing an external modem, the modem cable might be missing.

Bright Idea
If you find yourself trying to get your hands on a replacement keyboard long after the local computer supply stores are closed, you may still be in luck. You can get things such as mice, keyboards, and even toner cartridges at discount stores that you might not think would normally stock computer supplies. Check stores such as Wal-Mart, many of which are open 24 hours.

Aside from the missing items that should be in the box, most printers don't come with a connecting parallel cable, and network cards don't usually come with the cable necessary to hook them into your network. You definitely want to check local store hours before you start assembling your new system.

Think about where you want to install your system before you start the assembly process. If the only electrical outlets available are hidden behind a couch or bookcase, consider a short extension cord with a right-angle plug on one end, as seen in Figure 4.1, and a four- or six-way plug receptacle on the other.

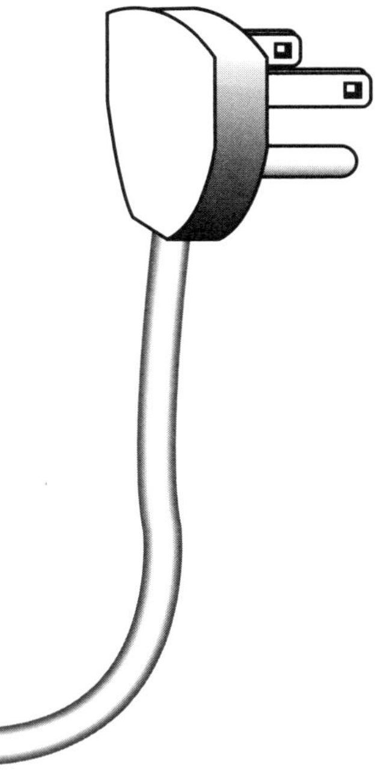

Figure 4.1
A right-angle extension cord for plugs blocked by filing cabinets, bookcases, and the like.

Check Availability of Tech Support

Consider the hours of operation for your computer manufacturer's telephone support line when you plan to assemble your PC. To do this, you need to know going into the adventure where your support will come from. Your support source might be the store you purchased the PC from, or it might be the manufacturer of the PC itself. Always check with the place you purchased your system from (preferably before you make the purchase) about who to call if you start plugging things in and you run into trouble. You definitely do not want to start assembling your PC right after technical support has shut down for the night. Sometimes this is not an issue; for example, Micron has 24x7 (24 hours per day/7 days per week) telephone support, so you can call anytime and get help (or at least someone on whom to vent your frustrations).

Taking this one step further, you might also want to keep in mind where the manufacturers of the minor system components are located and their normal business hours. We've run into issues that were more quickly resolved by making a phone call to Adaptec, for example, in the case of a SCSI card question, than by going to the mail-order company that sold us the system. Because few of the smaller component manufacturers maintain around-the-clock phone support, you have to consider where their offices are located and the time zones involved relative to your own. The various manuals for the different pieces of your system usually have contact information, hours of operation, and the applicable time zones.

Assembling the PC

Generally, putting together a system is a fairly straightforward and painless process. The key is to do a little preparation before you start opening boxes and plugging in devices. To make your assembly go smoothly, you'll need to have some things on hand before you start. And preparing the area in which you'll be setting up your system helps quite a bit as well.

Things You'll Need Checklist

You may not need everything on this list, depending on the type of system you're assembling and where you'll be setting it up, but odds are that you'll need most of them. They are items you probably have handy, but you might have to pick up one or two things on the list before you start unpacking your PC.

- Flashlight—You may not realize it, but it's dark under your desk. When installing a tower chassis on the floor, you usually wind up trying to plug cables into the back of the chassis one-handed while lying on the floor. A flashlight can make this chore a bit easier.
- Screwdrivers—If you get a tools-free case, you may not need a screwdriver to pop open the chassis, but it's a good bet you'll need one at some point. As long as you're gathering up tools, get both a flathead screwdriver (the slotted-blade type) and a Phillips screwdriver (the crosshead type).
- Manila Folder—Every invoice, packing slip, and loose sheet of paper goes here. Also, your original shopping list, your notes, and anything related to your purchase of this computer system goes into the folder.
- Notebook—A plain, 79-cent, spiral-bound, 8½×11-inch college-ruled notebook is all you need (well, maybe a pen, too). This is going to become your System Journal, in which you'll record anything that happens during the set up and configuration of your system (both here and in Chapter 5). This notebook will stay with your system from here on; every glitch and crash gets recorded here, which we'll discuss later in this book. By keeping a record of what's going on with your system, you can see patterns in its behavior. These patterns can clue you in to potential problems that may be developing.
- Surge Suppressors—This includes the power strips used to plug in the external modem, the speakers, your desk lamp, the fan on your desk, the radio, the coffee warmer, and so on. In other words, all the electrical flotsam and jetsam that seems to collect in your office will be plugged in here. The computer and monitor also require the protection afforded by a surge suppressor, although more and more people are opting to go with an uninterruptible power

supply (UPS) for these two key components—a trend we heartily agree with.

- Cable Ties—It's amazing, but have you noticed that computers displayed on TV and in magazine ads don't seem to need cables to connect them to anything? Our computers always have a dozen or so cables snaking every which way. And it seems that cables come in only two sizes: too long and way too short. It's an unwritten rule—a corollary of Butler's Law of Assembly, naturally—that when you replace a cable that is too short, the replacement cable will invariably be too long. So stock up on some cable ties (either the nice nylon ones you can buy at your local computer supply store or even the plain plastic-coated twist-tie variety that come with large trash bags). This way, you can coil the excess cable footage and tie it off, preferably somewhere where the coil won't hinder you from vacuuming up the enormous dust bunnies that will invariably collect.
- Largish Plastic Box—*This may be the single most important thing your new system needs.* This box should be about double the size of a large shoe box. We favor the Rubbermaid brand of plastic containers, about 12 inches wide and 16 inches long and 8 inches deep. Into this box goes every disk, manual, CD-ROM, license, and any other leftover parts, screws, cables, twist ties—in short, the works! This box is used only for things related to the computer you are currently assembling. What we're trying to get across here is that everything goes in the box. Call it your "New computer Emergency catchAll Trunk," or NEAT for short. If you set up another computer, you get another separate NEAT box for that system. Label this box with the name of the computer or its brand and model number.

You may want to consider a number of miscellaneous things as well. If a printer is part of your assembly project, find out whether it comes with a toner cartridge (most do, but you should check anyway). Make sure that you have some paper to test your printer. Having a music CD on hand lets you test your

CD-ROM drive's music-playing capability, as well as your speakers. You'll also want some blank 1.44MB floppy disks on hand for creating emergency startup disks and labels for same.

This covers nearly everything you'll need for installing a preconfigured PC, new from the factory.

Preparing the Installation Area

As tempting as it may be to tear into that big box like a kid on Christmas morning, restrain yourself and get the area where you'll be setting up your system ready to receive your new toy.

As part of preparing your shopping list in Chapter 1, you measured the space you have available for the system chassis and decided on either a desktop system or a tower (full-size or mini) model. This usually determines whether you'll be setting up the chassis on the floor for a tower (although some mini-towers fit nicely on top of a desk) or on your desktop. Clear everything out of the way so that you'll be able to place the chassis in the spot you picked out for it. Keep in mind that you'll want as much ventilation around the chassis as you can get (remember, heat is the enemy). If you're installing a tower chassis on the floor under your desk, you want it as far from where you'll put your feet as possible.

Watch Out!
Keep the monitor and system chassis out of direct sunlight. Heat is the primary enemy of your CPU. That's why one or more fans are present in the unit to draw cooling air into the chassis and across the chips inside the system, and why you need adequate ventilation space around your system.

Remove wastebaskets and that stack of binders and magazines you've been meaning to read for the past few months. You're going to want as much available floor space as possible after you start opening boxes, so you might think about rolling your desk chair into the next room until you need it. Next, clear all the available work surfaces that you can—the desk, the tabletop, the sofa, or whatever you have in the room.

Power Considerations

If you're planning on installing a computer, a monitor, an external modem, a printer, speakers, a telephone answering machine, a boom box, a desk lamp, and what-have-you, and you find that you have only one available electrical outlet, you're probably putting too much strain on a single electrical circuit. If every time you turn on your modem, the lights dim

Bright Idea
A lot of the gizmos you want to plug into your power strip have huge, bricklike power blocks built into the end of the power cord. This is bad because traditional strips have their receptacles aligned so that the brick covers the maximum number of plugs, thereby rendering two or three adjacent plugs useless. The hot tip is to get power strips that have the receptacles rotated 90 degrees. Another option is to get a few short three-prong extension cords and plug the brick into the extension cord and the cord into the power strip.

or go out, you might have to call in an electrician and have a few more circuits added to your cubicle/office/den.

One thing is sure: you want all your critical computer equipment protected by some sort of surge-suppressor technology. For most of us, that means one of those power strips you plug into the wall and into which you plug five or six power cords.

Surge-Suppression Strips

Make sure that any power strips you use are actual surge suppressors that filter electrical spikes, thereby protecting your equipment. However, keep in mind that the protection they afford you is minimal. Most of the run-of-the-mill, $15–20 strip suppressors (which use metal-oxide varistors, or MOVs) are rated for somewhere between 5 and 6 kiloamps by way of an electrical spike. This means that if the power goes out while your computer is turned on, your surge suppressor will probably protect your system from the small spike that's likely to occur when the power company turns the juice back on. But if lightning strikes the power pole down the block, you're looking at anything from 50 to 500 kiloamps charging down the line, and your computer is going to be toast (perhaps literally). Take our advice and during electrical storms, unplug any electrical equipment you're fond of.

To protect your home electrical system and assorted electronics from the occasional lightning strike requires hundreds of dollars for suppressor equipment, starting at the main panel where power comes into your house from the pole. Most people can't justify spending that kind of money. Unless you live in an area with severe power problems, it's probably not needed.

The reason most people opt for a cheap surge suppressor that utilizes MOV technology for stopping spikes is that for most users, it's all that's needed. Most of us don't have regular lightning storms, power outages, spikes, or brownouts. For us, the cheap power-strip surge suppressor is enough, although you might want to replace your power strips periodically. (Suppressors based on MOVs wear out with use.) The problem is that no good rule of thumb exists for when to replace them. As an alternative, you can get surge suppressors that do not rely on MOVs. ZeroSurge products, for example (`http://www.zerosurge.com/index.html`), do not use MOVs and therefore do not wear out over time.

Watch Out!
If lightning strikes a nearby telephone pole, you can get a spike running down your modem line and right into your computer. Many of the newer surge suppressors let you run your modem line through them to give you some measure of protection from spikes on your phone line. We recommend that you unplug everything if you are experiencing a lightning storm.

Uninterruptible Power Supplies (UPS)

Using a UPS system makes sense if your local power is a bit flaky or if having your PC suddenly shut down while you're working would be catastrophic. In this case, you'll want to get the UPS set up well ahead of your computer.

UPS systems come with a backup battery, and you'll want to get the UPS plugged in to allow the battery to become fully charged. The battery must be charged prior to your using the UPS, or you'll have no backup power in the event of a power failure. And not only are the batteries not charged when shipped from the factory, but they're usually not connected. You can spend the better part of an hour trying to figure out why the nifty new UPS is not working, when all that's needed is to connect the battery and plug the thing in to start charging it.

Watch out for UPS units that aren't integrated with Windows. These units only delay the inevitable, disruptive power loss. When their batteries give out, so does power to your PC—unless you get there first (remember, smaller UPS battery-power life spans are measured in minutes, not hours). Windows-integrated UPS units cooperate with Windows to shut down your system when only a few moments of battery charge remain and you haven't intervened.

The main components you want filtered though the UPS are the computer itself, the monitor, and the modem line (both the telephone cord running from the wall to the modem, and the modem power supply if it's an external model).

Whether you're using power strips, a UPS, or a combination of both, make sure that you have enough outlets to plug everything into without creating a fire hazard.

Unofficially... UPS systems by American Power Conversion (`http://www.apcc.com/english/power/index.cfm`) are relatively cheap and very reliable. The company's customer service can't be beat. American Power Conversion has UPS models that it claims will protect your equipment even from lightning strikes. The company stands behind this claim by offering a $25,000 guarantee against protected equipment loss. We haven't studied the fine print on this guarantee, but it sounds as though the company believes in what it sells. It also offers software that can be programmed to shut down Windows and then power down your system in the event of a power failure.

Unpacking the Monitor

First, open the box that contains the monitor. This is, of course, the most fragile component of your system, and you'll want to give a little thought to getting it out of the box safely. Even a 15-inch monitor is bulky—and heavier than you might think. Adding to its general awkwardness is its uneven weight; it is a lot heavier toward the screen.

It's a very good idea to get someone to help you uncrate the monitor and set it into position. Wrestling a 21-inch monitor can easily throw out your back, so be careful. It will be wedged tightly into the box with Styrofoam blocks bracketing the front and back. After the monitor is clear of the box, you need to get those blocks off, and you'll need one of those nice clean flat surfaces you cleared earlier to set it on. If the CPU is not going to sit under the monitor, go ahead and get it positioned where it will live when everything is connected.

Put the Styrofoam blocks from the monitor back into the box, along with any other packing material. Close the box and move it out of the assembly area. The less clutter the better.

Next, hook up the power cord for the monitor (some monitors have separate power cords that plug into the monitor at one end and into your power strip or UPS outlet at the other).

The NEAT Box

It's time to open the big box your computer system came in. Inside are usually a couple of small boxes containing the keyboard and one holding all sorts of software, CDs, manuals in plastic bags, and so forth. Set the keyboard aside and open the box containing all the other goodies.

Take this veritable avalanche of cards, disks, manuals, instruction sheets, diagrams, and assorted miscellaneous objects and start stuffing it in the plastic NEAT box we listed in the "Things You'll Need Checklist." We want you to put everything—and we do mean everything—that comes with your PC into this new, clean, airtight plastic box. All the paperwork associated with your new system goes into the manila folder we mentioned in the checklist, and then the folder goes into the box, along with the shopping list you developed when you decided on what type of system you needed, and the packing list and the invoice. As you toss in each manual (and there will be several), you should take the time to flip though each one to familiarize yourself with what resources are available should you need to start looking things up. While you're at it, if you notice any of the technical-support contact numbers (telephone numbers, email addresses, URLs, and such), you might mark those pages with a yellow sticky note or a paper clip.

Bright Idea
Save the box that the monitor and system chassis come in. If you have to return either component, you'll want the original box it came in for shipping. Plan on saving all the original boxes for at least 30 days after you get everything working—longer if you have the available storage room.

Now all the loose stuff is in one place. We'll talk about the NEAT box again—it's where you're guaranteed to find your system's emergency recovery CD or that extra SCSI cable when you really need it. If you have multiple computers, you should have one NEAT box for each one. Here at the Unofficial Lab, we name the computers, and each NEAT box has the name of its corresponding computer written across the side.

Make, Model, and Manufacturer

Next we tackle the computer itself. The chassis may be as heavy as the monitor, but it won't be nearly as awkward to handle. One person can usually lift it out of the box and set it down on a table or desk. Even if it's a tower chassis destined to sit on the floor under your desk, you should first set it up on a table or desktop where you can get a good look all the way around the system (remember to save the box and packing materials).

System Specifics

Pull the manila folder out of the NEAT box and extract the paperwork that shows how the system you purchased should be configured. Take a visual inventory. If you ordered a system with a CD-ROM, make sure that a CD drive bay is in the front of the system. Match the model number on the chassis to what you ordered and inspect the back of the unit for the correct peripheral cards. You may not be able to identify every card in the system from looking at the back, but you should be able to pick out some of the cards you'd expect to find (depending on what you ordered), such as a network card and an internal modem. While you have the system up where it's easy to inspect, you should record the model and serial number, which invariably are hidden somewhere on the back, in your System Journal notebook.

If you don't find the obvious components that you know should be installed on your system, it's possible that you've been shipped the wrong system unit. This does not happen often, but it does happen. If this is the case, contact the manufacturer or the store you purchased the unit from, and discuss the situation with a manager *immediately*.

Component Specifics

Your system comes with various components (video card, sound card, mouse, and so on), some of which you may have specifically ordered, others of which were chosen by the manufacturer for the system. It's a good idea at this juncture to specifically identify what components you do in fact have in your system. You'll want to do this foremost to determine that you've received the peripherals you were promised, and secondarily so that if you have a problem with one of them, you'll know its exact make and model.

Watch Out!
Be careful if you are relying on the manual for a given component to tell you that component's exact model name or number. Often to save printing costs, a manufacturer will include information for several similar models in a single manual, and you have to thumb to the section for your specific component. If you're not sure whether you have the 2140L or the 2140XL SuperWidget card, you'll be hard-pressed to look up relevant information in the manual.

If your invoice shows the component detail down to the type of cards in the system, the mouse, and so on, you can use this document as your starting point. If not, get a sheet of paper to record your inventory list. First, check to see what documentation has been provided with your system (this should all be in the NEAT box). If you have a manual for a particular model SCSI adapter, it's reasonably safe to assume that this is the model installed in your system.

Knowing the model number of a given card can be a tremendous help should you have to download an updated driver from a manufacturer's Web site. Every model will probably require a different driver, so you'll have to know the exact card you have installed.

Setting Up the Chassis

Before you place the system where you want to install it, carefully inspect all the ports and connections on the back of the chassis. Make sure that the keyboard, mouse, video, speakers, parallel ports, and serial ports are all clearly marked.

Unofficially... Although most systems today have icons clearly marking connectors such as the mouse and keyboard ports, "clearly marked" is a relative term, especially when you think about lying on the floor under your desk while trying to connect a cable by touch alone. Consider drawing a diagram of each port and connector on the back of your system before you start connecting cables. That way, you'll always know that the sound card's microphone connector is the third plug receptacle from the right.

Position the system chassis where you want it and connect the monitor cable to the video card adapter. Plug the telephone line running from the wall into the modem. Most modems (external or internal) have two plugs, one for the incoming phone line (usually marked "line") and the other for plugging in a telephone handset (marked "phone") so that you can dial out on that line. Although with some modems it doesn't matter which line you plug into which receptacle, with others it does, so make sure that you get the lines plugged in correctly. Connect your printer (if you have one). Next, plug in the mouse and the keyboard. Be careful because on systems with PS/2 style plugs, the mouse and the keyboard can have identical connectors, and you'll want to get each one plugged into the right receptacle on the chassis.

Most of the cables (monitor, printer, modem, and so on) should come with thumb knobs that allow you to screw the cables to the port connectors on the PC. This feature is nice because you don't need tools to connect the cables. It's tempting to just shove the cable into the connector and not bother with cinching the cable down with the thumb knobs, but take the few extra seconds to seat the connection by tightening the screws (just hand-tighten them; don't over-tighten them). You'll get a better, more solid connection that way.

Plug in your speakers. Usually, one speaker plugs into your sound card (or the dedicated connector on the system chassis) and the other speaker plugs into the first speaker. Speakers usually need to be powered separately, so make sure that you have an outlet available for them. Turn the volume down because every speaker we've ever installed has come from the factory turned all the way up. That can really get your heart started. Check the A: (floppy) drive on the front of the system, and if a cardboard insert is in the drive, this is an excellent time to remove it. Don't laugh! We've gotten calls from clients setting up new machines wondering why the unit would not boot up. They had left the cardboard in the A: drive.

Make sure that the power strip or UPS you're going to plug the system into is turned *off.* This keeps the system from suddenly starting up as you're connecting the power cord.

Finally, connect the power cord from the computer to your power strip or UPS. That's it. Take a last look at everything. Check that all your cables are plugged in and that you haven't forgotten anything. Now you're ready to enable power to your power strip or UPS and (if the system didn't just spontaneously start up because its on/off switch was in the on state) to turn on your new computer. With any luck, you can turn on the monitor and computer and your system will boot up without a hiccup.

System Glitches and Troubleshooting

Hit the switch. If your system purrs like a kitten and boots up without a hitch, you can safely skip this part and go on to the next section. However, should things not go smoothly, read on.

Unofficially... A saying in astronomy is that if you observe something but don't write it down, it never happened. This is good advice for troubleshooting a system problem. If you get an error message, write it down verbatim. In many cases, not writing down the entire error message is as egregious as not writing down the message at all. Note the sequence of events carefully. All this information can save time and trouble when you get technical support on the phone.

Some fixes are relatively easy, such as replacing a DOA (dead on arrival) component or reseating a loose cable. For the more serious problems, you can try various reality-check items, and if the system still does not work, you'll want to contact the outlet that sold you the system. Either way, at the first hint that something is not going as well as you'd like, pull the notebook out of your NEAT box and write the date, the time, and what has happened. Record all your observations as you try to get your system working, because this will be invaluable information should you have to call technical support.

Have You Tried This?

Anything seriously awry with a new system always involves a call to the company that sold you the system. Don't get too carried away trying to troubleshoot a problem until you've called technical-support personnel and have their blessing on whatever procedure you are about to try in an effort to fix the problem. Your system may be exhibiting a known symptom that technical support will instantly recognize and that requires special handling; you don't want to make things worse. Under no circumstances do you want to open the chassis of a new system that's not working and start tinkering with it, unless you have the manufacturer's technical-support representative on the other end of the phone, because some warranty and onsite service implications may exist.

That said, you should try certain things *before* calling for help to rule out any simple gaffs or easy fixes.

DOA Input Device

If everything seems to be working except that you can't get the mouse to interact with the screen, you may have a bad rodent. When the system doesn't recognize the keyboard, you get a "keyboard failure" error at boot-up time, with the admonition to press F1 to continue. You won't continue very far without a keyboard, however. First check that the mouse and keyboard cables are plugged into the correct receptacles on the back of the system unit and that they are firmly seated.

Assuming that you have a good connection, it's possible that the new mouse or keyboard is dead on arrival. The quickest way to test this is to borrow the component in question from another computer and see whether you get a better result. Keep in mind that if you grab the old keyboard from that 386 PC you gave the kids or a dusty relic from the storeroom at work, you may run into a problem with the connector not fitting the new system. As shown in Figure 4.2, newer systems have a small PS/2 connector about the size of a pencil eraser, whereas older keyboards have a five-pin DIN connector the size of a car cigarette lighter. You can get adapters for converting a keyboard's smaller connector to the larger style and vice versa. Confusing the issue is that most modern mice have the same type PS/2 connector port (standard serial mice that plug into a serial port on the system are still available). Be certain that you have the mouse in the mouse PS/2 port and the keyboard in the keyboard PS/2 port—not the other way around—when you connect these peripherals.

If you determine that you have a bad mouse or keyboard, the dealer from whom you purchased your system should be more than willing to ship you—at their expense, and overnight—a replacement. Some of the less customer-friendly outfits, though, may require that you send them the bad component first. This is massively inconvenient, and you might consider purchasing a replacement input device so that you can start using your new system right away.

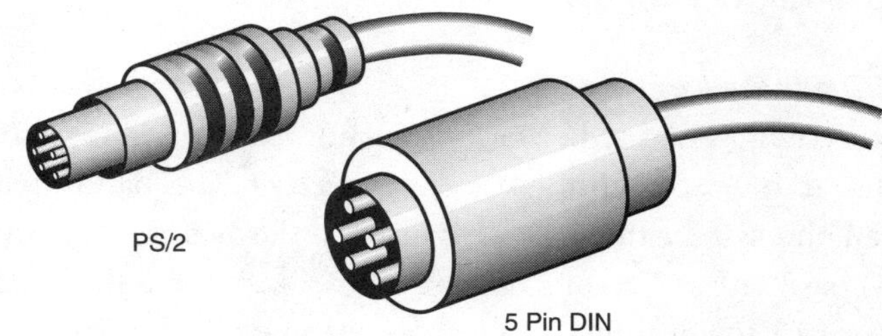

Figure 4.2 A PS/2 connector versus a five-pin DIN connector.

Jiggle the Wires

Before you toss in the towel, take the time to recheck all your cabling. It's much harder to hook things up wrong these days than it used to be, but it's still easy to forget to connect a cable or to not have a cable firmly seated. Trace each cable from peripheral to system and make sure that you don't have anything stretched too far to make a good connection. Make sure that you haven't overlooked a cable somewhere. Most of us have turned on a system and sat waiting for the monitor to come to life only to find that although we plugged in the screen's power cable, we overlooked the cable from the monitor to the system's video card.

Finally—and this may seem obvious—make sure that the power outlets you're connecting to have juice and that a dial tone exists on the modem line.

Before You Call for Help

We've covered the easy stuff, so if your system is still giving you problems, you probably need to call the company you purchased it from. If it's a local computer store, it might have you pack up your system and drive it over so that store technicians can check it. For a mail-order system, you have to get a return authorization number, and the odds are good that you'll have to deal with the company's technical support staff, who will try to diagnose and fix the problem by phone before authorizing a return. It's also possible that you might be entitled to an onsite service call by a repair technician. It all depends on where you purchased your system and what service policy it came with, or what policy you purchased separately.

In any event, here are some observations you can make (and record in your notebook) before you make that phone call. These notes will be extremely helpful when you talk to someone about your system:

- System Fan—When you turn on power to the chassis, does the fan built into the power supply come on? In a quiet room you should be able to hear the fan running, or you can put your hand over the vent by the power supply and see whether you can feel air being drawn in or blown out of the chassis. If the fan does not come on, you could have a bad power supply.
- Motherboard—Does the computer beep a second or two after you turn it on? No beep is a bad thing and can indicate anything from a bad motherboard to a motherboard that needs its power connector to be reseated (that is, it may have worked loose during shipment). Technical support will definitely want to know whether the system is beeping on startup.
- CD Drawer—With the power on, push the button for the CD drive. The CD-ROM tray should slide out of the PC case. If it does not, the CD drive (and possibly the other drives in the system) is not getting any power. (Press the button again to get the tray to slide back inside the chassis.)
- Monitor—Are you seeing anything on the monitor? If the fan is working and the system is beeping on startup but you're not seeing anything on the screen, the problem could be a bad monitor or video card.

At this point, you're ready to call the store or manufacturer's help line and discuss all your observations with them. Based on what you tell them, they may have you return the system or they may have you try specific troubleshooting procedures on the system. Have your notebook handy!

Chapter Ending

- Determine the best day of the week that will give you half a day, uninterrupted, to assemble your PC.
- Start at a time of day that will enable you to contact technical support should you need to.
- Review the checklist of materials to have on hand before you start, and prepare the installation area beforehand.
- Keep all necessary materials in your NEAT box.
- Record all manufacturer, make, and model information for all your system components.
- Assemble your system.
- If you have trouble, run through the troubleshooting tips and record the information listed in the "Before You Call for Help" list.

Chapter 5

Configuring Your New PC

By now you've gotten all your PC's hardware components assembled, connected, bolted down, and inventoried in accordance with the checklists in the previous chapter. Hopefully, you hit the ON switch and did not have to read the troubleshooting section at all but skipped ahead to this chapter. In any event, this chapter assumes that your computer is up and running.

What happens next depends entirely on what the manufacturer did in the way of preconfiguration at the factory, and on this score, every manufacturer is different. We'll cover all the bases in this chapter.

Configuring System Properties

The place to start when you're configuring your system is with the BIOS. As described in Chapter 1, "Decisions on the Basic System Components," the BIOS is a little bootstrap program that jump starts your PC into being able to deal with the peripherals attached to it. A small read-only memory chip on your PC's motherboard contains the BIOS and the date/time, and this chip gets power from its own small battery so that when your PC is turned off, this critical information isn't lost. CMOS stands for "Complementary Metal-Oxide Semiconductor," a term describing a commonly used type of semiconductor, and this is precisely the type of chip used as the storehouse for the PC's BIOS.

Bright Idea
Before you tinker one iota with your BIOS, write down each BIOS screen's values. Then put these papers in your NEAT box. If you think that writing this stuff down is tedious, well, yes, it is, but it is essential when it comes time to troubleshoot or upgrade your PC. Don't forget to update these BIOS records whenever you make a change. The section "Utilities for Formal Testing and Diagnosis," lists utilities that report your BIOS values for you.

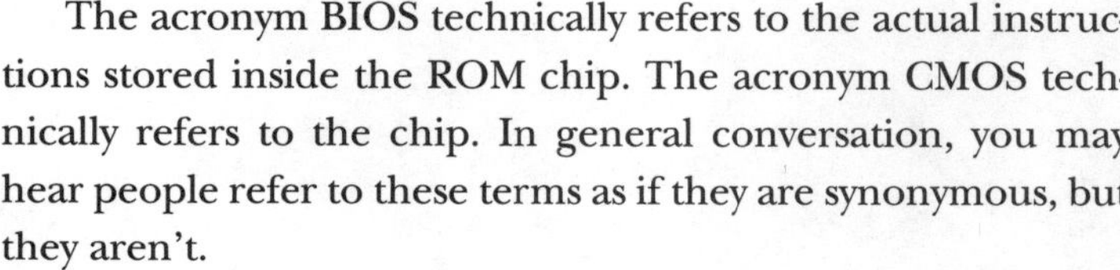

The acronym BIOS technically refers to the actual instructions stored inside the ROM chip. The acronym CMOS technically refers to the chip. In general conversation, you may hear people refer to these terms as if they are synonymous, but they aren't.

Verifying and Optimizing BIOS Settings

The key combination for getting into your BIOS varies from one PC to the next, but nearly all PC manufacturers refer to this process as the BIOS setup utility, or the BIOS setup program. For Micron PCs, an explicit prompt during the PC's POST (power on self-test) process reads `Press <F2> to enter SETUP`. For other computers, no prompt may occur (you have to know when to press the proper keys). In some instances the key is Esc or a key combination of Ctrl+Alt+Esc. Consult your PC user's guide if, during POST, you don't see an explicit prompt for starting the BIOS setup utility. When you're in the BIOS setup utility, instructions for navigating from field to field or page to page, as well as for changing values, getting help, saving, or canceling, are provided along the bottom or right side of the screen. Note that your mouse probably won't work in the BIOS, and key strokes are required for navigation.

Verifying the Main Screen

The main BIOS setting screen you see is somewhat different from one PC to another, but in the following subsections we cover the major areas you need to be aware of:

Watch Out!
If you're using a SCSI controller and hard disks, these hard-disk-related fields will say something like "none" or "not installed." Don't panic; that's perfectly normal for SCSI devices.

- **System Date and Time**—Here you can check, and update if necessary, the system date and time.
- **Disks and Hard Disks**—Here you set your floppy disk drive information. Also, one PC may say "hard disk" and another may say "IDE adapter," but whatever the term, this is where you set up your ATA/IDE hard disks.
- **Num Lock**—The world is divided into two camps: those who like their Num Lock state automatically on when their PC is running, and those who don't. Whichever

camp you belong to, here's where you can change things to your liking.

- **Extended Memory**—This category automatically detects how much memory is installed over and above the base memory of 640KB. You can change this value only by adding or removing memory modules.
- **Other Settings**—The rest of the settings likely to appear in the main screen are ordinarily of the "set once at the factory and forget" variety. However, you might want to check some—or all—of these and research them at your own discretion. These are settings such as key click (on or off), keyboard auto-repeat rate and delay, cache video BIOS, cache system BIOS, and system cache.

Verifying the Advanced Screen

This screen usually provides settings for integrated peripherals such as serial and parallel ports, disk and PCI IDE controllers (this is where you disable the PCI IDE controller if you're using a SCSI controller instead), and integrated sound cards, among others. The details vary somewhat from system to system.

If this screen includes a Plug-and-Play O/S setting, set it to Yes. Frequently, the factory default for this switch, even if the factory included a PnP operating system, such as Windows 95 or 98, is off. Go figure.

Verifying the Security Screen

This screen usually offers Supervisor and User password options. Whatever you do, *don't set any BIOS passwords.* The only justifiable exception would be if this is a policy imposed by your Information Technology staff, and they—not you—are responsible for storing the passwords in a safe place. If you enable and later forget a Supervisor, User, or boot password, you would either no longer be able to access your BIOS setup program or, in some cases, you would not be able to boot your system. You would have to resort to some very low-level, dangerous tricks to reset your CMOS: tricks such as performing a

Watch Out!
Plug and Play, power management, and individual software packages are a troika, the members of which have yet to see eye to eye. We have little confidence in the precise interplay among these three aspects of a delicate equation. So your best bet when it comes to power-management settings is to start out clean—leave all power management settings *off*. This way, you'll have far fewer variables to worry about while configuring or troubleshooting your PC. Later, when you're satisfied everything is kosher, you can begin to tinker, enabling power management one setting at a time. If nothing behaves strangely, you're in luck.

flash BIOS upgrade, using some special startup keys that—in some PCs—clear the CMOS (contact your PC manufacturer for information about these special keys), setting a CMOS clear jumper on the motherboard, or disconnecting the CMOS battery.

This is such important advice that we'll repeat it: *Don't set any BIOS passwords.*

Verifying the Power Screen

The factory default for all power management settings is Off, so if you want to reap any power savings, dig in. However, as explained shortly, during the configuration phase for a new PC, we strongly suggest that you leave all power management settings off.

Although no standard setting names or categories exists, you're likely to see settings similar to these:

- CPU Fan Failure—Enable this setting so that your system will prompt you should your CPU's fan ever fail.
- APM (Advanced Power Management)—Usually, one single setting sets all power-management settings on or off. To engage or customize the individual settings, turn this one on.
- Power Management Mode—This selection provides a range of options from off to maximum (power savings), and includes a customize mode. Pick the setting that makes the most sense for your use of the PC and your power bill.
- Standby Timeout—Standby mode isn't quite as deep a power-saving mode as Suspend. This setting determines how long your system is idle before dropping into Standby mode. Ordinarily, this setting is available only if you choose the customize APM mode.
- Suspend Timeout—This is a deeper power-saving mode than Standby. This setting determines how long your system is idle before dropping into Suspend mode.

Ordinarily, this setting is available only if you choose the customize APM mode.

- Standby CPU Speed—This involves a range of settings that govern the CPU speed during the power-saving mode. Ordinarily, this setting is available only if you choose the customize APM mode.
- Fixed Disk Timeout—Before enabling this setting, check with your disk drive manufacturer to be sure that your drive supports a spin-down mode. Ordinarily, this setting is available only if you choose the customize APM mode.
- CRT—Before enabling this setting, check with your monitor and display adapter manufacturers to be sure that these devices support reduced-power-consumption modes.
- Miscellaneous—Other settings manage how the system should "wake up" in response to an event for a mouse, modem, or other device (set by IRQ).

If your BIOS has this option, simply choose a global maximum power-savings mode. This way, you don't have to dig into each suboption and calibrate accordingly, but you can still see in the BIOS Setup program's screen what effect this has on each suboption.

Unofficially...
The BIOS Survival Guide at `www.lemig.umontreal.ca/bios/bios_sg.htm` is an excellent source of very detailed, very technical BIOS and CMOS information.

Verifying the Boot Screen

This screen includes a setting that controls the order of bootable drives (floppy drive, hard drive, CD-ROM drive, or network). Other settings are Setup Prompt (should always be enabled) and POST Errors (should always be enabled).

Verifying the Other Screens

One or more screens of additional settings may be available, depending on your system and its BIOS. Refer to your PC's user's guide for more information.

Verifying Year 2000 Compliance

You can use a free utility called YMARK2000 to verify whether your PC's BIOS is Year 2000-compliant. Go to the NSTL Web site, www.nstl.com/html/nstl_y2k.html, download Y2000.exe (a mere 35KB file), and then self-extract it into its two component files: 2000.exe and Readme.txt. Reboot into MS-DOS mode and run 2000.exe from its host folder. The test results are displayed on your monitor. For more information about possible outcomes, and in particular what to do if your PC fails the test, see NSTL Online at www.nstl.com.

In the case of a Micron Millenia Plus 166 in our lab, Micron's Web page indicated that it was Year 2000-compliant. When we ran the YMARK2000 utility, it reported that the system correctly supports the Year 2000. Here's the exact output of that test:

```
YMark2000
Year 2000 compliance test program, version 98.02.15
Copyright 1997 - 1998, NSTL (msp)
NSTL is a division of The McGraw-Hill Companies
This Software is copyrighted material of The McGraw-Hill
Companies.
All rights reserved.
YMark2000 license agreement accepted
    - MC146818 compatible hardware clock.
    - Progression to Year 2000 occurs
    - 21st century leap year test passes
Summary: (0)
     - This system correctly supports the Year 2000.
YMark2000, version 98.02.15
NSTL (National Software Testing Laboratories), a division
of The McGraw-Hill Companies, offers this Year 2000
compliance test program free of charge and royalties per
license agreement.
The purpose of this test is to determine if an "industry
standard" or "compatible" PC supports the Year 2000.
Questions, comments or requests for additional testing
should be directed to:
    internet - Year2000@nstl.com
    fax - +1 610 941-9952
```

Here's a partial log of the output for an old 486. This computer failed the test but should be able to deal with the year 2000 with a manual reboot and a manual resetting of the year:

```
<snip>
YMark2000 license agreement accepted
    - MC146818 compatible hardware clock.
    - Progression to Year 2000 fails_
    - Manual transition to Year 2000 supported_
    - 21st century leap year test passes
Summary: (2)
    - This system will not automatically transition to the
    Year 2000, but the system may support the Year 2000
    once the date is set manually.  This is less than ideal
    since corrective user intervention is required, only
    once, when the Year 2000 arrives.
    Do not use this system to run date sensitive software
    that must run 24hrs a day, such as voice messaging or
    satelite tracking.
    A manual Year 2000 reboot test is highly recommended.
    Please see the README file for more information.
<snip>
```

Unofficially... The NSTL's FAQ at `www.nstl.com/html/ymark2000_faq.html` (and, in part, YMARK2000's `Readme.txt` file) provides very detailed and useful information about the Year 2000 compliance issue as it applies to PCs. If you're interested in understanding this issue, this is a great resource.

Handling a Troublesome Component, Operating System, or Application

Windows itself comes with extensive online help material specifically designed around troubleshooting device, operating-system, and application problems. Naturally, these materials are available to you only if your PC is working, so you might want to check out the *Microsoft Windows 98 Resource Kit* from your local library, or purchase your own copy (Microsoft Press, ISBN: 1-572-31644-6).

The Resource Kit doesn't come preinstalled, so you'll have to do the job. Here's how:

1. Insert your Windows 98 CD-ROM.
2. From the CD's \tools\reskit folder, click `Setup.exe` and follow the instructions.
3. When setup is finished, you can access the Resource Kit in online help format by selecting Start, Programs, Windows 98 Resource Kit, and then Resource Kit Online Book.
4. You can browse at your leisure through the Resource Kit's extensive table of contents (click the Contents tab). Or you

can search for keywords (click the Search tab, type the words to search for, and press Enter), as shown in Figure 5.1.

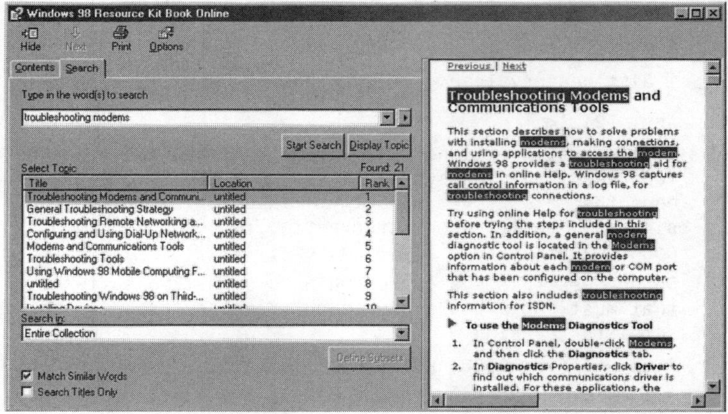

Figure 5.1 The Windows 98 Resource Kit Online Book in Search mode.

There's yet another great built-in feature in Windows 98 that can help you troubleshoot a problem. It's called, not surprisingly, Troubleshooting, and 15 Web-format question-and-answer Troubleshooters are bundled into Windows's help system. To try Troubleshooting, follow these steps:

1. Select Start, choose Help.
2. Click the Contents tab, click the Troubleshooting chapter title, and then click the Windows 98 Troubleshooters title. (You can get to the Troubleshooting chapter from any Windows help file's Contents tab.)
3. Choose from the extensive topic list; then answer the questions that appear in the right-hand panel, and click the Next button to progress to the next possibility, or hopefully, a solution. See Figure 5.2.
4. One of the most useful aspects of the Troubleshooting feature is that each question gives you the option I'd Like to Skip This Step and Try Something Else instead of locking you into a Yes/No logic path. Another excellent flourish is that when you get to the end of any Troubleshooter's questions list, you have the option I Want to See the Questions That I Skipped. Kudos to the designers of this interface!

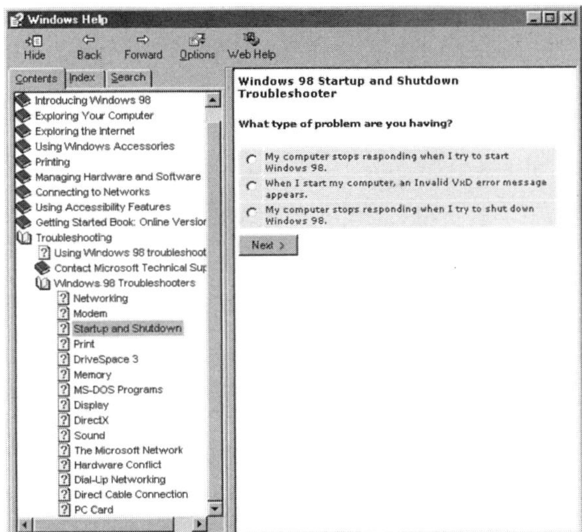

Figure 5.2
The Windows 98 Startup and Shutdown Troubleshooter in action.

5. The Troubleshooting chapter also includes a section called "Contact Microsoft Technical Support," so in the event that no solution is available from a Troubleshooter, you can browse this handful of additional options, one of which is to jump directly to Microsoft's Support Online center on the Web at `http://support.microsoft.com/support/c.asp`.

Watch Out!
Although this is a great tool, accidentally or indiscriminately changing values for any device can have serious consequences—such as your system not working. So always remember to use the Cancel button to dismiss any of these dialog boxes unless you definitely want to implement a change to a device.

Quickly Validating Your Devices

Windows 98 (and its predecessor Windows 95) provides a convenient way to quickly examine the list of devices installed in your PC, along with their configuration and resources. Simply right-click My Computer and choose Properties to bring up the System Properties dialog box. This dialog box has four tabs. The topmost General tab is a simple system summary, but an important piece of information is lurking quietly here. If you ever need to know your Windows 98 registration number, and you didn't write it down when installing Windows, you can find it right here.

The System Properties dialog box includes four tabs. We've already covered the General tab. The remaining three are the Device Manager, the Hardware Profiles, and the Performance tabs.

Bright Idea
If you have a Windows-enhanced keyboard, the fastest way to display the System Properties dialog box is to use your keyboard's Windows key and then press the Pause key.

The Device Manager Tab This tab lists all the devices in your PC. Any devices that have a problem are flagged with an exclamation mark inside a yellow circle. Disabled devices are flagged with a red X, but some questionable terminology exists in the Windows help file. The help text reads "disabled" for a red X, but when you examine a device that's flagged with the exclamation mark inside a yellow circle, you frequently see the term "disabled." Regardless of the help file's confusion, you need to research both types of flags. You can investigate any specific device by double-clicking its category, or by single-clicking the + symbol to the left of its icon. For example, the category CDROM expands to reveal one device, PLEXTOR CD-ROM PX-8XCS, as shown in Figure 5.3.

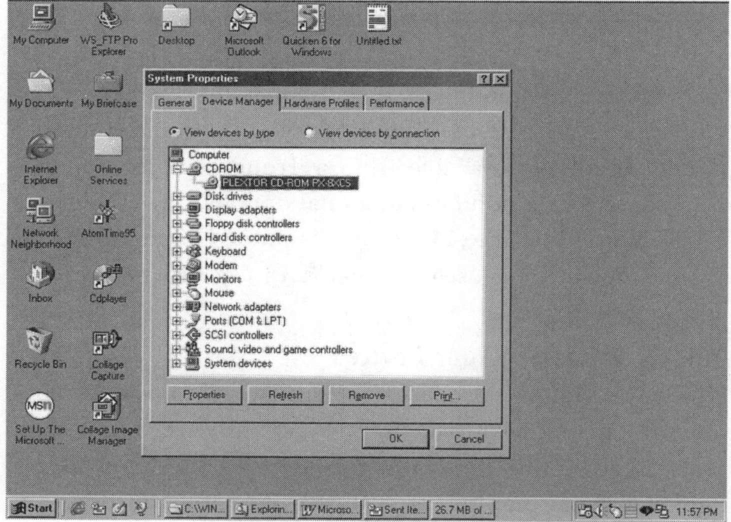

Figure 5.3
The Device Manager tab's device listing, expanded to show the CD-ROM device.

If you don't have any problematic devices, congratulations! If you do have any problematic devices, focus on them first. Double-click the first such device category, choose the specific device (shown in the next branch down), and then click Properties. This selection displays yet another dialog box, typically with three tabs: General, Driver, and Resources. If you carefully inspect these tabs, you can glean much information about this device and its configuration, sometimes including advice on correcting the problem, as shown in Figure 5.4.

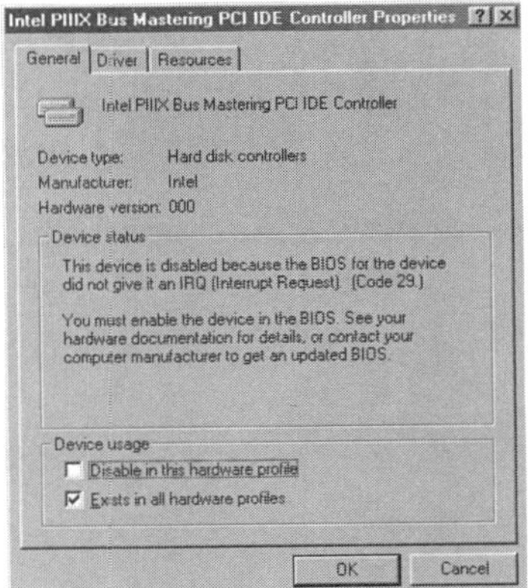

Figure 5.4
The General tab offers further information about a disabled device.

Now you can get to work checking the values for all the unflagged devices because occasionally, even though a device isn't marked with a red X or a yellow circle, the device's properties are incorrect or indicate a more subtle problem. Double-click each category, select its devices and click Properties, and examine the values in all the tabs of the resulting Properties dialog box.

When you're done looking at all these devices and settings, print a complete system report: from the Device Manager tab, click the Print button, select the All Devices and System Summary option, and then click OK. Put this important document in your NEAT box for safekeeping.

If problems persist with one or more devices, refer to the "Handling a Troublesome Component, Operating System, or Application" section.

The Hardware Profiles Tab You probably don't need to use the hardware profiles feature (see Figure 5.5). One likely scenario for using it would be if you use a laptop that has a different configuration when docked than when undocked. For information on this feature, search on "hardware profile" in Windows help.

Watch Out!
If you're using a SCSI controller and hard drive and/or CD-ROM drive, and you've got a PCI IDE hard disk controller on your motherboard, you'll see the exclamation mark inside a yellow circle icon for the PCI IDE controller. That's the way it should be because the device was disabled at the factory to avoid a conflict with your SCSI controller.

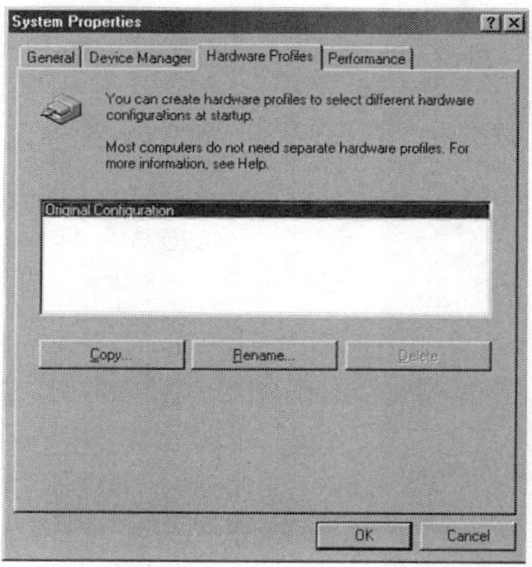

Figure 5.5 The Hardware Profiles tab on the System Properties dialog box.

The Performance Tab On the Performance tab, you want to make sure that you see the phrase "Your system is optimized for optimal performance" and that you do *not* see any references to MS-DOS real mode, as shown in Figure 5.6. If this is not the case, one or more devices aren't fully optimized for Windows 98. The Advanced Settings area, located near the bottom of the window, contains three buttons: File System, Graphics, and Virtual Memory. You want to inspect each one.

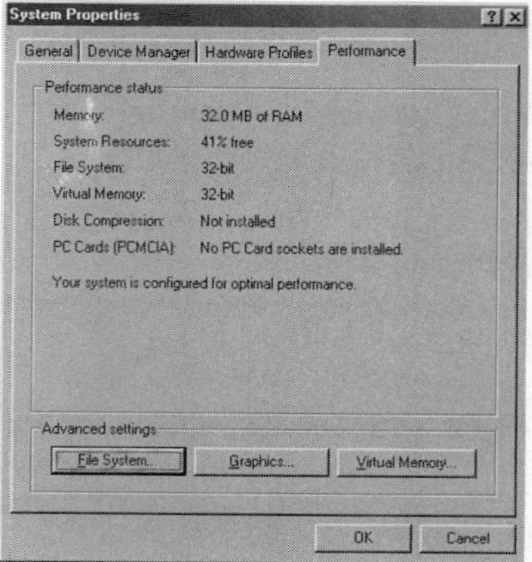

Figure 5.6 The Performance tab on the System Properties dialog box.

Nearly all modern PCs should have the following File System property settings (see Figure 5.7):

- Hard Disk—Set to Desktop Computer and full read-ahead optimization.

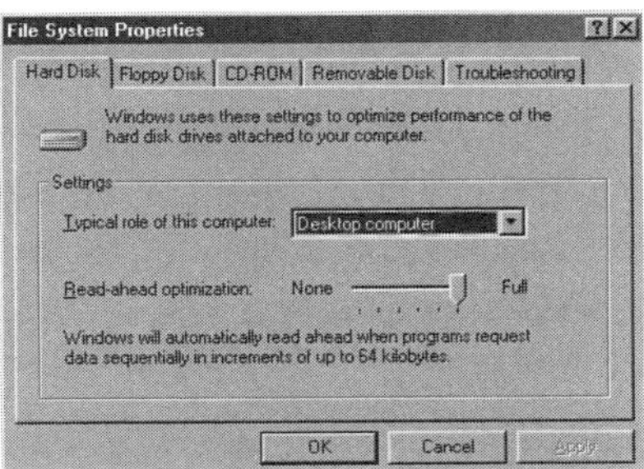

Figure 5.7
The File System Properties dialog box.

- Floppy Disk—You can reduce how long it takes your PC to start by clearing the Search for New Floppy Disk Drives Each Time Your Computer Starts check box. On a test system, clearing this check box reduced total boot-up time by about five seconds (four percent).

Bright Idea
While you're evaluating your Device Manager settings, compare what devices Windows *thinks* you have installed with what you *know* you have installed. Use the inventory list you prepared and stored in your NEAT box as your comparison basis.

- CD-ROM—Set supplemental cache size to Large and unless you have a CD-ROM that's less than a 4X speed, choose Quad-speed or higher in the Optimize Access Pattern for control.
- Removable Disk—This setting is ignored unless you are using a removable disk drive, in which case the ideal setting is to check the Enable Write-Behind Caching on All Removable Disk Drives check box.
- Troubleshooting—Heed the warning and leave these check boxes unchecked.

When you click the Graphics button, you see the Advanced Graphics Settings dialog box, as shown in Figure 5.8, and hardware acceleration should be set to Full.

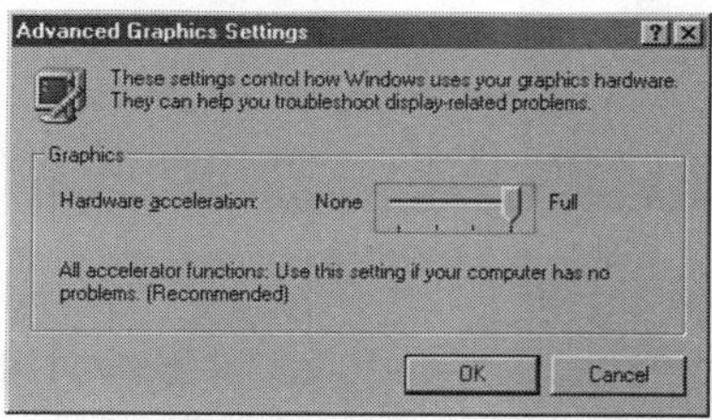

Figure 5.8 The Advanced Graphics Settings dialog box.

When you click the Virtual Memory button, you see the Virtual Memory dialog box. Unless you have thorough knowledge of Windows virtual memory and swap file settings, leave this set to the value Let Windows Manage My Virtual Memory Settings (Recommended).

Burning In Your System by Hand

Inspecting your device settings, as discussed previously, is the first step to your PC's shakedown cruise. But it's equally important to physically exercise each device. That's what this section is all about.

Moneysaver
If you like clever utilities and hoard them like treasures (we do), check out CDROMINF at `http://www.ncf.carleton.ca/~aa571/index.html`. From the folks at Computall Services (Jim McLaughlin), this MS-DOS command-line program makes calls to your CD-ROM's device drivers and displays the results. For audio CD lovers, it displays any textual information such as song titles or lyrics stored on the loaded CD.

The expression "burn in your system" refers to the process of testing all the components of your PC. By doing so early in its life, you can quickly identify any bad devices and get quick action on the part of the manufacturer. Two ways exist to burn in a system. The first way is to do one physical test of each device. The second way is to use third-party diagnostic and testing utilities that you can operate once or even set to run repeatedly, as well as to log results to log files you can study at your leisure.

To start, we recommend that you print a screen shot of your Device Manager listing. Then exercise each device, one at a time, and if it works satisfactorily, put a check mark next to it. We'll do it together.

CD-ROM

Insert an audio CD and play it; do you hear it?

Insert a software CD and use Windows Explorer to browse its contents; then pick a file at random and copy it to the root folder of your C: drive. Does the file copy properly? (You can delete the file from your C: drive when finished with this test.)

Another excellent test of the CD-ROM drive is to install a program from a CD. Does it install properly?

Disk Drives

To test your floppy drive, make a Windows startup disk: Insert an empty, formatted 1.44MB disk into your floppy drive and choose Start, then choose Control Panel, then Add/Remove Programs, Startup Disk, and then choose Create Disk. Does the process complete satisfactorily? Leave the disk in the floppy drive, reboot your system, and let it boot from the floppy. (You can remove the floppy disk now and press Ctrl+Alt+Del to restart your system normally.)

You already performed one test of your hard disk when you copied a file from a CD-ROM to C:. You also manually use some handy tools that ship free with Windows 98. One is called ScanDisk and one is called Disk Defragmenter. We'll cover Disk Defragmenter in much greater detail in Chapter 12, "Cleaning Up." For now, we'll do a one-time test of your hard disk using each tool. (If you have multiple physical hard disks, test each of them individually using these tools.) Later, in the section "Task Scheduler," we describe how to use a Windows 98 tool called Task Scheduler to further test your disk drives.

When running ScanDisk for the first time as a burn-in tool, follow these steps:

1. To start ScanDisk, close all running applications and then select Start, choose Programs, choose Accessories, choose System Tools, and choose ScanDisk. The ScanDisk dialog box opens, as seen in Figure 5.9.

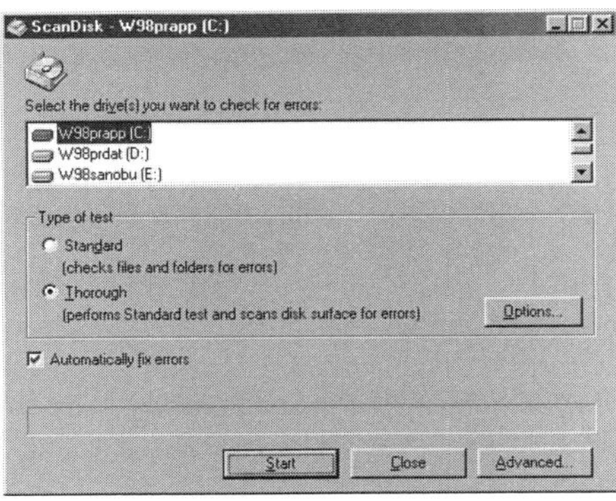

Figure 5.9
The ScanDisk dialog box.

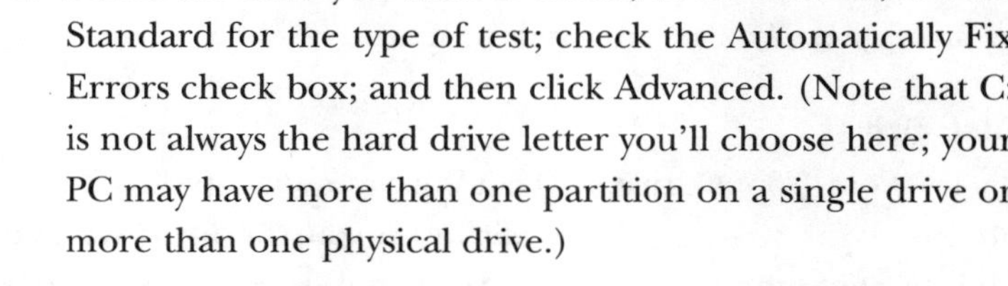

2. Select the drive you want to check, in this case C:; choose Standard for the type of test; check the Automatically Fix Errors check box; and then click Advanced. (Note that C: is not always the hard drive letter you'll choose here; your PC may have more than one partition on a single drive or more than one physical drive.)

   At this point, make sure that the settings are set this way: Always (Display Summary), Append to Log, Make Copies (Cross-Linked Files), and Convert to Files (Lost File Fragments). Also, Invalid File Names and Invalid Dates and Times should be checked, Check Host Drive First should be checked (irrelevant unless you're using drive compression), and Report MS-DOS Mode Name Length Errors should be checked. Now click OK.

3. To begin the scan, click Start. How long a Standard scan takes is strictly a function of how large your C: drive is; figure *roughly* 15 seconds per gigabyte on a classic Pentium system.

Watch Out!
In the earlier steps, you set Append to Log to have a running log of everything that happens for the next day or so in the PC's life. Don't forget to change this back to Replace Log when you finish the burn-in process. (By changing from Append to Log to Replace Log, you avoid the log file growing to an unwieldy size as your PC continually appends to it.)

When the tool is finished, you'll see a ScanDisk Results dialog box, as shown in Figure 5.10. Examine it and make sure that no errors occurred, or if there were, that they were all fixed. You can view ScanDisk's log file (typically `C:\Scandisk.log`) in any Windows-based text editor to see the behind-the-scenes details of what has been scanned and fixed. If you use an MS-DOS program to view this file, some of the characters may appear incorrectly.

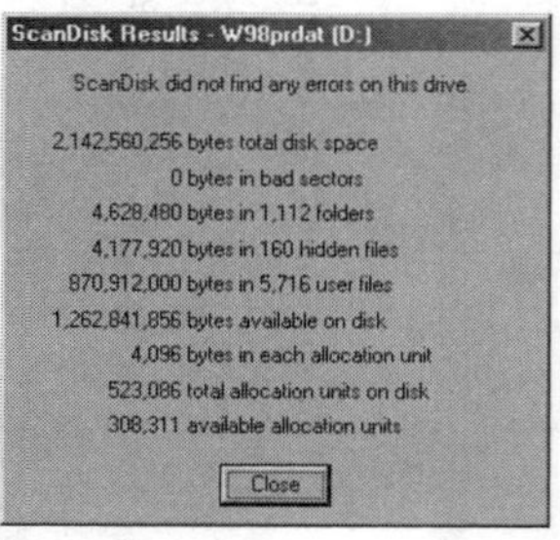

Figure 5.10 The ScanDisk Results dialog box.

Next, run a Thorough ScanDisk on the same drive by following these steps:

1. Select Start, choose Programs, Accessories, System Tools, and then ScanDisk.
2. Select C: again and choose Thorough. Click the Options button; then be sure that System and Data Areas is selected, and be sure that Do Not Perform Write-Testing and Do Not Repair Bad Sectors in Hidden and System Files are *not* checked; we repeat, *not* checked. Then click OK.
3. To begin the scan, click Start. When the tool is finished (for a Thorough scan figure roughly 14 minutes per gigabyte on a classic Pentium system), you'll see a ScanDisk Results dialog box. Examine this dialog box and `Scandisk.log`, as described earlier.

Unofficially...
By running the Standard ScanDisk, you identify any obvious, glaring problems. Consider it the equivalent of a doctor listening to your heart with a stethoscope. If no glaring problems are discovered, go to a Thorough ScanDisk. The Thorough scan, regardless of the Standard scan outcome, tests the drive more extensively—right here, right now—before putting any more time into configuring the PC. The Thorough SD is analogous to an EKG of a human patient. Any corners cut here can have a tremendous cost later.

After doing both a Standard and a Thorough ScanDisk of C:, it's time to defragment this drive. Because your system is fresh from the factory, it's not likely to be very fragmented. That's okay, because you're using this tool simply as a way to exercise the hard disk. Follow these steps:

1. Before using Disk Defragmenter, take special care to disable any screen saver (right-click on an open space on your Windows desktop, select Properties, Screen Saver, then select (None) and click OK). This is because we have known some systems to crash while being defragmented when the screen saver kicks in.
2. To start Disk Defragmenter, select Start, then select Programs, Accessories, System Tools, and Disk Defragmenter to bring up the dialog box shown in Figure 5.11.
3. Click the Settings button and make sure that the settings are as described here: Rearrange Program Files So My Programs Start Faster should be checked; Check the Drive for Errors should be checked (even though we just did a ScanDisk, go ahead and let defrag perform this error check because the objective is to thoroughly exercise the drive); and select the Every Time I Defragment My Hard

Watch Out!
Even if your disk is fresh from the factory, before running Disk Defragmenter, always close all running applications, including Task Scheduler and your screen saver.

Drive option. Then click OK. While the utility is running, you may want to click the Show Details button to see a full-screen representation of what it's doing.

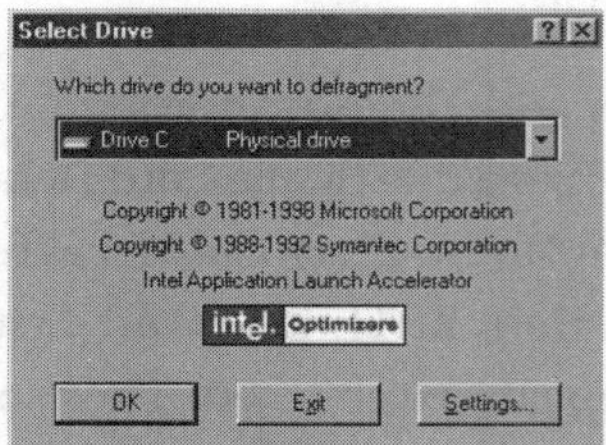

Figure 5.11 The Disk Defragmenter dialog box.

Unofficially... Symantec Corporation's Web site includes a knowledge base that has one article of particular interest to those of you yearning to delve into the nitty-gritty of hard drive configuration. See "How to Check Hard Drive Configuration" at `http://service1.symantec.com/SUPPORT/nunt.nsf/docid/1996112575859`.

Display Adapters

If you can see your Windows desktop, at least you know that your video card is sending signals to your monitor. To dig a bit deeper, right-click any open space of your desktop and choose Properties (see Figure 5.12). (Another way to access the same dialog box is to go into Control Panel and click the Display applet.) Now click on the Settings tab and make sure that the monitor and display adapter names match what you know to be installed. If not, you'll want to install the proper driver. It could be that the specific driver for your hardware is not on the Windows setup CD or that Windows is confused as to what hardware you have. In Chapter 8, "Staying Ahead of the Game," we'll talk at length about updating drivers.

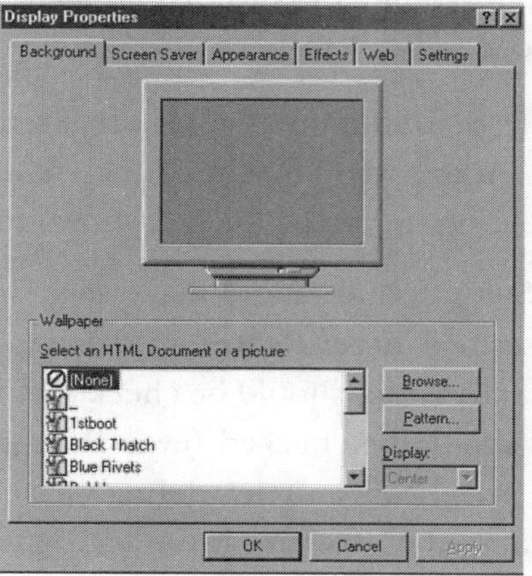

Figure 5.12 The Display Properties dialog box.

Try changing the Screen area setting, first to one resolution higher than the current setting, then to one resolution lower, then back to where you started (unless you prefer one of these different settings). While making these changes, observe how your display behaves, and look for any unusual disruptions in the screen image. Perform the same test with the Colors setting. Use what you learned about the What's This? button if you want to find out more about any of the Display Properties dialog box's controls. If you don't like what you see during this test, refer to the "Handling a Troublesome Component, Operating System, or Application" section.

If you have an Energy Star–compliant monitor, to activate its power-management features, click the Screen Saver tab, click the Settings button, on the Power Schemes tab choose Home/Office Desk (if your PC will always be on, select Always On), and then choose how many minutes to wait before turning the monitor off in the Turn Off Monitor control. As a quick test, select the After 1 Min setting; click OK; click OK again; and then take your hands off the keyboard and mouse and wait one minute, at which point your monitor display should go dark (in addition, some monitors have a color scheme associated with their LED indicator, such as Yellow for Stand By and Orange for Suspend, so look for this change if it's supported by your monitor). If you don't like what you see during this test, refer to the "Handling a Troublesome Component, Operating System, or Application" section.

Floppy Disk Controllers

The test you performed earlier that involved creating a Windows start disk is an adequate initial test of the floppy disk and its controller.

Hard Disk Controllers

The tests you performed earlier that involved ScanDisk and Disk Defragmenter are adequate initial tests of the hard disk and its controller.

Unofficially...
Sadly, many dialog boxes produced by Windows itself don't include a Help command button that allows you to dive into the details of an associated program or component's help file. However, Windows dialog boxes do include a feature called the What's This? button that appears as a ? button in the dialog box's title bar. When you click the What's This? button, the mouse pointer changes its appearance to include a black question mark. Now when you click a dialog box control, you'll see a small pop-up window with a sentence or two (sometimes more) explaining what that control does. The keyboard shortcut is F1; when you press F1 you'll see context-sensitive help for the control that has the input focus.

Keyboard

All the tests you performed thus far have required some use of the keyboard, so if you can type, it's probably working satisfactorily. You'll thoroughly test the keyboard with diagnostic software later in this chapter.

Modem

Windows comes with a modem diagnostic tool built right in. From Control Panel, click the Modems applet, click the Diagnostics tab, select the port that has a modem defined in the Installed column, click the More Info button, and after a few seconds you should see a dialog box like the one shown in Figure 5.13. Click OK twice to dismiss these dialog boxes.

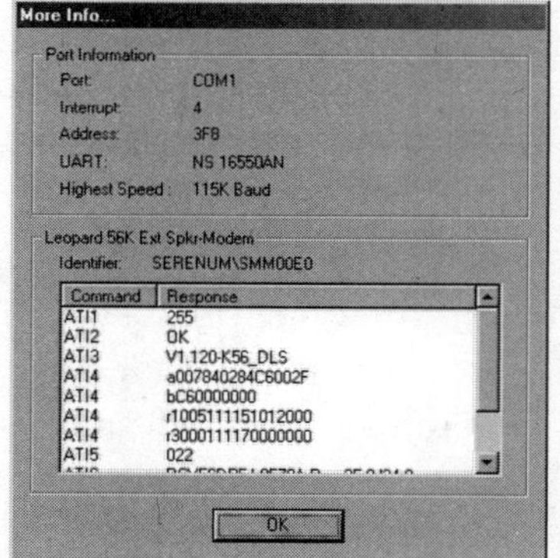

Figure 5.13
The result of a diagnostic test on a PC's modem is displayed in the More Info... dialog box.

Another easy way to test your modem is to connect to the Internet and browse the Web, or check your email. If you get connected, you know that your modem is working. Next you should check your modem properties to make sure that Windows and the modem are in agreement. From Control Panel, click the Modems applet, click the General tab, and then work your way through all the subsequent settings.

Monitor

The tests you performed earlier in the "Display Adapters" section provide a good initial test of the monitor. But you can do one more thing now. Not only will this exercise put your monitor through some additional paces, but it also gives you an opportunity to learn how to adjust these settings (which, by the way, are typically "set once and forget," but as we mentioned in Chapter 1, it's something you need to know how to do).

Each monitor manufacturer has its own peculiar configuration of buttons, knobs, and dials, in addition to onscreen menus and controls—all for the purpose of adjusting settings such as position, size, color, geometry, contrast, and brightness. Look in your monitor's user's guide for details on each control, and work your way through each of them right now. In fact, most user's guides include a section titled something like "Recommended Use," so read that material thoroughly and apply its suggestions now.

Mouse

All the tests you performed thus far have required some use of the mouse. You'll thoroughly test the keyboard with diagnostic software later in this chapter. Naturally, if your mouse has been working thus far, it's probably just fine.

Network Adapters

If you have a network card installed in your PC, you can test it by attempting to log on to the network. Otherwise, skip this step.

Ports (COM & LPT)

By testing your modem, you've tested the COM port that the modem is attached to. To test the LPT port, test your printer. Here's how to quickly test your printer: Select Start, choose Printers, right-click your printer in the list, choose Properties, and then click the Print Test Page button. You should take the time now to verify that Windows has your printer's properties right; we've found that Windows often is incorrect about the amount of memory in printers (see the Device Options tab). Work your way through all seven tabs in your printer's Properties dialog box, verifying each setting.

SCSI Controllers

The tests you performed earlier that involved ScanDisk and Disk Defragmenter are adequate initial tests of the hard disk

Unofficially...
If you're using SCSI, the SCSI software that loads at bootup probably includes a feature for testing your hard disks. Jump into this utility the next time your PC boots up, and check it out.

and its controller. This statement applies whether the controller is SCSI or ATA/IDE.

Sound, Video, and Game Controllers

If you played an audio CD (as recommended earlier as a test of your CD-ROM drive) and heard it through your speakers, that's a good sign. You can do some more testing by inserting your Windows 98 CD and choosing Cool Video Clips.

Utilities for Burning In Your System

The manual testing discussed up to now should point out any major problem areas in your new computer, but we don't recommend that you call it a day just yet. Windows 98 comes with various testing and diagnostic tools that you can (and should) use to burn in your system initially, and that you can schedule to run periodically to help keep your system operating trouble free.

Unofficially...
If you search the Web for diagnostic and testing utilities, you'll undoubtedly find dozens that have features similar to the ones we recommend in this section. However, when you read the fine print (or waste time downloading and installing them), you'll be disappointed to discover that they don't have a graphical user interface. Some don't run under Windows at all, only under MS-DOS mode *outside* the Windows shell. So many outstanding applications in this tool category are true Windows applications that you shouldn't bother with any that are DOS only.

In addition, you should be aware of some third-party diagnostic tools. These run the gamut from free utilities that will pluck up a single bit of useful system information for you (such as MMXTest, which verifies the CPU installed in your computer), to low-cost, full-blown shareware diagnostic programs (such as Sandra) that can report on every aspect of your system, to high-cost, full-blown commercialware diagnostic programs such as Norton Utilities. Adding a diagnostic package to your system-maintenance arsenal is a very good idea, and in this section we enumerate some of the more popular third-party packages available. Many of these products have troubleshooting features that walk you through locating and documenting a problem, which is half the battle of fixing it.

Windows Troubleshooting Tools

We strongly recommend that you familiarize yourself with Windows's built-in troubleshooting utilities because you'll undoubtedly be using them at some point. By using them now, you benefit by familiarizing yourself with them while you're burning in your PC. You should also plan on having at least one third-party application on hand for testing purposes.

Microsoft System Information Tool This tool (aka MSInfo) comes with Windows 98. As shown in Figure 5.14, it displays information about hardware resources, components, and the software environment. Consider it an extension to the Device Manager dialog box. You can also use MSInfo as a front end for other Microsoft troubleshooting tools by selecting the Tools menu and selecting the desired tool (more on these shortly).

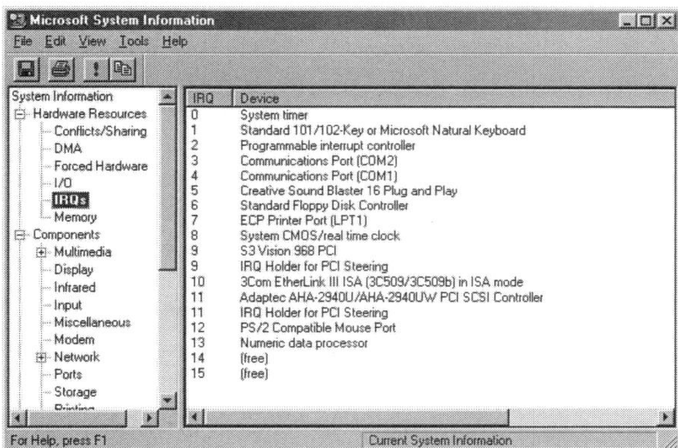

Figure 5.14
The Microsoft System Information tool.

To use MSInfo as a burn-in test, follow these steps:

1. Select Start, Programs, Accessories, System Tools, and then System Information.
2. Double-click the Hardware Resources category and then select the Conflicts/Sharing item, snooping for any trouble spots.
3. Double-click the Components category and then click the Problem Devices item to see whether MSInfo thinks you have any errant components.

Windows Update This Web-based facility examines your system and determines—across numerous categories ranging from the essential Critical Updates to the sometimes whimsical Additional Windows Features—where you could benefit from updated drivers or other software components. We cover Windows Update thoroughly in Chapter 7. For now, you can use Windows Update as a reality check to see whether the factory shipped you the latest and greatest software or stuff that's as moldy as a three-week-old loaf of bread.

Task Scheduler Although we'll spend more time on the Task Scheduler in subsequent chapters, here you'll quickly set it up to help you burn in your new PC. You access Scheduled Tasks by selecting Start, Programs, Accessories, System Tools, and then Scheduled Tasks; or you could create a shortcut to `Mstask.exe` (typically in `C:\Windows\System`). This tool allows you to set a date, a time, and intervals for tasks (programs) to be run automatically by Windows (see Figure 5.15). The tool also includes a wizard that helps you select and schedule a task.

A typical Windows 98 installation includes four predefined tasks: Disk Defragmenter, Low disk space notification, and ScanDisk (two tasks: one Standard and one Thorough). For your burn-in testing, follow these steps:

1. Start Task Scheduler.
2. Set Disk Defragmenter to run once every 3 hours for the next 12 hours, starting at 9:00 p.m. (adjust this time to suit your situation; for now simply make sure that it's a time *ahead* of the current time). Right-click Disk Defragmenter, choose Properties, click Task, and make sure that the Enabled (Scheduled Task Runs at Specified Time) check box is checked; click Schedule, set Schedule Task to Daily, set Start Time to any time before the current time, set Schedule Task Daily to Every 1 Days, click the Advanced button, check the Repeat Task check box, and set for every 3 hours until (Duration) 12 hours. In the Settings tab, make sure that the Only Start the Scheduled Task if Computer Is Idle For and Stop the Scheduled Task if Computer Is in Use check boxes are clear, and click OK.
3. Disable the Low Disk Space Notification Task. Right-click the task, choose Properties, in the Task tab make sure that the Enabled (Scheduled Task Runs at Specified Time) check box is cleared, and then click OK.

4. Disable the ScanDisk for Windows (Standard Test) and ScanDisk for Windows (Thorough Test) tasks for the purposes of this exercise.

5. To kick off the scheduled series of defragmentation tasks for your burn-in testing, you need to do only one thing: Set the value in the Start Time field (in the Schedule tab) to a time *before* the current time. That task will start immediately and proceed to perform its recurring tasks at the intervals you've defined.

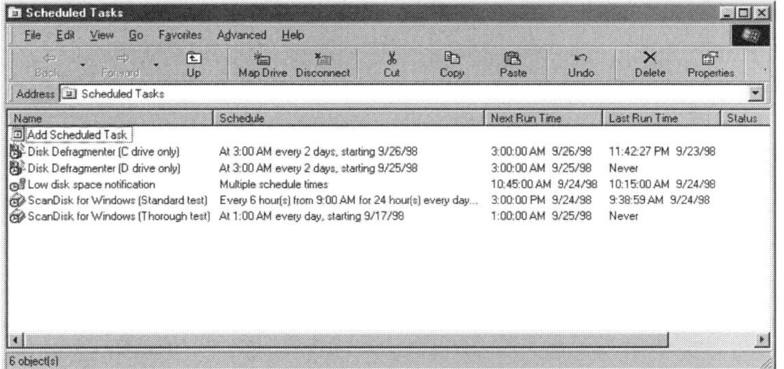

Figure 5.15
The Task Scheduler tool.

Watch Out!
Because you've turned off some options that under normal operating conditions should be on and your use of Task Scheduler for burn-in is finished, let's set things back. Check the Settings tab for the appropriate tasks and make sure that the Only Start the Scheduled Task if Computer Is Idle For and Stop the Scheduled Task if Computer Is in Use check boxes are checked (unless you explicitly want them cleared for a particular task). Then proceed to reset Disk Defragmenter the way you want it to run normally. Also remember to check the Task tab's Enabled check box for each task.

Other Microsoft Troubleshooting Tools

Several other troubleshooting tools come with Windows 98 but don't apply to the process of burning in a new PC. We'll cover many of them in subsequent chapters. You can also find out more about these tools in the Resource Kit by going to the "Troubleshooting Tools" chapter (or by performing a search on "troubleshooting tools").

Sandra We highly recommend that you check out Sandra from SiSoft Software (see Figure 5.16). The product name is derived from the phrase "System Analyser, Diagnostic, and Reporting Assistant," and Sandra delivers mightily on all these fronts. It is one of the most well-designed, informative, and easy-to-use Windows applications—in any category—that we've run across in a long while. Sandra's 50-plus reports (which it

Unofficially... Microsoft has a neat but well-hidden tool that can help you sniff out some problems related to entering low-power consumption modes. You can find `Pmtshoot.exe` on your Windows 98 CD in the `\tools\mtsutil\pmtshoot` folder. You can also go online to `http://support.microsoft.com/support/kb/articles/Q185/9/49.asp` for the tool and details.

calls modules) are presented on the screen much like applets inside a Windows Explorer folder and file listing. These modules are chock full of documented—and undocumented—information about your system and its components, all presented in a very clear and easy-to-digest style. You can choose how much of the nitty-gritty to view, too. Want to know the *exact* model information for your CPU? Then go into the CPU & BIOS Information module. Curious to know the manufacturer's name and version number of your motherboard, how much system memory (and of what type) is in each bank, or even how many banks you have? Then go to the Mainboard Information module. It's all there in stunning detail. You'll also find numerous tips at the end of each module that apply specifically to your system.

You can use Sandra's Create a Report Wizard to generate printed, file, or fax reports on any or all its modules. Sandra provides graphic bar-chart benchmarking statistics right inside its information dialog boxes. For example, it compares your CPU performance against four CPU configurations. You can use the CPU, drives, CD-ROM/DVD, and memory individual benchmarks as an aid to burning in your system. Or just use the Performance Tune-up Wizard that runs all enabled information and testing/diagnostic modules and then gathers all Sandra's performance-enhancing tips, errors, and warnings into a single list.

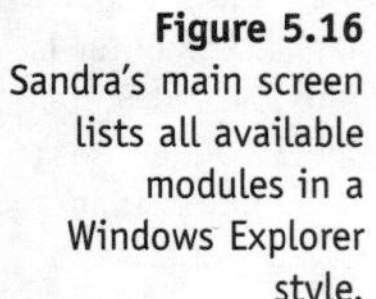

Figure 5.16 Sandra's main screen lists all available modules in a Windows Explorer style.

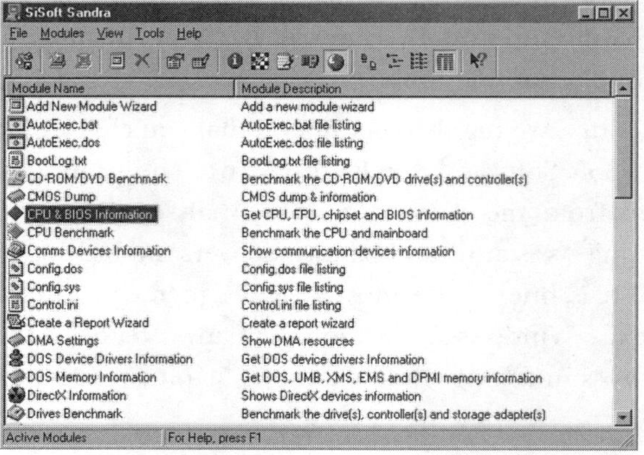

Sandra is shareware, and you can register for $29; the 2.2MB download is available at www.sisoftware.demon.co.uk/sandra/. Registering gets you the Professional edition, which includes fully functional modules (a few modules are disabled in the shareware version), free updates, and free technical support.

Sandra is a top-notch, reasonably priced utility, and we recommend it highly for both novice and experienced users.

Norton Utilities Norton Utilities from Symantec Corporation is the king of the hill when it comes to the wide-open Windows utilities category. It's a veritable 25-pound Swiss army knife, including these features (with dozens of wizards, doctors, subfeatures, and impressive background processes): problem diagnosis and repair, crash guard, automatic driver update, system rescue, antivirus, disk optimization, Registry optimization, file delete protection, and system information. If it can be done, Norton Utilities does it.

No shareware or demo version is available, however, so dig deep into your pockets because the street price on this hummer is $89.95. Check out the product page at the firm's Web site: http://www.symantec.com/nu/fs_nu3-95.html.

CheckIt 98 CheckIt 98 from TouchStone Software Corporation is a diagnostic utility for Windows 95/98 (and DOS) that also includes system information, backup/restore for critical system files, a system change monitor, Year 2000 test and fix, and a troubleshooter, among other items. CheckIt has a Web-style user interface (modules are listed along the left in a navigation frame), plus a traditional menu bar and toolbar. The interface is easy to use and presents resulting information clearly.

A 15-day trial version of the Windows 95-only version of CheckIt is available from the ZDNet Software Library, and you can register/upgrade to CheckIt 98 for $49.95. The 6.5MB download (remember, this is for a Windows 95-only version) is available at http://hotfiles.zdnet.com/cgi-bin/texis/swlib/hotfiles/info.html?fcode=000NTN.

The QuickCheck test will be most helpful during PC burn-in testing. If you have a problem during burn-in or sometime later, you'll benefit from CheckIt's Thorough Troubleshooter feature, which you can follow simply by clicking buttons.

PC Medic Network Associates's PC Medic is a diagnostic utility for Windows 95 systems. (At the time of this writing, the manufacturer hadn't confirmed whether PC Medic is suitable for use with Windows 98, so use it at your own risk.) Additional features include a Crash Monitor that intercepts many GPFs (general protection faults) so that you can stop and save your work before the crashing application *really* crashes, a "second opinion" knowledge base, backup/restore, a diagnostic undo that acts as a safety net so that you can roll back changes made by the Diagnostic Wizard and Crash Monitor, a detailed log of all PC Medic activity, system inventory, and Year 2000 testing. It displays a goofy splash-screen checklist that persists, and each module runs in a separate Wizard-style window. This makes for an awkward two-window arrangement at all times and makes it unnecessarily difficult to get to the product's main help table of contents.

A trial version of PC Medic is available from the ZDNet Software Library. The 32.7MB download—yes, that's right, 32.7 *megabytes*—is at `http://hotfiles.zdnet.com/cgi-bin/texis/swlib/hotfiles/info.html?fcode=0000OP`, and the price for a registered copy is $39.

Frankly, although PC Medic is listed in all the computer magazine reviews of this utility category (thus we've included it here), we don't like PC Medic's user interface.

Data Advisor Data Advisor is a free testing and diagnostic utility for hard disks and memory. It works like a small, special-purpose operating system. You create a bootable disk with Data Advisor on it, exit Windows, and reboot from A:. Data Advisor takes over and runs a quick check of your hard disks; then, if you so choose, it performs a series of tests including a complete surface scan, file structure test, and system memory test (all of which may take five or more minutes per hard disk, but a timer and potentiometer keep you posted throughout). Data

Advisor also includes a virus scanner that's frequently updated to detect the latest viruses, including macro viruses (but this component is only a scanner; it has no eradication or prevention capabilities).

Data Advisor was developed by ONTRACK Data International, Inc., a company that markets itself as the "world leader in data recovery." The tool can be used to remotely connect to ONTRACK's network so that its engineers can potentially help you recover data from a PC with a damaged disk drive (we cover this process in Chapter 19, "Recovering from a PC Disaster"). Go to www.ontrack.com for the free 1.3MB download.

Data Advisor is a useful utility that focuses strictly on your hard disks and system memory and is a must-have in your diagnostic tool kit. During burn-in, you can use it to exercise those components. Best of all, it's free.

BCM Diagnostics BCM Diagnostics (from BCM Advanced Research, Inc.) performs testing and diagnosis for Windows 95 systems. (At the time of this writing, the developer had not responded to our inquiry about Windows 98 compatibility or a timetable for a product update.) You can test these components: processor, memory, audio, video, modem, graphics, hard disk, floppy disk, and CD-ROM drive.

BCM Diagnostics is shareware, and you can register for $25; the 4.4MB download is available at www.bcmgvc.com. During the 30-day trial period, the only limitation is 10 maximum loops on the stress test.

We like BCM Diagnostics because you can both run benchmarks and perform hardware stress testing on your system. This latter feature is the most useful when burning in a new system, and sports a friendly user interface. We're hoping that Windows 98 support is added before this book hits the shelves.

Dr. Hardware Like Sandra, Dr. Hardware is a system analysis and reporting tool. However, it does not provide tips specifically catered to your system, so, unlike Sandra, it doesn't qualify as a diagnostic tool in the strictest sense of the word. Dr. Hardware has a pleasing user interface with plenty of graphics displays where appropriate; we find it easy to use.

Dr. Hardware, developed by P. Gebhard, is shareware, and you can register for $28; the 1.2MB download is available at `http://ourworld.compuserve.com/homepages/pgsoft/`. Registering gets you a fully functional version (some features are disabled in the shareware version), free updates for the next year, and access to technical support (none for shareware users).

All told, you'll find 60-plus modules to assist you in studying and reporting on your system and its components, and the reporting feature—although not as cool as Sandra's wizard interface—provides lots of options.

Unofficially... The folks at California Scientific Software tell an interesting tale in the `Readme.txt` file that accompanies MMXTest. We won't spoil all the fun, but they debunk the notion that the acronym MMX really stands for anything meaningful. Heh heh heh.

MMXTest MMXTest is a neat little no-interface utility that reports what family of processor you have, tests to see whether your CPU supports MMX, and if so, performs an "MMX versus non-MMX" speed comparison. MMXTest is freeware from California Scientific Software, and all 43KB can be downloaded at `www.calsci.com/`. Use this tool during burn-in to verify that you got the processor you were promised.

MMXTest is another special-purpose tool, but the price (free) is right and it provides useful information about your processor.

ZDNet Virtual Labs ZDNet maintains an online laboratory that's a good place to scope out tools for testing both hardware and software. You can actually test components attached to your PC *right now*, in real time, via your Web browser. However, this Web site doesn't replace a stress test that loops; instead, this facility is good for quickly testing something on your system. The site is by no means an alternative to buying a third-party testing/diagnostic package, but it is free.

The ZDNet Virtual Lab lives at `www.zdnet.com/vlabs/index.html`.

Upgrading to Windows 98 from Windows 95

If your "new" PC is one you inherited from another department, a coworker, or a friend, but it has Windows 95 installed on it, this section's for you.

Upgrading to Windows 98 from Windows 95 can be an easy process if you prepare for it. How? By carefully following our upgrade checklist. It's time for a spring cleaning of your Windows 95 system anyway, right? Expect to spend about one hour working through this checklist, then about one hour for the actual upgrade.

1. *Important*: Make sure that you have a working, write-protected Windows 95 start disk (also called a boot disk) that includes real-mode drivers to allow you to see your CD-ROM drive. If you didn't get a utility disk with your CD-ROM drive, or if it came from the factory without one, you can contact your CD-ROM drive's manufacturer. Typically, the company will have a utility on its Web site, or technical support can email it to you. Other alternatives? Format an empty 1.44MB floppy via `format a:/s`. After you have the drivers on the disk and set up `Autoexec.bat` and `Config.sys` properly, turn off your PC, insert the boot disk, turn on your PC, and verify that it boots properly and that you can see all your hard drives and CD-ROM drives. (By verify, we mean to literally type each drive letter and a colon, then press Enter and do a `DIR` command on the drive to be sure that it's available. It's of paramount importance that you do this for your CD-ROM drive. While doing countless upgrades in the field, on many occasions we've discovered a problem with the start disk's real-mode drivers such that the CD-ROM drive wasn't actually available. Better to find this out and correct it before you start the upgrade than afterward, when it's too late.)

2. Check your BIOS for Y2K (as discussed earlier in this chapter) and PnP compliance. If you need to upgrade your BIOS, do so now.

3. Clean up your existing main drives. (See Chapter 12, "Cleaning Up," for a handy checklist on how to clean up your hard drives and recover wasted space.) This gives Windows 98 setup the best chance of having adequate free space.

4. Fully back up your existing main drives. (See Chapter 11, "Backing Up," for this checklist.)

5. Defragment your existing main drives. *Important:* Before running Disk Defragmenter, always close all running applications, including Task Scheduler and your screen saver.
6. Print a hard copy of your current System Summary (Click My Computer, then select Device Manager, Print, then All Devices and System Summary. Click OK and then click Cancel.) and store this in your NEAT box.
7. In addition to getting a printed copy of your system settings, take screen shots of each device's current dialog box settings and save these in a WordPad or other word processing file, and then put them in your NEAT box. For example, the Advanced Connection Settings for your modem's Properties dialog box (Click My Computer, then select Properties, Device Manager, and then choose the modem device. Select Properties, Connection, and select Advanced.) could prove invaluable when—for some unanticipated reason—you next need to reinstall your modem.
8. Print a hard copy of your current CMOS settings and put these in your NEAT box.
9. Copy your production `Autoexec.bat` and `Config.sys` files (if you have any) to a disk, and then write-protect it. (`Autoexec.bat` and `Config.sys` files are present on the Windows start disk that Windows 98 produces for you, but these are specialized for use by the boot disk. You want to preserve your own boot files.)
10. Print hard copies of your current `Autoexec.bat` and `Config.sys` files, and store them in your NEAT box.
11. Verify that you have disks or CD-ROMs for all your latest device drivers. If you've downloaded and upgraded any drivers since you last set up or configured your system, be sure to copy these drivers from your hard disk to standalone disks, if you haven't done so already (see Chapter 7). Although in some cases Windows 98 will have its own updated drivers for devices, when it comes to upgrading a PC's operating system, you can't be too prepared.

12. Clean all the dust from your PC's interior and exterior. (We discuss this procedure further in Chapter 10, "Good Habits for a Trouble-Free System.") Okay, okay, so we're sounding a bit compulsive. But you'll read in Chapter 10 about how damaging the simple accumulation of a few months' worth of dust can be, so take this opportunity now to do a little dust busting.

13. If you intend to upgrade any peripherals or components—for example, system memory—do this *before* you upgrade to Windows 98. Test the new components for a few days before proceeding with the Windows 98 upgrade, too.

14. Cold-boot your PC; close *all* running applications, including those in your System Tray, and disable any antivirus software. Insert the Windows 98 upgrade CD and follow the installation instructions from there. When you're asked to register online, we recommend that you do so, but refrain from having the installer send an inventory of your computer to Redmond. The choice of whether to save your prior Windows 95 installation is strictly up to you, and a function of your available hard disk space. To date, of the many Win95-to-Win98 upgrades we've done at our companies and in the field, we have never found it necessary or useful to retain that prior installation. Still, use your own judgment. You'll notice that your PC boots and reboots itself many times during the upgrade; that's normal for this upgrade.

15. After you've been running Windows 98 satisfactorily for a few days, you can free up considerable hard disk space by converting to FAT32. Note that after you convert to FAT32, you can no longer uninstall Windows 98, so if you kept your Windows 95 installation around, this is the time to dump it. To convert to FAT32, close *all* running applications, including those in your System Tray; select Start, Programs, Accessories, System Tools, and then Drive Converter (FAT32); and follow the instructions from there.

Unofficially...
V Communications, Inc., makes a great utility called System Commander. Actually, there are two flavors, Regular and Deluxe. If you want a fail-safe safety net that also provides hand holding throughout the entire Win95-to-Win98 upgrade process, grab a copy of System Commander Deluxe and fire up its OS Wizard. The OS Wizard analyzes your system and recommends exactly how to upgrade, and it allows you to preserve your existing operating system. Additional features include dynamic repartitioning, multiboot options, and even multiple operating systems in the same partition.

Chapter Ending

- Start by verifying the settings of your PC's BIOS, a small bootstrap program that jump-starts your PC into recognizing the peripherals attached to it.
- Out-of-the-box failures come in three flavors: component, Windows itself, or an application. Each requires a specific approach to solve.
- It's easy to use our checklists to "burn in your system" by hand.
- If your new PC came to you from another department, coworker, or friend, and it has Windows 95, you need our checklist for upgrading to Windows 98.

PART II

Making the PC Yours

Chapter 6

Customizing Your New PC

NOW THAT YOU HAVE your PC assembled and running, it's time to start customizing it for your own use. We're big on customization because we fervently believe that wherever possible, the computer should adapt to the way you want to work, and not the other way around. In this section you learn how to customize your desktop, your menus, and other objects for quick and easy task management. You will have your top applications at your fingertips, and you'll be quickly moving and classifying files the way you want. Follow our lead here and we guarantee that you'll spend less time on the mundane stuff and more time being productive or just having fun.

Differences Between Windows 95 and Windows 98

Windows 95 was quite a departure from Windows 3.x, and it provided various user customizations to make your computing life easier. The apparent differences between Windows 95 and Windows 98 are not as easily seen, but some fundamental changes occur at the core of the Windows 98 interface and in the different ways you can customize it.

Probably the most visible change is Microsoft's attempt to integrate the Web browser interface with the Windows computer desktop. The Windows 98 Desktop can actually be a Web page stored on your local hard disk, and as you'll see in the next section, you can manage your folders and files in a very browser-like manner.

Improvements have been made in the taskbar with the addition of the Quick Launch feature (which we'll talk about in Chapter 7, "Going Further with Additional Customizations"); most of the menus (Start, Favorites, and so on) can be rearranged now just by dragging-and-dropping menu options; and overall stability has improved (or so Microsoft is fond of saying). And although not directly related to customization, the help system in Windows 98 has undergone a bit of a change. First and foremost is a change in file format. Previously, all Windows help files had a file extension of .hlp. The new format uses .chf, which stands for Compiled Help File. To see help specific to Windows 98 and its new features, select Start, Help, or open a Windows Explorer window and press F1. You'll find lots of good information here and many jumping-off points for further exploration.

Unofficially... When you call Microsoft's technical support staff, the first thing they do is look up your problem in the Microsoft Knowledge Base (MSKB). This database contains 83,000 articles (and growing daily) on every Microsoft product, package, OS, and then some. Check the database yourself before calling Microsoft. Bookmark `www.microsoft.com/support` for your troubleshooting resources.

In Chapter 5, "Configuring Your New PC," we talked about the troubleshooting features in the Windows help system. If you didn't do so already, we recommend that you open the help file and familiarize yourself with the troubleshooting resources that are available should the need arise (press Start, Help, and then type `troubleshooting`. Double-click About the Windows 98 Troubleshooters in the displayed list).

Another feature to look for is the capability to create shortcuts to help topics or add help topics to your Favorites list. This feature is wonderful, but a bit difficult to find. To create shortcuts or add topics to your Favorites list, right-click the topic text on the right side of the Help dialog box. The context menu, as shown in Figure 6.1, gives you the options Create Shortcut and Add to Favorites. Create Shortcut puts a shortcut to the current help topic on your desktop for quick access later. Add to Favorites lets you put an entry in your Favorites folder for the current help topic. Why would you want to do this? Suppose you find a help topic that looks interesting but doesn't pertain to what you are currently doing—something like Keyboard Shortcuts for the Windows Key. Will you remember where you saw it later? Possibly, but it's better to be sure by creating a shortcut to that topic while you are thinking about it. You can always delete the shortcut from your Favorites folder later. This can be the beginning of your own personal knowledge base when combined with the Favorites you add from the World Wide Web.

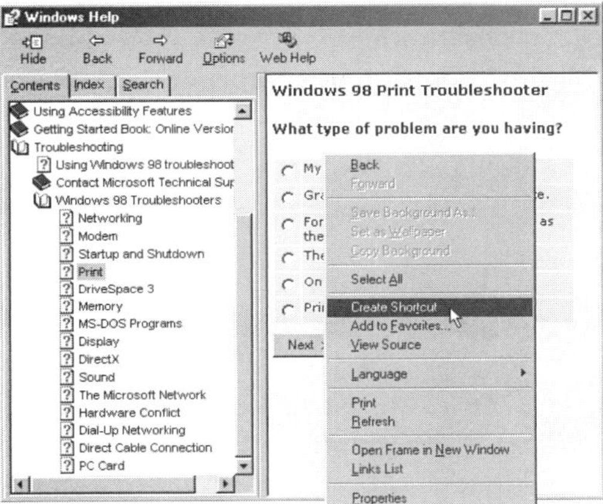

Figure 6.1
Make shortcuts to Help file topics that interest you.

Using the Windows 98 Interface

Here are the basic changes you should make to your system, and options you should seriously consider. When we install Windows for the first time or reinstall it for others, these are the first changes we make and lead people through. If you make a change and find that you don't like it, you can always change it back. The important point is that you need to know what your choices are and how to make your computer work more the way you want it to, not the way someone at Microsoft or the factory decided it should.

A quick note before continuing. Many of the changes you'll be making require your Windows 98 CD-ROM, so make sure that you have it handy. Almost all the changes recommended for Windows 98 will work with Windows 95 if Internet Explorer 4 is installed. You can download Internet Explorer 4 free of charge from `www.microsoft.com/ie/`.

Windows Explorer: Folder View

The changes you make in this section only affect the way you work with files and folders inside Windows Explorer. The program that displays your files and folders is Windows Explorer. Explorer gives you two views, or presentation formats, for representing your files and folders.

The first view is known as Folder view. Double-click the My Computer icon in the upper-left corner of your screen, and you get an Explorer window in Folder view, as shown in Figure 6.2. This view shows you your drives, folders, and files represented by icons. To look inside one of these drives or folders, double-click it.

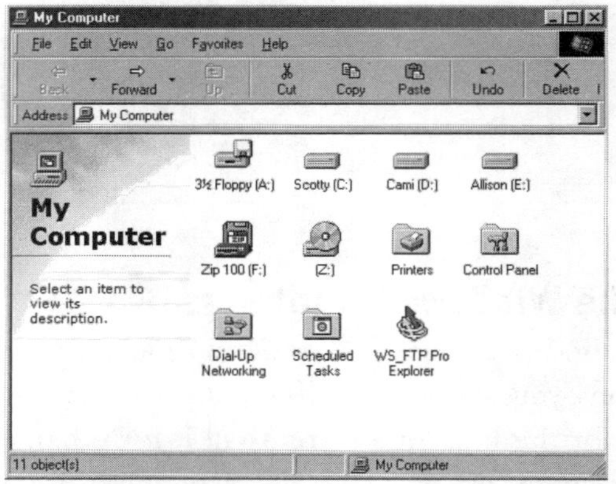

Figure 6.2 Explorer displaying files in Folder view.

Unofficially... Microsoft gives the term *Explorer* quite a workout. There's Windows Explorer, the program you use to work with files and folders on your computer; and then there's Internet Explorer, the Microsoft browser you can use to surf the World Wide Web. When we refer to Explorer, we mean the file management tool Windows Explorer. For Internet Explorer, we'll either use its full name or abbreviate it as IE.

Windows Explorer: Explorer View

The other way to view your drives, folders, and files is Explorer in Explorer view. Close all your open windows and then right-click your My Computer icon. From the pop-up menu choose Explore. The window that appears is Explorer in Explorer view (sounds confusing, but don't let Redmond's overuse of the term Explorer throw you). The main difference here is that the pane on the left side of the Explorer window lists all the drives, folders, and files on your computer as an expandable hierarchy, as shown in Figure 6.3. Any item with a small + sign to the left of it contains more items underneath it. Just click the little + with your left mouse button to expand that branch of the hierarchy. The Explorer view is a good way to get a quick overview of your system resources.

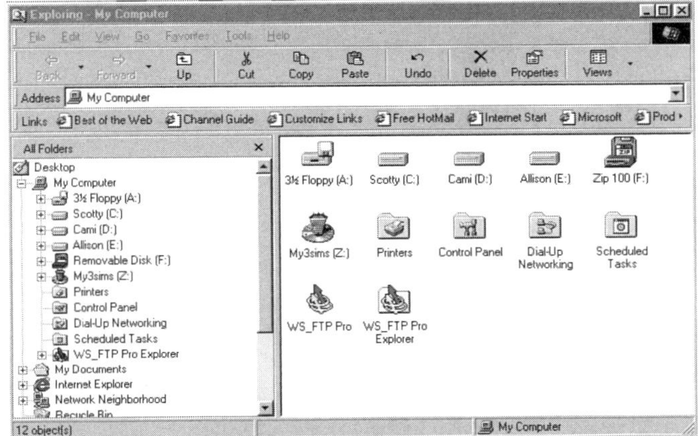

Figure 6.3 Explorer displaying files in Explorer view.

Configuring Folder Options

To control the options Explorer uses when you work with your files, start by opening the Folder Options dialog box:

1. Click the Start button on the taskbar.
2. Click the Settings option.
3. Click Folder Options on the cascading menu.

Bright Idea
If your keyboard has the special Windows keys, you can open Explorer in Explorer view quickly by pressing the Windows key and the E key on your keyboard at the same time. When you release the keys, Explorer opens.

As shown in Figure 6.4, you'll see that the Folder Options dialog box has three tabs: General, View, and File Types. The General tab controls the way Windows browses for files. The View tab gives you fine control over each aspect of an individual folder and lets you customize each folder's settings separately from the rest. The File Types tab controls which applications are activated when you select a particular file when you are file browsing. In this chapter, we'll stay focused on the options available on the General and View tabs.

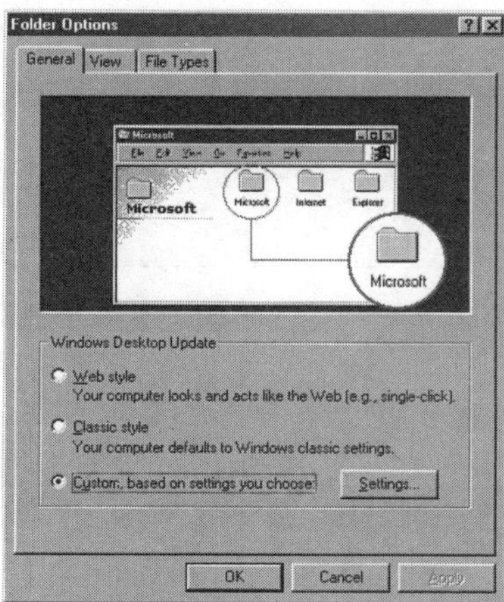

Figure 6.4 Customize Explorer in the Folder Options dialog box.

The General Tab: Web, Classic, or Custom

The General tab gives you three choices for your Windows Desktop Update. These choices have more impact on your overall Windows experience than any other change you can make. This is certainly the most visible change you'll make. Web style causes Explorer to behave like a Web browser. How much you'll like this depends on how well you like the way a Web browser browses! If you are an old-time Windows user or are very comfortable with the way the Explorer in Windows 95 handled file browsing, you may find that you don't like Web style. That's okay; you have choices; you are empowered. We'll outline the basic choices you'll be faced with, and then you'll have a good idea of where you want to go from here. We recommend that you at least try Web style for a while before writing it off as completely useless.

Web Style

Web style makes Windows Explorer behave like a Web browser. It also changes the way your Windows Desktop works. When you choose Web style, you'll notice the Channel bar, which is a collection of Web-site connections that Microsoft is promoting. Your desktop is actually a Web page you can customize. We've never liked the Channel bar or having your desktop pretend it's a Web page. We recommend that you do the following:

1. Click the Start button on the taskbar.
2. Click the Settings option.
3. Click Active Desktop and then click View as Web Page once to uncheck that option.

This action restores your desktop but still lets you use Explorer in Web style. Moving your mouse over an item in an Explorer window selects it. Click once on the icon or the underlined titles to launch them. One nice feature is a file-preview and object-information pane on the left side of the window. To see how this works, go ahead and select the Web Style option button and then click OK.

Now move your mouse around in your Explorer window. You should see each icon light up as you select it by simply moving the mouse over it. In addition, you'll see information on the current icon displayed in the pane to the left. Click your mouse button once on any file and it opens or launches. As you switch between folders, you can use the familiar Forward and Back buttons on your toolbar, along with a box in which you can type the path and name of a folder you want to view. All in all, your Explorer window now behaves exactly like your Web browser. This can be a plus if you or others in your household are new to computers.

Bright Idea
If you accidentally delete, rename, or move a file while in Explorer but you don't like the result (or aren't sure what you did), take a look at the Edit menu. Next to the Undo choice, the last action you performed appears. Clicking the Undo option undoes this action, whether it was renaming, copying, moving, or deleting a file.

Classic Style

The next choice on the General tab is Classic style. Classic style makes windows and folders behave the way they always have under Windows 95 (and as they did in the old Win3.x File Manager utility). You single-click a file or folder to select it and double-click to launch or open it. If you've used Windows 3.x, Windows 95, or Windows NT in the past, you are probably already familiar with this way of working.

If you want to compare the Web style and the Classic style, it's easy. Just switch the setting and play around a little bit in the file windows.

We recommend that you try both styles for a while, just to become familiar with what the options do and don't do. Then give Custom a try. In the next section we'll talk about the various choices Custom gives you.

Custom Settings

The last option on the General tab is Custom. With Custom you choose the exact options you prefer, using some features normally associated with Web style and retaining some of the Classic options—the best of both worlds.

Check the Custom option button and then click the Settings button. See Figure 6.5.

Figure 6.5
The best of both worlds—Custom Settings.

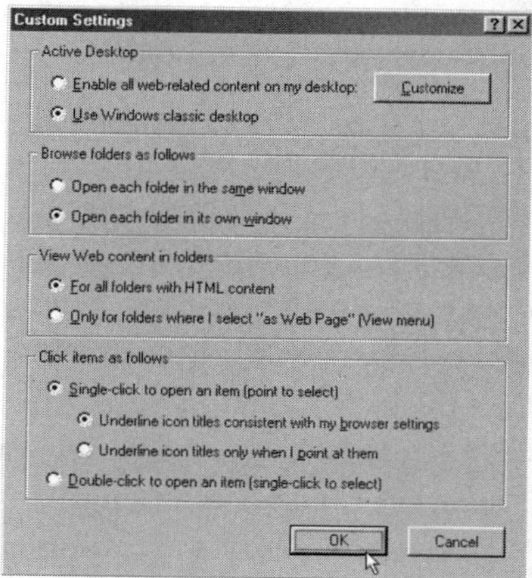

Unofficially...
Taking the Web flavor to an extreme, you can assign different wallpapers to display within the Explorer window when you view folders, and you can even make a little Web page for each folder, complete with hot links. In Explorer, click the View menu, then Customize this Folder, which starts a wizard that walks you through this process.

The first choice you are faced with in the Custom style is the Active Desktop settings. If you choose the Customize button here, the Folder options dialog box closes and the Customize Desktop options dialog box opens. We'll cover the Customize Desktop options later in this chapter.

The next section, Browse Folders as Follows, dictates how you browse folders and how it applies only to Folder view and not to Explorer view. Choosing Open Each Folder in Its Own Window opens a new window every time you double-click a folder. If you start in My Computer, double-click C:\, double-click Windows, and double-click Start Menu, you'll end up with four separate windows on your screen. Although this feature can be handy if you want to drag files from one window to another, it quickly clutters your screen.

Choosing Open Each Folder in the Same Window leaves only one window on the screen and changes the contents of that window as you click your way through your system. We recommend this option because having dozens of windows open on your desktop is extremely bothersome. When you want to drag files between windows, you can always open two Folder view windows and work from there. Even better is to use Explorer view for all file management, because it gives you quick access to all the files on your system and makes dragging files and folders from one place to another in the hierarchy a snap.

Bright Idea
After opening several My Computer windows, you can close all of them by holding down your Shift key and clicking the Close icon, the little X in the upper-right corner of the last window you opened.

The third section determines how folders that contain Web content are displayed. Web content in this case can be a custom background color, a font, or additional hyperlinks to other parts of your system that you have added to a particular folder. Unless you already know HTML (Hypertext Markup Language), you probably won't be doing much customizing of your folders in this manner.

Watch Out! HTML Experience Required
If you know HTML and want to customize your folders, you may do so by choosing the View, Customize This Folder menu item at any time you are viewing a folder. This selection brings up a little wizard to step you through your options. Be forewarned that if you are changing anything more than the background of the folder, you are thrown into an HTML editor with lots of JavaScript and such to wade through. If you aren't sure what that means, don't be in a big hurry to start inserting HTML into your folders.

We leave this option set to For All Folders with HTML Content in the interests of simplicity and conformity—simplicity because it's one less thing to wonder about, and conformity so that all folders act and look the same.

Last is the Click Items As Follows section. We find this option to be somewhat misnamed. Instead of Click Items As Follows, it should be called Underline Items As Follows. This section is relevant only if you choose Single-Click to Open an Item (the default for Web style, as mentioned earlier). If you've used a Web browser before, you know that clickable hyperlinks in Web pages are typically blue and underlined. Windows gives you the choice here of having all clickable items in your folders appear with underlines or without. If you choose Underline Icon Titles Consistent with My Browser Settings, all your icon titles will be underlined, as shown in Figure 6.6. If you choose Underline Icon Titles Only When I Point to Them, the only icon title that appears underlined will be the current selection.

We find the Explorer windows too busy looking with all the icon titles underlined, so we recommend choosing Underline Icon Titles Only When I Point to Them. If you choose to

Double-click to Open an Item, the underline issue really doesn't affect you.

Figure 6.6 Folder view with the selected icon title underlined.

Watch Out! If you set your folder to underline icon titles but you never see any underlines, check your setting in Internet Explorer. Make sure that the Underline Links setting is not set to Never.

After you've made your choices in the Custom dialog box, click OK. That takes care of all the settings you'll want to consider on the General tab. Click the View tab and we'll continue.

The View Tab

As mentioned earlier, the choices on this tab enable you to customize each folder individually. This tab also sets the options you use on a global basis when you're viewing your system through Explorer. We'll cover each option in turn and tell you why we do or don't recommend your choosing it. As a basic guideline, we keep our options set so that similar things appear in a similar manner. So if we are using Explorer to look at our files, we want to make sure that it is using the same rules to display all the files. Likewise, we turn off settings that limit the information your system gives you. You have enough to think about without wondering whether the file you're looking for is hidden or has part of its name hidden. Follow along and we'll work through these myriad choices.

Files and Folders

The options in this section control how Windows displays information about your files and folders. Checking the box preceding an item activates that option or turns it on. Unchecking deactivates an option and turns it off.

Remember Each Folder's View Settings—This setting, on by default, tells Windows to save different settings for different folders as you set them. This benefits you when you decide that one folder should have large icons and another should show files sizes and attributes. Initially, you'll view all folders the same way, so this setting has very little effect on your work overall. We recommend leaving this setting on.

Display the Full Path in Title Bar—This setting is off by default. With this setting turned on, you won't be wondering where in the drive/path hierarchy the folder you're looking at is located. Why Microsoft turned it off in the first place is beyond us. Don't spend your time guessing which folder you're looking at. We recommend you turn this setting to on.

Hide File Extensions for Known File Types—On by default, this setting hides the extensions, the part of the filename after the last period in a filename, only for files that are registered on your system. An example of this is Microsoft Word documents, which use .doc for a file extension. Not knowing the extension for a file can be very confusing. No doubt you've got better things to do while you are working than to keep track of which files have their extensions hidden and which do not. We recommend you turn this option off.

Show Map Network Drive Button in Toolbar—We recommend that you turn this option on if you will be connecting to computers that let you map network drives. Although this is possible with the Internet, you will not be using this option in that context. Usually you map drives on a computer at your place of work or on a small network in your home. If you aren't sure whether you'll be mapping drives, you probably won't be, so go ahead and turn the option off.

Show File Attributes in Detail View—We recommend that you turn this option on to add a column to your Detail listing in any Explorer window. Just a glance tells you which files are read-only, hidden, or system.

Show Pop-up Description for Folder and Desktop Items—Leaving this option on causes little yellow notes to pop up as you move your mouse over various objects, such as icons on your desktop or in an Explorer window. If you need more information than you get from just looking at a file listing or if you use really long filenames—for example, more than 30 characters—then leave this option checked. Long filenames may not display entirely depending on the size of your windows, and this option lets you know at a glance what the names of items are just by hovering the mouse over the name. On the other hand, if you don't use really long filenames, you may find it annoying to see the little yellow notes popping up all the time. Set this option at your discretion.

Allow All Uppercase Names—Do you want to name your files in all uppercase letters? If so, turn this option on. We prefer to leave it off and name files the way we want to name them. These files are often case sensitive, and this setting will give you problems more often than not.

- Hidden Files

  Under Hidden Files you have three option buttons instead of check boxes, which means that you can select only one of the following three options:

  Do Not Show Hidden or System Files—On by default, this option seems sensible at first. What it does is hide your system and hidden files from view when you are in an Explorer window. These files are critical files to your operating system, and great havoc can be wreaked if you accidentally delete or rename one of them; therefore, Windows hides these files from your view to protect you from yourself. The problem occurs when you try to locate a system file and it just isn't showing up. Your system registry is an example of this type of file. Usually you are trying to find these files when your system is messed up and you've run out of patience. Spare yourself the agony and do not check this option button. Windows will still warn you if you try to delete or rename a system file, so you aren't leaving yourself totally unprotected.

  Do Not Show Hidden Files—All the caveats we mentioned about showing hidden or system files apply here as well.

From a practical standpoint, there isn't a great deal of difference between this setting and the preceding one. Most system files are set as hidden also, so the effect is roughly the same. Again, we recommend not checking this option button.

Show All Files—Of the three Hidden Files settings, we recommend turning this setting on to eliminate frustration and maximize productivity. This lets Explorer display all your files to you all the time. Hidden system files icons will be slightly dimmer than regular files, so you'll still have visual clues as to any file's system status.

- Visual Settings

  These settings affect how Explorer and other programs respond visually. An important note here is that some of these settings may not work on your system. This can be due to either your video card or the related video driver. If one of these settings does cause problems on your system, uncheck it to turn it off, and don't worry about it. You want to avoid making lots of changes to your system trying to get one of these settings to work. You don't want to mess things up accidentally.

  Hide Icons When Desktop Is Viewed As Web Page—If you have chosen to view your desktop as a Web page, this option hides all the icons normally found on your desktop. You'll still see your files in Explorer windows and File Open and Save dialog boxes, but they won't appear on the desktop. We like having key folders, applications, and text files visible on our desktop at all times, so we recommend setting this option to off. On the other hand, if your desktop contains a jillion icons, they might cover up the important parts of the underlying displayed Web page (hot links, for example).

  Smooth Edges of Screen Fonts—Turning this option on fills in the jagged edges of fonts displayed onscreen. This feature is useful if you are working with large type or doing any kind of graphics design work. This setting is especially useful with certain foreign-language fonts, such as Greek and Hebrew. This slows your computer down slightly, but that is a minor trade-off compared to less strain on your eyes. We recommend turning this setting on.

Show Window Contents While Dragging—When you move or resize a window onscreen, this setting lets you see the contents of the window while you are resizing or moving. Turn this option off and all you see is a thick outline where the window you are resizing or moving will be. If resizing or moving windows causes a lot of jerkiness on the screen, you might consider unchecking this box, but on most systems this is not a problem.

Our recommendations will save you time and frustration when dealing with your PC. If you decide that setting things up differently works better for you, then by all means go for it. The important part is to take control. The remaining tab in this dialog box, File Types, does not need customizing, and the default settings there should serve you well.

The Basics: Everybody Do This

These are procedures you may want to perform periodically on your system, much like dusting your furniture or other regular housekeeping chores.

Organizing the Windows Start Menu

As you install programs, you'll quickly find your Start menu and its various cascading submenus filling up with entries. You'll also find that little rhyme or reason exists to the entries it contains or the order in which they appear. Many companies install their programs under the company name rather than the program's name. This can be frustrating when you are trying to locate an infrequently used program's entry on the Start menu. Nearly every computer we've come across has been in need of some basic reorganization of the Start menu.

It's important to note that the Start menu is really just a collection of folders on your hard drive. Each of these folders contains shortcuts to the applications on your computer. In this way it is somewhat dynamic. Any shortcut you put in that group of folders appears on the Windows Start menu system. Delete something from the folder and it disappears from the Start menu. On most systems you'll find this special folder at `C:\Windows\Start Menu`. You can open this folder in an Explorer window by right-clicking the Start button and choosing Explore from the pop-up menu. As you customize your Start menu, keep in mind that you are working with shortcuts to programs and not the programs themselves.

Think of your Start menu as a grouping tool. All the software you install will try to group itself within your Start menu. Unfortunately, most of the grouping behavior will be for the benefit of the company that wrote the software, not for you. A good example of this is Microsoft products. When you install Microsoft Office, all its icons go on the Start menu at the Start, Programs level. When you install the Microsoft game Return of Arcade, its icons show up under Start, Programs, Microsoft Games, Return of Arcade. If you were looking for a game, is that where you would look? You might look under Start, Programs, Accessories, Games, but this won't find all your games unless you do a little housekeeping. The following are some general guidelines to keep in mind when you start cleaning up your Start menu:

- Classify your programs in groupings according to where you think they should go. If you think Return of Arcade more properly belongs in the Start, Programs, Accessories, Games group, go ahead and move it there.
- Use multiple menu pointers to the same program if it makes sense. Nothing prevents you from having multiple Start menu entries to the same program. If it makes sense to put Return of Arcade in both Start, Programs, Accessories, Games and Start, Programs, Microsoft Applications, then put it in both places.
- Give meaningful names to your shortcuts. Can't remember what Start, Programs, Accessories, System Tools,

System Monitor does? Rename it something like "System Monitor—watches File System, Cache, and Kernel Processes."

- Create task-oriented names to some shortcuts. If you always use Word for Windows to write letters, name its shortcut something like "Write Letters." This technique is especially useful if you are setting up a system for a new computer user.
- Organize shortcuts by task. Consider creating Start menu groups that refer to tasks and placing all the programs you need for that task in that group. You might create a Church Newsletter group with pointers to your Desktop Publishing, Graphics Editor, Clip Art CD, and Reference programs in it.
- Give your Start menu items meaningful icons. *Meaningful* means meaningful to you. Choose icons that remind you of what the program does or that inspires you to want to use the program in ways that may be more creative. You'll learn how to change icons in Chapter 7, "Going Further with Additional Customizations."

That advice may seem like a lot to think about, but it's really just common sense. What's more, you'll be very pleased with the overall result of the effort. Having a Start menu organized in a way that makes sense to you and the way you want to use your computer goes a long way toward making you feel as though you're in control of the machine and not the other way around. The names and icons on the Start menu are not set in stone, and neither are the groups that are created for you. Even better is that Windows 98 provides easy ways to edit and rearrange the Start menu. We'll cover these techniques briefly and then jump into actually customizing your Start menu.

Before we start moving things around, you'll want to open an Explorer window. It doesn't matter whether it's Explorer view or Folder view, just open one. You'll find out why you opened this window shortly. Next, open your Start menu and have a look around. You already know how to select things by clicking them. But did you know you can drag items around in the Start menu by clicking and dragging with your left mouse button? Don't like where that menu option sits? Grab it with your mouse and drag it where you want it, even to a cascading submenu. Try the following:

1. Open your Start menu to the Start, Programs menu, and then look for the MS-DOS Prompt entry.
2. Grab it with your left mouse button and drag it over to just under the Start, Windows Update entry. Windows draws a thin black line on the screen showing where your icon will appear when you release the mouse button.
3. Drop the MS-DOS Prompt under the Windows Update entry. It should appear there after a few seconds. On some machines you have to close the Start menu and reopen it before your change shows. Pretty easy, isn't it!

At this point you are probably wondering what happens if you make a mistake or if you drag something you didn't mean to drag and don't know where you dropped it. That's where the Explorer window you opened comes in. Switch over to your Explorer window and take a look at the Edit menu. The top item is the Undo item with a description of the last action you performed, as shown in Figure 6.7. In this case, it should say Undo Move. Go ahead and select Undo Move, and then take a look at your Start menu again. The MS-DOS Prompt item should be right back where it started.

You can rearrange your Start menu directly in Explorer, but you will not be able to put the items in any special order. Rearranging them on the Start menu enables you to place the icons in the order most useful to you.

If you want to copy an entry rather than move it, you'll need to hold your Ctrl key down while you drag the entry around on your Start menu. You know that you are in Copy mode rather than Move mode when you see the + sign added to your cursor. Try dragging a Start menu entry and then press and release the Ctrl key several times to see the little + come and go. If you change your mind while dragging, simply press the Esc key before releasing your mouse button.

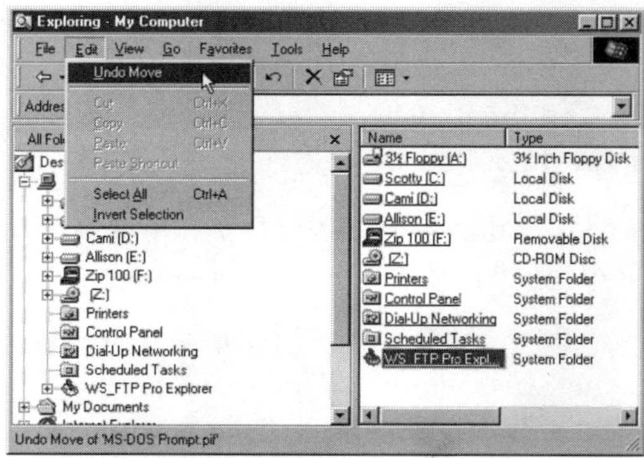

Figure 6.7 You can undo Start menu edits in Windows Explorer.

A couple of other activities are deleting entries and changing their icons. You start both of these actions by right-clicking the menu entry you want to alter. If you want to delete the entry, choose Delete. To change the entry's icon, choose Properties and then click the Change Icon button.

To rename an entry, create a new folder, or rename a folder, you'll need to edit the Start menu from Explorer, as shown in Figure 6.8. Navigate in your open Explorer window to the `C:\Windows\Start Menu` folder. All the actions you learned for copying, moving, and deleting work the same in Explorer as they did on the Start menu itself.

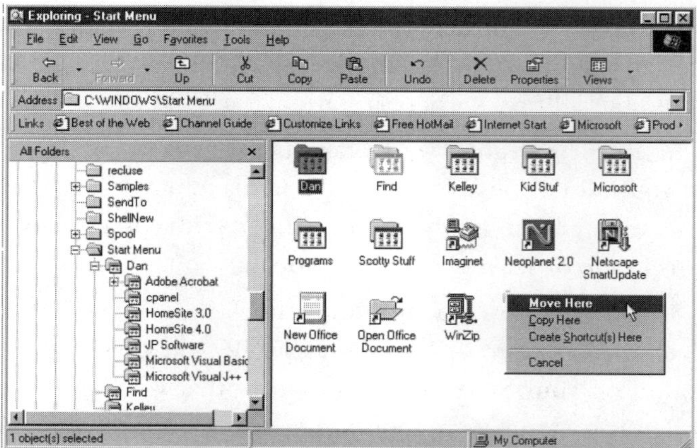

Figure 6.8 Editing the Start menu with Explorer.

Explorer gives you more flexibility in your dragging than the Start menu does. You'll want to try clicking, dragging, and dropping objects with your right mouse button. This opens many possibilities. Using the right mouse button pops up a little menu with choices on it when you drop the object you are dragging. You can see this menu in Figure 6.8. (This menu is called both the "pop-up menu" and the "context menu.") You now have the capability to copy or move using the same action. That's one less thing you'll have to remember, and one less action to take. Windows uses different rules depending on whether you are moving things from one drive to another or whether your files are executable. Moving with the right mouse button eliminates these ambiguities and makes your task much more straightforward. Learn to use the right mouse button for all your tasks.

Bright Idea
All the techniques for editing the Start menu work just as well with your Favorites menu. You'll usually find it located at `C:\Windows\Favorites`.

Note that dragging items with the right mouse button doesn't work when you are dragging directly on the Start menu. You must be in an Explorer window to drag with your right mouse button.

Now that you know how to edit the Start menu, we'll start editing by dragging the Windows Update entry to a more logical place. Windows Update can be a good thing, but you won't be using it often enough to warrant a top-level spot on your Start menu. Because you are just going to move the entry, you can edit directly on the Start menu. Click Start; then drag the Windows Update icon using your left mouse button to Start, Programs, Accessories, System Tools, and then drop it there. System Tools is a good place for Windows Update and a place you would naturally look for it.

Bright Idea
In Windows 98, the entries do not need to be in alphabetical order, so feel free to put your programs at the top of their groups and the uninstall, readme, and miscellaneous files at the bottom.

In Chapter 7 you'll create new Start menu groups designed to reduce the time you spend looking for your favorite programs and getting your work done. For now you can continue dragging entries around on your Start menu to put them on the submenus and in the order you prefer.

Organizing Your Windows Desktop

The next area you want to customize is your Windows Desktop. Simply put, the desktop is what you see when all your applications are minimized. It's also the top-level choice in an Explorer window and most other file-selection dialog boxes. Don't let this fool you, though! *The Desktop is really a folder on your hard drive.* In most cases you'll find it at `C:\Windows\Desktop`. Anything dropped into this folder appears on your desktop, and anything deleted from this folder disappears from your desktop.

Typically, you'll want to use your desktop to store temporary items or files to which you'll need quick access. We find that it's a good place to download files to. It's easy to find the file after the download, and if you need to keep the file, you can move it to a more permanent location (in Chapter 8, "Staying Ahead of the Game," we'll discuss how to store downloaded drivers and program updates). It's also a good place to leave a file for someone else on the same computer to look at later.

Having files and shortcuts so visible, however, makes it easy to quickly clutter up the desktop. Before we start adding shortcuts to your desktop, let's clean up the mess that Microsoft left for you! The first thing to delete is the icon to sign up with the Microsoft Network, or MSN for short. Of course, if you are planning to sign up for the service, leave this icon alone for the time being; otherwise, grab it with your mouse and drag it directly to the Recycle Bin. Windows gives you a message about not being able to undo this action, which you can safely ignore.

Remember our tip earlier about dragging objects with the right mouse button instead of the left? This tip applies on the desktop as well. It's a good habit to get into, and it can keep you out of trouble when you accidentally drop an object in the wrong spot, because you can safely click Cancel on the pop-up menu.

The next change you want to consider is whether to keep Network Neighborhood around. If you connect to a network to share drives and files between computers, you'll want to keep Network Neighborhood. If you have no idea what it does or if you'll ever need it, grab it with your mouse and drop it on the Recycle Bin. Oops! You can't drag Network Neighborhood to the Recycle Bin. Windows treats some of these icons as system folders and prevents you from deleting them. Network

Neighborhood is one of these. To remove Network Neighborhood, you can either dive in and take your chances fussing with the system registry (decidedly not something we recommend) or use a tool such as TweakUI, which lets you remove system folders that appear on your desktop. We'll talk about TweakUI in greater detail in Chapter 7 and show how you can use it to remove system folders from your desktop.

Bright Idea
While you are customizing your desktop, go ahead and rename the My Computer system folder. It's easy. Right-click My Computer and choose Rename. Type the name you would rather have and press Enter.

The other thing you can do with your desktop is put shortcuts to your favorite folders or your most-often-used programs on it. Any file you drag onto one of these icons will be opened or processed by that application. For instance, if you have a shortcut to your printer on the desktop, you can drag a file out of Explorer and onto the printer's shortcut icon to quickly print the document. To create a printer shortcut, follow these steps:

1. Locate your printer in Explorer from the My Computer, Printers folder.
2. Using your right mouse button, drag the printer icon to the desktop and release it.
3. Choose Create Shortcut Here from the menu that pops up.

Putting shortcuts to your favorite filing folders on the desktop lets you quickly move a document to that location by simply dragging and dropping the file onto the shortcut. How do you create a shortcut to a folder? The same way that you created the printer shortcut. Locate the folder, right-drag it to your desktop, and then choose Create Shortcut Here.

Removing Unwanted Applications

If you've had your computer for any length of time, you already have programs that are just taking up space—space that could be put to better use. Likewise, when Windows was installed, it left files and directories scattered about on your hard drive. We'll start by removing these programs and then do some looking around to make sure that all traces of the unwanted programs are gone.

An example of what we will remove is the Online Services starter kits folder that Windows has supplied. This is the sign-up software for AOL, AT&T Worldnet, CompuServe, and Prodigy. You'll find a folder full of shortcuts on your desktop, pointers in your Start menu, and files in your Program Files folder. If you are planning to sign up with any of these services, you may want to make use of these icons. We're guessing that you would prefer to be rid of the extra sign-up files, so rather than searching out all these entries, we'll use your Control Panel to get rid of them.

Start by opening your Control Panel, Add/Remove Programs utility. You'll notice that this utility has the following three tabs on it:

- Install/Uninstall lists all your installed programs that have been registered as having an uninstall routine.
- Windows Setup lets you add and remove programs from the Windows 98 CD-ROM.
- Startup Disk creates emergency start disks to use when Windows won't boot up.

Watch Out!
If you want to add or remove a Windows Component using the Windows Setup tab in Add/Remove programs, don't make the mistake of unchecking boxes of things you want to keep. When you click OK after making your choices, Windows installs everything with a check and uninstalls everything without a check.

To remove the Online Services files, we'll use the Windows Setup tab, so select that now. Look through the list of available Components. The choices on this list are either unchecked, gray and checked, or checked. To install a component, simply check the box next to it. Likewise, to uninstall a component, merely uncheck its box. Some components such as System Tools are really a category. Click the Details button to see the individual choices available in a category.

Because we want to remove the Online Services component, scroll through the list and uncheck the box next to Online Services, as shown in Figure 6.9. Click OK, and the Online Services are toast.

Figure 6.9
Remove Online Services by unchecking the box.

Whether your computer is brand new or an old family friend, programs are probably on it that you either don't want or won't use. Look through your Start menu and make a list of the programs you want to remove from your system. Most programs have an uninstall routine accessible from Control Panel's Add/Remove Programs utility, but unfortunately some don't. Look in the following places when you are trying to uninstall a program:

- On the Start menu—The program may have an entry on the Start menu for uninstalling itself. If this is the case, run that uninstall program now.
- In the Control Panel, Add/Remove Programs utility—Look through the list on the Install/Uninstall tab. Remove the program from here by selecting it from the list and then clicking the Add/Remove button. (If a program gets removed but its entry remains on the Add/Remove list, you can use the TweakUI utility discussed in Chapter 7 to remove it.)
- In the folder the program is installed in—Right-click the entry and choose Properties to see the folder name. Then use Explorer to view that folder and see whether an uninstall program is available or whether uninstall instructions are in the documentation or readme files.

Adding Missing Applications

Control Panel's Add/Remove utility can be used to add any missing components or applications to your system as well. Go ahead and look through this list for other components you might want to add if they are not already on your system. The following is a list of components we recommend:

- Accessibility—This component adds options and wizards for making it easier for people with disabilities to use their computers. Even if you aren't disabled, you might consider adding this to get more options for your keyboard, mouse, sound card, and display. Run through the Start, Programs, Accessories, Accessibility, Accessibility Wizard to see the types of enhanced features that are available.
- Accessories—You can use this component to add Desktop Wallpaper, Mouse Pointers, and Screen Savers. Some people love wallpapers and like to change the look of their systems regularly, and some think it's nonsense. If you're in the former group, by all means install some of this neat eye-candy that comes with Windows.
- Desktop Themes—If you want to give your computer a different look, add this component. Windows 98 installs only a handful of the themes on the Windows CD by default. Check the ones that interest you and uncheck the rest. You change your themes using the Control Panel, Desktop Themes applet. Again, we realize that some people love this type of fluff, er, stuff and some don't.
- System Tools—You should add System Monitor and System Resource Meter if they aren't checked already.

Unofficially... If themes really tickle your fancy, head over to the outstanding Winfiles site at `www.winfiles.com/apps/98/themes.html`. You'll find desktop themes to satisfy every taste grouped by categories.

Use our list as suggestions only, and don't remove anything you want or need! After making your selections in the Add/Remove Programs list, click the OK button to begin the Install/Uninstall process. Depending on the choices you've made, Windows may want to restart your computer. If so, go ahead and reboot.

Some really useful applications are located on your Windows 98 CD-ROM that are not installed during the regular installation process. They're sort of like hidden gold—you have to ferret them out and install them.

The first program we want to focus on is actually a series of programs. The Windows 98 Resource Kit and its associated program files offer many ways to work with and customize your system, often at an advanced level. You can find detailed instructions on installing the Resource Kit's Help file in Chapter 5, so refer to that if you haven't already installed the kit. After you have installed the kit, you can access the Tools Management Console by selecting Start, Programs, Windows 98 Resource Kit, Tools Management Console. As shown in Figure 6.10, the Tools Management Console groups the Resource Kit tools both in categories and alphabetically.

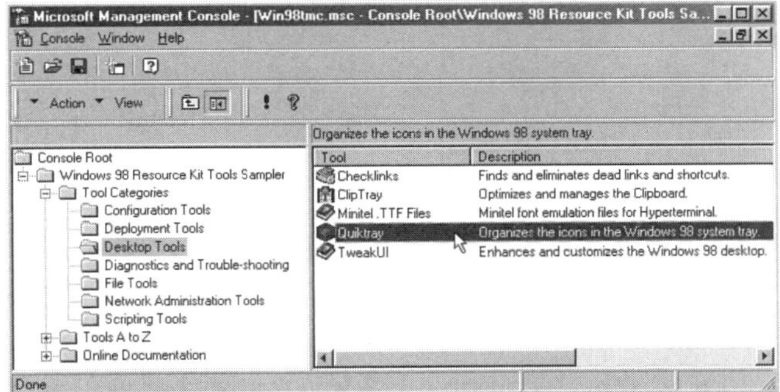

Figure 6.10
The Windows 98 Resource Kit Tools Management Console.

The following are the tools we think you'll find especially useful:

- Configuration Tools, Time Zone Editor—This tool is useful if you travel and use a laptop in different time zones.
- Desktop Tools, Clip Tray—The Clip Tray extends your Clipboard to allow you to store more than one chunk of text at a time. This capability can be useful if you are a writer, Web developer, or programmer, or if you otherwise need to store more than one thing in the Clipboard at a time. Your entries are saved between sessions, so you can easily keep your favorite snippets at your fingertips.
- Desktop Tools, Quiktray—This tool lets you use your System Tray as a file launcher. Consider this if you want another easy-access program launcher.

Unofficially...
Quitting Clip Tray is a tricky little operation. You can't close it from its dialog box (clicking the Close (X) button doesn't shut the utility down; it only minimizes it back to the system tray). And no direct Close or Exit command is available on the right-click pop-up menu. You have to right-click, choose Options, and then choose Exit Clip Tray.

- Desktop Tools, TweakUI—This is a tool for modifying many system settings that would otherwise require you to edit the system registry. We'll talk more about using this tool in the next chapter.
- Diagnostics and Troubleshooting, Microsoft File Information—This gives you information about the Windows 98 and Internet Explorer 4 files. It's good for checking version numbers or locating files from your Windows installation CD.
- File Tools, WinDiff—WinDiff lets you compare the contents of two files by displaying the two files as one and marking any lines that are different. WinDiff will also compare two file folders and mark files as identical, different, or in only one directory.
- Scripting Tools—You'll want to look through these tools if you plan to write scripts using the new Windows Scripting Host language.

Maximizing and Monitoring Performance

If you've followed along so far, you're well on your way to making your new computer work the way you want. In this section we'll look at some additional housekeeping changes that help improve your overall system performance and avoid trouble in the future. These changes are not as visible as some of the changes you made earlier, but they have a big impact on your overall computing experience.

The first recommendation is to change your CD-ROM's drive letter to Z:. Why should you do that? Whenever you change the partition structure of your hard drive, your CD-ROM drive letter also changes. I know you aren't planning to change your partition structure, but you might add a second hard drive. Or perhaps you'll install a Jaz or Zip disk. Many things causes drive letters to change, and many of your programs can wind up looking for the CD-ROM in the same location it started in. So follow these steps to set the letter to Z: and you won't have any surprises down the road.

1. Open the Control Panel System utility.
2. On the Device Manager tab, locate your CD-ROM and then click the little + sign to expand the entries.
3. Click your CD-ROM, and then click the Properties button near the bottom of the System Properties dialog box.
4. Switch to the Settings tab of the dialog box that opens.
5. Near the bottom of the box, you'll see the current drive letter for your CD-ROM along with two settings for Reserved Drive Letters: one for the Starting letter and one for the Ending letter. Set both of these to Z:, as shown in Figure 6.11.
6. Click OK, and then click OK again to close the System utility.
7. You'll be prompted to reboot your system to make the change active, and you should do it.

If you have a CD-ROM changer (a CD that accepts more than one disk at a time), you'll want to set the range of drive letters accordingly. For instance, if your CD-ROM holds three disks, set the Start drive letter to X: and the End drive letter to Z:.

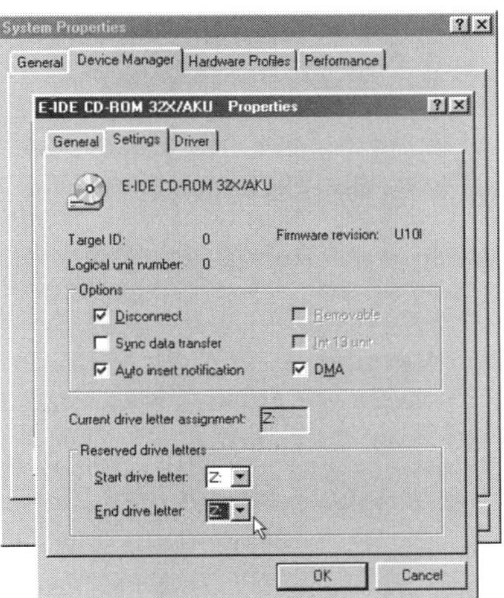

Figure 6.11
Set your CD-ROM drive to be the Z: drive.

While we are talking about disks, we'll change some settings that affect how Windows treats your drives. Specifically, we are concerned with how much space is occupied by various files that Windows produces. We know that you have plenty of disk space now, but you'll run out soon enough! Better to cut down on these space wasters now while you are thinking about it.

Unofficially...
Don't leave sensitive files sitting in the Recycle Bin. After you've selected the file or folder you want to delete, press and hold the Shift key, then do what you normally do: press the Delete key, click the Close (X) button on the toolbar, or right-click and choose Delete (all these actions have the same effect). The file is *permanently* deleted after you confirm.

Size Down the Recycle Bin

One of the biggest wastes you'll find on your new system is the Recycle Bin. Microsoft sets it by default to use 10 percent of your hard drive. This may not sound like much, but on a 4GB hard drive, this amounts to 400MB! Now having Windows save deleted files for you in case you make a mistake is a good idea, but we seriously doubt you'll need to keep track of 400MB worth of deleted material. Follow these steps to take back some of your hard drive right now by setting the Recycle Bin to a reasonable size.

1. Right-click the Recycle Bin and choose Properties.
2. Choose the Global tab.
3. If the Maximum Size of Recycle Bin is higher than 3 percent, go ahead and lower it to 1 percent. If you aren't comfortable setting it that low, leave it at 2 percent or 3 percent.
4. If you don't want Windows to ask for confirmation every time you delete a file, uncheck the box labeled Display Delete Confirmation dialog box.
5. Click OK to close the Recycle Bin Properties dialog box.

Bright Idea
Norton Utilities and other packages interact with your Recycle Bin to ferret out additional space savings. Check the settings for any of these utilities that might be running on your system.

Size Down the Internet

Our next stop is Internet Explorer's Temporary Internet Files. From your desktop, right-click Internet Explorer and choose Properties. In the middle section of the General tab, you'll see Temporary Internet Files. Click the Settings button, which brings up the dialog box shown in Figure 6.12. Look for the slider bar showing how much of your hard drive is being used by the Temporary Internet Files folder. Use your mouse to adjust this slider down as far as it will go, usually 1 percent. If you have a 4GB hard drive, Internet Explorer will use 40MB of your hard drive for storing Temporary Internet files. This is still a very large number. By contrast, Netscape Navigator typically sets aside 5MB to 10MB for the same purpose.

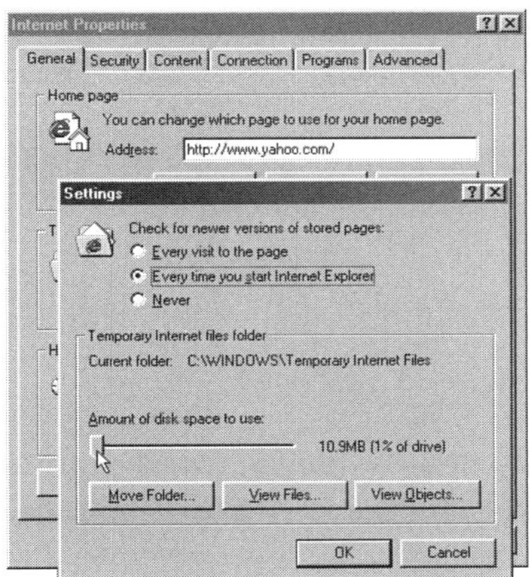

Figure 6.12
Limit how much disk space Internet Explorer sets aside.

Fine-Tuning Options in Explorer, Taskbar, and Elsewhere

By now you know that when you want to view the contents of your computer, you'll be using an Explorer window. Earlier, we went through many of the detailed options available for customizing Explorer. This section covers the other settings used with Explorer, along with settings for the taskbar.

The View menu in Explorer is where you set the major settings that determine how Explorer appears to you onscreen. The following are the options we keep checked for maximum productivity:

- Toolbars, Standard Buttons—Quick access to most file management functions.
- Toolbars, Address Bar—Either type an address or use the drop-down box to choose a folder on your computer.
- Status Bar—Provides real-time feedback based on the currently selected object.

- Explorer Bar, All Folders—Displays the list of your folders down the left side of Explorer.
- Details—Lets you see the details of your files at a glance, including the type, the size, the last modified time, and the attributes.
- Arrange Icons, By Name—Puts the files in alphabetical order by name.

Your next stop is your taskbar. In Chapter 7, "Going Further with Additional Customizations," you'll make changes to the taskbar to turn it into an actual tool kit and not just a switching mechanism. For now, right-click your taskbar and choose Properties. On the Taskbar Options tab, these are the settings we keep checked:

- Always on Top—Prevents the taskbar from disappearing behind other applications. Leave this checked to always have access to it.
- Show Small Icons on Start Menu—When you click Start, the icons on the first menu will be the same size as the other levels of your Start menu.
- Show Clock—Puts the current time at the far-right end of the taskbar. Hovering your mouse over the time displays the date.

Also while you're here, grab the taskbar with your mouse and place it on any edge of the screen. We find that it works best across the bottom and choose to leave it there.

Chapter Ending

- Show key differences between Windows 95 and Windows 98 that increase customization.
- Work with different Windows Explorer views.
- Configure the folder options to suit how you want to manage your folders and files.

- Clean up and organize your Start menu to make application access more efficient.
- Give your desktop a facelift.
- Add and remove Windows components and applications.
- Reclaim disk space from the Recycle Bin and temporary Internet file creep.

Chapter 7

Going Further with Additional Customizations

AFTER FOLLOWING THE RECOMMENDATIONS in the preceding chapter, you now have a very functional copy of Windows. The customizations we're recommending here are more personal. Some you'll use, some you won't, and in every case you'll be customizing your system to suit your individual needs. The idea is to make your system, specifically the Windows operating system, adjust to you, to work the way you want instead of your having to change the way you work. After you have Windows fine-tuned, you'll find it far less frustrating.

One concept that presents itself repeatedly is Windows' use of folders as menus. You see this with the Start menu, the Send To menu, Favorites, and Taskbar toolbars, among other things. All the techniques we discussed in Chapter 6, "Customizing Your New PC," for editing the Start menu directly or through Explorer work equally well with these other special menus. We cover each one in this chapter. You will do well to become familiar with them and master the menu-editing process because of the customizing power it affords.

We believe that your main criteria when customizing is to increase ease of use and decrease the time you spend getting your most common tasks done. This approach leaves more

Bright Idea
Keep your customizations focused on productivity by listing every task you perform for one week. Use this list to plan your Start menu groups with an eye to making the things you do most often the most readily available on the menu.

time for you to surf the Internet—or better yet, spend the extra time with your family or friends. Don't let Windows make you a slave to the mundane idiosyncrasies that the system brings to your computer via its default settings. You can master it and take control of your desktop. So grab your mouse and come along for the ride.

The customizations discussed in this chapter and back in Chapter 6 are the kinds of changes that put actual time back in your day. It's not enough just to learn how to do things on the computer—you want to remove as much thought as possible from mundane tasks, such as starting programs. It's easy to spend valuable brain power on remembering where each program is and what it does rather than solving the actual task at hand. Follow the tips here and you'll be less frustrated and far more productive in very short order.

Revisiting the Start Menu

For starters, let's create a Window that will house your personal stuff. Right-click the Start button and choose Open. Then right-click on an empty area of the Start Menu Explorer window; from the pop-up menu, choose New, Folder. The newly created folder is named New Folder, which you change by typing a new name and pressing Enter. Use your first name for the folder title, and set up a new folder for each person using the computer. We'll name the folder in this example "Dan" and refer to it by that name. See Figure 7.1.

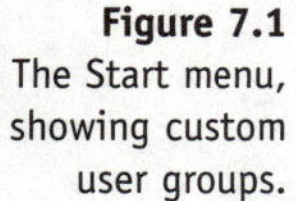

Figure 7.1
The Start menu, showing custom user groups.

The Dan subfolder appears on the Start menu, and selecting it causes any programs or shortcuts you put in this folder to appear as menu options on a cascading menu. The shortcuts you'll want to put in this folder are those to programs or files you use day in and day out. If you're like us, you'll find that you run the same five or six programs most of the time, and the Start menu options to start them are probably scattered over various menus and submenus. Gather all these menu options in your new folder by locating them on the Start menu and its cascading submenus and then dragging them to the Dan folder. To copy the menu options instead of actually moving them, hold down the Ctrl key while dragging.

The next set of folders to create is task-oriented folders. Think about the tasks you do on a regular basis. If you create Web pages, for instance, you will often use an HTML editor, a graphics program, and an FTP program, among others. Create a subfolder called Web Tools and put a shortcut to each of these programs into this folder. Now when you create Web pages, all your tools will be accessible from a common location, making it easy to get to the tool you need when you need it. If you produce the newsletter for an organization you are a member of, you might use a word processor, a graphics program, a desktop publishing system, email, and a calendar. Put a shortcut to these programs in a Start menu subfolder called Newsletter, and you're ready to get productive without having to look all over for your tools. By using shortcuts, you can have numerous menu options to the same program—your graphics program, for example—from everywhere you might want to access it.

Bright Idea
Do you have some novice computer users at your house or business? Why not rename the folders and shortcuts on your Start menu with descriptions of their tasks rather than the program names? Then these users can click Write Letters rather than trying to figure out which program to use to write letters.

If you have small children in the house, you know that they love to get on the computer. The problem is that you don't want them messing up your data or running certain programs. The solution is simple and works great for us. Create a Kid Stuff group with all the programs the kids are allowed to run (see Figure 7.1). Now create a shortcut to the Kid Stuff group on your desktop for easy access by the children. This clearly lets them know what they can and can't use on your computer.

This technique eliminates frustration and gives them a sense of control over what they are doing. The children also find it quite a treat when they open their special icon and find new programs to explore. To further customize this, give the Kid Stuff group on your desktop a unique icon. How? Simply right-click Kid Stuff, choose Properties, and click the Change Icon button. Let your children choose the icon and go from there.

The following is a list of files on your system that contain icons you can use. To use one of these files, either type its name into the File Name box or click the Browse button; then locate the file you want. Either way, all the icons available in your chosen file will be displayed on the screen. Click the one you want, and then choose OK.

- C:\WINDOWS\Progman.exe—arrows, hands, symbols, and the Mona Lisa
- C:\WINDOWS\SYSTEM\Cool.dll—high-color folders and disk drives
- C:\WINDOWS\SYSTEM\Shell32.dll—computers, folders, disk drives, and a tree
- C:\WINDOWS\SYSTEM\Wmsui32.dll—folders, briefcases, and email-related icons
- C:\WINDOWS\SYSTEM\setupx.dll—networking related
- C:\WINDOWS\SYSTEM\pifmgr.dll—airplanes, boats, cars, balls, and cards

This list is by no means complete. If you can't find an icon you like, try searching the Internet for `icons` and the type of icon you are looking for. You are sure to find something you can use.

Taskbar Toolbars

You want some programs at your fingertips at all times. For us, that includes our email program and word processor, among other things. The place to put these programs is on your taskbar. Windows 98 includes the Quick Launch toolbar as a component of the taskbar. Look at your taskbar and you should see a set of small icons on either the right or the left end. If you don't have the toolbar showing on your taskbar, simply right-click on an empty area of the taskbar, choose Toolbars on the pop-up menu, and then click Quick Launch. You should now see the Quick Launch toolbar on your taskbar, as shown in Figure 7.2. The application icons that appear by default are mostly Internet Explorer related, so you'll want to add your favorite programs to the list. Suppose, for example, you want to add Solitaire to your taskbar for quick access. Simply locate the program entry on your Start menu and drag it using the right mouse button to your Quick Launch toolbar. You'll see a thick black line showing you where the icon will appear on the toolbar. Choose a spot and drop your icon there. A menu pops up asking whether you want to Move, Copy, or Create a Shortcut. Choose Copy and your new icon should now be operational. Do this with the primary programs you use most often, and you'll save enough time to actually work in a game of Solitaire.

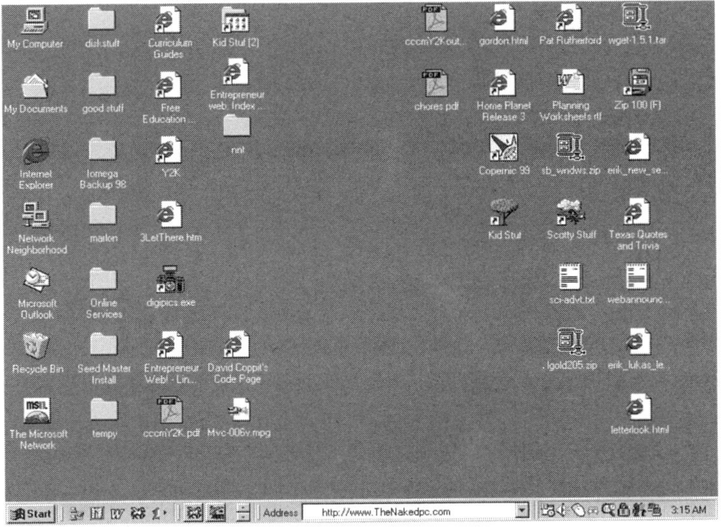

Figure 7.2
The taskbar with Quick Launch and the Address toolbars turned on.

Any time you want to update a program on your taskbar, simply right-click it and you'll get the usual choices: Open, Delete, Properties, and so on. The settings for the Quick Launch toolbar are actually stored in the folder `C:\Windows\`

Bright Idea
A tip to make the Address toolbar take up less space is to right-click on a gray area of the Address toolbar and uncheck the Show Title option, which removes the label "Address" from the URL launch box.

`Application_Data\Microsoft\Internet_Explorer\Quick_Launch`. This menu will become your own personal launch pad for your most-used programs. By putting them in a prominent place, you'll find yourself spending less time getting ready to use your computer and more time actually being productive.

If you find yourself looking up a lot of URLs, you might want to consider turning on the Address toolbar. This puts a URL launch box directly on your taskbar, as shown in Figure 7.2. Now just cut and paste or type a URL into this box, press Enter, and Internet Explorer launches and displays the URL for you. To display your Location toolbar, right-click on an empty area of the taskbar, choose Toolbars on the pop-up menu, and then click Address.

No matter which toolbars you choose to display, don't feel that you are limited to having them on your taskbar. Grab any toolbar with your mouse by clicking and dragging near the left end of the toolbar. You can drag the toolbar to any location on your screen.

Desktop Again

Your desktop is a very important folder and is a good place to keep things you need to be visually reminded about. One reason is that the desktop is quickly accessible from most File, Open and File, Close dialog boxes via the View Desktop button, as shown in Figure 7.3. It is always the top folder in the Look In drop-down list box in these dialog boxes, as well.

Remember, your desktop is another folder on your system. Windows gives you multiple ways to access the information you have stored there. The following are several ways you can access your desktop:

- From any Explorer window, click your Desktop icon, which is always at the top of the hierarchy.
- Click the Desktop button in most File, Open and File, Close boxes.
- Click the Show Desktop button on the Quick Launch toolbar, which minimizes all open windows on the first click and restores the screen on the second click.

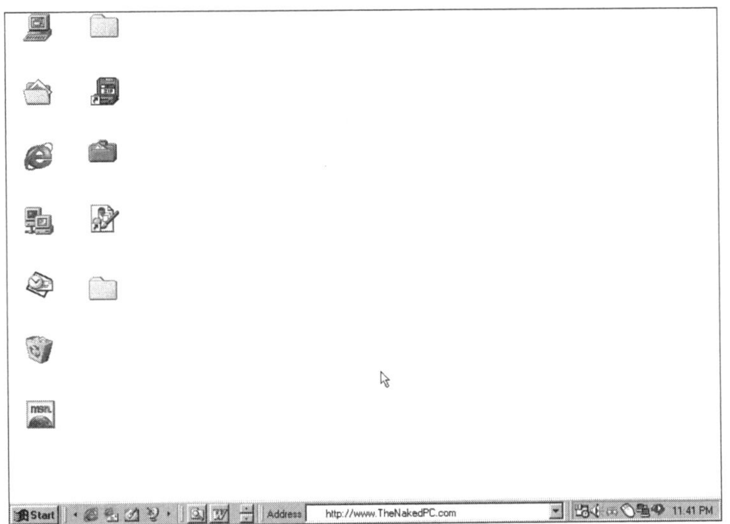

Figure 7.3
The desktop is easy to access in File, Open and File, Save dialog boxes.

- On keyboards with a Windows key, press Windows+M to minimize all windows and Windows+Shift+M to restore all windows.
- Navigate in Windows Explorer to `C:\Windows\Desktop`.
- In the Start, Run box, type `Desktop` and press Enter.

As you can see from the list, it is easy to get to your desktop from almost anywhere in Windows. Later in this chapter, you'll learn about the Send To menu and how to use it to automate moving and creating items on your desktop.

Earlier in this chapter, we described how to create a shortcut on the desktop for a Start menu group by using the right mouse button while dragging. You can do the same thing with any folder or document to which you want quick access. It's important to keep in mind the differences between putting a file or folder on the desktop, putting a copy of the file or folder on the desktop, and putting a shortcut to a file or folder on the desktop. To accomplish any of these three tasks, open an Explorer window and then drag the desired object to the desktop with your right mouse button. Release the mouse and from the pop-up menu, choose from the following:

- Move Here—Moves the actual item from the source location to your Desktop folder.
- Copy Here—Places a copy of the original object on the Desktop.
- Create Shortcut(s) Here—Places a pointer to your original file on the Desktop.

Refining the StartUp Folder

Of all the special folders in Windows, perhaps the StartUp folder is the most important. On the Start menu you'll find this option at Start, Programs, StartUp. In Windows Explorer you'll find the folder at `C:\Windows\Start Menu\Programs\StartUp`.

Any program (or shortcut) in this folder is launched automatically every time you start Windows. So if you always open a certain program after you start Windows, locate that program in your Start menu, right-click and drag it to StartUp, and then choose Create Shortcut Here. This is a great way to get in the habit of checking your calendar every morning or just to launch your Web browser with the weather page pulled up.

There are also some things you don't want in your StartUp folder. If you run Microsoft Office, for example, a couple of entries are automatically placed there that are prime candidates for removal. Specifically, we are talking about Fast Find and Office StartUp. Fast Find indexes your hard drive to supposedly make it quicker to find documents when you search for them. In our experience, it's just a big headache. Go ahead and remove this entry by right-clicking it and choosing Delete. Remember that you can do this on the Start menu without having to open Explorer itself.

Unofficially... Just removing Fast Find from your StartUp folder isn't enough. Finish the job by starting the Fast Find applet from the Control Panel. Select each drive listed, pull down the Index menu, click Delete Index, and then click OK.

Office StartUp loads the common system files for running any of the Microsoft Office programs. The purpose is to reduce the time it takes to load one of those applications. Unfortunately, if you aren't running a Microsoft Office application, those files are still taking up space in your memory. Besides, the first time you start an Office product, the files are loaded at that point. Nix this entry the same as you did the other one, by right-clicking and choosing Delete. If you use the Microsoft Office products constantly, you might consider leaving this file in place. Otherwise, just send it to the bit bucket where it belongs.

This example of the Microsoft Office files is just that—an example. There is no way to know which programs are in your StartUp group. (See Figure 7.4.) Even so, you should have a look there and load only those things that are necessary for your day-to-day sanity. If you aren't sure whether a program in your StartUp folder is needed, don't delete it; instead, move it to your desktop temporarily, reboot, and see whether you can live without it. Run through your normal routine for a few days; then when you are sure that the file is disposable, move it from your desktop into your Recycle Bin.

Bright Idea
After you put shortcuts to data files (an Excel spreadsheet, a Word document, and so forth) into StartUp, the parent application opens and the data file loads automatically. This technique works for any data file that has a program associated with it.

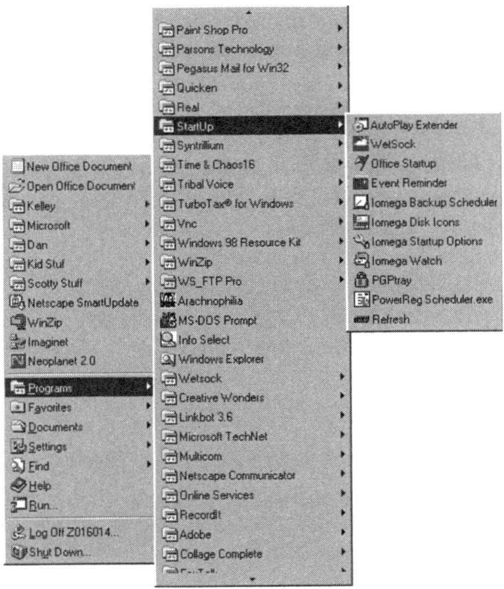

Figure 7.4
Keep only the necessities in your StartUp folder.

Now that your StartUp group is cleaned out, let's fill it up again! Think of the programs you use every time you start your computer. They might be the Calendar file, your email program, a financial package, or a Web browser. Decide which files you want loaded when your computer starts, find the entry for that program on your Start menu (or in Windows Explorer), and then drag it to your StartUp folder while holding down the Ctrl key. The next time you boot your machine, your program will run.

Don't get the idea that you can't change things after you have your StartUp folder populated. If you're working on a project for the next couple of days that involves running Excel, Notepad, and your FTP software—by all means, put shortcuts to them in StartUp. Every time you fire up your PC, all your apps are running. When that project is complete, remove the shortcuts. StartUp is a great tool you should use to make yourself more productive on a day-to-day basis.

Unofficially...
If you ever want to bypass your StartUp group while booting your computer, simply hold down the Shift key when you see your Desktop while Windows loads. Doing so can quickly tell you whether a problem you are having is coming from the StartUp group or some other source.

Using the Send To Command

One of the most underused features of the Windows interface is the SendTo folder. The Send To command offers a lightning quick way to move things around on your system. When you are in Explorer, simply right-click an object with your mouse, choose Send To, and then pick the place or application to which you want to send the object (see Figure 7.5). The object is immediately sent or copied to the destination. Whether the item is sent or copied depends on what the target of the Send To does to the selected object. For example, if you Send To Microsoft Excel, Excel opens and loads the file. If you Send To the A: drive, Windows copies the file from your hard drive to the floppy disk.

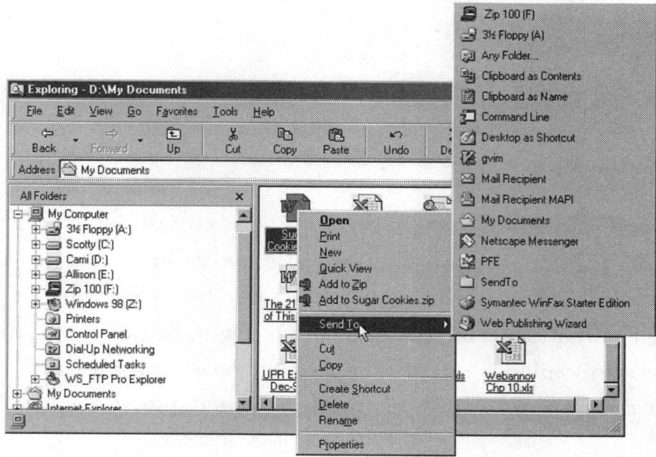

Figure 7.5
The Send To menu.

You'll find the SendTo folder at `C:\Windows\SendTo`. Any shortcut placed in this folder appears on the Send To menu. The first item we suggest you place here is a shortcut to the SendTo folder itself. Open Explorer and simply right-click and drag the SendTo folder back into the SendTo folder. When you release the mouse, choose Create Shortcut Here, and your new entry will be in place. Why do you want a shortcut to SendTo on the Send To menu? To make it easy to add new items to the menu without having to open the folder first.

The following is a list of some of the places you'll find the Send To menu waiting to go to work for you:

- In Windows Explorer
- From the Start menu
- From the Favorites menu
- In File, Open and File, Close dialog boxes
- From your desktop
- From within Microsoft Office applications

Watch Out!
Putting a shortcut to your desktop into Send To can be tricky. If you try to right-click and drag the desktop in Explorer, nothing happens. Instead, right-click in your SendTo folder and choose New, Shortcut. In the dialog box that pops up, type `C:\Windows\Desktop` for the command line. Your Send To menu now has an entry for your desktop.

Spend a moment to think about the various things you might want to put on your Send To menu. Good choices are Printers, File Viewers, and Editors. Several useful entries are your Desktop, Favorites, and StartUp folders. The Windows Fax utility should already be there; to quickly send a document out as a fax, you can right-click, choose Send To, and then select the Fax entry. Your fax program should launch and your document will soon be on its way. The PowerToys, discussed later in this chapter, also add several very useful entries to the SendTo command folder.

Windows 98 adds a new entry to the Send To menu called Desktop As Shortcut. Choosing this sends a shortcut of the current item to the desktop rather than the item itself. Combining this with a Send To entry pointing to the actual desktop gives you a lot of power. Now with a click of the mouse, you put a quick pointer to any file or the file itself on your desktop. If you are working on a document and want quick access, try these steps:

1. Create the document and save it to your preferred location, which for most people is My Documents.
2. Open the File, Save As dialog box.
3. Right-click the file you just created and choose Send To, Desktop As Shortcut.

Unofficially... One use of Send To that is rarely mentioned lets you expand the Send To menu by creating subfolders of items as well. Simply create folders inside your SendTo folder and group similar entries together. This approach helps keep your menus to a manageable size.

Navigating with Favorites

Favorites are Microsoft's way of helping you organize all the files and Internet sites you use the most often. Previously, the My Documents folder was the way to store these files, but Favorites is now the favorite way to track things. The trick to using Favorites effectively is to create a hierarchy of folders and subfolders within the Favorites folder to keep your favorites organized. This is easy enough to do: open the Favorites folder and create categories of Favorites exactly the way you did with your Start menu. To help you with your customizing, think of your Start menu as your program organizer and your Favorites menu as your information organizer.

The following are a few of the places in Windows from which you can access your Favorites folder:

- On your Start menu
- In the File, Open and File, Close dialog boxes of Microsoft Office applications
- On the menu bar in Windows Explorer
- On the menu bar in Internet Explorer

The Favorites folder is actually located at `C:\Windows\Favorites`. You can quickly open your Favorites folder for editing by typing `Favorites` into the Start, Run dialog box. As you create folders and make your hierarchy, you might want to review the list of guidelines we recommended when you cleaned up your Start menu back in Chapter 5. Those tips apply equally well to your Favorites folder.

PowerToys

When Windows 95 was released, it was a major change to the Windows interface. Some of the developers of Windows 95 created some handy add-in tools that Microsoft never supported, known as the PowerToys. Some of these have been integrated into Windows 98, some were just curious novelties, and the rest were useful additions to the standard interface. At Microsoft's site to download these tools, you will see disclaimers stating, "This download is not intended for use on PCs running Windows 98." Some of the PowerToys are now part of Windows 98; therefore, you should not download and install all the PowerToys. The short list in the following subsection provides a simple road map for you to follow when you install the PowerToys—pick the ones that help you the most. Some people find the PowerToys indispensable, whereas others find that they never use them.

Bright Idea
Not sure which category (subfolder) to put one of your Favorites into? No problem—create more than one entry for the same Favorite. Put each in a category that makes sense, and you'll always have your Favorites at your fingertips.

Here are a couple of important notes on how to install the PowerToys. First and foremost, you must install them from a directory that has no long filenames (more than eight characters) in its path. For example, `C:\Windows\Desktop\Toys` works fine, but `C:\My Documents\Toys` does not. For this reason, we recommend that you create a folder on your desktop called Toys, and then download and install the programs from there. Additionally, Microsoft seems to change the URL for the PowerToys every time we publish an article on them! The last time we looked, they were at the following URL:

```
http://www.microsoft.com/windows/downloads/default.asp?Cust
➥Area=bus&Site=
family&Product=&Category=Power+Toys+%26+Kernel+Toys&x=6&y=6
```

Unofficially...
Having trouble finding what you want on Microsoft's Web site? Join the club and do what we do—surf over to Bob Cerelli's Windows Page (`www.halcyon.com/cerelli`) and find direct links to all the important files, Knowledge Base articles, and product pages at Microsoft. You can always find a current link to the PowerToys at our Web site, `www.TheNakedPC.com`.

Key PowerToys to Consider

Read through this list and download the Toys that give you enhanced functionality. When a Toy is part of Windows 98, we'll tell you how to access it.

- Quick Res—Changes your screen resolution without rebooting. This utility is now built into Windows 98, and to access it, you right-click on your desktop, choose Properties, switch to the Settings tab, click the Advanced button, select the General tab, and check the box labeled Show Settings Icon on Task Bar. Then click OK twice. You'll then have what looks like a little computer monitor sitting on your system tray. Click this monitor and you can switch among different video resolutions at will (see Figure 7.6). Why would you want to do this? Some games require a certain screen resolution or color depth. Quick Res lets you switch quickly between the various options available to you. Other times, you'll want to switch resolutions to make reading a certain document easier or to test something on a different-sized screen. This utility makes it easy. Download the Quick Res PowerToy only if you're still running Windows 95.

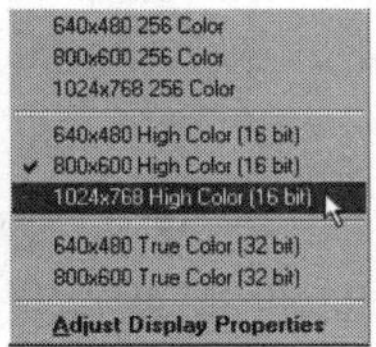

Figure 7.6 Using Quick Res to change screen resolutions.

- Explore from Here—Right-click an Explorer folder and choose Explore from Here. Another Explorer window opens with your selected folder open. Useful when you want two windows available for copying or moving files.
- Command Prompt Here—Right-click an Explorer folder and choose Command Prompt Here. A DOS window opens, already focused on your chosen folder.
- Contents Menu—Right-click an Explorer folder and choose Contents. A little menu flies out, showing you the contents of your chosen folder. Choose an item from this menu and it opens as if you had selected it in Explorer. Useful for seeing what's buried down in your folders or for quickly launching an item from a folder on your desktop. Works with a shortcut to a folder as well.
- Send to X—Includes a host of additions to your Send To menu. Send to AnyFolder: A true workhorse if there ever was one. Send to Clipboard as Contents: Sends the full

contents of the current file to the clipboard. Useful only with text files, and small ones at that. Send to Clipboard as Name: Sends the name of the current file, including the full path, to the clipboard. Command Line: Sends the name of the current file, including the full path, to the Start, Run dialog box. The next option lets you configure your Send To menu to send email. Not all mail programs work with these utilities, though. For the MAPI setting, Netscape Mail, Outlook, and Eudora are known to work correctly, although most will put their own entry onto the Send To menu, making this entry obsolete. We recommend turning all the mail options off.

- Shortcut Target Menu—Lets you access the properties of the file or program to which a shortcut points.
- TweakUI—If you are running Windows 98, you'll want to use the version of this that comes on the Windows 98 CD-ROM, so don't install this PowerToy. Full instructions on how to install the Windows 98 version can be found in Chapter 5, "Configuring Your New PC," where we talk about the Windows 98 Resource Kit. For Windows 95, download the version on the Web site.

After you've downloaded the PowerToys you want to install, what do you do next? First, uncompress the files by double-clicking them. Next, look for the file with an extension of .inf. Right-click the file and choose Install from the pop-up menu. Do this for each PowerToy you downloaded. When you are finished, you can delete all the files in the temporary folder you created.

Fine-Tuning with TweakUI

TweakUI is probably the most useful tool of the bunch. Make sure that you installed TweakUI from your Windows 98 CD. Start TweakUI from the Control Panel. The resulting window has several tabs, as shown in Figure 7.7. The changes we recommend make your system *seem* to run faster by eliminating all the sliding and other animation your menus and windows go through.

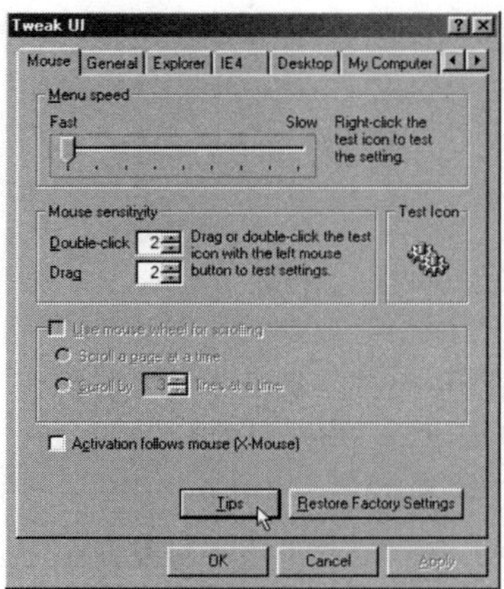

Figure 7.7 TweakUI in action; note the Tips button, which opens the Help file.

- Mouse tab—Set the Menu Speed to Fast. Click the Apply button and then try your Start menu. The menus should open faster than before—too fast for some people. Adjust the speed until you are comfortable.
- General tab—Under Effects, uncheck all the boxes that control animation. Changing these settings makes your computer appear faster by speeding up the response time of your windows and menus. Set the Internet Explorer option to point to your favorite Internet search engine. If you don't have one yet, just leave this setting alone.
- Explorer tab—Under Settings, uncheck the Prefix "Shortcut to" on New Shortcuts box. This makes all the file-maintenance and menu-organization tips we've given you work more smoothly. You'll no longer have to rename your files just to get them to sort correctly.
- Desktop—Controls which of the system icons are displayed on your desktop. In Chapter 6, you saw that Network Neighborhood cannot be dragged into the Recycle Bin. This is where you eliminate that and any other system icon you don't want. Simply uncheck the box of those that you don't want, and check the box of those that you do.
- My Computer—Works the same as the Desktop tab except that this tab controls which of your drives are available in an Explorer window. Generally, you'll leave this setting

alone, but occasions might arise when you want to protect a certain drive from curious eyes.

- Add/Remove—Lets you remove entries from Control Panel's Add/Remove Programs list. Useful if you deleted a program directory instead of uninstalling it. Removing an entry here does not uninstall the application; it only removes it from the list of programs you can uninstall from your Control Panel. Use this with caution!
- Repair—This tab repairs some fairly technical problems, such as altered file associations, special folder behaviors, and default icons. You should familiarize yourself with this tab so that you'll know where to look should any of the problems it repairs crop up on your system. Some of them won't make much sense to you until the problem occurs on your system.
- Paranoia—Clears various lists that report a user's activity. If you need to keep someone from knowing what you are looking at and where you have been Web-surfing, look through these options.

That does it for our quick tour of TweakUI. Many more options are available in this dialog box, and you should read through its Help file as well. The Help file is located on the Mouse tab under the Tips button, as shown in Figure 7.7.

Active Desktop: The Internet on Your Desktop

We covered the various components of the Active Desktop in Chapter 6. The full extent of the Active Desktop includes Stock Ticker tapes, news reports, and other updates delivered on a schedule that you set. The available objects change almost daily, so any list we give would quickly be obsolete. If you want to look into these options, here's how to go about it:

1. Right-click on your desktop and choose Active Desktop, Customize My Desktop.
2. Check the box labeled View My Active Desktop as a Web Page.

Unofficially...
Use a service such as Company Sleuth (`www.companysleuth.com`) to track information on companies in which you hold stock. The information is delivered right to your email box, keeping you current while saving you tons of time.

3. Click the New button.
4. Windows asks whether you want to go to the Active Desktop gallery at Microsoft's Web site. Click Yes.
5. Choose the Channels you want to view.

After completing these steps, your desktop will look similar to Figure 7.8. It's a simple process, and it's easy to load up on lots of free information. Unless you have a high-speed Internet connection, this is also an easy way to bog down your computer while it is gathering this information for you. We recommend looking at free email newsletters for the same types of data. Email is much quicker to download, and you have more control over what happens to the data.

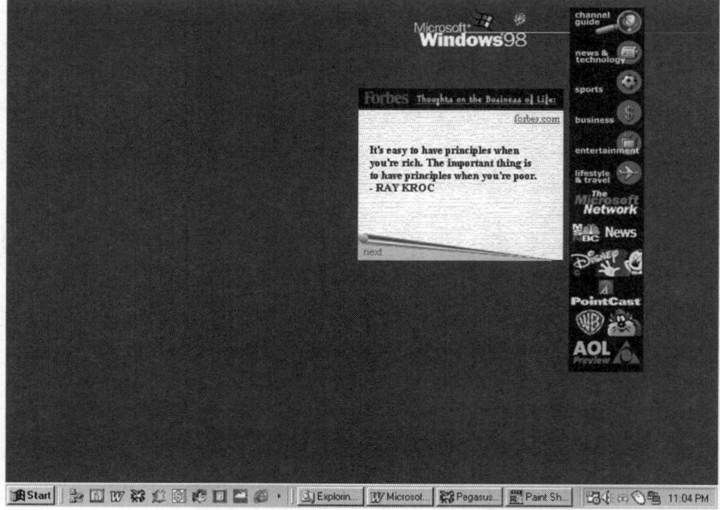

Figure 7.8
The Active Desktop with the Channel bar and an active window embedded.

Chapter Ending

This chapter and the preceding one have quite a bit of information in them. The following is a quick summary of the changes we recommended:

- Make your own personal reference list from Help files and Web sites.

- Configure Windows Explorer to work the way you want it to work.
- Organize your Start menu and Favorites by person or by task.
- Use your desktop to speed up your work.
- Remove unwanted applications and add missing applications and utilities.
- Change your CD-ROM drive letter.
- Size down your Recycle Bin and Temporary Internet Files to conserve disk space.
- Put your most frequently used programs on the taskbar.
- Maximize the use of your Send To menu.
- Clean out the StartUp file.
- Use the PowerToys.

Chapter 8

Staying Ahead of the Game

IT WOULD BE NICE if we could say that after you had assembled your PC, configured it, loaded it with software, and generally customized the heck out of it, you were home free—that all you had left to do was use and enjoy your new system. Unfortunately, the computer world does not work that way. The pace at which computer technology moves is staggering. And in the mad rush to get hardware components shipped out the door and to get the latest software versions on store shelves, a lot of what you might find on your new system is probably just a tad underdone.

Almost immediately, you'll find that new hardware drivers need to be downloaded and installed to correct minor and major problems that weren't quite worked out before that nifty sound card was shipped, or to fix some incompatibility with the latest and greatest operating-system software. You'll have driver upgrades to deal with and software that needs to be updated with bug fixes, maintenance releases, service releases, service packs, and patches.

Installing almost anything new on your system (after you have it up and running) inevitably entails a trip to the Internet and a search for a driver or a software upgrade you need to download before everything works.

Unofficially...
The PC industry has coined many confusing, obscure terms in an attempt to steer its customers away from one cold, hard fact. Operating systems, software applications, and drivers are bug-infested products. Sure, some are more buggy than others, and it's fair to say that bugs are inherent in software currently being developed. Bottom line: the terms *update, maintenance release, service release, service pack,* and *patch* all mean effectively the same thing: a set of bug fixes with—if we're lucky—some new features thrown in. Yes, down at the bits and bytes level, a patch operates differently from a service release, but all these terms are effectively synonymous. To keep things simple, in this chapter we'll simplify by using the noun *upgrade* wherever possible.

This chapter covers driver and software upgrades in three stages. First, in the "Ongoing Upgrades" section, we'll go over the most common components you'll be updating and upgrading as you work with your system. If you're not aware of what is likely to need an update, you can be blindsided when you install something new on your computer only to have something else suddenly stop working or start misbehaving.

In the "Tracking Down Upgrades" section, we'll take a look at how you can find out which of your many installed drivers and applications might benefit from an upgrade or a newer version. Various built-in tools and third-party applications are available to do this, as well as some Web-driven upgrade processes you should know about.

Finally, in "Installing Upgrades on Your System," you'll get our recommendations on how to deal with downloadable upgrades, how to keep track of the files, and how to go about installing them. We'll walk through some real-world examples of what's involved with actually performing upgrade downloads and installations.

Ongoing Upgrades

Keeping your system tuned and running is not a full-time job—it just seems that way if you get caught flat-footed by a problem that requires you to install a new driver or a software upgrade, and you don't know where to begin. Not to worry; we'll show you the ins and outs of updating your system and your application software on an ongoing basis.

Know What You Have Installed

The key to upgrading drivers and maintaining your system software is knowing exactly what you have installed. To get the right upgrade, you need to know the exact piece of hardware you are trying to find a driver for, or the specific version of software you currently have installed. For hardware, that includes the manufacturer, the make, and the specific model number. We discussed how to gather this information as you were assembling and configuring your computer back in

Chapter 4, "When and When Not to Assemble Your PC," and Chapter 5, "Configuring Your New PC." One of the tools we discussed for this task is the Device Manager in Windows.

To open Device Manager, follow these steps:

1. Right-click the My Computer icon on your Windows desktop.
2. Select Properties from the pop-up menu.
3. Select the Device Manager tab in the Properties dialog box (see Figure 8.1).

Figure 8.1
Using Device Manager to find out exactly what you have installed.

Hardware Versions * Installing software—especially upgrades to the operating system—can actually be the cause of some hardware problems. After installing software, including an upgrade to Windows 98, on a system here in our labs, the system started experiencing some odd screen glitches in some of the applications we regularly run on that PC. Taking a quick peek at Device Manager (see Figure 8.1), we checked each item against our last inventory sheet, which of course we had handy in the NEAT box for this system.

Although the monitor was listed correctly in Device Manager, the display adapters and mouse settings had changed and no longer reflected the actual hardware installed on the system. As you can see, after a fairly common event (upgrading

Moneysaver
In addition to keeping your installed programs up-to-date, you'll no doubt want to find the best in new software and hardware to add to your system. For this, you can't beat Review Finder (`http://www.reviewfinder.com`), where you can get the latest reviews on hardware and software before you shell out any hard-earned bucks.

Bright Idea
If you have a keyboard that sports the Windows keys, you can instantly pop up the System Properties dialog box using the Windows key + the Pause key combination. This makes getting to the Device Manager tab in the System Properties dialog box a snap.

or installing new software), we were suddenly faced with having to reinstall some hardware drivers. Rather than use the original drivers that came with the video card and mouse, the best course of action is to check with the manufacturers of these components (via their Web sites) and download the latest drivers. We'll cover how you go about this process later in this chapter.

Software Versions * Figuring out what version of a given software package you have is far easier than version-sniffing your hardware, although it's not foolproof. Generally, you need only to start the application, pull down its Help menu, and click the About option. The program's version number should appear in the resultant dialog box. Determining which software version you have gets tricky when you're dealing with maintenance releases or service releases. Rarely will an interim release cause the version number to increment an entire left-of-decimal value. Instead, something like "SR-1" might get appended to the end of the current version number (as Microsoft did with its first service release for Microsoft Office 97). For patches or minor maintenance releases, you'll more often get a right-of-decimal increment of some kind.

Bright Idea
When something suddenly starts acting up on your system, always check out Device Manager and see whether any warning flags are displayed. It's easy to overlook this handy troubleshooting tool.

As you can see in Figure 8.2, Outlook shows a version number of "8" with a right-of-decimal sub-version number of ".5.5603.0." The hows and whys of version numbering are a dark and mystical science rumored to be understood only by software makers and the ancient scholars of the lost continent of Atlantis. Staying with our Outlook 98 example, we recently had to patch this software twice in response to the discovery of a security bug and the release of two patches. Outlook 98 originally had a version number of 8.5.5104.6. We applied the security patch immediately after it was released, and the version number didn't change at all. Without tediously comparing dates of key files, no easy way existed to tell that the application had been patched. We complained loudly to Microsoft that it was going to be difficult for customers to determine whether their machines were patched. They must have listened, because when it was discovered that the patch did not deal completely with the security issue, Microsoft issued a second patch, and this time the application version number changed (to 8.5.5603.0).

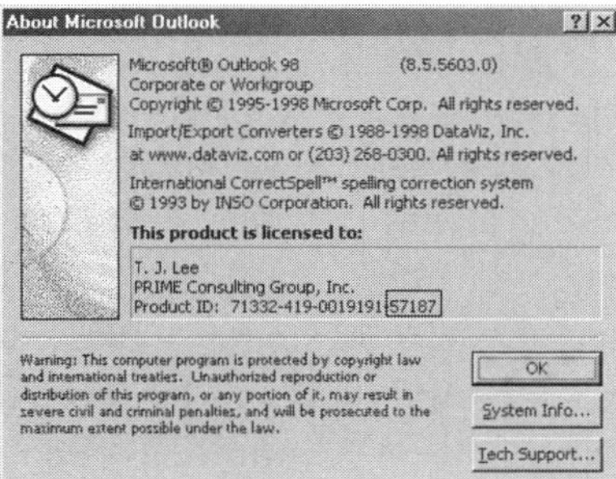

Figure 8.2
Microsoft Outlook 98 version 8.5.5603.0.

Common Hardware Driver Updates

Unofficially... Upgrades, however minor, should be recorded in the notebook that is in your NEAT box. Although you usually can determine the current version numbers of software applications from their Help, About dialog boxes, occasionally you may run into an update in which the version number is not incremented; therefore, your journal might be the only way you can later determine whether you in fact installed the upgrade. Also, the journal gives you a chronological record of which upgrade you applied and in what order. This can help you troubleshoot problems that might be traced back to a specific update.

Which drivers are most subject to requiring the occasional update, and what happens that necessitates updating a driver? As you can imagine, the answers depend a lot on the type of system you have and the various components you have installed.

Installing a new operating system "on top" (upgrading from Windows 95 to Windows 98, for example) can cause new or different drivers to be installed over existing drivers without any warning or explanation. Windows 98 is notorious for installing old drivers over newer ones. You might suddenly find yourself getting unexpected results and have to reinstall the drivers you had *prior* to your operating-system upgrade. Occasionally, installing a piece of application software causes drivers to be overwritten with versions that are incompatible with other programs on your system. This was an acute problem with the Winsock.dll driver for a time when every communications program seemed to come with its own version of this dynamic link library, which was incompatible with every other version. The good news is that this problem seems to have been resolved among the software manufacturers within the past year.

Should you update a driver just because you discover that a newer version is available? For the most part, we go along with the adage that if something is not broken, don't try to fix it. A few exceptions exist, especially where software is concerned, but for the most part, you don't need to worry about your hardware unless it stops working or starts causing you grief. The following subsections cover the most common drivers you might have to upgrade or fuss with over time.

Unofficially... Be sure to keep track of all the disks that come with your hardware peripherals (as we've said, the best place to keep them is in the system's NEAT box). Because everything comes preinstalled, it's easy to become careless with the floppies that accompanied your system, but these disks contain drivers you might desperately need some day.

Video Drivers * The video display adapter in your system can make your computing life a pleasant experience or a living nightmare. Screen artifacts (dots and other screen-pixel garbage appearing in an application), color distortion, or even outright system crashes can be the result of a video-driver problem. One way to keep your system (and yourself) happy is to use the latest and greatest driver for your particular video adapter.

Given that the video driver is so critical to your system, it makes sense to drop by the Web site of your video-display card manufacturer to see whether the manufacturer has posted a newer video driver for your adapter—newer than the one you have installed. However, first you have to know which driver is currently installed on your system. One way to determine this is to look at the disk(s) that came with your video adapter. Often the version number appears on the disk label, in the Readme file, or in the documentation file included on the disk.

You can also check the video-driver version by starting Control Panel.

1. Click the Start button on the Windows taskbar.
2. Select Settings and then click Control Panel on the cascading menu.
3. Double-click the Display icon and select the Settings tab.
4. Click the Advanced button and then the Adapter tab (see Figure 8.3).

After you know what version you have installed, it's a good idea to record that information in your journal in case you have to reinstall that driver (the updated driver might not solve your current problem or, worse, might introduce a bigger problem of its own).

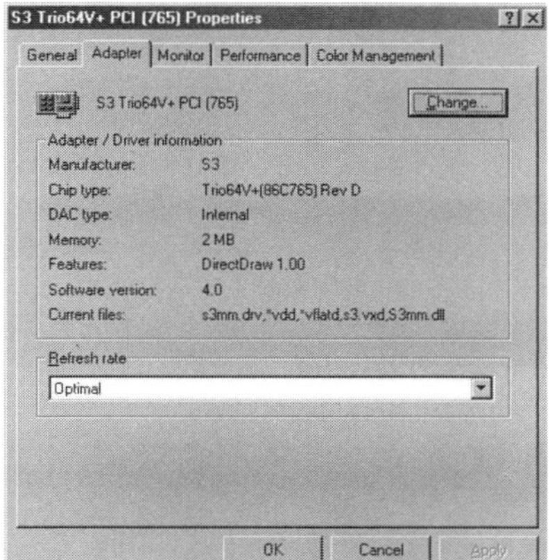

Figure 8.3
Get detailed information on the version of your video-display adapter.

Sound Cards * After sound cards are installed and working, they are usually stable, but we have had problems when upgrading operating systems or when trying to get a game to play its sounds and music properly. Fixing the former problem required downloading a more current driver for the PC's sound card. The latter problem is usually a glitch with the DirectX drivers (discussed in the next section).

Watch Out!
When Windows boots up, if the driver and Windows don't see eye to eye, you may not see *anything* on your monitor. This situation brings everything to a screeching halt, so before you install a new video driver, make sure that you know the name of the old driver in case you have to reinstall that, and make sure that you are familiar with booting your computer into Windows Safe Mode.

Checking the currently installed version of a sound-card driver can be a bit tricky. In the Device Manager dialog box, expand the setting for Sound, Video and Game Controllers, and select your installed sound card. Clicking the Properties button displays the properties for the selected card. The Driver tab probably will not give you exactly what you are looking for because most sound cards use several drivers to make your PC the auditory wonder that it is. Click the Driver File Details button and you'll see a list of the various drivers used by your sound card.

As shown in Figure 8.4, the PC in this example is running a Sound Blaster 16 Plug and Play, by Creative Labs. The first driver in the list is the SB16.VXD, and the version number is displayed in the dialog box: 4.37.00.1998. A visit to the Creative Labs Web site (`http://www.soundblaster.com/wwwnew/tech/ftp/`

`ftpnew.html`) shows us that an update is available for this card, and that it includes several drivers:

SB16.VXD v4.38.14

SB16SND.DRV v4.38.13

SBAWE.VXD v4.38.2

SBAWE32.DRV v4.38.0

SBFM.DRV v4.12.1

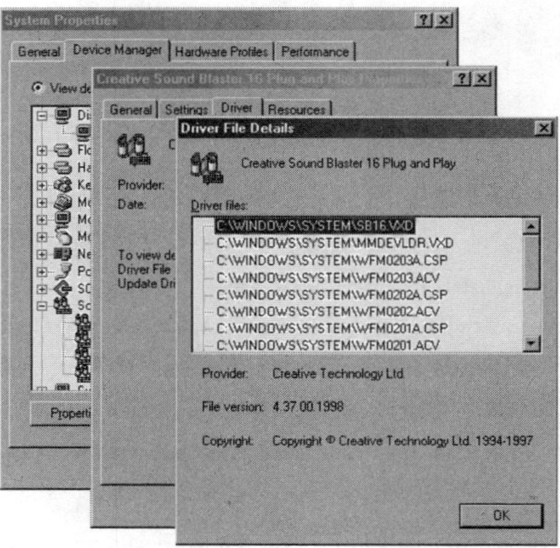

Figure 8.4 Determining the version of the sound-card driver.

By comparing the filenames and their version numbers from the Creative Labs site to those shown in the Driver File Details dialog box, we can determine that the sound driver we currently have installed is out-of-date. We can then download a newer driver from the Creative Labs site and update the system.

DirectX Drivers * If you play computer games, you should read this section. If you're not a game aficionado, you can skip this because it pertains to how gaming works under Windows 95/98 and why you might find yourself installing updated DirectX drivers.

In the past, most computer games were strictly DOS based, meaning that they did not run under Windows (running only under DOS increased performance). Windows requires that all activity be passed through it to the hardware so that it can manage disputes when two running applications try to access something, such as the video card or the printer at the same time. Back then, going through Windows proved too slow for the games being designed.

Windows DirectX drivers is a technology Microsoft came up with to fix this problem, and now most games are written specifically to run under Windows 95/98. DirectX comprises various application programming interface (API) calls that let games get the performance they need from the computer hardware, while still running under Windows. So far so good.

The problem is that DirectX is constantly evolving, and newer versions appear regularly. You might install game A, which, as part of its installation process, puts the latest and greatest DirectX drivers on your system. Later you install game B, which overwrites your newer DirectX drivers with older drivers. Technically, this is not supposed to happen, but it's not unknown for games with poorly designed installers to do this. After this, game A is not going to be happy. This situation is complicated because, if you are like us, you're not sure which of your various games has the most current drivers. Easier than shuffling game disks is to download and install the latest drivers from the Microsoft site (`www.microsoft.com/directx/default.asp`).

Mouse Drivers * Mice used to be simple and uncomplicated. Point, click, occasionally clean the lint and dirt from the mouse's innards, and buy a new one every other year or so. Things are more complex these days. Now the newer mice come with fancy wheels and support software you have to install so that you can set this feature, fine-tune that feature, and so on.

With this complexity comes the inevitable driver and software updates to fix little glitches that weren't fixed when the mouse was shipped. Microsoft's Intellimouse has already gone through at least two updates. Of course, the possibility of an update is not really something you pay much attention to unless you're having a problem with your mouse. But if you have problems with your mouse, be aware that a new and improved driver for it might be available to download from the mouse manufacturer's Web site. In fairness to Microsoft's Intellimouse, version 2.2 does offer a compelling new feature (along with bug fixes): it lets you use the cool, wheel-based scrolling feature in *any* Windows application, not only those specifically designed to support the Intellimouse.

Modem Upgrades * The good news is that you'll probably never have to fool around with upgrading the firmware in your modem. But *field-upgradable* modems are a hedge against new protocols that can make the modem you just bought obsolete.

At one point in modem history, two competing high-speed modem protocols existed, K56flex and x2, which are incompatible with each other. Manufacturers rushed these modems into production before any of the standards bodies had a chance to bless one protocol over the other. Users were wary of the two protocols but were assured that the protocols that controlled the modems could be upgraded. When the V.90 specification was finalized, manufacturers of field-upgradable modems posted software you could download and run to update the instructions stored in the modem. Like magic, a K56flex could become a V.90 modem.

Watch Out!
You won't get any high-speed benefits from your modem if it does not use the same protocol as the modem to which you are connecting. Always make sure that you know what protocols your ISP supports before you upgrade your modem.

Some modems support multiple protocols, which means they negotiate with the modem they're connecting to and choose the highest-speed protocol that both modems support, but some support only one specific high-speed protocol. And not all modems are field upgradable. If you don't know whether your modem could benefit from a field upgrade, check the manufacturer's Web site.

Printers * As with the mouse, you'll probably never have to mess with your printer driver after you install the printer and get it working.

Of course, if you get a new printer, you'll have to install the drivers for it. Most of the mainstream printers have drivers already on the Windows 98 installation disks, but we suggest that you use the driver disk or CD-ROM that accompanies any new printer you are installing to make sure that you get the latest driver. You might want to check the printer manufacturer's

Web site as a matter of course to see whether an even newer driver is available for your printer. In some ins. .nces, the manufacturer has added new features to a given printer by issuing a new printer driver.

The Unusual Suspects * In addition to drivers for common components, you might have to deal with any exotic hardware you've installed, such as a scanner or a digital camera.

The basic premise is the same, though. If you're not having problems, or if an upgraded driver doesn't offer a nifty new feature, you don't have to worry about tweaking the driver. But when you have a need for a new (or replacement) driver, the place to start is always at the manufacturer's Web site.

Unofficially...
It seems that some of the Hewlett-Packard DeskJet printer drivers that come with Windows 98 might have been rushed. We've heard reports that updated drivers from the HP Web site provide a tad more functionality for some models. Check the HP site and see whether your DeskJet printer might benefit from a driver upgrade (www.hp.com/cposupport/eschome.html).

Common Software Upgrades

The application software you run on your computer is something you'll upgrade far more often than your hardware drivers. A "new and improved" version is always available—one that you simply must have. "Must" because you hope it will fix the bugs that are driving you crazy in the current version of the application.

In this section, we'll look at software upgrades in general and try to answer the question "To upgrade, or not to upgrade?" Sometimes the answer is obvious; sometimes it is not.

Software is in a very sorry state today, partly because software manufacturers are trying desperately to change the software sales model. In the past, an application has been treated by everyone as a purchasable product. Never mind the licensing small print and the accompanying legal mumbo-jumbo—you slapped your credit card down on the counter and walked out of the store with a box under your arm. Software companies competed for your dollars by creating feature-laden programs that worked well, and they tried to entice you to switch from a competitor's product to theirs whenever possible. But that model has been changing.

The Changing Software Sales Model * That doesn't sound any different from what's happening today? Well, the change is subtle but it's there. Consider the applications you are currently using. We'll bet you did *not* walk into a computer store, evaluate a number of competing products, and choose one for purchase. More likely, you took the best bundle that came with your computer and are using that software mainly because it came preinstalled from the factory. This probably is true at least for your major applications, and we doubt that you're going to dump these applications anytime soon and purchase new ones. Therefore, to get more money out of you, the software company lucky enough to have its products land on your hard disk initially has to get you to spring for the next upgrade.

Unofficially...
We've seen great features in software applications we were beta-testing just disappear in the final released version of the software. Now, these features were working flawlessly, mind you, so why they were pulled was a puzzle until we found them touted as the big improvement in the *next* version. We reasoned that rather than put too many goodies in any one version, the software manufacturer wanted to add only enough good stuff to ensure a good upgrade cycle. Everything else, even if it was already tested and working fine, was held over to the next upgrade.

Software upgrades come fast and furious these days—the operating system, applications, utilities, you name it. An upgrade has to be available to keep you shelling out hard-earned bucks to stay current and to keep the software companies in cheese and crackers.

This approach is shifting the entire software industry to a "subscription model" like that used in the magazine business. We won't be surprised when the time comes that you pay once a year and get the current version and all maintenance upgrades (probably released once per quarter). The next year you get to "renew" your subscription. That's exactly the way it works with antivirus software programs today. The secondary fallout is that upgrades come more often to keep the upgrade cash-cow milk flowing. More upgrades, shorter beta cycles with products rushed out the door—no wonder interim upgrades are becoming a way of life for most computer users. And beta tests are really just presale programs in which you can buy into the beta program by purchasing the beta software.

The Software Upgrade Cycle * That said, how often should you upgrade your software? Personally, we keep current on everything we use regularly. We automatically go for the maintenance releases (mainly because these always seem to include some bug fixes), as well as the major new version releases. However, if you are using a piece of software and it's doing everything you need it to do, no need to upgrade exists unless the next version provides some new, compelling feature. The rub with this "practical" approach is that if you exchange documents and data with other users, you might find that they've upgraded, and the file formats between the two versions of the same product are now incompatible. Usually in this situation, the newer version can read your (older version) files, but the older version of the software can't work with files created by the newer version of the software.

Watch Out!
Not staying current with the latest upgrade of your favorite applications can make getting support for those applications more difficult; software companies don't like to support older applications (even though you usually have to pay for that support).

As you can imagine, these factors make staying with an older version of your software difficult at best, and the problem compounds with each new release. Is there a way out of the endless cycle of upgrades? Probably not. For example, you should always upgrade when security fixes for programs you use become available. But we've seen a situation in which a security bug affected both the current version of a piece of software and the previous versions. But the patch to fix the bug could be applied only to the newer version. The software company simply told users of the previous versions that they should upgrade to the newest version and apply the patch if they wanted to fix the security hole. Fortunately, this was a free upgrade, but many people we know had to change to a new version of the application to get a security issue dealt with when they would have preferred to stay with the earlier version.

Of course, whether you upgrade each application you own is up to you, but some upgrades you should always consider making.

Windows System Upgrades * As anyone who has used Windows can attest, it is a vast and complex operating system. It is made up of literally thousands of utilities, programs, drivers, dynamic link libraries, and the like. Staying up-to-date with its copious upgrades is definitely worth the trouble, and we highly recommend that you keep current in this arena.

Security fixes, new and improved utilities, fine-tuned DLLs—these can all make your computing experience a better one. Mindful of how difficult it can be to stay on top of the updates to a complex operating system such as Windows, Microsoft has implemented an automated Windows Update system that lets you update Windows 98 over the Web.

Browser Upgrades * The browser wars have shaken out every product except the market leaders: Netscape Navigator

(Navigator) and Microsoft Internet Explorer (IE). The question of upgrading your browser every time a new version is available is not as simple and as straightforward as you would think, even given that both browsers are free for the downloading.

First, both Internet Explorer and Navigator are works in progress, in a perpetual state of beta testing no matter what the press releases say. Both browsers try every trick they can think of to outdo the other. They try to get Web-page developers to support page features that only their browser will display. Or they make their browser the default Web page viewer (assuming that you install both on your system) and quietly "undefault" the other. Or as Microsoft recently did, they make the browser an integral part of the operating system itself. All this one-upmanship necessitates a very short development cycle, so you can spend a lot of time downloading the current version of each browser every time a new upgrade is released.

Watch Out!
This problem of an application being in a perpetual state of beta testing is not limited to browsers. Therefore, it's very important that you have a way to find out what's being reported about various software releases. Paid services such as BugNet are one source (`www.bugnet.com`), and most of the computer trade publications have pages on the Web, such as PCWeek Online News (`www.zdnet.com/pcweek/news/news.html`). Email newsletters like our own *The Naked PC* are also good sources for current news on upgrade problems (`www.TheNakedPC.com`).

Each new release brings with it a new round of glitches, bugs, security panics, and the like. So, should you upgrade your browser whenever you can?

If you are a Navigator user, the decision is easier because you can keep the older version installed on your system by installing the newer version to a separate folder. You can have several versions of Navigator installed on the same computer this way. Internet Explorer is a tougher decision because you can't generally install multiple versions of this browser on the same machine. Microsoft has integrated version IE 4 with the Windows operating system, thereby precluding installing multiple versions—or even completely removing the browser from your computer.

We recommend that you avoid the public beta releases (both Internet Explorer and Navigator have open betas in which you can get the latest version in development, hot off the Web), but we recommend that you do get the final release (the version that's not clearly marked as "beta"). But not right away. Don't be among the first to download the final release the second it's available. People who do that are called pioneers and are easily recognized by the arrows protruding from their backs. Seriously, wait a few weeks to make sure no nasty surprises surface in the code at the last minute.

System BIOS Upgrades

You should have a very compelling reason before fooling around with a BIOS upgrade. Generally, the only thing that would warrant such action is a system problem that cannot be resolved in any other way. Some of our customers had to upgrade their system BIOS before they could install Windows 98 and get it to run properly. In some cases, a new peripheral might require an upgrade to the machine's BIOS. Note that we're talking about only the newer systems that allow a BIOS to be upgraded via software, a process known as *flashing* the BIOS. Older systems require that you physically change the BIOS chip in your system—not something we recommend that you do yourself.

The addition of new hardware is one of the main reasons that a BIOS upgrade might be necessary. For example, throughout PC history, BIOS constraints have limited the size of a hard drive that could be supported. Every time a size barrier has been shattered by drive manufacturers, a new BIOS has been required (for example, drives greater than 8.4GB have been supported only since 1998).

What's tricky is figuring out exactly which BIOS you have. When your system boots up, the BIOS manufacturer and the version number usually appear onscreen. Unfortunately, this information might appear for only a few seconds (perhaps not even long enough for you to write it down without rebooting your PC several times). You can try your keyboard's Pause key to see whether you can freeze the display long enough to read the BIOS information, but if you followed our advice in Chapter 5, "Configuring Your New PC," and printed a complete system report from Device Manager, you'll find your BIOS information on page one. If you did not print the report, we suggest that you do it now by going into Device Manager and clicking the Print button. Select All Devices and System Summary, and keep the printout in your NEAT box.

Watch Out!
If your BIOS has already been updated, *the update might not have changed the version number*. Unfortunate but true. Therefore, any update to the BIOS is something you should record in your NEAT box, where it will stand out!

If you ever add hardware that did not even exist when your computer's system was originally put together, you'll probably have to update the BIOS. Another common reason to upgrade your BIOS is for Year 2000 compliance, as mentioned back in Chapter 5. Otherwise, leave the system BIOS alone. In the next section, we'll show you how to determine whether a newer version of your BIOS is available for your system.

Tracking Down Upgrades

We talked about the types of upgrades that keep your computer humming—primarily drivers to keep your hardware happy—as well as software upgrades (to both your Windows operating system and your applications). In this section you'll learn how to discover what upgrades are available for your system. The best place to go for information on what's available is, of course, the manufacturers of your PC's software and hardware. Unfortunately, keeping track of the current whereabouts of a half dozen or so manufacturers' phone numbers and Web addresses can be daunting. The good news is that in addition to the manufacturers themselves, various clearing sites for updates are on the Web, and even third-party software packages are available that monitor your system and notify you when a relevant upgrade becomes available.

Finding Manufacturers

If you have a problem that requires a specific driver or software fix, always start at the Web site of the application or device manufacturer. First, check the documentation you have collected in your NEAT box for hardware, or the documentation that came with your software (assuming you actually got any software documentation). The software itself might provide you with contact information for the application in its Help, About dialog box, as shown in Figure 8.5.

A tremendous resource for tracking down drivers is the WinDrivers.Com site (`www.windrivers.com/`). WinDrivers.Com keeps track of where to find drivers by keeping tabs on the peripheral manufacturers. The WinDrivers.Com database enables you to search for a given company. Each firm's listing has links to relevant Web pages for downloadable drivers, addresses, telephone numbers, email contact information, and the hardware categories applicable.

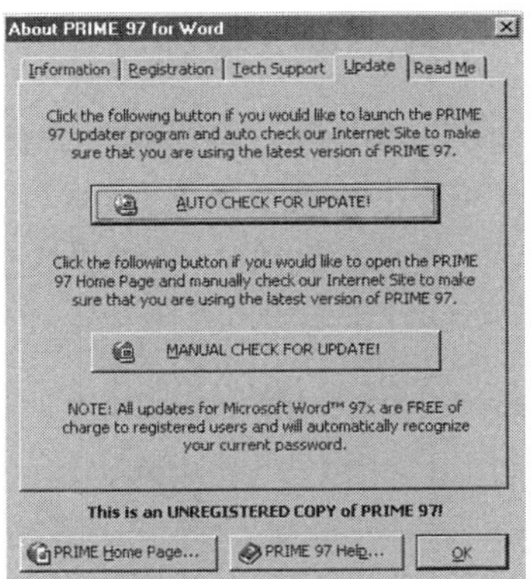

Figure 8.5
Update and Web site information is frequently available in the Help, About dialog box.

Manufacturers can be searched for alphabetically, by product category, or even by the FCC ID number that you'll find on most peripheral cards. WinDrivers.Com maintains a page on Windows 95, 98, and NT service packs and driver updates, with links to the appropriate Microsoft Web site pages. You can sign up to get an email notification when your virus software has a new update available (assuming that your virus package is one of the packages WinDrivers.Com is tracking).

Two similar sites for tracking down manufacturers are the WinFiles drivers database (`www.winfiles.com/drivers`) and PC Drivers HeadQuarters (`www.drivershq.com`).

Should all that fail to turn up the company information you need, try the Computer Company Information Center page maintained by Microsoft at `http://library.microsoft.com/compcos.html`. Microsoft's Computer Company Information Center page enables you to search for a specific manufacturer by name, or you can click the Get Big List link to see the entire 1,800-plus list of computer companies in the Microsoft database. As with most Web listings, you'll run into outdated links, and some of the companies listed might not be around any longer, but overall this is a great resource of last resort.

Bright Idea
While visiting the Web site of a vendor that built one of your system components, always check the main page to see whether the vendor offers an electronic newsletter or email notification when new or updated components are available. If it does offer such a service, sign up so that you'll be kept aware of the latest news.

Unofficially... The Microsoft Computer Company Information Center is not the only handy resource that Redmond maintains on the Web. Check out `http://library.microsoft.com/comp.htm` for general computer information, a listing of computer industry publications, standards-setting bodies, and other handy information.

Another Web resource lists various computer companies and shows their Web site addresses, their FTP sites (if they maintain one), and even their telephone numbers. It's part of a general computer FAQ that covers Internet newsgroups. Find this list at `http://www.faqs.org/faqs/pc-hardware-faq/part5/`.

Third-Party Upgrade Trackers

The process of upgrading computer software via the Internet is still relatively new and a bit clumsy. Expect to see refinements making the process easier as time goes on. Eventually, the process might become completely seamless and trouble free. Right now, though, it's a very disorganized process that puts most of the onus of finding out about available upgrades on you, the customer.

To ease this burden, several third-party products purport to keep track of updates that your system needs to keep it running smoothly. As with most things, pros and cons exist with this approach to keeping your system current. Using one of these third-party packages is certainly convenient in that you have only one service to check for your updates. But several problems occur with this solution that keep such products from being a panacea.

First, two of the most popular of these software packages—Oil Change (`http://www.cybermedia.com/products/oilchange/`) and TuneUp (`www.tuneup.com`)—require you to subscribe to their updating service (usually for one year) to get your ongoing updates. This means that in addition to the initial cost of the update tracker software, you'll be paying an annual fee if you keep using it. The third package we discuss is freeware, so the price is certainly right. But all three share the same caveat: it's not feasible for one update-monitor application to update every single item installed on your particular system. The sheer volume of component, peripheral, and software manufacturers, along with their product lists, is overwhelming.

Here's how these packages work. The update software inventories your installed drivers and applications and checks these against the service's own online database of drivers and software upgrades. When an item in your system inventory matches an entry in the online database, the software determines whether the online library contains a more current version, and you can then get the update.

We think that eventually more and more software vendors will incorporate automatic updating into their products. Most likely, "smart" software applications will themselves (or via some mechanism in the operating system) watch for idle time on your Internet connection to check the vendor's Web site to see whether an upgrade is available and then offer to get it and install it for you. Quite possibly, smart "update agents" or "update-bots" will just handle the whole process automatically in the background.

For now, however, these third-party upgrade-tracker packages can save you time and trouble updating some, if not all, of the software components installed on your system. The best bargain, however, is the Catch-UP freeware package.

Catch-UP takes a very different approach compared to the subscription services. First, Catch-UP is free. Second, instead of being a standalone software package, it's an add-on to your Web browser. Download the Catch-UP executable and run it, and it finds your browser (Navigator or Internet Explorer) and installs itself. One of Catch-UP's more endearing features is that you can review the software, drivers, and dynamic link libraries that Catch-UP keeps track of on its Web site before you decide to install it. After installing the product, you start the Catch-UP scan by clicking the Catch-UP Now button on the Catch-UP Web site. As with the other third-party packages we've discussed, a scan is run on your computer (you specify which of your hard drives are to be scanned). See Figure 8.6.

Catch-UP builds an inventory list of the software you have installed that it recognizes, and it compiles this into a Web page that is stored on your computer (*not* on the Catch-UP site). This inventory list shows each item next to a check box. Uncheck any items for which you do not want update information. Click Find Updates and get back a list of updates available for your installed software.

Figure 8.6 Catch-UP scans your installed software.

Here again, Catch-UP takes a different approach than either Oil Change or TuneUp. What Catch-UP gives you on the Results page is a listing of each upgrade it has determined your system can benefit from and a link that downloads the driver from the manufacturer's Web or FTP download site. Catch-UP finds what needs to be updated on your system and then provides you with the upgrade directly from the manufacturer's site. Simple and elegant. You can look over the suggested upgrades and download any you want. You do have to install the upgrade yourself, but that's usually just a matter of double-clicking an executable file and following onscreen instructions, as you'll see in the "Installing Upgrades On Your System" section of this chapter.

Catch-UP is free and can be found at `www.manageable.com`. Although it's not as automated as the two subscription services we previously covered, we think Catch-UP is the way to go and recommend it as a part of your update arsenal. The lack of automation helps you to remember that this is just one tool you can use to keep track of upgrades, and that you are ultimately responsible for finding the upgrades you need in order to keep your system running smoothly. And you can't beat the price.

Finding Browser Upgrades

Web browsers—we're talking about Netscape Navigator (Navigator) and Microsoft Internet Explorer (IE), which cover

99 percent of the browser market—will keep you busy with upgrades. As discussed earlier in this chapter, browsers are in a constant state of upgrade. You download the current beta and then the released version, only to find that a beta of the next version is available for download.

Our position is to avoid the beta versions and upgrade only when a new release version is available. Even with a released version, we suggest that you wait a couple of weeks after it becomes available before you download and install it; this is to see whether early adopters report any significant problems. This advice applies to whichever browser you favor—Navigator or Internet Explorer.

Staying current is easy because both Netscape and Microsoft have dedicated Web pages that can determine which version you are using and let you download the latest components.

Unofficially... Keeping up-to-date on information about Microsoft products can be a full-time job in itself. Microsoft is aware of this fact and tries to offer the latest information on bugs and upgrades in an extensive Knowledge Base. You can get a periodic email notification of the latest articles added to the Microsoft Knowledge Base by subscribing to the Windows and Internet Explorer Support News Watch newsletter. You can sign up for various Microsoft newsletters at `http://register.microsoft.com/regwiz/personalinfo.asp`.

Windows Operating System Upgrades

When it comes to Windows 98, Microsoft has taken the complexity of the Windows operating system into account and has built an update mechanism right into the operating system itself. From the Start menu on the task bar, you can select the Windows Update option. This option fires off your browser and takes you to the Windows Update site on the Web, where you can get the latest and greatest upgrades for Windows 98.

Tracking Down Flash BIOS Upgrades

As we've said several times already, you don't want to fuss around with your BIOS unless absolutely necessary. However, should the need arise, you'll want to deal with the manufacturer of your current BIOS. In the earlier "Finding Manufacturers" section, we discussed some resources for tracking down drivers published by various peripheral manufacturers. You can use the Web sites listed in that section to find BIOS manufacturers. In addition, we've had luck tracking down BIOS upgrades for various motherboards on the Motherboard Manufacturer List page (`www.ping.be/bios/`) maintained by Wim Bervoets. You'll find various helpful pages, including a FAQ that can answer almost any questions you have on updating a BIOS—from what to do if you don't know the name of your motherboard to how the flash process that updates a BIOS works. You will definitely want to check out this FAQ before upgrading your BIOS.

Installing Upgrades on Your System

The third-party upgrade services such as Oil Change and TuneUp automate this process to the largest extent possible, but it's not rocket science. You can use some tricks to make things easier. Remember, after you upgrade something via a download from the Web, you have an inventory problem.

Suppose you have a piece of software that you originally purchased at your local computer store or directly from the manufacturer. The box containing the CD-ROM and documentation is sitting on the shelf over your desk. If your application gets corrupted, you can always pull the CD off the shelf and reinstall it. Ah, but then you upgrade this program by installing a patch or bug fix downloaded from the manufacturer's Web site. Now the application in the box is no longer the full and complete copy of the software. If you had to reinstall it, you would have to install the application from scratch using the original CD-ROM and then remember to reapply the patch. You have to keep copies of the upgrades you download so that if you need to recover a piece of software, all the components are on hand. Most inconvenient, and prone to error.

In this section we'll talk about storing downloads and describe some typical upgrades.

Storing Downloaded Updates

Most upgrades involve downloading a file to your local hard disk from the Web and running through an installation procedure. Some of the third-party update trackers help automate this process, but even with the trackers, you'll find that you have to manually install something now and then. Often, upgrades are kind and considerate. After downloading such an upgrade, you double-click the downloaded file, it unpacks itself, and it runs an installation program. The installer tells you what it is updating and what it proposes to do, showing you at each step of the way what it's about to do before doing it. You follow the onscreen instructions and you're done. Nothing to it.

Other upgrades are less friendly. Some you download as self-extracting zip files. Double-clicking the .exe causes it to unzip a plethora of cryptically named files in whatever folder the file was in. It's left up to you to ferret out the executable file that actually starts the install/upgrade process.

Before you start downloading updates, you need to figure out how you are going to store and track these files, which fall roughly into two groups. The first group is the upgrade in which you download a new version of the entire application—for example, when you download a new browser version. The second group is the upgrade that patches an existing file or application, or one that updates a handful of DLLs—for example, patching Microsoft Excel for a recalculation bug or updating the dial-up networking component of Windows.

Although you could simply download, install, and forget about it, we don't recommend that approach. If you download an entirely new version of an application, you can forgo storing the downloaded application because you can always download it again, should you need to reinstall it. But if you want to keep a copy around, storage becomes a problem because many of these files are several megabytes in size. For most users, the answer is to keep a copy of the compressed, uninstalled version of the downloaded file on a high-capacity removable drive (such as the popular Zip or Jaz drives).

On our machines, we initially store any downloads (whether they are updates or new applications downloaded from the Web) on the target system's hard disk. We create a folder structure like this:

d:\Downloads\Applications\

d:\Downloads\Drivers\

d:\Downloads\Utilities\

d:\Downloads\Temp\

Unofficially...
It's always a good idea to carefully read any Readme.txt files (or any file with a filename of readme) for instructions or cautions regarding the upgrade you are about to install. You might also want to save a downloaded file's associated-instructions Web page to your disk as an HTML file; we suggest that you keep it in the same folder to which you're downloading the file.

Bright Idea
Some patches might fit on a floppy disk, which makes it simple to copy the update files onto a disk and toss that disk into the original application box. You can also do this with a Zip disk (if you have disks to spare). Or you can keep a disk library of all your upgrade files, and in each application box, put a note with the upgrade information (the date and version of the update) and a reference to which disk in the library the upgrade is stored on.

Here, the *d:* drive is a data drive, purposely kept separate from our application/OS drive (C:). Create a subfolder in the appropriate category (applications, drivers, or utilities) and download the file to that folder. For example:

```
D:\Downloads\Applications\Netscape405_Pro\cp32e405.exe
```

If we're going to store the file on removable media, we copy the file to the appropriate drive and store the media (usually a Zip disk) in a safe place. Then we execute the update file and follow the installation instructions.

If we're going to store the download on our hard disk, we copy it to the `\Download\Temp` folder to perform the actual installation. Some patches require that you place the download file into the same folder as the application you are patching before running the update, but for most updates, you just need a folder to hold the files while you start the installation process. After a successful installation, the `\Temp` file is cleared of all residual files, and we still have the original file we downloaded in case a reinstall is required.

Bright Idea
Whenever you install *anything* on your system, shut down all unnecessary applications. Usually this means you have only Windows Explorer running. Should anything go wrong with the installation, this precaution avoids lost data or possibly corrupted applications. At the end of most driver updates, you'll have to reboot Windows anyway for the new driver to be loaded, so the less you have running at the outset of the installation process, the fewer worries you have when it's time to restart Windows.

Updating Peripheral Drivers

Drivers sometimes come with an installation program that is triggered when you double-click the downloaded file. But sometimes running the downloaded file simply unzips a group of files you have to install manually (this is why you should run an update file only from an otherwise empty folder). If you are left with a dozen or so unzipped files, you'll know that they all relate to the same device, and you won't have them mixed up with other files.

Manually installing updated drivers in this situation is simple.

1. Open the Device Manager.
2. In the device list, find the peripheral you are updating and select it.
3. Click Properties, and then in the Properties dialog box for this device, click the Drivers tab and then the Update Drivers button. This selection starts the Update Device Driver Wizard.

4. Click the Next button and you'll see the panel displayed, as shown in Figure 8.7.

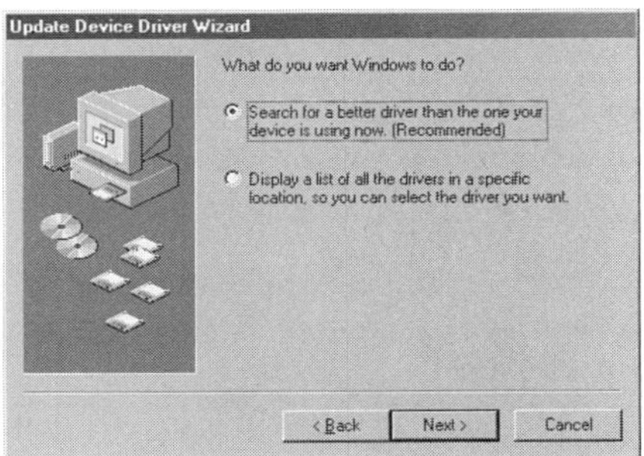

Figure 8.7
Choosing where to search for updated drivers.

5. In this panel you can choose either to have the wizard search for a better driver (the recommended choice according to Microsoft) or to have it display a list of all the drivers in a specific location.

The first option is useful because you can specify the resource to be searched: the A: drive, the CD-ROM drive, the Windows Update Web site, or a specific drive/folder location. You can search any or all of those locations in one operation by checking the appropriate boxes.

However, because we downloaded and unzipped the new driver files and know where they are stored, we usually go with the second option button, which lists all the drivers in a specific location. This panel displays a list of the compatible drivers that Windows is aware of and has a button marked Have Disk. Clicking Have Disk displays the Install from Disk dialog box, into which you enter the path to the unzipped drivers. See Figure 8.8.

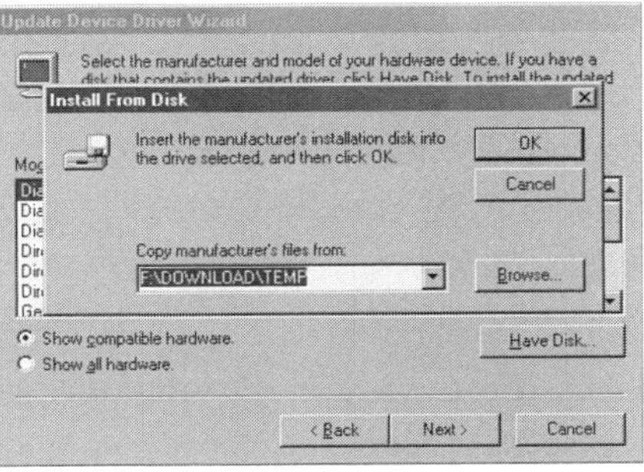

Figure 8.8
Specifying the folder location of the new drivers.

After the new driver is selected, follow the instructions in the wizard, and the new driver is installed.

Let us stress that the most important thing you can do is read any documentation that accompanies the downloaded update. If an automated installer exists, follow the directions carefully. If a readme file is present, make sure that you understand what has to be done, and then follow any instructions contained therein.

Updating Your Browser

Browser updates are fairly straightforward. Internet Explorer is a bit scarier than Navigator because it is integrated to such a degree with Windows itself. If something goes badly wrong, you could wind up with Windows malfunctioning. Navigator, a standalone application, is less likely to take the operating system with it if things go wrong.

Both browsers make it easy to find and download the latest version, as well as add-on components.

Unofficially... Although we like SmartUpdate and think that this technology will only improve, a case can be made for bypassing all the automated bells and whistles (which, although automating the process, keeps you from seeing exactly what is going on), downloading the version of Navigator you want, and installing it yourself. You can download Navigator in its various flavors directly from the Netscape Web site at `http://home.netscape.com/download/index.html`.

Netscape's SmartUpdate * To upgrade your version of Navigator to the latest version or to add various Netscape components and add-ons to Navigator, follow these steps:

1. Start Navigator.
2. Select the Help menu.
3. Click the Software Updates option.
4. Click the Click Here to Begin button on the resulting Web page.

This action takes you to the SmartUpdate page of Netscape's new Netcenter Web site. This page is smart enough to recognize the version of Navigator you have currently installed. It lists the available updates, the various Netscape components (marking which are already installed), and some third-party add-ons from companies that have a relationship with Netscape.

Each download displays the file size and estimated time to download. Check the boxes for the upgrades you want, and click the Start Download and Installation button on the Web page. You have to be a Netscape Netcenter member to actually start the download, but this is simply a matter of filling out a form (although you are required to enter a unique username and password for your membership).

Internet Explorer Download * The people at Microsoft experimented with a dedicated Internet Explorer Update page for a while, but when they came up with the Windows Update system, they folded all the Internet Explorer updates into the newer page. In Internet Explorer, you click Help, About, and then click Product Updates, which connects you to the Windows Update Web site. The section "Updating Windows Itself" discusses how this site works.

Updating Windows Itself

Keeping Windows 98 running smoothly has been made easier, thanks to the new Windows Update feature. This is Microsoft's first step toward automating the updating of drivers and system software. Microsoft has taken a lot of flak over how difficult and expensive it is to run Windows systems, so the company is making a big effort to convince everyone that Windows Update, the "online extension of Windows 98," as the marketeers call it, is going to make your update woes fade away. In the long run this might be how it works out, but expect a few bumps along the way until Microsoft gets the kinks worked out.

Bright Idea
Before you install any piece of software (whether an application, a driver, or an upgrade of any kind), it's a very good idea to save all your work and close any unnecessary applications that are running. If anything goes wrong and you have to reboot your system, you won't lose any work. You also want to make sure that you have adequate free disk space when performing an update. You should also pause Microsoft Task Scheduler to avoid any conflicts with pending tasks.

Like it or loath it, Windows Update is the future of software upgrades.

1. To use Windows Update, select Start, Windows Update. This action causes your browser to start (if it's not already running) and to bring up the Welcome to Windows Update page at `http://windowsupdate.microsoft.com/default.htm`. Alternatively, you can surf to this URL from within your browser. Click the Product Updates link to start the process.
2. If you have never utilized the Windows Update before, you'll see the Security Warning dialog box shown in Figure 8.9.

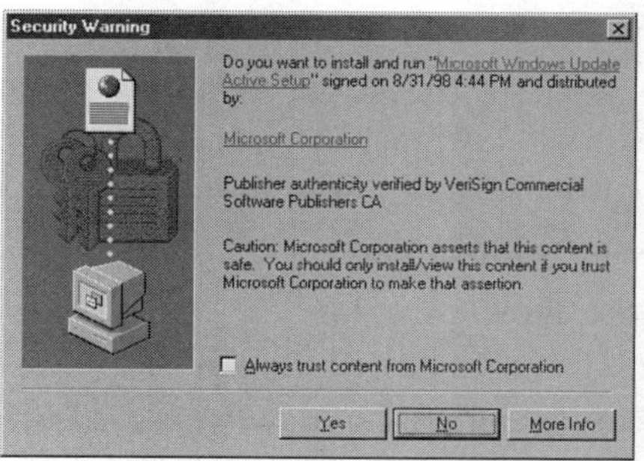

Figure 8.9 Installing the Microsoft Windows Update Active Setup.

3. Microsoft wants to install a program, the Microsoft Windows Update Active Setup, that can check to see what you have installed on your system so that it will know what can be updated. Select Yes and the program is installed without further action on your part.
4. Next, you're told that your system is ready to be checked, and you are assured that no information about your system will be sent to Microsoft. (If your system already has the Update Active Setup installed, the Windows Update page appears and you click Product Updates.)
5. Click Yes and Windows Update analyzes your system to see what you already have installed. You'll then be able to pick from an assortment of downloads arranged in categories such as Critical Updates, Picks of the Month, Recommended Updates, Additional Windows Features, and Fun and Games. Only downloads you do *not* already have installed on your system appear in this list.

You need not acquiesce to the automatic system checking performed by the Microsoft Windows Update Active Setup. You can either decline to install this utility or answer No when the message box appears asking whether your system can be checked to see what is currently installed. When you get the list of available downloads, however, *all* downloads appear in the list, even things you might have previously installed. It's up to you to keep track of what you need versus what you have, unless you let Windows Update analyze your system.

You'll want the Critical Updates (especially those that deal with security issues), and you should carefully look over the Recommended Updates. Check the box next to each item you want updated on your system. As you pick items to be downloaded, the total download time is estimated and shown at the top of the page next to the Download button.

Click the Download button and you get another page that lists three steps:

Step 1 shows all your chosen selections. This gives you a last chance to change your mind about any of your selected items.

Step 2 lets you view the installation instructions for the items you've selected by clicking the View Instructions button. For most of the updates, installation is performed automatically, but you should check the instructions to see whether you have to perform any manual steps as part of the install.

Step 3 is where you click the Start Download button to begin the process in earnest. A dialog box appears, showing the progress of the download as well as the installations of each update (see Figure 8.10). After the download/setup process gets underway, Windows automatically pauses Task Scheduler to avoid any conflicts with pending tasks.

Unofficially...
We recommend that you download only those things you really need because, like your garage, your computer can rapidly accumulate an awful lot of stuff that does not serve any useful purpose except to take up space and add to the general clutter. But if something such as one of the desktop themes really tickles your fancy, go for it.

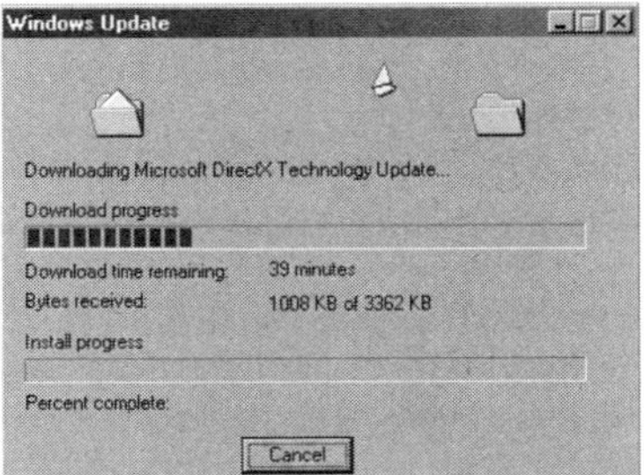

Figure 8.10
The download and installation progress is tracked automatically.

Because some updates involve very large files, you won't want to sit and stare at the screen while your chosen updates are copied to your hard disk and installed. But given the various problems you might experience in downloading large files across the Internet, you need to know how the update went, especially if you do multiple updates at one time. Fortunately, Windows Update displays a summary message box at the end of the process, as shown in Figure 8.11, which shows the final status of each update.

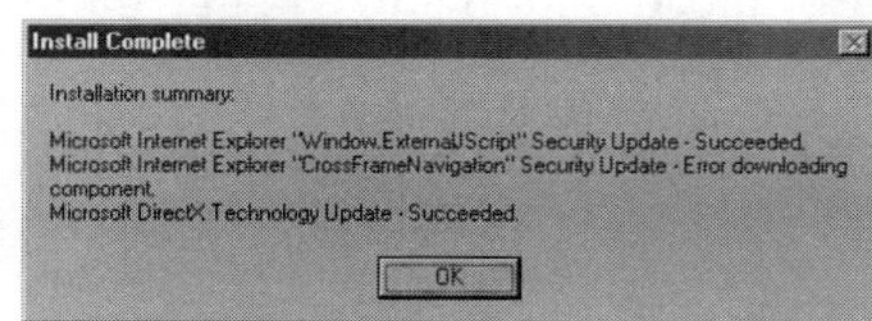

Figure 8.11
On completion, you get a summary of each item installed.

Notice in Figure 8.11 that the second item—the CrossFrameNavigation Security Update—experienced an error while downloading. When you encounter a problem like this, restart the Windows Update process and reselect the errant component. On the second attempt, this item downloaded and installed without a problem.

Depending on the item installed, you might have to restart Windows for the changes to take effect. If this is the case, you'll see a message box offering to restart Windows for you.

Watch Out!
If things go awry when you are performing a BIOS upgrade, your system can wind up unusable. Clearly, you don't want to start a BIOS upgrade late Friday night when you know you'll need your computer running all weekend so that you can have that important report on your boss's desk on Monday at 8:00 a.m.

Updating the System BIOS

A system BIOS update is not to be undertaken lightly. You need to carefully prepare and plan before you start the update. Should something catastrophic happen, such as a loss of power to your system at a critical moment, your computer becomes an expensive paperweight until you can get it into the repair shop. At a minimum, you need to do the following things:

- Have a current backup of your system.
- Have an emergency plan in case your computer becomes unusable.

Again, it's vital that you follow the instructions that accompany the BIOS upgrade. We recently upgraded the BIOS on a Pentium system with an AMI BIOS, and to give you an idea of what's involved, we'll discuss the steps we took to perform the upgrade. Note that these specific instructions are applicable only to the particular BIOS we were upgrading and might not apply to your specific situation. We took the following steps:

1. Backed up the system's 4GB primary hard drive to the duplicate 4GB backup hard drive installed on the system.
2. Made the following emergency plan in case something went wrong: Typical for systems that allow a BIOS to be updated via software, the manufacturer usually provides a jumper on the motherboard that, when set per instructions, resets the BIOS to the original factory defaults. In case the system becomes unusable, we located this jumper and checked the motherboard manual for the settings to restore the BIOS to the factory settings. If this fails to get the system operational, the backup hard drive can be pulled from the chassis and popped into one of our other computers until we can get the dysfunctional system back up and running.
3. Looked outside to see whether we were in the middle of a thunderstorm. Seriously, if you expect any possibility of a power outage, don't do a BIOS upgrade.
4. Checked the system's NEAT box and pulled out the pamphlet that was our only motherboard documentation. Found that we had an Intel Advanced/ML motherboard. Went to `www.ping.be/bios/` (discussed earlier as one of your best bets in finding BIOS update sites), drilled down on Intel, and then found the link for the Advanced/ML. This link went straight to the Intel page, where we reviewed the instructions and then downloaded the latest BIOS for this motherboard.
5. Ran the self-extracting file and printed the readme file. In this case, however, the readme file was named Bioinstr.txt. It's a good idea to review all .txt files for information after extracting the files.
6. Rebooted the system and went into the CMOS settings utility (discussed at length in Chapter 5). Manually recorded all CMOS settings from all screens. Any of these current

settings that are different from the factory defaults will have to be reset after the BIOS upgrade.

7. Followed the instructions and created an MS-DOS boot disk (not a Windows start disk). All this boot disk needed, according to the instructions, was to have Sys.com installed on it and be capable of booting the computer. Extracted the Bios.exe file to the floppy disk. This put about 18 files on the floppy, including an Autoexec.bat.
8. With the new boot floppy in the A: drive, rebooted the system. When prompted, pressed Enter to go to the Main menu. Selected Update Flash Memory From a File and then Update System BIOS. When prompted to enter the path and name of the file, highlighted the filename and pressed Enter. Next came a warning that the BIOS was about to be changed (your last chance to change your mind). Pressing Enter updated the system BIOS.
9. Rebooted the system after removing the upgrade floppy from the A: drive.
10. Entered the CMOS and pressed the function key that restored all factory settings. At this point, we compared all the prior CMOS settings to the new factory defaults and made changes where necessary, to restore any settings to their pre-update values.
11. Shut down the system, powered it off, and then restarted the system.

Bright Idea
On reboot we verified that the BIOS version number reflected the newer BIOS. All this should be recorded in the journal or notebook that's part of your system's NEAT box.

Our upgrade came off without a hitch, but as you can see, this process is not something you want to endure without a compelling reason. Again, we stress the importance of being sure that you have the right BIOS upgrade for your system and that you carefully follow the instructions that accompany the upgrade.

Chapter Ending

- Know the version number of whatever component you are updating.
- Common hardware-driver upgrades include the video adapter, sound cards, DirectX drivers, mouse drivers, modems, and printers.
- The most important software upgrades on your PC are the operating system itself, security fixes for applications, Web browser updates, and the system BIOS.
- Several Web resources can help you track down manufacturers to get the latest upgrades. Third-party software is also available to help you stay up-to-date with upgrades for your specific system components.
- Store downloaded update files at your location (using whatever inventory method you favor) in case you ever have to reapply the update.
- Drivers can be updated through the Device Manager's Update Device Driver Wizard; most software upgrades include their own installation programs.
- Windows Update makes it easy to upgrade Windows 98 components.

PART III

Avoiding Problems

Chapter 9

Preparing for Disaster

SOME OF YOU MAY WONDER why we don't discuss backing up data in this chapter. This book is organized to guide you step-by-step through the acquisition and customization of a new PC. At this point in the book, the assumption is that your new PC has been subjected to only those actions described so far in this book. Therefore, no proprietary data is on it yet. So literally, nothing is there to back up. Although it's technically correct to say that it is possible to back up the system in its entirety right now (more on this in a moment), no production data is stored on it at this time. What your PC does have on it are an operating system and a set of peripherals that have been tested and tweaked to your liking.

Most of those settings reside in your Registry. If the system were to crash during your work based on this chapter, the PC would most likely be flawed in some fundamental way. This would be an early burn-in failure and the PC would need considerable reworking. That reworking would probably render unusable any of the operating system, peripheral, or application changes you've made to date. This means that restoring them from a backup would probably be a disaster on top of a disaster because the backup version of the Registry would be out of whack with the misbehaving system's current Registry. Simply put, you'd be asking for trouble if you used a restore operation as a panacea for a system problem at this point in your new PC's life.

But some of you may be coming to this chapter in a different sequence. Also, it's possible that some of you went ahead and—even as you read along with us chapter by chapter—added some proprietary data. To accommodate all possible PC states at this point, consider the following important note:

If you prefer to make a backup of your system now, refer to Chapter 11, "Backing Up."

Just assembling and configuring your PC isn't enough to get your PC ready. You should perform another set of tasks as well, although it's fair to say that many folks (and yes, that includes us, too) don't spend enough time preparing for problems with their PC. This chapter, along with Chapter 10, "Good Habits for a Trouble-Free System," Chapter 11, "Backing Up," and Chapter 12, "Cleaning Up" are all part of a very important section of the book. The section is titled "Avoiding Problems," and that's exactly what we're doing. This section helps you lay a foundation of preparedness (that's what this chapter is all about), gets you going with a set of routines that will quickly and easily become good habits, and then teaches you the mechanics of backing up and cleaning up your system.

Creating Rescue Disks

One of the ancient and honorable rescue programs is Norton Utilities' Rescue Disk, which, in version 3.0, has added the capability to boot up into Windows 95 or 98 and perform the rescue functions in that environment. You need to have an Iomega Zip or Jaz drive for this—Norton Rescue uses a floppy to start your PC, and then runs the Windows system files off the Iomega drive. After you are up, the program launches a Wizard interface that steps you through various system fixes, including a check for viruses and a check of your CMOS information, boot records, and partition tables; it also runs various other Norton Utilities components, such as Disk Doctor, as needed. Although cool in its own way, Zip Rescue doesn't add new capabilities so much as it simply allows you to make use of the Windows interface. The traditional MS-DOS version of Rescue (now called "Basic Rescue") is still available, and it allows you to boot to DOS to perform the recovery.

The central premise behind Norton Rescue is that your system has stopped working because of a correctable hard-disk problem, generally an issue with the boot record or partitions, which can be corrupted by defective software or by viruses. Rescue tries to fix the problem by restoring previously working settings, so if you don't update your rescue disks regularly, they won't do you much good. Of course, if the hard disk itself has failed mechanically or electronically, you are pretty much out of luck with this or any other rescue software.

Windows 98, relative to its predecessor, has considerably improved the type of automated, behind-the-scenes operations that occur to keep your system running smoothly. One of the most important of these operations is the application called Registry Checker. Registry Checker has the following features:

- It runs automatically every time you start your PC.
- It can be used to recover a specific Registry backup.

In a nutshell, when your system starts, Registry Checker scans the current Registry for any problems, and if none exist, it makes a backup for the current day (it keeps the most recent five "known good" Registries in compressed CAB files on your hard disk in the hidden system folder `C:\Windows\Sysbckup`, in addition to copies of Win.ini and System.ini, as shown in Figure 9.1), and optimizes the current Registry by eliminating superfluous space.

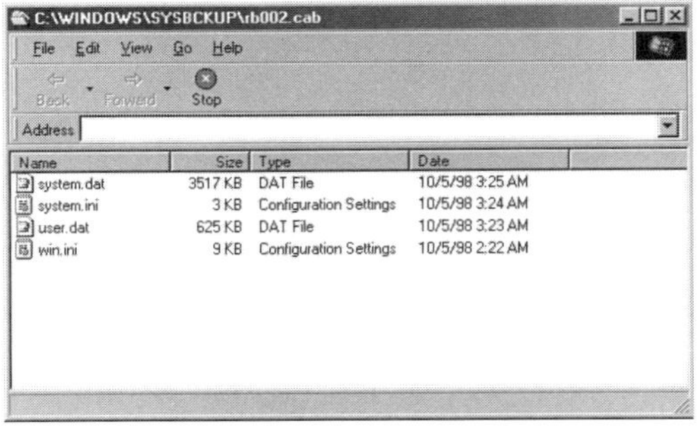

Figure 9.1
A Registry Checker cabinet file's contents revealed.

Unofficially... You can view the contents of CAB files by using the Windows 95 PowerToy called Cabinet File Viewer. However, at the time of this writing, the only PowerToy that has been released for Windows 98 is TweakUI. The Windows 95 PowerToy utilities are available at `www.microsoft.com`; then search for powertoy.

Registry Checker doesn't produce "rescue disks" per se; rather, it stores its backup CAB files on your hard disk. It's very likely that each compressed CAB backup file is close to or greater than the capacity of a 1.44MB disk, and these files don't compress when zipped because they're already highly compressed. However, these five backups of your Registry are part of your system's rescue infrastructure, so we mention them and their associated tool Registry Checker here.

To manually restore your Registry, follow these steps:

1. Select Start, Shut Down, Restart in MS-DOS Mode, and click OK.
2. From the MS-DOS command prompt, type `scanreg/restore`.
3. You'll see a list of the last five backups (named Rb*nnn*.cab, where *nnn* starts at 000), along with their date/time stamps. The screen also indicates either Started or Not Started for each backup file, which means that the particular copy of the Registry has successfully started your system or it hasn't, respectively. Pick the backup file you want to restore. Usually this is the latest known-good backup, but you may, under certain circumstances, want to go back one or more levels.
4. Choose Restore. If the restore is successful, Registry Checker tells you so. Likewise, if a problem occurred in restoring the CAB file, an error message appears. In this case, try restoring the next-oldest CAB.

Bright Idea See the Windows 98 Resource Kit for additional documentation on using Registry Checker. Look up the topic "Administrating with the Registry," which describes how to manage the Registry and, in turn, how to use the Registry to manage your system.

Creating and Using Windows Startup Disks

Creating a Windows startup disk has always appeared to be a foolproof process, at least on the surface. As you might already know, Microsoft forgot one very important thing under Windows 95: automatically loading real-mode drivers and extension software to allow you to access your CD-ROM drive from a DOS prompt. Under Windows 95, you had to perform a tortuous process and manually update the startup disk to get it to see your CD-ROM drive. Fortunately, Windows 98 corrects this omission for 99 percent of Windows 98 users (more on the one percent in a moment). A Windows 98 startup disk automatically includes real-mode support for most IDE and SCSI CD-ROM drives. What's more, when you boot off your Windows 98 startup disk, a new multistart menu exists, so now you can choose to boot with or without access to your CD-ROM drive.

To create a startup disk, follow these steps:

1. Insert an empty, formatted 1.44MB disk into your floppy drive.
2. Choose Start, Control Panel, Add/Remove Programs, Startup Disk, and Create Disk.
3. When the disk has been created, remove it from the drive, flip its tab to write-protect mode, and clearly label it with "Windows 98 startup disk" and today's date.

To test the startup disk, follow these steps:

1. Put the startup disk into the floppy drive and reboot your system, which will now boot from the floppy drive. (You can remove the startup disk and press Ctrl+Alt+Delete when you want to restart your system normally.)
2. You'll see three options: one to start your PC with CD-ROM support, one to start it without CD-ROM support, and one to view the Help file. Pick the first option. When you get to a DOS prompt, you'll notice that your CD-ROM drive letter is one higher than usual (this is because when the startup disk boots, it automatically creates a 2MB RAM drive).
3. Switch to each drive letter, type the `DIR` command, and then press Enter to verify that each drive is properly recognized.
4. When your test is complete, remove the disk and finish labeling it by adding "Tested okay" near where you wrote today's date. Then file it in your NEAT box and hope that you never have to use it.

All the files and utilities that you need to start your system to an operational DOS prompt in an emergency—and that assist you with problems in setting up or starting Windows—are supplied on your startup disk. To see what these files are, browse your startup disk with Windows Explorer. (Note that many key files are hidden away inside the compressed Edb.cab file, a new feature of Windows 98's startup disk.) A typical startup disk will have about 250KB free. It's not ordinarily necessary to add any files or make any changes to this startup disk.

Unofficially...
The "Ebd" in the esoteric filename "Ebd.cab" stands for "Emergency Boot Disk."

If your CD-ROM drive (or tape drive or removable media drive) isn't supported by the generic drivers, you can update your startup disk as follows:

1. Refer to the discussion in Chapter 8, "Staying Ahead of the Game," on how to locate the driver for a particular device.
2. Copy the driver file to your startup disk.
3. Use Notepad to edit the startup disk's Config.sys file. In the last section labeled [COMMON], add the necessary statement to load the driver. For some devices, you might also have to modify the startup disk's Autoexec.bat file. For more information about editing Config.sys and other boot files, see the Win98 Resource Kit section "System Startup Files" or search on `config.sys`.

Watch Out!
You might read tips in magazines, on the Web, or elsewhere about how to create a leaner Windows 98 startup disk. Our advice: don't do it! A simple problem occurs with trimming down your startup disk. It takes more time to jump through the technique's convoluted hoops than you'd ever save by having a marginally faster bootup. Besides, you're going to need to use that disk only once in a blue moon—hopefully never. Stick with the plain vanilla startup disk and you'll be just fine.

Crash Prevention

Applications crash for various reasons, including fundamental programming errors within the applications themselves or bugs in the operating system that aren't manifested until certain conditions are met (for example, low system resources). Whatever the root cause, the results of these crashes range from easily recoverable, in which you are able to save your work before the application shuts down completely, to those that completely hang up your system so that your only option is to punch the Big Red Switch and power down the system. In the latter case, you lose all unsaved files and are inconvenienced by the hassle of having to restart your system and all the applications you were using at the time of the crash. Into this vacuum comes a class of programs known as "crash guards."

Aptly named, Norton CrashGuard is a top-notch crash-prevention application from the market leader for system utilities. CrashGuard goes even further: it can remove a frozen application from your desktop display (a feature it calls Anti-Freeze), it keeps a detailed log of all crashes it has intercepted, and it allows you to test how it responds to many kinds of crash scenarios by offering its own (safe) crash-inducing code.

As shown in Figure 9.2, you can direct CrashGuard to intercept 16-bit application crashes, 32-bit application crashes, or both. You can turn the Anti-Freeze feature on or off. From the Properties dialog box you can also test CrashGuard's protection capabilities or view historical statistics (click the Advanced button).

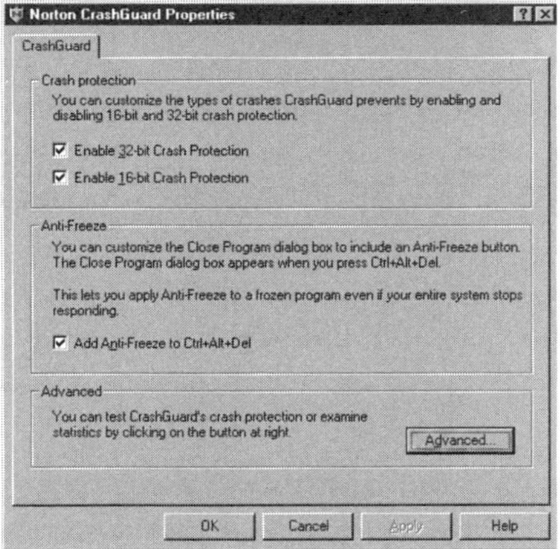

Figure 9.2
Norton CrashGuard's Properties dialog box is where you set how you want the application to prevent and intercept crashes.

If you find that your system is prone to application crashes, we highly recommend Norton CrashGuard as a way to isolate any patterns and possibly help you detect the root cause of the problem. You can download a free trialware version of CrashGuard (it's a large 12.9MB download) at `http://shop.symantec.com/trialware/`.

DLL Show from Gregory Braun is another gem we recommend. Although it has some features primarily appreciated by hard-core Windows C/C++ programmers, you can still learn something from studying its informative, well-designed display

Bright Idea
DLL Show is shareware, and you can register for $20; the 135KB download is available at `http://www.execpc.com/~sbd/index.html`. Note that Gregory has developed literally dozens of other cool shareware Windows 95/98/NT utilities, so check out this site.

of running processes and file dependencies. More importantly, what you'll most likely benefit from is its listing of documented Windows Error Codes (the utility supplies them for Win95/98/NT). In some cases, a program you have might generate an error-code warning but without an explanation of what the error means. Wonder no more!

Virus Scanning and Protection

This section focuses on scanning for and protecting your system from viruses, but not disinfecting your system. That comes later, in Chapter 19, "Recovering from a PC Disaster." However, an important disk (or set of disks) to have on hand is a virus-recovery disk. Having excellent scanning and protection tools installed is great, but in the unlikely and unfortunate event that your system is attacked by a virus, you'll be left holding the bag if you don't have a virus-recovery disk handy.

NOTE: Throughout this chapter, we'll use McAfee VirusScan and its set of antivirus tools as an example package. Most other antivirus packages have similar features, procedures, and steps for those procedures. The only thing that might be different from product to product are the actual names of the features and procedures. McAfee has free, fully functional evaluation versions of its antivirus tools available. Go to `www.mcafee.com` for more information and download details.

The steps for creating an antivirus emergency disk are similar to the steps you've learned for creating rescue or startup disks. However, keep in mind that the specific steps may vary slightly among different vendors' antivirus tools.

As you complete this process for McAfee VirusScan, it verifies that the disk is free of viruses; it keeps you posted with a progress meter as it copies key files; and when it's finished, it provides a helpful, informative dialog box that reminds you to write-protect the disk, and then explains how to reboot your PC and test the disk. See Figure 9.3.

To test the emergency disk, leave it in the A: drive and turn off your PC's power (if you don't, McAfee's utility will tell you to turn off the power and will refuse to run until you do so). Then restart your PC and follow the onscreen instructions.

WARNING: McAfee's online help is *incorrect*; it advises you to test the disk by rebooting from it, then switching to C: at the prompt. This is not possible—*after the disk's scanning functions start, no way exists to stop it short of powering off your PC.* So if you have a large C: drive or several drives, be prepared for a very, very long wait during the scan, or be willing to abruptly kill the power on your PC (never a good idea, in our opinion, while the drive is busy).

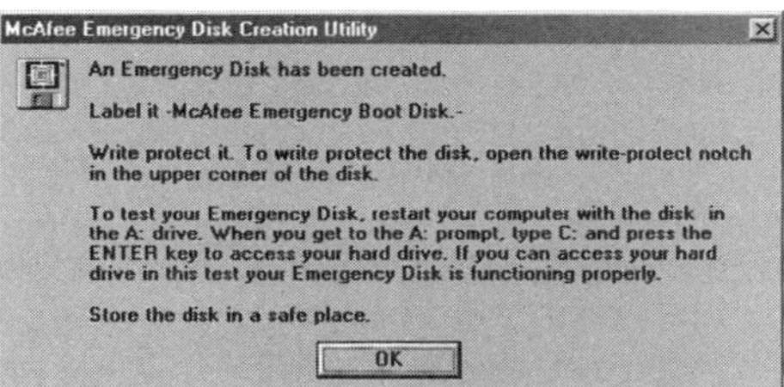

Figure 9.3 McAfee Emergency Disk Creation Utility's final dialog box offers good advice.

Virus Overview

A virus is a program that infects files, typically without your knowledge. Originally, viruses propagated using program files such as .com or .exe files, but within the past several years "macro viruses" have been developed that propagate via such sources as Microsoft Word documents or Excel workbooks. Some antivirus experts estimate that 75 percent of all viruses today are macro viruses. Although viruses often do carry out destructive or annoying actions, not all do. To get a sense of the scale of the problem, check the more than 2,300 virus descriptions at the AVP Virus Encyclopedia (`www.avp.ch/avpve/`); the list will make your head spin.

Your PC can get infected from many kinds of sources: a document or file from a coworker, the Web, a shrink-wrapped product, or any other source that gives a program a chance to be executed on your computer. You should suspect each and every document that arrives on your PC from an outside source, no matter its lineage. Your single best solution to the problem of viruses—whether they are boot viruses, file viruses, macro viruses, or other malware—is to consistently use (and update) an antivirus program.

Performing a Full System Scan

You've already created and tested an emergency disk, so the absolute first priority has been taken care of. Now you need to do a full-system virus scan, even if this is a brand-new PC fresh from the factory. Most antivirus tools have an option to scan portions of your system while they're installing themselves. But you need to go one step further and do a *full* system scan. Here's how:

1. Eliminate operations that could interfere with or slow down the scan.

   Close all running applications, disable your screen saver, and disable (pause) Microsoft Task Scheduler.

2. Scan only the nonremovable drives physically attached to your PC.

   Start McAfee VirusScan and then select Tools, Advanced. Click the Add button, and in the Select Item to Scan area, select the All Fixed Disks option. This action sets up a scan of all hard drives attached to this computer and excludes any removable media or mapped network drives.

3. Scan all files, including compressed files such as zip files, not just program files. In the Detection tab's What to Scan section, select the All Files option button and check the Compressed Files check box. By scanning all files, you might have a slightly longer scan, but you'll be sure not to miss any potential virus hosts. If you don't scan all files, and instead scan just those files your tool thinks have the right "program file extensions" settings, then you'll have to spend time meticulously verifying that all the file extensions are listed. (In McAfee VirusScan, this is controlled from the What and Where tab; select the Program Files Only option and then click the Extensions button.)

4. Configure the tool to prompt you for what action to take upon detecting a virus, rather than have it proceed automatically. Later, you might want to scan in automatic clean/disinfect mode, but not now.

In the Action tab's When a Virus Is Found section, select Prompt User for Action. Check all check boxes in the Possible Actions section so that you'll have the maximum number of options when prompted that a virus has been detected.

5. Configure the tool to write its results to a log file.

   In VirusScan, click the Report tab and check the Log to File check box to automatically write to the log file VSCLog.txt in its primary program folder (typically, `C:\Program Files\Network Associates\McAfee VirusScan`). This way, when the scan is finished, you'll be able to study a record of what happened. Also check *all* the check boxes in the What to Log section so that the log will actually log every conceivable activity.

6. Start the scan.

   Click the Scan Now button, sit back, and brew a new pot of coffee. Depending on the size of your drives, this process could take a while.

7. When the scan is finished, study the log file.

   Remember that log file we mentioned earlier? Open it and study it carefully. If any viruses were detected during the scan, your antivirus tool should have provided an interface for eliminating the virus from your system.

Routine Scanning

You can scan your PC for viruses in three ways, none of them mutually exclusive:

On-demand scanning—Scanning can be done "on demand," meaning whenever you start the tool and click Scan. This type of scanning can be as simple as clicking a button to scan your entire system, creating a complex set of drives to scan, or right-clicking a specific file—for example, a Microsoft Word document—in Windows Explorer and selecting Scan for Viruses from the pop-up menu (see Figure 9.4). McAfee's tool for scanning on-demand is

VirusScan. Earlier we walked you through the steps using McAfee VirusScan for configuring a full-system scan, including all local hard drives (not removable media drives and not mapped network drives). You can repeat those steps at any time, fine-tuning the scan parameters to suit your needs, and then save those parameters to a VirusScan settings file.

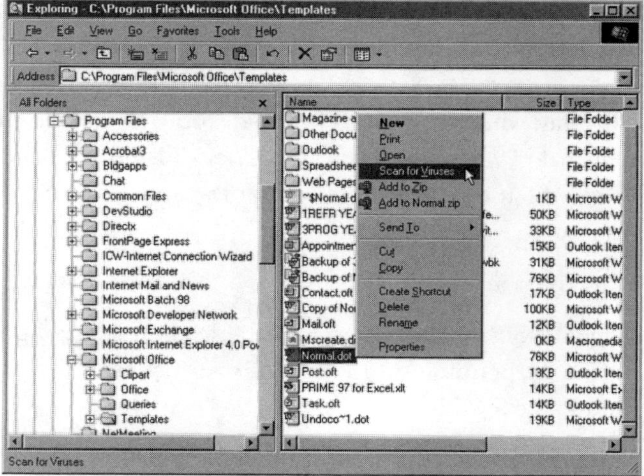

Figure 9.4 Scan a file for viruses from inside Windows Explorer with a simple right-click.

On-access scanning—Scanning can occur "on access," meaning in the background in response to certain file- and system-related events—for example, when files are created, run, copied, renamed, or when your PC starts and shuts down. Think of this as a behind-the-scenes scan operation. On-access scanning is managed in McAfee by VShield, which runs constantly in the background. See Figure 9.5 for the types of activities that can trigger a scan in the background, along with options for when to scan, what to scan, and what actions to take if an infection is identified.

On-schedule scanning—Scanning can be done "on schedule" by using either your antivirus tool's schedule feature or Microsoft's Task Scheduler. This is accomplished in McAfee VirusScan via the VirusScan Console (see Figure 9.6), which is similar to Microsoft's Task Scheduler. You could also use Microsoft's Task Scheduler.

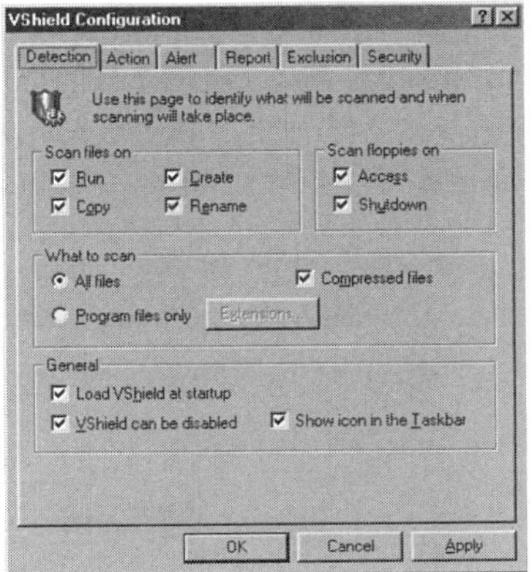

Figure 9.5
McAfee VShield controls on-access scanning.

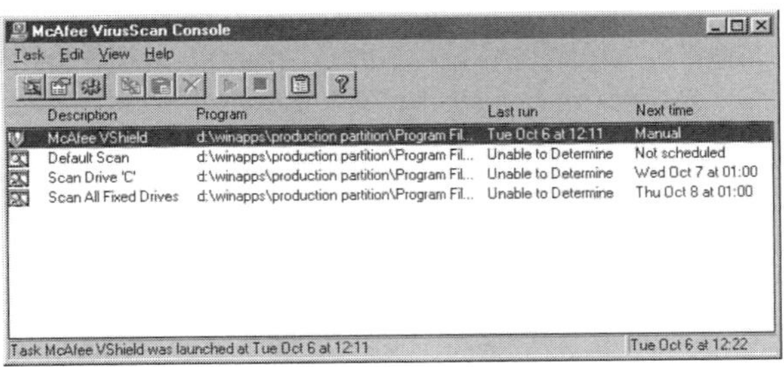

Figure 9.6
Using McAfee VirusScan Console to schedule virus-scanning tasks.

The most important thing to do when scanning, apart from the obvious step of actually doing the scan, is to use the very latest virus table. You can get an update from your antivirus tool developer's Web site. For McAfee, start VirusScan, select File, and then choose Update VirusScan. If updates of either the VirusScan product itself or the virus table are available, you'll be informed; then just follow the wizard's instructions.

McAfee's installation default is for VShield to run at startup. You can configure McAfee's antivirus package so that it doesn't, though. This is a decision you need to consider carefully. With VShield always running, you stand a better chance of detecting a virus, no question about it. However, a considerable performance downside exists. If you have all of VShield's Scan Files On options turned on, many operations will take much longer

Watch Out!
Here's what McAfee has to say in its readme file about disk defragmentation and its own products: "Disk defragmentation programs move files as they work to maximize hard disk efficiency. If you have VShield, VirusScan, or other applications active during a disk defragmentation operation, your disk defragmentation program might tell you that it cannot find the active application files. This is normal and does not mean that the files do not exist. To avoid error messages like this, close all open applications and disable VShield, then run your disk defragmentation operation again. We're here to tell you that running these tools at the same time might cause you much more grief—as in a locked-up system—than the readme file's statement implies. Don't do it.

than normal. In essence, your system will feel sluggish. (In one extreme example, it takes Microsoft Outlook 98 14 seconds to print an appointment without VShield running, and with VShield running, this same operation takes 78 seconds—five times longer!) You'll also run into trouble if you happen to leave VShield running and a disk defragmentation operation starts. The following is an effective compromise strategy:

- Schedule regular (daily or at least weekly) full-system scans with VirusScan, making sure that they don't coincide with any automatic defragmentation tasks.
- Do not load VShield at startup.
- Manually scan foreign disks and documents you receive via email.

These are the steps to prevent VShield from running at startup: right-click VShield's system tray icon, select Properties, click the Detection tab, clear the Load VShield at Startup check box, and click OK.

Testing Your Antivirus Tool

The material in this section may, at first blush, seem inconsequential or overly technical. *Please read it anyway; trust us.* You really owe it to yourself and your PC's integrity to run the test at the end of this section to see what would happen if you had all the McAfee antivirus safety nets in place and your system did actually get assaulted by a virus.

Naturally, now that you've purchased an antivirus tool, installed it, and configured it, you're curious about what would happen if it actually detected a virus on your PC. Excellent question. With the smoke alarm in your home, you don't test it by starting a real fire. Instead, perhaps you hold up a warm skillet containing a tiny bit of smoking cooking oil to the detector (and cover your ears). Similarly, you don't need to infect your PC with a real virus. The folks at the European Institute for Computer Anti-Virus Research (EICAR) have created a safe test file called the EICAR Standard Anti-Virus Test File.

It's not a virus; it doesn't even include any fragments of viral code, so it's completely safe. Most antivirus tools react to it as if it were actually a virus and report it with a name like EICAR-AV-Test. It's also a legitimate DOS program; when you run it, it prints the message "EICAR-STANDARD-ANTIVIRUS-TEST-FILE!" as shown in Figure 9.7. (If you have VShield enabled when you do this, it intercepts the execution of the file, beeps, takes over the screen with a bright blue background and a red dialog box, and prompts you with options to Clean, Delete, Continue, Stop, or Exclude.) Finally, it's easy to create without actually having to pass around a specific file (more on this shortly). Any antivirus tool that supports the EICAR test file should detect it in any file starting with these 68 characters:

```
X5O!P%@AP[4\PZX54(P^)7CC)7}$EICAR-STANDARD-ANTIVIRUS-
➥TEST-FILE!$H+H*
```

Unofficially...
In McAfee VirusScan, you can perform a scan at system startup by placing a special settings configuration (.vsc) file in your StartUp folder. For more information about this configuration file (created and managed automatically by VirusScan), see the VirusScan help file.

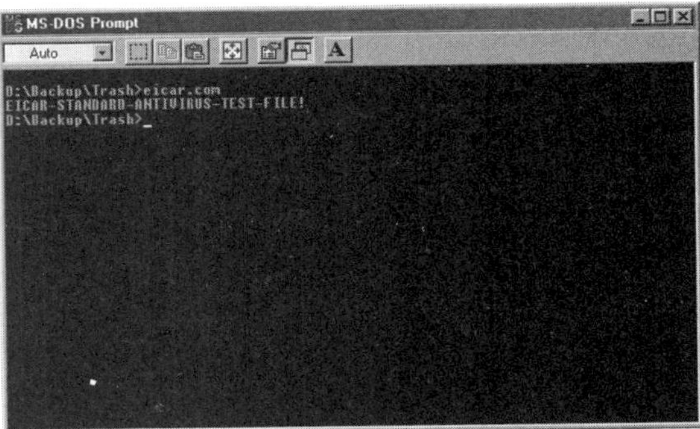

Figure 9.7
Here's what happens when you run the EICAR Standard Anti-Virus Test File in an MS-DOS window.

To create your own EICAR antivirus test file, follow these steps:

1. Using Notepad, copy the line at the end of the preceding paragraph into its own file and then save the file as `Eicar.com`.
2. Start VirusScan and scan the folder containing Eicar.com. When VirusScan scans this file, it should detect the EICAR-STANDARD-AV-TEST-FILE virus, as shown in Figure 9.8.
3. As mentioned earlier, if you enable VShield (and you should, just to have the experience we're describing right

here), when you run the Eicar.com file you should see VShield unmistakably take over the screen and prompt you for what action to take.

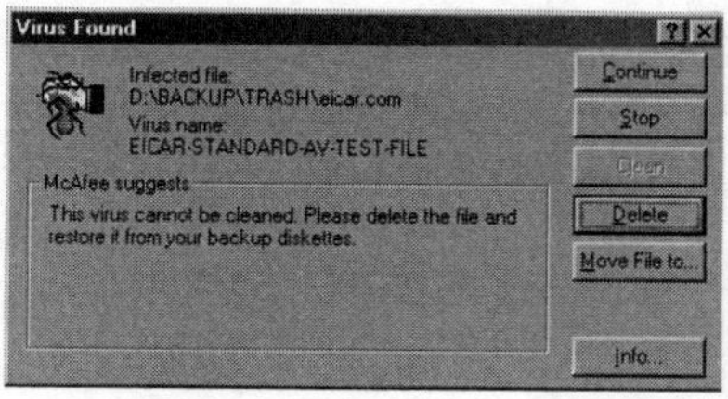

Figure 9.8
How McAfee VirusScan reacts to the EICAR Standard Anti-Virus Test File.

Chapter Ending

Bright Idea
For more information on EICAR, go to the Web site at `www.eicar.com` and look for the local link to the test file.

- Learn how to create rescue disks from Windows itself (in particular, find out about the built-in Registry Checker tool) and by using third-party utilities.
- Create a Windows startup disk (also called an emergency boot disk) to have handy when your system experiences a problem when booting from your hard disk.
- Prevent system and application crashes with third-party utilities.
- Scan your system for viruses and learn about the different types of scanning operations you can perform manually or with a task scheduler.
- Protect your system from viruses by implementing our suggested ongoing regimen.

Chapter 10

Good Habits for a Trouble-Free System

IN CHAPTER 9, "PREPARING FOR DISASTER," you learned about virus scanning and Windows startup disks. If you didn't prepare those items already, now is a good time to do so. In Chapter 11, "Backing Up," you'll learn everything you need to know to make sure that your important files won't be lost in case of a disaster. In this chapter you'll learn about some habits you should form that will help keep your system trouble free. Obviously, we can't guarantee that your system will remain completely trouble free, but we can show you the ongoing habits you need in order to minimize the problems you encounter when using computers in general and Windows in particular.

Logging Maintenance, Performance, and Upgrade Info

An important consideration of your ongoing maintenance routine is keeping track of exactly what you've done to your system and when you did it. Why do you need to track this type of information? When a problem occurs on your system, a well-kept log of all your ongoing maintenance, upgrades, and system performance is a great starting point. Go to your NEAT box and dig out the notebook for keeping a record of everything that happens

Bright Idea
You did make Windows startup disks, didn't you? Now make them easy to find. Label all your rescue disks with a brightly colored label and large bold lettering. Your important disks will then be hard to lose when you are in the middle of troubleshooting.

with your PC. The following is a list of the sorts of things you should be noting in your system journal:

- System files you delete.
- Types of maintenance you perform.
- Circumstances surrounding system crashes.
- "Glitches," odd behavior you notice as you use your system.
- Programs and utilities you install.
- Programs and utilities you uninstall.
- Modifications you make to your system files.
- Solutions you use to resolve any problems you encounter and where you found the solution.
- Any changes in your system's performance.
- Notes on any phone discussions you have with technical support people regarding your computer.
- Additions you make to the scheduled programs in your Task Scheduler.
- Patches and upgrades to programs and your operating system. Be sure to include the version numbers before and after the upgrade.
- Where you found update files or patches and the names of the update files.

This list is just a beginning, of course. The items you'll want to log generally fall into three categories: maintenance you perform on your system, things—either good or bad—that affect your system's performance, and any upgrades you perform. System upgrades were covered in Chapter 8, "Staying Ahead of the Game." We'll cover some maintenance steps in this chapter and then even more in Chapter 12, "Cleaning Up." Do you have to slavishly follow our suggestions? Yes! Well, not really. We give you lots of guidelines in this book and suggest that you at least try them. Keep the ones that help you and discard the rest. Over time, the ongoing maintenance and your system journal will give you a strong advantage in troubleshooting problems that is hard to beat.

Take a look at the following entries from one of our system journals, for example. The first things you want to list, as a reference point, are the details of your basic system. Be sure to include the version number of the display driver. Display drivers typically change much more frequently than other drivers, so expect to update this entry more often than the others. After that, record each action, upgrade, or problem that affects the performance of your system. The following is an excerpt from one of our system journals:

166 MHz Pentium (Hysterium)

32MB RAM

4GB HD W 1.5GB Free Disk Space

800×600 Display Using Small Fonts

Diamond Stealth 64 Series (Diamond GT)

Display Driver Version 4.02.268

7/9/98: Closed Internet Explorer 4.0 while it was loading a Web page. Outlook was the underlying application, but it only partially displayed when the screen and mouse froze. No mouse or keyboard action could get PC to respond. Used reset button to force a reboot.

8/8/98: On boot (working partition) got "insert bootable media" message before Windows loaded. Ctrl+Alt+Delete rebooted system but the "D" physical drive (Drive 1) was not recognized. Powered down and opened case. Reseated SCSI controller and all ribbon cable connections. Rebooted and everything came up with no errors.

9/16/98: Updated via Windows Update:

External JScript Security update

Cross Frame Navigate Security update

DirectX 6 update

10/13/98: Upgraded flash BIOS from 1.00.03.db0 to 1.00.08.db0.

Unofficially... How do you know whether you record enough information about a given incident? If you review your log book and find yourself trying to remember the rest of the details, you probably aren't recording enough detail. If you have to err, do it on the side of having too much information.

Keep careful notes in your system journal and include as much detail as you need to refresh your memory on what happened. Our sample log might be too detailed for you, or it might be too sparse. The key is to record enough information to keep you from doing a lot of guesswork later. When problems start cropping up on your system, you'll want to look through your system journal, keeping your eyes open for patterns. You'll look for things that have been going on for a long time, problems that started after installing a particular piece of software, and so on. You'll also want to note any solutions you might have discovered. Spending just a small amount of time in keeping your system journal current can save you a lot of troubleshooting down the road.

Implementing an Ongoing Maintenance Regimen

To keep your system as trouble free as possible, you have to take ongoing system maintenance seriously. Track everything you do to your computer in your system journal so that you can quickly determine what has and hasn't been done. In the following section, you learn about all the major maintenance areas, including several items that are commonly overlooked in planning your maintenance regimen.

Dust and Heat Abatement

Heat is your system's ongoing enemy, and dust serves to insulate components inside your computer and make them run hotter. Be sure to open your system every couple of months and blow it out. Get a can of compressed air at your local computer supply store, open the case, and blow out all the dust you can find. Dust all parts of your computer, including circuit boards, floppy drives, your CD-ROM drive, and your tape cartridge drive. Just a couple of small specks of dust could make any backup you perform ineffective—or even cause the tape drive to damage your tapes.

Be careful how you dust, though. One friend of ours set his shop vac up to blow the dust out of his PC. The problem was that he forgot to empty out the fireplace ashes he had vacuumed up the day before. When he turned on the shop vac, all those ashes went into his PC. No harm done, but it certainly wasn't the highlight of his day. When you get ready to dust out your PC, unplug the cables and take it to a different room entirely so that the dust you blow out won't be in the same location as your PC. Better yet, go outside and keep the extra dust out of your home or office. Note in your system journal the date on which you dusted out your computer so that you'll know when to repeat the process. While you are dusting things, don't forget your printer. You'll also want to keep the dust bunnies from collecting on the cables that coil up behind your desk and your computer. All this dust has a way of finding its way into your system over time.

Moneysaver
Inkjet printers can become clogged if you don't use them regularly. Be sure to print in color as well as black to keep the ink flowing freely. You'll actually spend less on ink in the long term, and the ink you use will go on your printouts and not be wasted on cleaning cycles.

Make sure that your system has the necessary clearances around the case so that the internal fans can pull in the air needed to keep things running cool. Over the weeks and months, things get shoved around and stacked up on other things—and before you know it, your computer can be choked off from its needed air flow.

Window exposure needs to be checked periodically. Direct sunlight is anathema to your PC and the monitor. You might have picked the perfect spot when you set up your PC in the dead of winter, only to find that it gets full sunlight in the summer months. Your computer will run better and last longer if you keep it running as cool as possible.

Electrical Spikes and Low Voltages

Keep tabs on the power going to your computer. Situations arise that could harm your computer; the most common is a lightning storm. No matter how good your UPS is, go ahead and unplug the whole thing from the wall during an electrical storm. While you are at it, be sure to unplug your modem line! Your PC can be completely disconnected from the wall and still be zapped by a power surge on the phone line going into your modem. Likewise, if electricians are doing work around the house, it would be a wise move to disconnect your PC from the wall.

Preventing power surges is a good start, but don't forget to supply enough power to your system. Don't keep plugging power strips into power strips so that you can run more appliances in your office and expect things to keep running smoothly. Having too little power can be just as bad as having too much. In fact, too little power can often result in unusual system activity as your computer struggles to keep running on meager electrical resources. Symptoms of power problems can include frequent lockups for no apparent reason. Your system journal will be useful in tracking down problems of this type, especially if a pattern exists. If you have problems at the same time every day, it might dawn on you that each afternoon when the kids come home, the TV goes on, Junior fires up his electric guitar amplifier in the garage, and you start having computer problems.

Backing Up

We have an entire chapter dedicated to the mechanical aspects of backing up your data (Chapter 11), but we wanted to touch here on how important it is to make backing up part of your regular routine.

You should perform a backup any time your data could be altered: before you install new software or drivers, when you need a duplicate of a key data file, before you perform any hardware upgrades, and so on. You also need to back up your files on a regular, ongoing basis. How often you perform regular backups depends on how your system is configured, your backup method, and how often your data changes, so we can't give you a one-size-fits-all solution. Still, backups are an important part of your ongoing system maintenance.

Bright Idea
When you want to find files on your drive with the Windows Find utility, open it quickly with this tip. Holding the Windows key down and pressing F opens the Find utility. Or, with all open windows minimized, press the F3 function key.

Ongoing Disk Cleanup

Your computer's hard disk is like your closet. It has a tendency to fill up with junk, making finding the stuff you need difficult, so some sort of ongoing disk cleanup is a necessary part of your maintenance regimen. Chapter 12 talks about deleting space-hogging files and provides you with detailed checklists, but for now we cover the basics and show you how easy it is to clean up unwanted files with the Windows Find utility.

To start the Windows Find utility, follow these steps:

1. Click the Start button.
2. Select the Find option.
3. Click the Files or Folders option on the cascading menu.

To demonstrate how you can quickly find a group of files for deletion, we'll gather a set of files that are good candidates for clean up. Microsoft installation programs create place-holder files called mscreate.dir, which serve no useful purpose after the installation; periodically, you should clear them out.

Watch Out!
Whenever you are in doubt about deleting a file, you should always view the file's contents in the application that created it, in Quick View (right-click in Windows Explorer and choose Quick View), or in Notepad (or WordPad if the file is more than 64KB).

In the Named text box of the Find dialog box, type `mscreate.dir`. Then click the Browse button and select the drive to be searched. Be sure that the Include Subfolders box is checked, and then run the search by clicking Find Now. Your dialog box should end up looking something like the one shown in Figure 10.1. On one test system we have, we found more than 200 copies of the file, which we promptly deleted. They aren't causing any harm, but that's 200 fewer files we need to worry about when doing our system maintenance later. To quickly select all the found files, click one of the filenames and then press Ctrl+A to select all the files. With all the files selected, press your Delete key to finish the job. Be sure to record in your system journal the date and the types of files you are deleting.

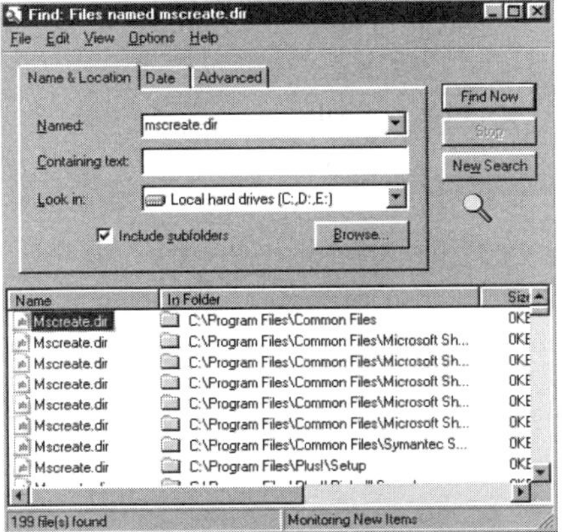

Figure 10.1
Use Windows Find to quickly locate and delete unneeded files.

Bright Idea
Make repeating these searches easy. Select File, Save Search. This action puts an icon on your desktop that will repeat that search at any time. Move these search icons to an ongoing maintenance folder to make cleanup a snap.

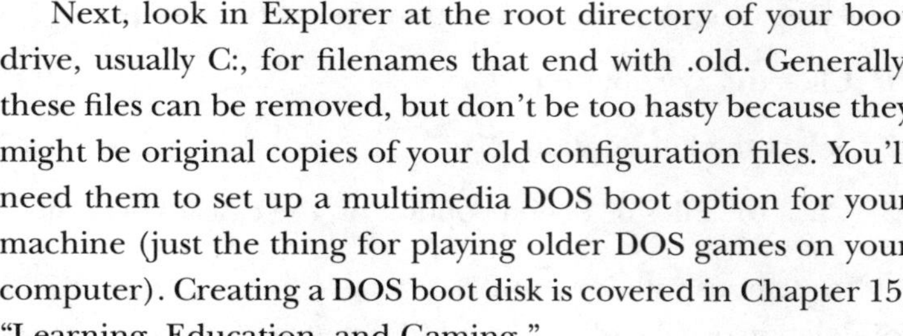

Next, look in Explorer at the root directory of your boot drive, usually C:, for filenames that end with .old. Generally, these files can be removed, but don't be too hasty because they might be original copies of your old configuration files. You'll need them to set up a multimedia DOS boot option for your machine (just the thing for playing older DOS games on your computer). Creating a DOS boot disk is covered in Chapter 15, "Learning, Education, and Gaming."

You should, of course, be cautious when deleting files, and some files you should not delete for any reason. All the following items are key folders and system files that can cause you much grief and aggravation should you mistakenly remove one:

- Your `C:\Windows\Sysbckup` folder or anything in this folder should be left alone. Windows uses Sysbckup to track changes to your system files and automatically keeps the most current version of a given file on your system at bootup. Modifying the contents of this folder will prevent Windows from being able to track those changes.
- The `C:\Windows\System.dat` file is the main part of your system Registry. Deleting this file will put you in the highly undesirable position of rebuilding your Registry by hand. It would be easier just to reinstall everything on your system from scratch! We know that you don't want to do that, so leave this file alone. Backing up the file, on the other hand, is a *very* good idea.
- The `C:\Windows\User.dat` file is the other half of your system Registry. Read and heed the same warnings and suggestions for System.dat.
- Don't delete files in your C:\ root directory willy-nilly unless you're a glutton for punishment. If you have any doubt, leave the file alone and save yourself some possible heartache.

Unofficially...
After removing a large number of files, it's always a good idea to run Scan Disk and Defrag to clean up your hard drive.

Task Scheduler

This section discusses how to put your ongoing maintenance on autopilot. You will learn how to use the Windows Task

Scheduler, so let's make sure that it's up and running before proceeding. When Task Scheduler is running, you'll see its icon in your System Tray, as shown in Figure 10.2. To start Task Scheduler, select Start, Programs, Accessories, System Tools, and Scheduled Tasks. You used Task Scheduler in Chapter 5, "Configuring Your New PC," to automate burning in your new system. Later, in Chapter 12, you'll use Task Scheduler to automate your day-to-day cleanup tasks.

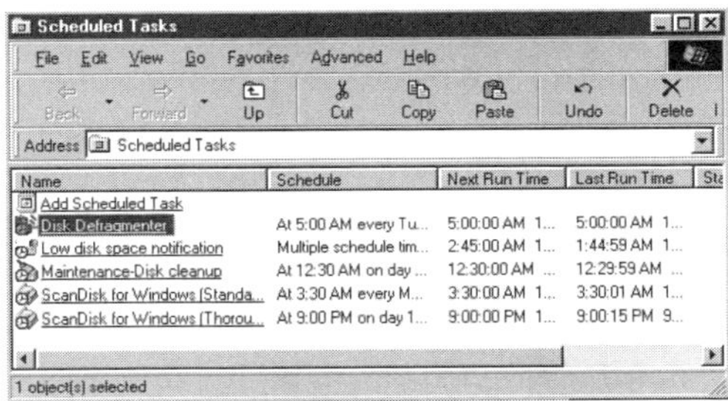

Figure 10.2
Task Scheduler running in the System Tray and opened to show scheduled tasks.

Task Scheduler comes preloaded with some system tasks. The following is a list of the programs already set up for you:

- Disk Defragmenter is set to run every Tuesday, Wednesday, Thursday, and Friday at 5:00 a.m. This removes any defragmentation on your hard disk. By default, it scans each of your drives and asks you before fixing errors. Asking is okay, but only if you are going to be around to answer the question! You don't want your system waiting half a day or more just to hear back from you. We'll delve deeper into Defragmenter in Chapter 12.

- Low Disk Space Notification runs every 30 minutes and alerts you when your C: drive has less than 20MB of free space. You can add other drives by right-clicking this item, selecting Properties, and then clicking Settings on the Task tab.

- Maintenance-Disk Cleanup runs at 12:30 a.m. on the first day of the month. This entry is configured by the Windows Cleanup Wizard. Look through the settings here to make sure that you aren't deleting files unwittingly. The default settings are acceptable and you shouldn't need to change them. You should, however, inform yourself of what is happening on your system. We'll look at all the options of the Disk Cleanup Utility in Chapter 12.

- ScanDisk for Windows (Standard test) runs at 3:30 a.m. every Monday through Friday. It checks your files and folders for lost file fragments, invalid filenames, and cross-linked files.
- ScanDisk for Windows (Thorough test) runs at 9:00 p.m. on the first day of the month. It performs the same checks as the Standard test, and then it scans your hard drive for physical errors.

Watch Out!
We do not recommend that you run these sorts of low-level disk utilities regularly without also backing up your disk regularly. The types of repairs and data moving performed by these utilities have the potential to destroy data!

Pay attention to the scheduled times of the defaults as well. The defaults assume that your machine stays on 24 hours a day. If this isn't the case, you'll want to adjust the entries to match whatever downtime your system has. Be sure to make a note of any changes to your Task Scheduler in your system journal.

Booting in Other Modes

Under normal conditions, which means your system is running without problems, you'll boot into Windows when you turn on your system. But when things go awry, you can find yourself having to boot your system into another mode, usually Safe Mode. In this section we'll cover the other modes you must be familiar with.

Safe Mode at Startup

Safe Mode can start automatically after your system encounters a major problem during bootup. Sometimes all you need to do is exit Safe Mode and reboot to be up and going. This turn of events can be frustrating because your system had a problem but you now have no idea what it was or how it corrected itself! As part of your maintenance routine, be sure to record in your system journal the details of what might have led up to the system's booting in Safe Mode. You can recognize Safe Mode by the words *Safe Mode* that appear in each corner of your screen.

When Safe Mode starts, you'll receive a message giving some general information about Safe Mode. See Figure 10.3.

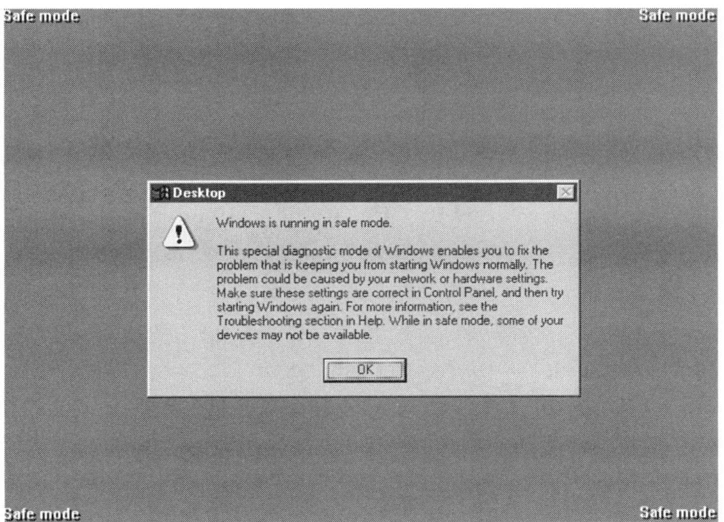

Figure 10.3
Safe Mode gives you information about itself when you boot into it.

Safe Mode eliminates many possible points of failure in Windows, most notably the video drivers you are using, and attempts to give you access to a plain-vanilla version of Windows in the hope that you can correct the problem you are experiencing. In Safe Mode your video resolution is set back to 640×480, 16 colors using generic Windows drivers, and several of your system devices are left inaccessible (your network access, for example). But perhaps the most frustrating missing device is your CD-ROM drive. If you need to restore files from the Windows CD, you have a problem. But you can anticipate this problem and work around it.

Because you won't be able to access your CD-ROM drive in Safe Mode, it's a good idea to copy the Windows 98 installation files to your hard drive for quick updates and installations. The folder you want to copy is Z:\Win98 (assuming that your CD-ROM drive is Z:), and you'll need 110MB to hold the files. A good folder name for the Win98 files is `c:\_win98`. The underscore forces this directory to the top of the list so you can find it quickly.

With these files on your hard drive, you can boot into Safe Mode and then reinstall damaged system components. If you find yourself in Safe Mode and you have not copied the install files to your hard disk, you can boot your system with the startup disk we described in Chapter 9. This emergency startup disk has your CD-ROM drivers on it, so you can copy the files from your Windows CD to your hard disk. Reboot into Safe Mode and you can finish your system maintenance. Make sure that you log all your actions into your system journal for future reference.

After your system is repaired and running smoothly again, you can delete the `c:\_win98` directory to free up the hard drive space.

Performing routine maintenance such as upgrading your video drivers can necessitate a visit to Safe Mode. Suppose you install the latest driver for your video card, and either it wasn't really ready for prime time when it was released by the manufacturer or you've got the resolution set to something the driver or card can't handle. The system might come up fine only to have the monitor display solid black. Fixing video problems is impossible if you can't see what you're doing. Safe Mode to the rescue.

Shut down your system and then hold down the Ctrl key, in Win 98, as your system boots up (under Windows 95, press the F8 key). Instead of the Windows splash screen, you'll see the Startup menu. The choices on this menu determine how your system boots up and what is and is not loaded when Windows starts. The following is a quick rundown of the choices on this menu:

- Normal—Boots into Windows normally.
- Logged (`\BOOTLOG.txt`)—Creates a file called bootlog.txt in the boot drive's root folder. Normally, this is `c:\bootlog.txt`. This text file contains a description of every file that gets loaded and whether any errors occur. Use this when you just can't figure out why Windows won't start.
- Safe Mode—Boots into Safe Mode as described previously. Uses generic mouse and keyboard drivers and Standard VGA for your video.

- Safe Mode with Network Support—Appears only if you are attached to a network. Boots into standard Safe Mode with the addition that you can attach to your network.
- Step-by-Step Confirmation—Steps you through the files Windows loads at startup. This is very helpful when you have your problem narrowed down to a particular component.
- Command Prompt Only—Boots into Windows command-line mode, processing the autoexec.bat and config.sys files. Start in this mode only if you know your DOS commands; otherwise, you'll get frustrated quickly.
- Safe Mode Command Prompt Only—Same as Command Prompt Only, except Windows bypasses your autoexec.bat and config.sys files.

Watch Out!
After you boot in Safe Mode, your Start menu displays large icons. To make them small again, just right-click on the taskbar, choose Properties, and check the Show Small Icons in Start Menu item.

Safe Mode gives you the opportunity to change your video driver (back to the previous driver if the latest upgrade is not working for you) or the resolution settings. Then you can try booting normally into Windows to see whether everything is working.

Booting from a Floppy Disk

You can always boot from your emergency startup disk when Windows is not behaving. This is the same as booting to Windows in DOS, except your emergency startup disk allows you to access your CD-ROM drive. Start in this mode only if you know your DOS commands; otherwise, you'll get frustrated quickly.

Using MSCONFIG and TweakUI to Control Startup

You also have two other ways to control how your system starts. Both of these utilities are launched from inside Windows. You may be more comfortable using these utilities to control how your system boots rather than working at the system level while your system boots.

One of your options involves using the MSCONFIG utility to gain access to arcane settings and to selectively run portions of your Win.ini and System.ini files. See Figure 10.4.

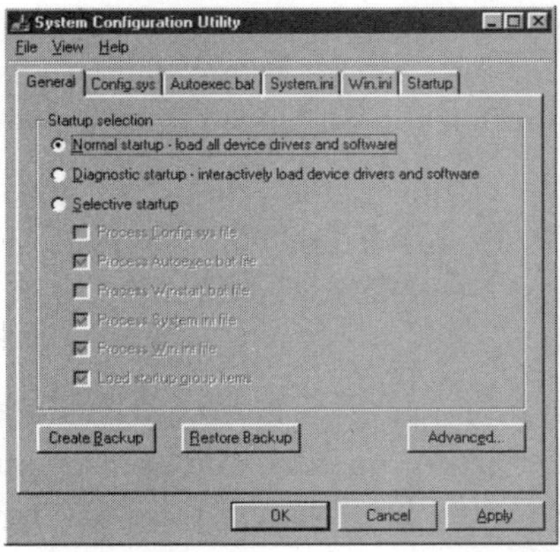

Figure 10.4 MSCONFIG gives you control over how your system starts up.

Start MSCONFIG by choosing Start, Run; then type `MSCONFIG` and click OK. On the General tab, you can choose a normal startup or the diagnostic startup, which simply calls up the Startup menu discussed in the preceding section on Safe Mode. Or you can use the Selective Startup option to selectively choose which files and processes are run at startup. The remaining tabs let you control which sections of the key system files are executed and what items in the StartUp folder are actually run. This capability can be tremendously helpful when you're troubleshooting a stubborn computer. You'll learn more about MSCONFIG in Chapter 19, "Recovering from a PC Disaster."

The other utility to keep in mind is TweakUI. One of the particular sections of TweakUI you want to look at regarding maintenance is the Boot tab, where you can turn on the Startup menu, which TweakUI calls the Boot menu, and set the length of time that the menu is displayed before the default option (Normal) is run. The other tab to look at is the Paranoia tab, shown in Figure 10.5. Here you'll find a section labeled Illegal Operations. Check the box, and any illegal operations your system generates are logged to a file named `C:\Windows\FAULTLOG.TXT`. This file is equivalent to the Bootlog.txt file we discussed earlier in this chapter and can be helpful in nailing down what's causing a specific problem.

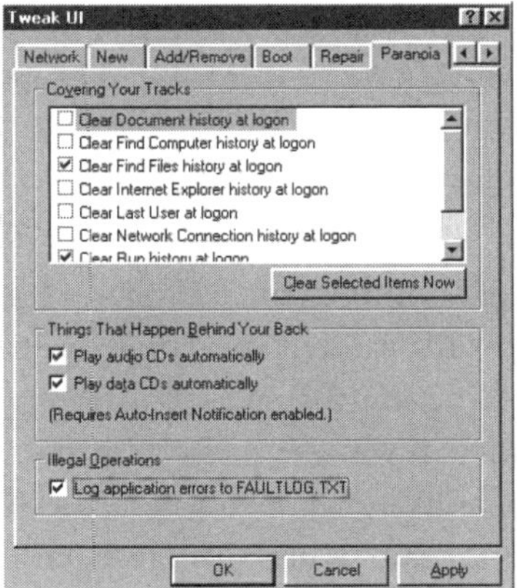

Figure 10.5
TweakUI can log your application errors for you.

Low-Level Utilities

When everything seems to go wrong and you just can't nail down that problem your system is having, it's time to turn to a good set of low-level utilities. These types of utilities are system diagnostic tools, disk repair tools, unerase tools, and the like, which we covered back in Chapter 5 when we covered testing and running diagnostics on a new system. Many of the utilities we discussed can be found on the Internet, and some of them are quite good.

If you're not comfortable with having various tools from different vendors, you should get a single, full-featured commercial utilities package. Our recommendation is the Norton Utilities by Symantec Corp. Norton Utilities costs less than $100, and you'll make that back the first time you use it to save your lost data (not to mention your sanity).

The key to using Norton (or any of these types of maintenance utility programs) is to not wait until you have a problem. Norton has component utilities that perform preliminary maintenance that make heavy-duty tasks easier. In the case of Norton's Disk Image, it makes some impossible tasks feasible. We say "feasible" and not "possible" because you would want to use some of these features only as a last resort. Disk Image does its magic by storing information about your system in a special location on your hard drive. The other Norton utilities know where to look for the file and can use the information it contains to repair damage to your system. The Disk Image stores information on your disk partition tables, fat tables, and directory structures, along with other information that can aid the Norton programs in repairing problems on your system.

An example of an impossible task made feasible is Norton's Unformat utility. This utility can actually unformat your hard drive after an accidental formatting. Although it can do this magic without your having run the Norton Disk Image program first, your results won't be nearly as useful. Also, don't get the idea that you'll run Unformat and have your computer running like new again. Instead, think of it as a *last resort* way to access important data you didn't have backed up.

Watch Out!
Don't use an old Norton Rescue Disk unless you want to add to your headaches. Update these disks regularly, especially any time you add hardware or make system-level changes to your hard drives. Restoring your system using an old Rescue Disk can quickly wipe out your entire hard drive or system configuration.

It's not just the utilities that make this package worth your time. We place equal value on the manuals and help files that come with it. What good is a utility if you don't understand what it does or how to make it work for you? Norton has troubleshooting sections pointing you toward which utility to use for which task. Pay close attention to the ongoing maintenance recommendations in the manuals as well. These utilities were made to keep your system running smoothly. It's smart to understand how they go about their tasks.

One of the most far-reaching tools in the Norton package is the Norton System Doctor, shown in Figure 10.6. This utility runs in the background and constantly monitors your system for changes that will affect you adversely. Think of it as protecting you from yourself. The System Doctor alerts you when it finds a problem and assigns a severity level ranging from Notice to Alert. It also makes suggestions as to which utilities to use to fix the problem. When System Doctor coughs up a warning, take the following steps:

1. Make a detailed note of the warning in your system journal.
2. Review your other system-journal entries, keeping an eye out for patterns.
3. Study the help file and manuals to determine what the causes and effects of the problem really are.

4. Make an informed choice on what to do with your system.
5. Make another note in your system journal describing what you did to fix the problem.

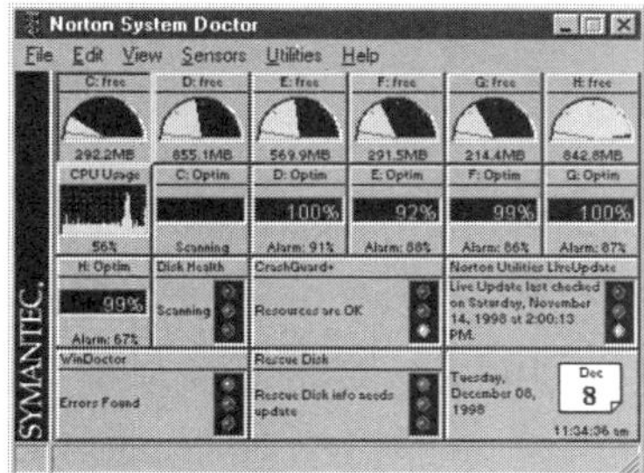

Figure 10.6 System Doctor watches your system so that you don't have to.

Although a utility such as Norton System Doctor can't fix every problem, it can often spot things you would overlook. Some people find this constant monitoring troublesome in itself and prefer not to be alerted every time something gets a little out of kilter. Then there is the issue of system performance. Symantec claims that the System Doctor runs in the background and you won't notice it. The cumulative demand of System Doctor, Anti-virus, Protected Recycle Bin, and assorted other utilities does take a toll on your performance—too much of a toll, in our opinion. Be sure to use your system journal and keep track of which utilities degrade your system's performance the most. Disable any utilities from the Startup group that you don't regularly use. Don't completely disable any of them until you understand the impact that action will have on your recovery efforts later. Your goal is to have a trouble-free system, and part of being trouble free is peace of mind, which might be worth a small performance hit.

Unofficially... When you evaluate utilities, don't just look for what they find or diagnose. You also want detailed help on what to do when a problem is found and descriptions of what all the processes are really doing. Become an expert on your system, and you'll have far fewer surprises.

This was just a brief overview of the complex subject of system utilities. Be sure to familiarize yourself with the capabilities of your chosen utility set before you need to use it. If you can't find a utility to do what you want to do, search the Internet. You're likely to find what you want, although sometimes the documentation is a bit sparse. On the other hand, you'll often be able to contact the utility's author directly. Regular use of low-level system utilities goes a long way toward keeping your system trouble free.

Chapter Ending

- Keep your system journal up-to-date.
- Dust out your PC and other components regularly.
- Monitor the power going to your machine.
- Clean up unneeded files.
- Keep your Task Scheduler under control.
- Be familiar with the different ways your system boots.
- Learn the capabilities of your low-level system utilities.

Chapter 11

Backing Up

IMAGINE THAT YOU'RE STANDING in front of a huge chalkboard. You're working feverishly, the click-scratch of the chalk on the board keeping a staccato rhythm as you put the final touches on the Unified Field Theory that the scientific world has been collectively searching for since $E=MC^2$. The next morning you return to your office, colleagues in tow, to show them that you've solved the riddle of the ages. Opening the door, you see that your chalkboard is now completely blank, having been scrubbed clean by the night cleaning crew.

The feeling you would experience is identical to the one you get when your hard disk crashes, taking all your programs and data with it. And notice that we said "when," not "if." With hard disks, it's only a matter of time and fortune. One day, fate will force you to think about your backup, and hopefully that thought won't be a simple, "Gee, I wish I had one."

Your hard drive is the most important piece of hardware inside your PC. Think of it this way: if some component of your PC crashes (excluding the hard disk), you can probably replace the bad peripheral with one swipe of your credit card. But if your hard disk fails, you've got a real problem. It's not just another piece of hardware, it's the central repository to which you've entrusted...well, everything. All your information, programs, updates, passwords, bookmarks—the list goes on and on. With a crashed hard disk and no backup plan, you might as well be walking around with a permanent case of amnesia.

What you need is a backup plan. Unfortunately, no one-size-fits-all plan exists. Several factors are involved: the type of work you do on your computer, the amount of risk you're willing to accept, and the medium you choose for creating backup copies of your programs and creative work (loosely referred to as *data*). This chapter covers what you need to know to formulate a backup plan that works for you.

Backup Media

Simply put, a *backup* is a copy of your electronic data—the files that make up everything you have on your computer. If something happens to one copy, you have another copy, so you don't lose anything. At least, that's the theory. Going from the theory to the reality is another thing altogether.

You need three things in order to create a backup:

- Something to back up—we'll leave that part up to you.
- A medium to back up to—a place, in other words, to copy all your information to.
- Software to copy your files from their primary location to your backup medium.

Right up front, you should know that we favor a backup strategy that differs from traditional methods. For a long time, the accepted method of backing up your files was to copy them to magnetic tape using a special tape backup device and related software. But tape has some drawbacks. First, tape is linear, so if a file you want to access is at the end of the tape, you have to search to the end of the tape to find it. This often makes the restoring of a single file a slow, time-consuming process. Then the problem exists of knowing whether your tape backup is any good. The only way to really know whether that tape sitting on the shelf with your backup on it is good, is to restore it and test to see whether everything works on a random-access device such as a hard disk.

We prefer and recommend backing up to a hard disk or an equivalent removable medium, such as the Jaz drive by Iomega (`www.iomega.com`) or a writable CD-ROM drive.

Hard Disk

Performing backup to another hard disk is a joy. It can be done with software already on your computer, such as the familiar XCOPY command (which we discuss in detail later in this chapter). It's very fast, and most importantly, your backed-up data is always available. Random access is the key. Unlike tape, in which the file you want to restore is invariably at the hard-to-reach end of the tape, a hard disk can access the data randomly wherever it resides. We used to fumble with tape backups until M. David Stone, a noted author and all-around computer genius, introduced us to the advantages of random-access storage for backups.

With the cost of hard disks dropping every time you turn around, this is a very attractive backup medium. Of course, it requires your adding a second hard disk to your system, but that is not any more difficult than adding a tape storage device. We usually have two drives of the same make and size installed when we order new systems for ourselves.

Watch Out!
When offsite storage is required, removable media or tape is the only way to go. But if you simply toss the "offsite" tape backups into a drawer next to the computer, you're kidding yourself. A fire or disaster sufficient to destroy the physical computer will get the tapes as well.

The added benefit of backing up to a second hard disk is that in the event that your primary drive fails, you can actually swap drives and be back up and running in short order. Let's assume that your primary hard drive has failed and won't boot, but that you have a current backup of the failed drive's contents on the secondary drive (which has the same partition and directory structure). You'll need to do two things:

1. Make your secondary drive your primary drive so that your computer will try to boot from this drive.
2. Make your secondary drive (now your primary drive) bootable.

Making a Second Hard Disk the Boot Drive

A bootable drive has to have an *active* partition. A partition is a physical division of your disk. You can break up a disk into multiple partitions to make organizing your files easier, to enable you to run multiple operating systems, and to make more efficient use of your hard disk space.

A partition can be set as active only on the primary drive. So first you have to make your backup drive the primary drive—the drive that the system tries to boot from. How this is accomplished depends on what types of drives you have installed on your computer. The combinations we'll tackle are two IDE drives, two SCSI drives, and a combination of IDE and SCSI drives.

These procedures usually require you to open your system case and tinker with the physical hard drives installed in your system, fiddling with jumpers and the like, so this approach might not be everyone's cup of tea. But whether you do the work yourself or have a technician do it, you must understand the process involved in restoring your drive so that you'll better appreciate what's involved in keeping it backed up. In any event, the result is a smooth recovery of all your data, so the effort expended is very much worthwhile.

Two IDE Drives

IDE drives are usually configured via jumpers on the hard disks themselves. One drive is set as the Master; the second IDE (your backup drive), as the Slave. Your computer boots the Master IDE drive. Consult the documentation for the drives installed on your system; rejumper the secondary drive as the Master, and then remove the former Master drive or rejumper it to be the Slave drive.

Watch Out!
Some IDE drives have jumper settings for Master, Slave, and Master with Slave. To avoid confusing the system, don't jumper the backup drive as Master with Slave unless you are going to install another drive as the Slave.

Two SCSI Drives

SCSI hard disk drives (all SCSI devices, actually) are identified by the system by their number, usually with 0 (zero) being the first installed SCSI device. On a typical two-SCSI drive system, the boot drive is drive 0 and the secondary drive is drive 1. Numbers are assigned to each drive via jumpers on the drives themselves, so you'll have to consult the documentation for your drives to reconfigure these settings.

SCSI controllers (the card in your machine that manages all your SCSI devices) usually boot the system off the 0 device (the lowest possible SCSI device ID number). But some SCSI controllers boot your system from the lowest device ID available; therefore, you aren't forced to designate the boot hard disk as drive zero. If this is the case for your system (check the controller's documentation), it makes sense to make the bootable hard disk drive 1 and the secondary hard disk drive 2. Should drive 1 fail, you need only to rejumper drive 2 to be drive 0, and the system will boot from the secondary disk. Alternatively, you should be able to just remove the ribbon cable from the failed drive, and the system should boot the next-higher ID device, drive 2, without your having to fuss with jumpers at all.

Unofficially...
To remove a drive, gently unplug the ribbon cable that connects it to the next device. One edge of the cable has a red stripe on it. Note which side of the drive the red stripe goes on for when you later reconnect the cable to a replacement drive. This applies to both SCSI and IDE drives. If you lose track of how the ribbon cable goes back, look on the connector on the drive; a printed "1" is on one end. The red side of the cable goes to the "1" side of the connector.

SCSI and IDE Drives

Most systems we've seen and worked on are either IDE systems or SCSI systems, and rarely are both types of hard disks installed on the same system. But because you could install both on a single system, we thought we'd better cover that possibility. With this configuration, the IDE Master drive is the boot drive, and the SCSI is the secondary or backup drive. To boot from the SCSI, you go into your system's BIOS settings and disable the IDE drive altogether, and the system then boots off the SCSI device. Make sure you have written down all your drive parameter settings before changing the IDE BIOS setting (or any BIOS setting, for that matter—you never know when you'll have to restore the settings to their original values).

Bright Idea
Use a program such as Norton Utilities Rescue Disk to make an easy-to-restore backup of your BIOS settings and Partition Table.

Making a Hard Disk Bootable

After the system is configured to boot from your backup hard disk, that drive has to be made bootable. We'll assume that you're running Windows 98 as your operating system. For a drive to be bootable, it has to have an active partition and must contain the key system files necessary for the drive to boot. To make the primary partition on the drive active, you'll boot your computer from your emergency disk to a DOS prompt and run the Fdisk.exe utility.

Watch Out!
Disk-management software such as Fdisk.exe is very unforgiving. Mistakes with Fdisk.exe can result in lost and unrecoverable data. Use care and caution when running this utility.

Chapter 9, "Preparing for Disaster," covered the emergency boot disk and how to create one. This disk is what you reach for first in the event of a major problem with your system, so make sure you have an up-to-date one in your NEAT box. After booting with the emergency disk (you select how you want your system started at the Win 98 Startup menu; boot the system to a command prompt), type `FDISK` at the A:\ prompt and press Enter.

If your primary hard disk is larger than 512MB, you'll be asked whether you want to enable large disk support. If you're using FAT32, you should click Y(es). See Figure 11.1.

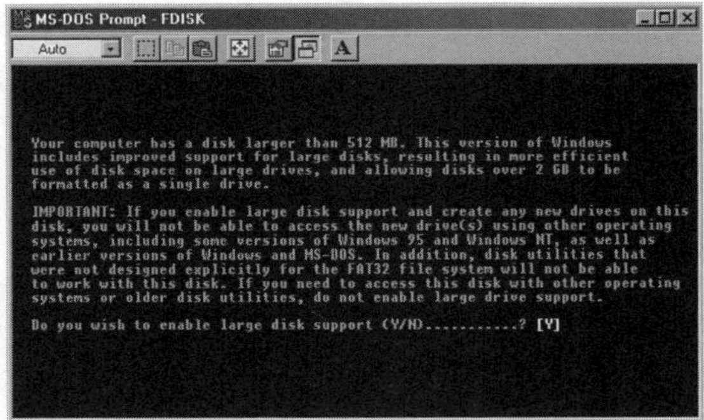

Figure 11.1
Be sure to enable large disk support if you are running FAT32.

The Fdisk menu is straightforward. Type the number of the menu option you want and press Enter (see Figure 11.2). Take your time because you do not want to make a mistake with Fdisk. Drives in Fdisk are numbered starting with 1 for the primary hard disk, 2 for the second hard disk, and so on. Menu option 5 lets you change the selected drive—the drive you are working with; make sure that you are working with drive 1.

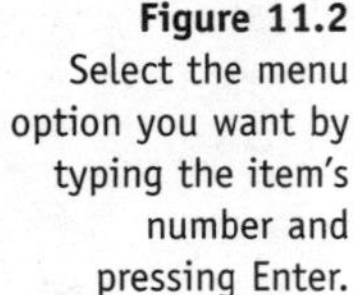

Figure 11.2
Select the menu option you want by typing the item's number and pressing Enter.

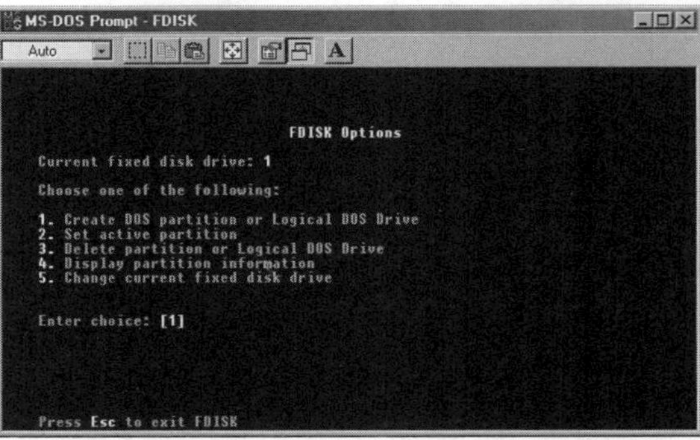

Select menu option 2 to set the active partition. You'll be shown another screen that lists the partitions on the current drive. Make the first (primary) partition active. Press the Esc key to return to the first menu and Esc again to leave the Fdisk.exe utility.

To complete the process of making the drive bootable, you need to transfer some key system files to the new boot disk. From the A:\ prompt type `SYS C:\` to transfer the system files to drive 1. When done, you'll see the message `System transferred`. The drive is now bootable.

Removable Media

When we talk about removable media, we're talking about cartridge systems such as the Iomega Jaz drive, which we'll refer to as *cartridge drives*, or a writable CD-ROM(CD-R) player. Both technologies are in the gigabyte or near gigabyte range. Smaller-capacity, removable media such as the Iomega Zip drives (in the 100MB to 250MB range) are suitable for backing up specific data (all the files related to a specific project, for example) but lack the space to back up a significant portion of the multi-gigabyte drives commonly found on most PCs.

Cartridge drives are basically removable hard disks with capacities in the 100MB to 250MB range all the way up to 1GB and 2GB, depending on the vendor and model. This might be the most attractive backup method because these drives approach the speeds of actual hard disks, and you have random access to backed-up information. This means that you can run programs and use your data right from the backup medium without having to restore the data to another medium first (as you do with tape). It also addresses the problem of needing offsite storage because you can toss the cartridges into your briefcase and take them with you at the end of the day.

Moneysaver
With removable drives, the cost of the cartridges can become a significant cost as you back up your data over time, especially if you maintain several generations of backups. For example, 2GB Iomega cartridges cost about $100 each. Hard disks, CD-R, and tape are all cheaper storage options on a per megabyte basis.

Writable CDs are also a viable backup medium but are best suited for long-term archive storage of data, given their relative small size compared to the Iomega drives. CDs are durable and take up very little storage space, and the actual medium, the compact disc itself, is inexpensive at $2 or less per disc and has a practically unlimited shelf life (although a vocal minority claims CDs begin to degrade significantly after 15 years). The main drawback is the 650MB size limitation, given the multi-gigabyte hard drives that are now standard on most computers.

When using removable media for backup and archive purposes, you need to give ample thought to how you create and store the information you'll be storing.

If you are keeping individual project files on smaller-capacity drives (such as Iomega's Zip or the Imation SuperDisk drives), you need to keep track of the total size of the collective project files and the size of the removable medium. You should organize your hard disk to store data files by project rather than by type (having all your Excel files in one folder or folder hierarchy, with Word files in another). Take into account what you'll do if the collective size of a given project's files exceeds the size of a single cartridge. By creating a series of folders under the general project folder, you can break up a number of files into chunks that would each fit on a single backup disk.

Bright Idea
You can boot your computer from your removable-medium drive. Suppose you have a SCSI cartridge drive and SCSI controller that boots from the lowest-numbered device. Set the hard disk as drive 1 and the cartridge drive as 2. Switch the cartridge drive to 0 and it can be used to boot your computer.

When it comes to backing up entire partitions on your hard disk, you can make things easier for yourself if you set up those partitions with your backup medium in mind. If you'll be backing up to a 1GB or 2GB Jaz drive, partition (or repartition) your hard disk so that no partition that you'll want to back up exceeds the size of the disk cartridges you plan to use. Ditto for the writable CD-ROM medium. Find out how much *usable* space you can write to your CD-R, and keep your partitions just under that size.

Tape

Traditionally, tape drives have been used to do complete backups of the largest hard disks (you can get a tape drive that will handle 20GBs of data to a single tape). Restoring data from a tape has always been a lengthy process, given that in the event of a drive failure, a new drive must be physically installed and formatted, the operating system must first be installed, and then the special software that recognizes and reads from and writes to the tape device must be installed.

Finally, you try to restore the data from the tape and hope that it is actually restorable.

If you get the impression that we don't favor tape (and have had some very unpleasant experiences with tape as a backup medium), you're absolutly correct. Some of the problems with using tape include the following:

- Unlike the random-access nature of a hard disk or hard-disk equivalent, a tape doesn't enable you to quickly access a given file if that file is way down at the other end of the reel, making speed an issue (especially if you are looking for only one file).
- The nature of tape itself, in which the physical medium is pulled back and forth from spool to spool, makes tape more prone to physical and mechanical failures than other media.
- In the past, tape drives have usually worked well only with specialized software that handles the process of moving your data from your primary medium to the tape, and vice versa for restoring. This situation has improved somewhat, and you can use a wider variety of software and utilities for copying files to and from tape.
- As we've said, it is awkward to test the integrity of a tape backup. You really know whether your tape is good only when you try to restore all the backed-up files to a new hard disk.

Utilities are now available that let you treat a tape drive just like a hard disk. Tape-it by PGSoft Inc., for example, assigns your tape device a drive letter, and you can copy files to and from the tape the same as you would a hard disk. You can even save a file from within a Windows application such as Word or Excel directly to tape. Although this utility simplifies the software side of things by making the tape appear to be a random-access device, it does nothing to work around the speed issues involved with searching the tape to find a file or with finding free space on the tape to back up the next file. Still, this is a

Unofficially...
If tape is your backup medium, test whether the tape is good by performing a restore of the backed-up files. Although it is rarely practical to perform a restore of the entire tape, you should test the tape by restoring a few files and then checking that those files are okay.

very slick utility and one you should consider getting if you use tape. Tape-it has a downloadable trial version at `www.pgsoft.com` (the full version costs $59.95).

When it comes to backing up and archiving large amounts of data from a file server, we recommend a high-capacity tape system. But for a personal computer, we don't think tape is worth the hassle, even given the substantial improvements surrounding tape backups. If you do settle on tape, be sure that you know how to restore your tapes if Windows won't run. In the event of a disk failure, this process might entail setting up a new disk, installing Windows, and then installing the tape software before you can restore the first file from your tape.

What to Back Up and When

After you've decided on a backup medium, you then must determine what information needs to be backed up from your primary hard disks and how often you'll perform these backup chores. The "how often" part has no single correct answer, but this one comes closest to fitting the most users: "Back up whenever you have done more work than you would care to do again."

The "what to back up" part is more objective, and it basically falls into two categories: full or incremental. A full system backup, in which you copy everything from each partition on a hard disk (remember, hard disks can also be set up as one large partition) to a backup medium, is straightforward in that you know exactly which files you'll be copying: all of them.

Incremental backups, in which you copy less than everything, are trickier. Maybe you want to back up only the files that have changed since the last full system backup. Perhaps only critical operating-system files, such as the Windows Registry, or only the data files—those files you create in such applications as Word or Excel—need to be backed up. This type of backup is faster than backing up everything, but makes restoring things a bit trickier. In the event you need to restore your information, you first restore the last full backup, and then all the incremental backups made since the last full backup was made. This technique restores your system to the state it was in at the time the last incremental backup was made.

Data files change more often than your program files, which is why it is generally advised that applications be installed to different locations than the data files that those applications create. In the days of DOS and even the first few versions of Windows, things were easier. You put your applications on one drive or partition and your data on another. That was before Registry files, DLLs, shared system files, and the like. Now the data for which you need to keep a current backup is scattered around everywhere. Still, you back up your data files regularly, your operating system maybe once, and your applications only occasionally or perhaps not at all, no?

No. Things are not as simple as they once were in determining what needs to be backed up. You might think that you have all your applications on CD or floppy disk sitting on a shelf in the original boxes that the applications came in, so *Why bother to back them up?* Well, what about all the software programs you downloaded from the Internet? Back in Chapter 8, "Staying Ahead of the Game," we talked about keeping track of downloaded programs as well as the patches, fixes, and updates you've downloaded and applied to your programs over time. You need to make archive copies of these applications and fixes so that in the event of a disk failure, you can recover all your programs in their patched, fixed, and updated state.

Also, we'd wager that some of your applications are "upgrade only" versions that required the preceding version of the program to be installed before you could install it. Windows itself is notorious for this. If your version of Windows 98 is the upgrade only version, you can't install it unless a previous version of Windows is already installed, or unless you have a disk of an approved Microsoft product to pop into the A: drive at the appropriate time, to prove your upgrade-worthiness. Relying on being able to restore all your applications from the stuff on the shelf is a chancy proposition at best. Make backups of your applications.

Speaking of the operating system, every time you install a new application it's even odds that DLLs get copied to the Windows/System folder, drivers get installed, the Registry gets changed, and who-knows-what-all in the way of hidden files gets tucked *here* and stashed over *there.* Then there are bookmarks, ISP dial-up information, passwords, and so on that change as you use your applications. Fortunately, most of these things are stored under the Windows folder and its folder hierarchy.

Making Practical Backups

In this section, you learn how to back up partitions and drives to our backup medium of choice—secondary hard disks. These procedures work just as well with most removable media, although with tape you would probably want to use a dedicated software backup program.

Windows 98 itself comes with a backup program, Microsoft Backup, (select Start, Programs, Accessories, System Tools, and Backup) that backs up folders and files (see Figure 11.3). It stores entire disks in what appears to be a single file with a .qic extension, and you can set the level of compression you want, if any (handy if you're short of backup space). You can recover your files by using Microsoft Backup to restore them to their original location or to another destination you designate. But after the files are backed up, you cannot access them until you perform the restore process because they are contained in the backup .qic file. This is a limitation of most backup software programs: first you must back up and then you must restore, and a failure in either process leaves you with a useless backup.

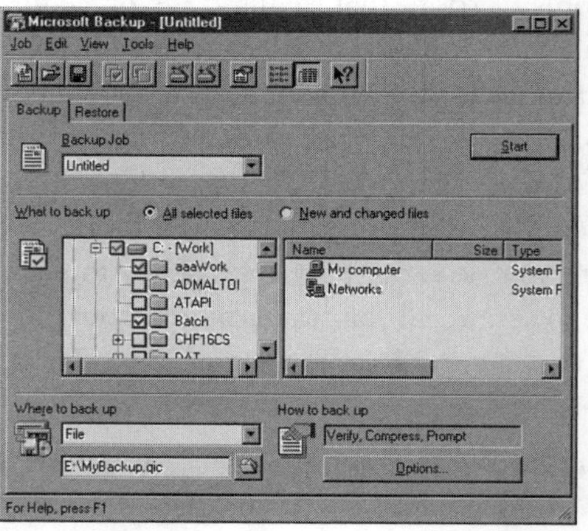

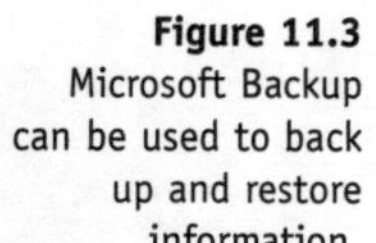
Figure 11.3
Microsoft Backup can be used to back up and restore information.

We favor a much simpler approach using lowly batch files and the XCOPY command. XCOPY is an old DOS command that is still available in Windows. It can be used to copy files to random-access media (hard disks and hard-disk equivalents, or even tape if you're using a utility such as Tape-it, as discussed earlier).

Full Backups

This is probably what most people think of when they think "backup": a complete copy of everything on a given hard disk or partition. If you need to duplicate your drive, this is the best type of backup from which to work.

Unofficially...
If XCOPY is Greek to you, you can get help on DOS commands by opening a DOS window (choose Start, Run, *type command*, OK) and, at the DOS prompt, typing the name of the DOS command you want help on followed by /?. For example, type XCOPY /? and then press Enter in the DOS window. Help for XCOPY then appears, including a listing of all the possible switches.

For our backup routine, we create batch files that use the XCOPY command and that take advantage of the various software switches that XCOPY supports to perform different types of backups. We keep a full and exact copy of our primary hard drive copied to our secondary backup hard drive, but the techniques described here can be adapted to do any type of backup you need to either hard disk or hard-disk-equivalent media.

The computer used in this example has a primary 4GB hard disk divided into four partitions (C:, E:, F:, and G:). The D: drive is the backup hard disk and has four partitions (D:, H:, I:, J:) that are the same size as those on C:. To make a complete backup of a given hard-disk partition, such as the C: drive, we start by creating a text file in Notepad that contains DOS commands that the computer executes when we run the file (known as a *batch* file):

1. Click Start.
2. Select Run.
3. Type notepad, and press Enter or click OK. (You don't have to use Notepad if you have another plain ASCII text editor you would rather use for creating batch files.)

   Type the following line in Notepad:

```
xcopy "c:\*.*" d:\ /e /c /h /r /k
```

This command backs up the entire C: drive, with c:*.*, to the destination medium, the D: drive. The quotation marks around the source ensure that long folder names and filenames are copied as is. The switches that follow the destination drive perform the following functions:

`/e`	Copy all subfolders, including empty folders.
`/c`	Continue copying even if an error occurs.
`/h`	Copy all hidden and system files.
`/r`	Overwrite read-only files.
`/k`	Copy files, including their attributes.

The command `xcopy "c:\*.*" d:\ /e /c /h /r /k` copies all the files, folders, and attributes to your backup disk (assuming that you have enough free space to accommodate the files you are copying; more on this issue shortly). Save this text file in Notepad to a folder where you'll keep your backup batch files, and give it a name such as BU_FULL.BAT (BackUpFULL).

Watch Out!
When you use XCOPY for full or incremental backups, keep in mind that the maximum number of characters allowed in a DOS command line is 127 when you're typing the command manually. Limitations also exist on the length of filenames (255 characters) and folder names (240 characters) in Windows.

We create batch files to copy C: to D:, E: to H:, F: to I:, and G: to J:. Of course, it is just as easy to create a single batch file with several XCOPY commands in it (one XCOPY command per line) and back up several partitions at once.

Incremental Backups

Now create a second batch file for the same drive or partition. Again, in Notepad type this command:

```
xcopy "c:\*.*" d:\  /m /e /c /h /r /k
```

This is identical to the first XCOPY command we created, with the addition of the `/m` switch. The `/m` switch tells XCOPY to copy only those files with the archive bit set to on, and then to set the bit for archive to be off. The archive bit lets the operating system keep track of when a file has been changed since it was last copied. When you change a file, the operating system turns the archive bit to on. When the incremental batch file is run, only those files that have changed (and so have the bit set to on) are copied; then the bit is set to off so that the file won't be copied in future incremental backups unless the file is changed again. This type of backup is a major timesaver because only modified files are copied.

Name this file BU_INCR.BAT (BackUp Incremental), and save it to the same place as the full backup batch file. Immediately after running the full backup for the first time, you need to run the incremental backup batch file so that all the archive bits are set properly. Then you just run the incremental backup periodically to keep all your files backed up on your secondary hard disk (or removable medium).

Bright Idea
It's doubtful that you want to back up the Recycle Bin from your primary drive to your backup disk, so it's a good idea to empty the Recycle Bin before you perform your backups. You might also purge any temp files and your browser cache (as discussed in Chapter 12, "Cleaning Up").

One drawback to making backups this way is something we call file-creep. When you make the initial full drive or partition backup, you get every folder and every file, which is exactly what you want. But what happens over time on your primary drive is that you delete, rename, move, and create files and folders. The things you create and rename get copied when you perform the incremental `XCOPY`. But nothing on the backup drive ever gets deleted. Because of the number of files and folders and the space they consume, your backup disk is eventually filled to capacity, even though it's the same size as your primary drive, which might not be anywhere near full.

To counteract file-creep, you need to completely clear the contents of your backup disk or partition when it approaches its maximum capacity. In Windows Explorer, delete each of the folders and the contents of the root from the partition that is near capacity; then perform a full backup followed immediately by a incremental backup from the primary disk or partition to get the archive bits set properly on your files.

Bright Idea
Windows Explorer dumps deleted files and folders into the Recycle Bin when clearing your backup drive or partition. Bypass the Recycle Bin by holding down the Shift key while deleting files and folders. Exercise *extreme* caution when doing this. Deleting is not something you want to do when you're distracted or in a hurry.

Backing Up Windows

Spreadsheets, word processing documents, address books, email, and the like are all-important and need to be regularly backed up. But first and foremost, you need to maintain a stable operating system. To that end, here's a backup routine that can help stave off the Windows gremlins when you're installing a new network driver or a piece of software. This trick can be done to your backup disk, or you can use it on your primary drive if you have the space.

What you want to do is create a backup Windows folder and name it something like `winback`. Then either execute the following command from a DOS command window or create a batch file for it:

```
xcopy "c:\windows" c:\winback  /e /c /h /r /k
```

Before you install new hardware or software, run this command to create a complete backup copy of the Windows folder structure on the system. Then perform the install. Should you encounter problems with Windows during or after installation, perform the following steps:

1. Boot the computer from your emergency disk into DOS mode.
2. Rename the folder c:\windows to c:\winbad.
3. Rename the folder c:\winback to c:\windows.
4. Reboot the system.

If, however, the newly installed equipment or software works as desired, you can delete the c:\winback folder (assuming that you won't need to roll Windows back to a pre-most-recent-install state) and perform a new backup of the current c:\windows folder. Doing this gives you a way to restore Windows to a working condition if it becomes unstable for whatever reason, and you won't have to reinstall the most recent hardware or software additions.

Automating the Process

By creating DOS batch files and then creating shortcuts to these files on your Windows desktop, you can run a backup process with just a few mouse clicks. To create desktop shortcuts, use the right mouse button to drag a batch filename from Windows Explorer to your desktop. Release the mouse key and choose Create Shortcut(s) Here from the pop-up menu. We discussed creating shortcuts in detail back in Chapter 6, "Customizing Your New PC."

In Chapter 12, we'll discuss and show you how to further automate this process by using Windows Task Scheduler to automatically run an XCOPY command.

Chapter Ending

- Determine the proper backup medium for your system.
- Boot from secondary drives if the primary fails.
- Make full and incremental backups.
- Keep Windows backed up.

Chapter 12

Cleaning Up

BACKING UP IS UNDOUBTEDLY the singlemost important task in anyone's computing repertoire, and the singlemost neglected. But you no longer have any excuses—the tools we provided in the previous chapter together with the automation capabilities of Task Scheduler described in this chapter are the keys to hands-free backups. Now you can sleep easy at night. Also in this chapter, we give you organizing and cleanup checklists that have been finely honed, like a Samurai master's sword, over years of hard-fought field experience.

Organizing and Cleaning Up Your Hard Disk

Picture this: Someone bought a home and its previous occupants left it trashed and disheveled to the point where one room's design was unrecognizable, and they left behind a pile of unidentified flotsam and jetsam. What's the first thing to do? Throw things out into the dumpster haphazardly, or create separate staging areas for different types of stuff? Keep in mind that some of the stuff strewn about in this hypothetical new home is potentially priceless treasure and some of it is pure rubbish, but it's too wildly mixed up to be able to tell which is which just yet. The best approach would be to organize first, then clean up.

A Cleanup Checklist

The technique of "organize first, clean up later" minimizes the number of items you mistakenly get rid of that you actually would have wanted to keep if you had carefully examined each item before tossing it. Here's our down-in-the-trenches cleanup checklist.

1. Before you can clean up, you have to perform a backup. Because this chapter follows Chapter 11 "Backing Up," we'll assume you've already done your backup.

2. Get organized.

   Secure in the knowledge that you've got a rock-solid backup on hand, it's time to get organized. Some folks prefer to clean up *before* organizing, but we discourage that practice. Establish a hierarchy first; then clean up. If you clean up first, you might accidentally delete a file or folder that you wanted to keep, simply because it wasn't stored in the right place.

3. Documents first.

   Start the drive housecleaning with your documents (by documents we mean word processing files, workbooks, presentations, databases, and such). If you're in the Microsoft Office coterie and still use the default My Documents folder for all your documents, a better way exists. Even with using all 255 characters of a long filename, you'll still get lost in the file forest if everything's stored in one folder. Instead, create one folder below the root and call it Data. If possible, keep all your data on a separate partition. Below the Data folder, if you're running a business, add a Clients folder; then add a subfolder for each client. (Apply whatever scheme works for you based on how you use the PC.) Below Data, create one folder for each main application (Excel, PowerPoint, and so on) where you can store nonclient documents. Perhaps you also want a Data\Church folder and a Data\Surfing folder; the key is to apply whatever cataloging scheme works for you, and then use it consistently to avoid growing an impenetrable thicket of files on your hard disk. Next, configure all your applications to save data outside their own host folders to the appropriate Data subfolder. (For example, in Microsoft Word you define the folder you want to be the default this way: choose Tools, Options, and then choose the File Locations tab, select the Documents category, click the Modify button; then browse to the desired location and click OK twice to dismiss the dialog box.)

4. Use long names for folders as well as files, use smart installation practices, and establish good habits.

   While you're moving stuff around in your new data regime, remember that folders can have long names, too. Also, from now on when you install a new application, if it doesn't lodge itself by default below the standard Program Files folder (typically `C:\Program Files`), forcibly redirect it there. This gives you a convenient roster of your installed programs, as shown in Figure 12.1. Remember to continue applying these organizational techniques (and the cleanup tricks discussed throughout this chapter) long after this one-time reorganization. Caveat: don't move application folders manually; instead, always use the Add/Remove Programs applet to uninstall and then reinstall an application.

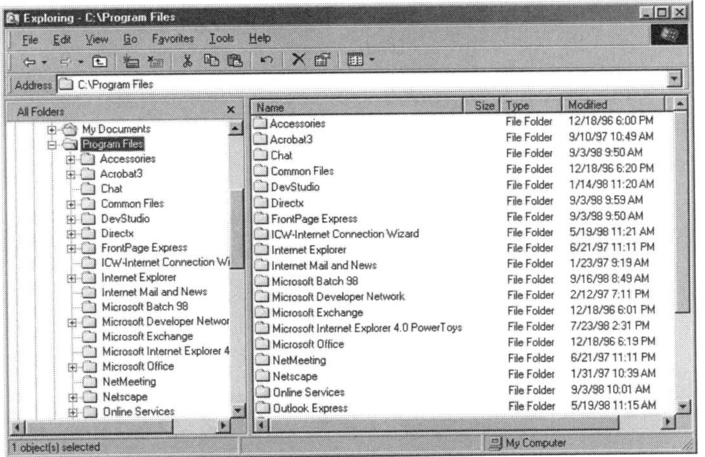

Figure 12.1
Use your Program Files folder as an application inventory.

5. Clean up the debris.

   So far so good. You've now organized the regions of your hard disk you routinely use, so it's time to sweep up the rubbish. Your first priority is to get rid of junk files you don't need any more and discard files that are too ancient to be of any use (and that you don't need to archive). You don't need fancy third-party disk management tools here; good ol' Windows Explorer and Control Panel fit the bill, and they're free. As we discussed in Chapter 6, "Customizing Your New PC," be sure Windows Explorer is set to view all files so you can see hidden and system files. Also, when using Find for drive-wide searches, check the Include subfolders box once (see Figure 12.2) and then forget about it. (This check box is a sticky control, which means that after you set it, Windows remembers the setting even across Windows sessions.)

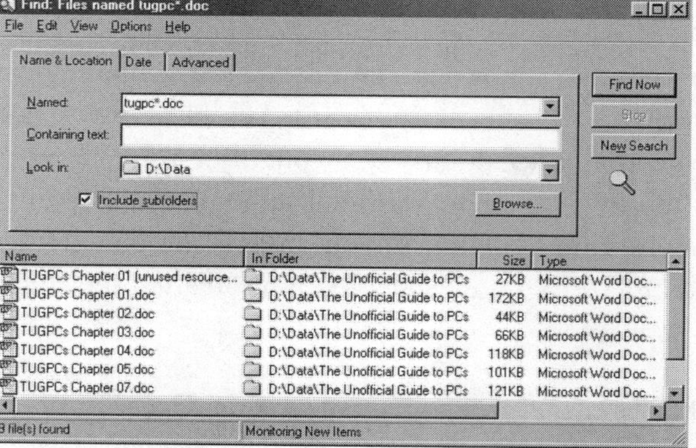

Figure 12.2 Keep Find's Include Subfolders box checked.

6. Special handling for rubbish files.

   A rubbish file is one that you don't have use for any more, period. Whatever its content or purpose, you don't want it around. For such files, only you can be the judge (as for entire applications, more on this in a moment). Be on the lookout for these files as you cycle through files in the "too ancient" category. Start at the root of your drive and examine each of your folders one by one, sorting files in reverse chronological order (oldest first), as shown in Figure 12.3. When you find obvious candidates for immediate destruction, delete them on the spot. For those you aren't sure about, here's a neat tip: fire up Notepad, then back in Windows Explorer select the prospective rubbish file, press F2 (same as right-click, Rename), Ctrl+C (copy to clipboard), switch over to a text file in Notepad, Ctrl+V (paste), and repeat for any other files you think might be litter but need to research before annihilating. When you're done, save this text file as your "nuke 'em" inventory. Avoid core folders such as Windows, System, Help, and so on; you'll still be amazed at how much space you can free up.

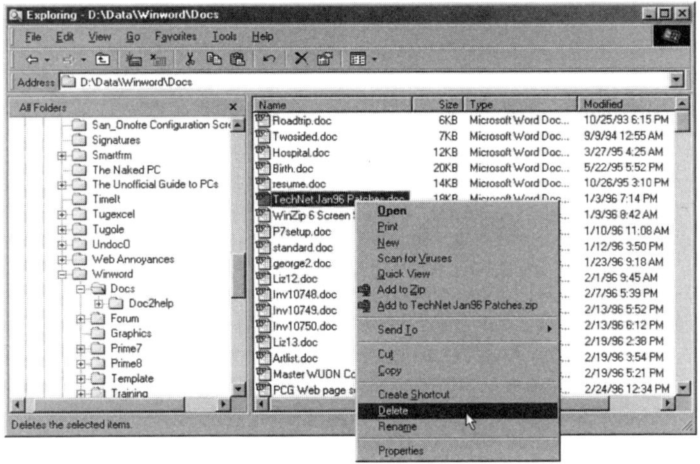

Figure 12.3 Use Windows Explorer to sort oldest files first and weed out the rubbish.

7. Zip 'em up.

   Zip any files you rarely access but that aren't yet ancient enough to be archived off your system. In fact, when you combine a third-party tool such as WinZip, which integrates seamlessly with Windows Explorer, you can easily zip frequently accessed files, too. You be the judge here in a contest between free disk space and the time it takes to unzip, edit, re-zip, and scrub a file.

Money Saver
You'll save time and money galore by using this elegant and smart compression/decompression tool—check out Nico Mak's WinZip. WinZip is worth its weight in gold, therefore, as with any shareware program you use, please buy a copy and get registered. See Appendix B.

8. Archive old files.

   In the case of files that are old—but not junk—that you need only for historical purposes, archive them to a removable disk cartridge, a writable CD-ROM, or to tape so that you can easily store them offdrive—or if warranted, offsite.

9. Use Windows 98's Disk Defragmenter. (Windows 95 also has a built-in Disk Defragmenter.)

   This doesn't affect disk space in quantitative terms, but it does optimize the time it takes to read from and write to your drive.

10. After your drive is clean, keep it clean.

    You can establish many of these steps as routine, automatically scheduled activities. For example, use Task Scheduler to alert you when free disk space falls below a threshold you set for each drive (partition); we check our systems every half hour.

11. Put data on a separate partition and be sure to use FAT32.

    Now that you've reorganized your hard disk, swept out the rubbish, and archived old files, consider two other changes. First, store your operating system and applications on one partition (typically C:) and your data on a separate partition (typically D: and higher). This makes incremental data backups and crash recoveries much easier, as discussed in Chapter 11, "Backing Up." Second, if you haven't already done so, upgrade to FAT32. The benefits, among others, are volumes up to 2 terabytes, smaller clusters, and no size limits on the root folder. Dividing huge drives into smaller partitions and carefully choosing the best cluster size can yield tremendous disk-drive space savings.

Finding Files Fast

The best way to find a file is with the Windows Find feature. Pure and simple. The hot tip here is that it's actually faster and easier to search for a file on a drivewide basis rather than struggling to remember or guess which folder it might be in.

Because the Find tool is fast and efficient (unlike other utilities that waste precious disk space with index overhead), consider it a vastly underrated tool. Find can do more than a simple search by filename, as shown in Figure 12.4. We urge you to look into its full-text and case-sensitive search features, among others. In Figure 12.4, for example, you'll notice we typed `Naked PC` into the dialog box's Containing Text edit box, which will search all the documents in the `D:\Data folder` (and its subfolders) for that text.

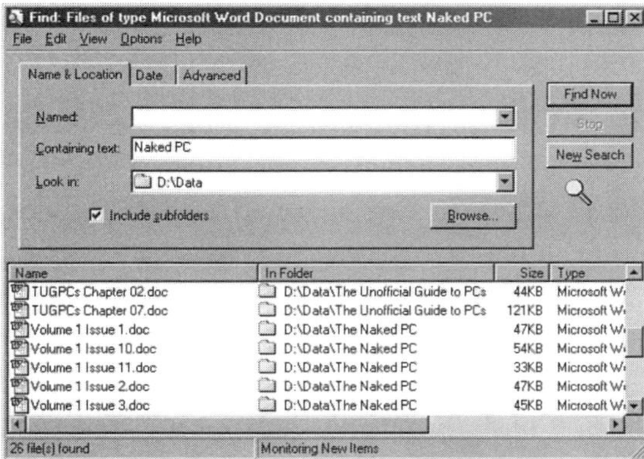

Figure 12.4
Find can find files by more than just their names.

Sources of Wasted Space on Your Hard Drive

If there's one thing we really dislike, it's a hard drive space hog. We all pay good money for our hard drives and the applications we grace it with. And naturally, our data is priceless. So any program that comes along—Windows itself, a Web browser, a word processor, or a game—and takes up unnecessary space on our hard drive is the sworn enemy. We have been refining a checklist for identifying and nuking space hogs over the years, and here it is for your benefit. Use it with relish!

Plenty of space hogs exist on your hard drive. Although Windows 98's Disk Cleanup tool is handy, we'll first work our way through all the nooks and crannies manually; then we'll cover how much of this you can automate using Disk Cleanup. For those of you using Windows 95, it has no such tool as Disk Cleanup, so very few of these activities can be automated; thus, we cover our checklist first and then describe the Windows 98 Disk Cleanup tool afterward.

1. We've said it before and we'll say it again—make sure you've got Windows Explorer set to view all files so you can see hidden system files and folders.
2. When you use Find for drivewide searches, always have the "Include Subfolders" box checked. This is a sticky setting, which means you select it once and then you can safely forget about it. In some rare cases, you might want to limit a search to a specific folder and thus clear the box, but remember to check the box again when you're done.
3. Use the Add/Remove applet's Windows Setup page to uninstall Windows 98 components you don't use (see Figure 12.5) and follow up with a manual deletion, if necessary. By manual deletion we mean hunt down and remove the component's main folder and any vestiges its uninstaller left behind. Windows' `C:\Program Files\Online Services` folder and its subfolders represents about 350KB of wasted space if you already have an ISP. Granted, this isn't a Grand Canyon-sized chasm in your hard disk, but every little bit helps. (The Disk Cleanup tool can help with this task.)

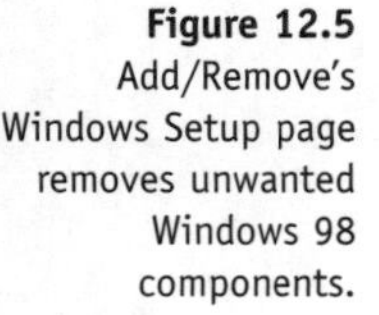

Figure 12.5 Add/Remove's Windows Setup page removes unwanted Windows 98 components.

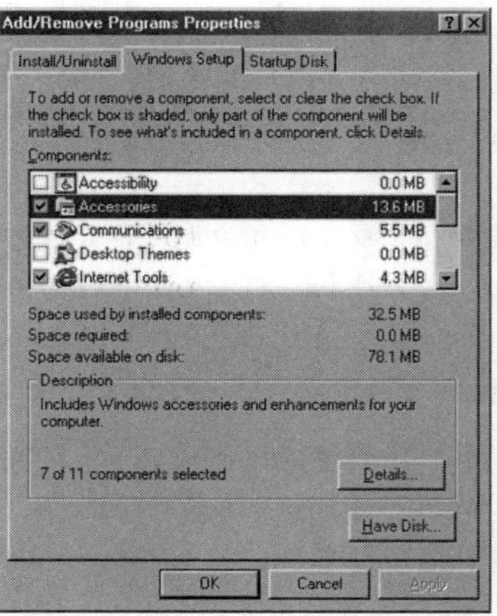

4. Use the Add/Remove applet's Install/Uninstall page to uninstall applications you don't use (see Figure 12.6), and follow up with a manual deletion, if necessary. (The Disk Cleanup tool can help with this task.)

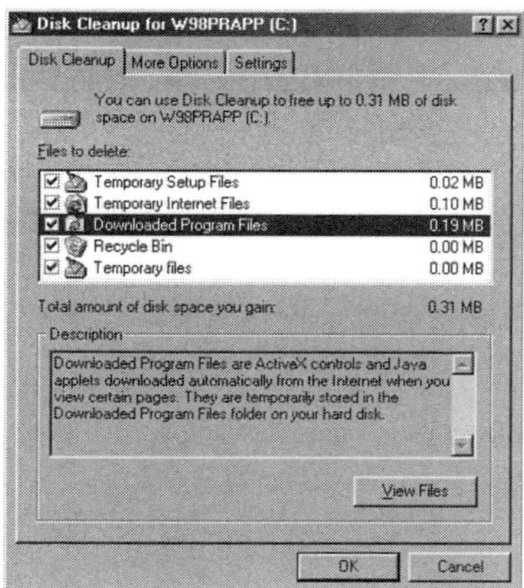

Figure 12.6
Add/Remove's Install/Uninstall page is the place to go to remove unwanted applications.

Dozens of third-party uninstaller utilities are out there vying for your hard-earned frogskins. *Don't use them!* These utilities purport to clean up the mess left behind by other software developers (Microsoft included), but this is like using kerosene to douse a roaring fire. Even one teensy-weensy mistake by such a utility, compounded by the problems left behind by a haywire uninstaller, can have disastrous consequences (the typical disaster is a corrupted Registry).

5. Manually uninstall unwanted 16-bit (or noncompliant 32-bit) applications that don't appear in the Add/Remove Programs applet's list.

6. Empty your Recycle Bin and your browser's temporary Internet cache. In Internet Explorer, select View, Internet Options. Next, in the Temporary Internet Files section, click the Delete Files button, and then click OK twice. In Netscape Navigator, select Edit, Preferences. Next, expand the Advanced node, choose the Cache node, click the

Clear Disk button, and then click OK. (The Disk Cleanup tool can help with this task.)

Bright Idea
The TweakUI PowerToy includes a Paranoia page in its dialog box, and from there you can choose to automatically clear a variety of history caches every time you log on.

7. Optimize your browser's history settings. The lower the history value, the less disk space is consumed.
8. Delete unwanted File*.chk files in each partition's root folder; these are left over from ScanDisk's cross-linked file correction operations.
9. Delete log files (typically with a .log extension) that you might have unintentionally set in Append mode instead of Replace mode. These files can reach gargantuan proportions.
10. Delete outdated document backup files. For example, candidates for deletion are a Word 97 document with a name of `Backup of Family Christmas Letter.wbk` (`Backup of...wbk`) and an Excel 97 workbook with a name of `Backup of Local Surf Forecast Compared to Actual.xlk` (`Backup of...xlk`), and so on. Check the help files in your individual applications for information about their backup file-naming conventions.
11. With Word closed (and Outlook/Exchange closed if you're using WordMail), delete any ~*.tmp and ~*.doc files left around by errant Word sessions inside your document folders.
12. If you're running Microsoft Office, turn off Find Fast as we advised earlier in the book.
13. Remove any unwanted messages from your email client's Deleted Items folder. First move or archive any important messages you might have floating around in Deleted Items. Make note of your email storage file's precompaction size. Next, use your email software to compress your email storage file (in Microsoft Outlook 98 the steps are to right-click the Personal Folders folder, select Properties, Advanced, Compact Now, and click OK twice). Check again to see your file's reduced size and notice the difference. The first time you do this, you'll be amazed!

14. Go into your Windows Help folder and delete all the large, useless Movie Clip (AVI) files you find there (7MB). (This tip applies only to Windows 95.)

15. Delete any vestiges of old versions of Windows 3.x and MS-DOS left behind if you upgraded to Win95 from Windows 3.x. For example, Win95undo.dat (hidden, read-only, in the root of C:) is present only if you upgraded from Win3.x to Win95, and it can be double-digit megabytes in size. (This tip applies only to Windows 95.)

16. If you've upgraded to Windows 95 OSR2, activate FAT32. (FAT32 is only available for the OSR2 version of Windows 95, sometimes called Windows 95.0b.) If you're not running OSR2 and don't have access to it, install PowerQuest's Partition Magic and optimize your cluster size.

Windows 98 Disk Cleanup Tool

To run the Windows 98 Disk Cleanup tool, select Start, then choose Programs, Accessories, System Tools, and Disk Cleanup. It first prompts you to select a drive to clean up, and then displays a progress meter as it calculates how much space you'll be able to save on that drive; finally, it displays a dialog box, as shown in Figure 12.7.

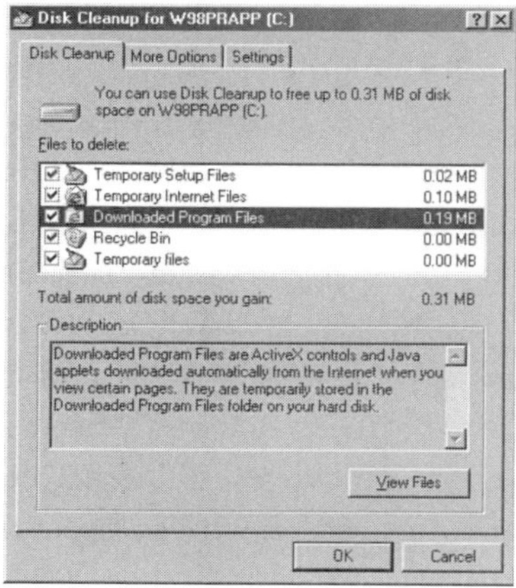

Figure 12.7
Windows 98 Disk Cleanup tool lists, describes, and allows you to view files that it recommends for obliteration.

You can decide which files to delete by checking or clearing each check box. As you navigate the list, the Description text changes to give you a brief idea of what types of files would be deleted for that group. For some (but not all) of the groups, you'll see a View Files button that you can use to view those files in an Explorer window. You can use the More Options page to clean up your Windows components and installed applications, and convert to FAT32. Finally, the Settings page lets you set whether Disk Cleanup should run automatically when the drive's free space drops below a built-in threshold (25MB to 65MB, depending on the volume size).

Unofficially...
If you start the Disk Cleanup tool from the General tab of a drive's Properties dialog box, when it has finished cleaning up, a bug may cause the amount of free hard-disk space reported on the Properties dialog box to not update. Workaround: close, then reopen the drive's Properties dialog box.

Defragmenting Your Hard Disk

After you've organized and cleaned up your hard disk, the next sensible step is to optimize it. To do this, use a tool called Disk Defragmenter.

Defragmenting Is Optimizing

When you defragment a hard disk, you're really optimizing it by rearranging files in a tightly packed fashion. This optimization minimizes the amount of time your hard disk has to spend reading a particular file into memory. Windows 98 goes one step further by incorporating a new watchdog called Task Monitor.

Bright Idea
To find out exactly what low disk space threshold triggers Disk Cleanup to run automatically on your drive, surf on over to the Microsoft Knowledge Base Article *"Hard Disk Is Low on Disk Space Message."* See Appendix B.

Task Monitor runs transparently and automatically; you don't need to do anything to run it. This feature monitors the programs you execute most often and logs this information to a series of files in your Windows\Applog folder. For example, the log file for Calc.exe would be named Calc.lg*n*, where *n* represents the drive letter where this program resides; on your system, this is probably Calc.lgc. When you next run Disk Defragmenter, it uses that logged information to reorganize these program files to the most swiftly accessible portion of your hard disk so they execute even faster. To see the listing of files that Defragmenter will attempt to optimize when it runs next, open Optlog.txt in your Windows\Applog folder as shown here. At the end of the log file, you can also see what programs are ineligible for optimization and why.

How to Defragment with the Disk Defragmenter

Follow these steps to defragment a hard drive:

1. Before using Disk Defragmenter, close all running applications and disable any screen saver (right-click an open space on your Windows desktop, then select Properties, Screen Saver, (None), and click OK). If other applications are running, they may have files open that Defragmenter needs to rearrange. We suggest disabling any screen saver because we have known some systems to crash while being defragmented when the screen saver starts.

   According to Microsoft, "You can use other programs while you are running the Disk Defragmenter tool. However, your computer will operate slower than normal." We challenge this first part of this assertion and agree with the second, but why tempt fate at all? It has been our real-world field experience that Defragmenter hangs, aborts, and generally causes you grief if other applications are running, even if they're just idling. Although it's true that you may statistically be the lucky reader who avoids any such catastrophe, we suggest running Defragmenter only when no other applications are running.

2. To start Disk Defragmenter, select Start, Programs, choose Accessories, System Tools, and Disk Defragmenter.

3. Click the Settings button and make sure the settings are as follows: check Rearrange Program Files So My Programs Start Faster and Check the Drive for Errors, select the Every Time I Defragment My Hard Drive option, and click OK. To see a full-screen representation of what Disk Defragmenter is doing, click the Show Details button.

Watch Out!
You can view Task Monitor's .lc*n* files and the Optlog.txt file with any text editor. *But don't ever save any manual changes to these files.* Occasionally when you view such a file, you might dirty it by accidentally typing a character, so be vigilant when closing them so that you don't unintentionally save changes.

Automating the Process

By working through Chapter 5, "Configuring Your New PC," to burn in your PC, you got some first-hand experience with Task Scheduler. Now we'll apply this tool to disk cleanup, optimization, and backup operations.

We recommend you clean up your hard disk weekly by working through this checklist from top to bottom. Naturally, the organizing part of the process happens once in a sweeping way, then good habits set in and you won't have much reorganizing to do from then on.

We recommend that you defragment your hard disk every two days. We also recommend that if you maintain separate volumes for your operating system and applications and data, you defragment these volumes separately so that if a problem develops with the defragmentation process, the problem's effects are isolated and you have a chance to intervene.

As we discussed in Chapter 5, a standard Windows 98 installation includes these predefined tasks: Disk Defragmenter, Low Disk Space Notification, and ScanDisk (one Standard and one Thorough). Fire up Task Scheduler and verify that your Disk Defragmenter task is set for a frequency of every two days. While you're at it, verify that you're running a Standard and a Thorough ScanDisk of all your drives at least daily (we actually run the former every six hours, the latter each day at midnight). Lastly, be sure you routinely run the Low Disk Space Notification task (we use a setting of every 30 minutes).

Now we'll add a weekly Disk Cleanup task.

1. Start Task Scheduler if it isn't already running.
2. Click the Add Scheduled Task item, which starts the Scheduled Task Wizard.
3. Select Disk Cleanup in the Application column and click Next.
4. Accept the default task name, select the Weekly option button, and click Next.
5. Select the desired start time, week recurrence cycle, and day of the week to suit your needs (we'll go with Friday evenings at 11:00 p.m.), then click Next, and in the next panel click Finish.

Next we'll schedule a daily incremental backup task via an MS-DOS batch file (see Chapter 11 for details about this file). To be sure none of the files that you need to have backed up is open at the time the backup batch file runs, remember to restart your system before leaving your desk in the afternoon or evening. Follow these steps:

1. Start Task Scheduler if it isn't running already.
2. Click the Add Scheduled Task item to start the Scheduled Task Wizard.
3. Click Browse in the Click the Program You Want Windows to Run panel, locate and select your `Bu_incr.bat` file (ours is in `D:\Data\Batch`), and then click Open.
4. Type in `Incremental data backup` for a name, select the Daily option button, and click Next.
5. Select the desired start time, week recurrence cycle, and day of the week to suit your needs (we'll go with 11:30 p.m.), then click Next, and in the next panel click Finish.

The Microsoft Maintenance Wizard is a nice idea, and if you really want to use it we won't discourage you. But you'll have much more direct control over your PC's ongoing self-maintenance regimen, and learn more in the process, if you interact directly with the tools that the Maintenance Wizard is a front-end for: ScanDisk, Disk Cleanup, and Disk Defragmenter, as well as the System Configuration Utility's (SCU) Startup options page. (To run SCU, select Start, choose Programs, Accessories, System Tools, System Information, Tools, System Configuration Utility, and Startup. Now you can see which utilities start when your PC boots up without manually opening your Registry, and you can prevent them from running by unchecking the box. Be careful when using this tool!) These tools in their standalone form all have more options than the Maintenance Wizard reveals.

Chapter Ending

- The first step in cleaning up is to organize the contents of your hard disk.
- The next step is to clean up using our checklist.
- When you defragment your hard disk, you're optimizing its performance by minimizing the time it spends reading files.
- Use the built-in Task Scheduler tool to do many of your hard disk cleanup, optimization, and backup chores automatically.

Chapter 13

Security at Work and at Home

SECURITY OF YOUR PC and its data is a very broad topic. Most people think very little about how secure their data is. What are the risks you should be worried about? Both intentional and unintentional security violations occur. This chapter discusses both of these risks and describes some simple steps you can use to minimize them. The second topic covered is privacy—on the Internet and off. Think of privacy as security for your personal data.

How do you prevent wandering, curious, or naïve children from damaging the important data on your home PC? How do you protect the important data at your business from wandering, curious, naïve, or malicious employees? It turns out that these two situations are not so different. A few simple concepts can help keep the task of securing your data in perspective.

Your computer probably has more sensitive data on it than you realize. If you have a home business, you clearly have a need to keep it secure. But even if you don't work out of your house, it's a good bet that at some time you've brought work home from the office. You might be surprised at how much of your employer's confidential information is sitting on your home PC's hard disk. Knowing that you have sensitive data on your computer, you'll want to protect that data from those who might accidentally compromise the information or even seek to gain unauthorized access.

In addition, dangers are associated with having your computer connected to the Internet; many of you have (or will have) more than one computer installed in your home, and chances are that you'll be networking these computers in an effort to share resources such as printers and Internet connections. You'll want to keep information on one computer secure from accidental or intentional access from any other local computer connected to it.

Watch Out!
Microsoft's Internet Explorer can store the passwords you use to access Web sites. This can be a good time-saver. What if someone logs in to your accounts while you aren't there? Are any of those Web sites ones you don't want other people looking in? If so, don't store the password.

Given all this, you have a compelling reason to approach the security of your PC seriously. The basic steps outlined here for securing the PCs in a business setting will serve you well as you work toward securing your home PC.

By following our simple three-point outline, you will have a flexible approach to solving security and privacy problems. Don't let its simplicity fool you. Security can be complicated. Having a simple outline helps you focus on solutions while accommodating complex situations.

The general steps you should follow are

- Make sure your policies are clearly defined, accessible, and visible. Think about what you're trying to accomplish.
- Require authentication by your employees when they gain access to company computers and information.
- Follow up abuses quickly.

First, we'll apply our basic outline to employees in a work situation, and then to children in a home situation.

Employee Proofing

We use the term *employee proofing* to refer to how you protect your company's data from those that would do your data harm. The term also refers to unintentional harm originating from curious or other well-intentioned employees.

Giving Them Access to Only What They Need

The first order of business is determining which employees have access to which data and systems. On the one hand, you don't want disgruntled employees having enough access to damage important data. On the other hand, you don't want to stifle the creativity of your employees. Often, employees find creative solutions to problems and processes that can dramatically increase their productivity. Putting too many restrictions on the way they use their computers only frustrates them as they try to use the tools they're given to improve their work life. It can also lead to further security problems as employees try to find ways "around the system" to do what they need to do.

Watch Out!
Small computer networks are becoming a way of life for many families. With the advent of cable modems for accessing the Internet, even a single computer becomes one of many on the neighborhood network of cable modem users. Make sure you know who can and cannot access your computer.

Using our outline, we want to establish policies that dictate who can access what information. The policies should be formal, written documents specifying which employees can access which system. Backing up this written document, the system administrators and security people should have the proper access controls in place to enforce the stated policy. Finally, in keeping with our simple outline, any abuses should be followed up quickly.

Securing Your Important Stuff from Them

You have important data that you don't want just anybody looking at both at a company level and on a personal level. Follow the same principles we just described to govern access to your systems: be clear on your policies, limit access to sensitive data, and follow up on abuse swiftly.

When you think of securing your important information, you have two things to think about: the data itself and the hardware on which it resides. It does you no good to prevent people from seeing the data if they can steal the machine the data resides on. Either way, you've lost your data. Therefore, the first step is to have a good backup program like the one we described in Chapter 11, "Backing Up." With your backup in place, you can recover even if the machine goes belly up or is stolen.

After you are sure that your data is securely backed up, use common sense to secure your hardware. Don't leave your computer unattended, do lock the door when you leave, do put passwords on your screen savers, and don't run programs unless you know where they came from. In addition to the common sense approach, the following are some uncommonsense solutions:

Unofficially... Keep in mind that at some point, your own memory's limitations become a factor. If you have too many decoy filenames to remember, you risk losing the data even from yourself. A related trick is to password-protect a single decoy file that in turn lists all your decoy files.

- Hide semi-sensitive files in plain sight by giving them benign filenames. Most casual snoops look for files titled passwords.txt or something similarly obvious. Go ahead and name your file something like dsb456.dll so that it blends in with every other file in the directory. Few snoops go looking at .dll files.
- Use encryption to protect really sensitive data from prying eyes. We'll talk more about how to encrypt files and email later in this chapter. The rule of thumb is if you don't want someone else to see the data, encrypt it. This is even more important if you travel and use a laptop. What would you lose if your laptop was lost or stolen? If the data that would be exposed would damage you, make sure you take steps to encrypt it. The program Pretty Good Privacy, otherwise known as PGP, can do this for you as well.
- Keep data you don't want seen on removable storage media like an Iomega Zip disk. Every time you get up from the computer, take your data disk with you. If this is the approach you take, make doubly sure you keep a backup of your removable disk. It's easy to forget that disk when doing your routine backups.

Monitoring and Disabling Web Usage

One of the more troublesome aspects of computers in the workplace today is the Internet. How do you give your employees access to the Internet without dropping all their productive time down the drain? That question is on the minds of many employers today. Our three steps can make your company's Internet access open, yet appropriate:

- Post your intended-use policy clearly. Make sure employees know what is and isn't appropriate use of the Internet. Make sure they know that their communications may be monitored. A good place to post the policy is on the front page of your intranet. To see examples of policies, search for `network usage policies` on any Internet search engine. This search also finds information on policies and legal developments regarding employers' monitoring of their employees' email and Web activities.

- Use a proxy server as your company's gateway to the Internet. This enables you to control what information is being sent to remote servers in the form of headers (see Figure 13.1) and logs which sites are being accessed. Having your users log in to the proxy server before accessing the Internet helps them remember to keep their Web browsing business related. It also gives you a log of who went where should the need arise to know. Netscape (`www.netscape.com/servers`) and Microsoft (`backoffice.microsoft.com`) have powerful proxy servers.

Unofficially... Your Web browser reports several pieces of information on you to remote Web servers. Don't let it be a mystery to you. Come by The Naked PC Web site (`www.thenakedpc.com`) and we'll show you what information you are passing along when you go Web surfing.

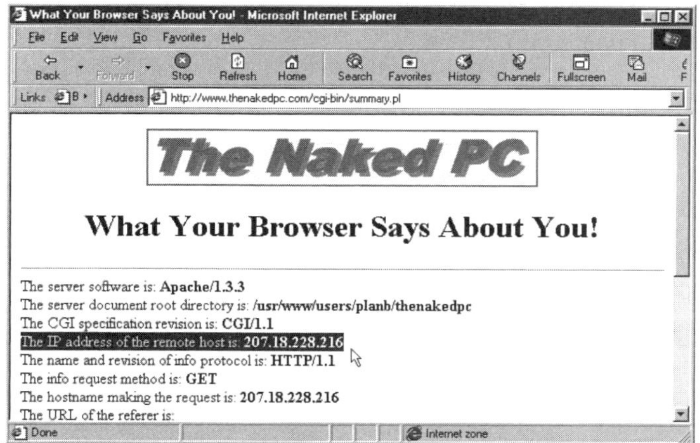

Figure 13.1 Your Web browser provides information to Web sites.

- If you feel a need to block access to certain Web sites, you can configure your proxy server to do this for you. If you need to control access on only one or two machines, you might prefer to use a tool such as Net Nanny. Net Nanny is also good for keeping a log of which programs and types of Web sites are accessed from a given PC. We'll talk more about Net Nanny later in this chapter.

- Don't be shy about following up on any indications of Internet abuse. The more quickly you deal with it, the fewer problems you'll have. When employees start to feel as if they are "getting away with it," your problems increase. Learn how to research the Internet history and cache files that Internet Explorer and Netscape Navigator leave behind. Yes, employees can erase these files, but the emptiness of the files is often as revealing as the contents of the files.

These steps are obviously more complex than what our brief descriptions reveal. But you can see how we are taking our basic principles and applying them to limit the access various people have to your data. You will be able to take these steps and evaluate any effort at protecting data in the future. Just ask yourself these questions:

- Do we have a policy?
- Is it posted publicly?
- Can we tell who has been where?
- What do we do when we have a problem?

Following the preceding steps will help you control the use of the Internet in your company. Here are some tips for keeping a modicum of personal privacy on the Internet. We recommend you share them with your employees as well.

- Use an email alias when necessary. We'll talk about aliases more in Chapter 17, "Making Internet Connections."
- Know what information is available on the Internet about you. In Chapter 17 you'll learn how to track down information on an Internet Service Provider. You can use the same general concepts to research information on yourself. You'll also want to look at the articles at Sherlock@ (`www.intermediacy.com/sherlock`), which we mention in the search engine section of Chapter 18, "Choosing Internet

Applications." Keep track of what is showing up about you so that you won't be surprised later.

- Don't include too much personal information in your email signatures. An easy test for deciding whether you should include something in your signature is to ask yourself this question. If a stranger used some of the information, would you be wary and ask "Where did you find that out?" If the answer is yes, you probably shouldn't include it.
- If you have a personal Web site, limit the amount of personal information you leave there. This includes phone numbers, addresses, and other information. It's a cinch to find a personal Web site after you know the person's email address. After that, you can locate the ISP to pinpoint a city. Most people live in close proximity to their ISP. Follow this with a quick lookup on a service such as AnyWho (www.anywho.com), and the snooper will have your phone number, address, and directions from their house to yours—complete with a map—all within about 15 minutes. Now we don't say all this to scare you. Just keep your common sense when you put information on the Internet.
- For transmitting highly sensitive information, use encryption. We'll talk about PGP later in this chapter.
- Protect the privacy of others with whom you come in contact.
- Read Esther Dyson's article on privacy at www.edventure.com/release1/0498.html.

Watch Out!
When you start seeing information about yourself that isn't accurate, always follow up privately first rather than publicly. Remember that everything you post on the Internet is stored and indexed somewhere. You don't want a message jotted off in anger and haste coming back to haunt you years from now.

Bright Idea
Esther Dyson has written a very good article on privacy and what steps you can follow to protect your privacy. Read *Privacy Protection: Time to Think Locally and Act Globally* to understand the issues with privacy today.

PGP: What Is It and Why Do I Need It?

Pretty Good Privacy (PGP) was written by Phil Zimmerman of Phil's Pretty Good Software and released on the Internet. Soon after, the United States government accused him of exporting munitions when people outside the United States downloaded PGP. The investigation, which went on for several years, has since been dropped. The PGP license is very specific about who and where PGP can be used. Obtaining your software from a recognized software dealer—in this case Network

Bright Idea
Don't waste time wandering around the Network Associates Web site. It's poorly laid out and confusing. Go to the site map and quickly locate where the information you are seeking is hiding. In this case, you are looking for PGP-related files.

Associates (www.nai.com)—ensures that you are not violating the law.

The Network Associates Web site has two versions of PGP to download. The free version of PGP uses the International Data Encryption Algorithm (IDEA) method of encryption. The fee-based version uses either IDEA or RSA from RSA Data Security. RSA was used in older versions of PGP, and you may need it if some of the people you exchange encrypted messages with use older versions. It should be noted that the freeware version of PGP is for personal use only. Limitations also exist on which version you can purchase or download depending on what country you live in.

PGP uses public key encryption to do its magic. With public key encryption, you create two secret keys: a public key and a private key. The public key is distributed to anyone who wishes to send you encrypted files. The private key should be kept private and never be shared with anyone. When an associate of yours encrypts a file to be sent to you, that associate uses your public key. After the file is encrypted with the public key, it cannot be opened by anyone unless the private key is used. Even the person who encrypted the message cannot decrypt the message without the private key. This is why it is important to keep your private key private. The advantage of public key cryptography is that the channel you use to exchange the keys and the data does not need to be secure. Therefore, emailing your public key to another individual will not compromise your encryption integrity.

After you install the software, you have a new icon in your system tray and, depending on your email client, a new menu to choose from when working on email. We'll talk about email clients and which ones support PGP in Chapter 18, "Choosing Internet Applications." The installation automatically steps you through creating your public and private key set. Your private key uses a pass phrase for authentication. When the installation prompts you for a phrase, be sure to pick one you can remember but that won't be easily guessed.

PGP offers you four major benefits:

- You can send and receive encrypted email for privacy. Without the private key and the pass phrase, mail encrypted with your public key cannot be read (see Figure 13.2). Without encryption, email is like a postcard. Anyone who sees it can read the message. If you are not comfortable sending a message that anybody can read, you should take steps to encrypt it.

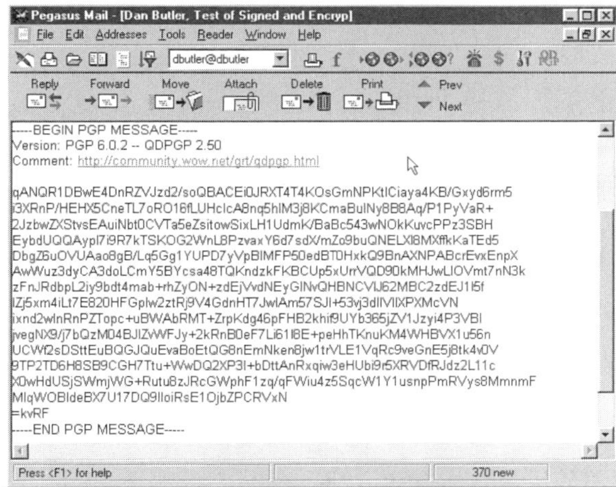

Figure 13.2
Mail encrypted with PGP is unreadable without the private key.

- Document signing. Rather than encrypt an entire document, you can have PGP place a small digital signature at the end of an email message or other document. Another person can then use PGP to determine that the document actually came from you and whether it has been altered since you signed it (see Figure 13.3). Think of it as verification that you really said what this document says you are saying.

- You can encrypt sensitive files on your hard drive to keep snooping eyes out of them. You can encrypt a file in addition to password protecting it. Running PGP on a file ensures that you will be the only one looking at the contents of that file.

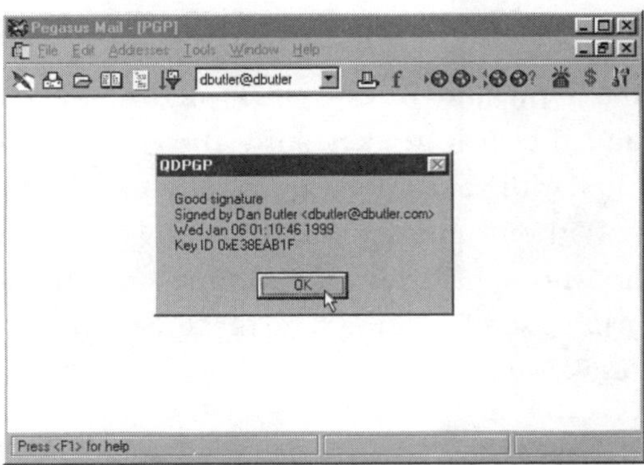

Figure 13.3
PGP can verify the identity of the sender.

- You can create PGP Disks on your hard drive. PGP Disks are areas of your hard drive set aside to hold encrypted files. Rather than encrypting each file, the PGP Disk encrypts everything stored on it. Without the private key and the pass phrase, a PGP Disk is unusable. This can be used very effectively to protect sensitive data on laptops.

Watch Out!
When you create your key set, make extra sure you can remember your pass phrase. If you forget it, you will never be able to read any document encrypted with that key again. Make sure you have a written copy stored in a very safe place.

Now you have PGP installed and know what it can do. The next step is to distribute your public key so people can send encrypted documents to you or verify the digital signatures on documents that you send them. Simply exchange public keys with each person you want to communicate privately with, and you'll soon be on your way.

Child Proofing

One day, on arriving home from work, we found Explorer open on the computer and all our Desktop files renamed to gibberish. Several long hours later, all the files were named correctly and moved to their proper locations. The three-year-old was no longer able to access the computer room!

Watch Out!
If you leave encrypted files on your hard drive, don't forget to back them up. Even though casual snoops won't be able to see the contents of your files, they may be inclined to delete them for you instead. Make sure you have a backup.

As the previous true story shows, children present special circumstances when it comes to protecting your data. Their actions aren't always malicious in intent but can cause a harmful end result all the same. We could easily make a comparison between an eager, yet untrained, employee and some of the children we know. They like to experiment and figure out how things work. The three-year-old mentioned earlier didn't know he was hurting anything; he was just doing what he saw daddy doing. Later in this chapter, we'll list a few easy-to-follow steps to help avoid problems of this kind.

Letting children have access to your computer presents many of the same problems that giving employees access does. Fortunately, the same solutions work in both instances; it's the implementation that changes.

Giving Them Access to Only What They Need

Again we refer you to our simple outline. Decide what access the children can have to your machine, make sure the policy is clearly understood, and follow up abuses promptly.

In Chapter 7, "Going Further with Additional Customizations," we talked about creating a program group for your children that contains all the programs you allow them to run. After you decide what access the children should have, put all the programs they are allowed to use in this special group. Show them how to open the group and launch the programs.

After giving them access to what they can run, take steps to deny access to programs they aren't allowed to run. The following are a few ways to do that:

- Many programs, such as Quicken, enable you to password protect your data files. Use these passwords as necessary.
- Put your important data on a PGP Disk to keep it safe from experimenting computer users. You could also keep your data on a removable Iomega Zip Disk.
- Set a password on your screen saver and require that the children ask permission to access the computer. Reiterate your policies as you open the computer for their access.
- Make sensitive files harder to locate by putting them on a different partition. Then hide that partition with Tweak UI's My Computer tab. Note that a knowledgeable child could make the partition visible again the same way.

- Use Net Nanny to turn off access to various system functions that your children don't really need to access (see Figure 13.4). Some of these include disabling the registry editor, the system device manager, and access to the DOS prompt.

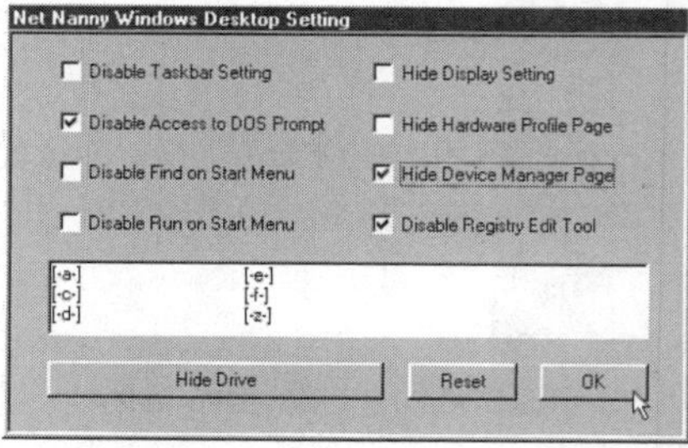

Figure 13.4
Net Nanny can control access to many parts of your system.

Securing Your Important Stuff from Them

Using the Net Nanny software, you can make changes that help protect your data from curious young eyes. In its Security settings you can set various hard drives to be invisible to Explorer, disable the MS-DOS prompt, disable registry editing, and disable most other ways to access and change your system data. When you need to use your PC or make these kinds of changes, simply turn off Net Nanny using the System Administrator password.

Watch Out!
The changes we talk about here protect you from curious eyes, but not from persistent, adamant, find-it-at-any-cost eyes. If your data is important enough to keep it hidden at all costs, be sure to use some sort of removable storage device to hold it.

Monitoring and Disabling Web Usage

The same suggestions we laid out for managing employees' use of the Internet apply to your children as well. Certainly, young children should not be allowed on the Internet unattended. This should apply to older children as well. A good practice is to keep the PC in a visible location in the house. Children are more likely to stay within their bounds when they know their actions can be seen.

Throughout this chapter we've mentioned Net Nanny from Net Nanny Software Ltd. (`www.netnanny.com`) as a tool for securing your PC and filtering the Internet. Although this is not the only filtering software available, it is one of the more flexible. With Net Nanny you can control access to any application on your computer. The software also lets you edit what it will or will not allow access to. Because it works on any application, the Net Nanny is always active. In Figure 13.5 we have opened an email that contains forbidden words, and Net Nanny has blocked them from displaying.

Figure 13.5
Net Nanny can block out objectionable text onscreen.

We like this product because it gives you control over the process. If you decide to block a certain application, Web site, or piece of data, you can. To see more products of this type, go to Yahoo!'s listing of Internet Blocking and Filtering Resources at `http://dir.yahoo.com/Business_and_Economy/Companies/Computers/Software/Internet/Blocking_and_Filtering/`.

If you don't want to actively filter what can be viewed on the Internet, you can set Net Nanny to work silently and keep a log of all activity. The log can help you determine whether you need to filter (see Figure 13.6).

It's important that you don't expect a filtering program to do the complete task of monitoring Internet usage for you. These programs are only tools that can help you in allowing the type of Internet usage that you deem appropriate for your household.

Security and Administration

By now you are probably wondering if securing your PC is going to be a full-time job. It doesn't have to be. Keep your security measures in perspective, and you will find them more of a help than a hindrance.

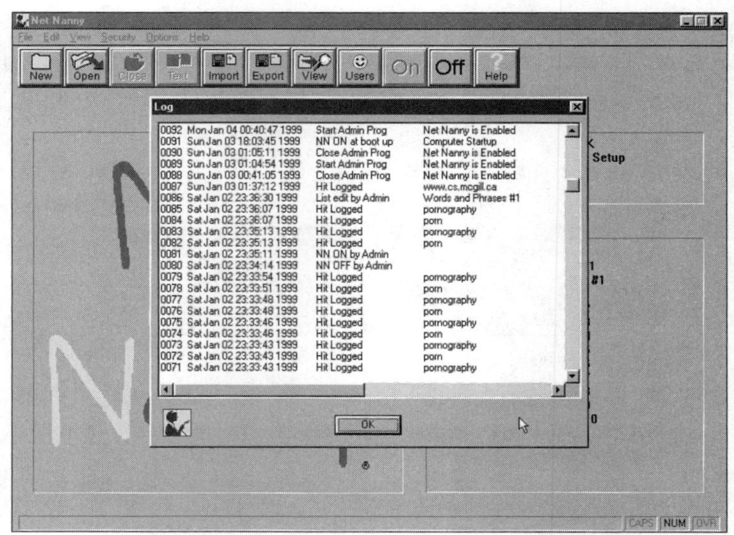

Figure 13.6 Net Nanny keeps a log of activity on your system.

How Far Do You Need to Go?

All the time you are putting security and privacy measures into place, keep asking yourself if it's really necessary. Yes, privacy is important. Yes, security is important. But is the time you are spending to secure your information more important than the information itself? Make sure you balance these factors. Don't spend time protecting data that isn't really that important. Here's a key question you can ask yourself: "What's the worst that can happen if this data isn't secure?" If you can live with the answer to that question, don't spend too much time securing it. However, that doesn't mean you should just put it out in the open.

Practical Security Measures

Use your common sense when implementing security measures. The more complex your system, the less likely you are to use it. The following are a few tips to make your task easier:

- Choose passwords that are easy to remember but difficult to guess. Use a combination of special characters, !@#$%^&*(), and words to create good passwords. An example is HaM&eGGS. Here we capitalized the consonants and tied the two words together with a special character.

- When you have visitors, turn your PC off to discourage even casual snooping. This is especially important when small children are visiting, because they seem to be drawn to computers.
- Although it's nice to have a good view for working, be careful how visible your PC is from outside your home. The same goes for your nice peripheral devices.
- When you buy new hardware such as a printer or scanner, don't just toss the box out on the curb with the rest of your garbage for pick up. That's like advertising what you have available. Instead, store the box in the attic for the next time you move.

Bright Idea
Don't put your system password on a Post-it note and stick it on your monitor! If you must write down the password, be sure to store it in a location away from the computer that uses the password. Don't tell anyone about this location, either.

Administering a Secure PC

Administering your secure PC does not have to be a daunting task. Follow these simple steps to keep on top of things:

- Look through any log files regularly for activity that you deem suspicious. By looking at the logs frequently, you'll learn what they contain and will be able to spot inconsistencies or changes quickly.
- Be aware of which programs are on your PC and watch for recent additions.
- Never install software from an unknown source without first scanning it for viruses. Eliminating viruses before they start is the best prevention. We covered virus scanning in detail in Chapter 9, "Preparing for Disaster."
- Be aware of any changes in your system's performance. Be sure to keep detailed notes in your system journal.

Chapter Ending

- Clearly state your policies.
- Authenticate access to your systems.
- Follow up problems swiftly.
- Use encryption to protect your data.
- Monitor usage of your system.

PART IV

Choosing More Software

Chapter 14

Deciding on Common Applications

CHOOSING THE PRIMARY SOFTWARE APPLICATIONS for your computer depends on the type of work you need to accomplish. If you do computer-aided design work, you'll have some very specific software requirements that differ from what you would need for general office management (for example, word processing and a spreadsheet program). But some common computer tasks everyone needs to perform, and this chapter focuses on the best software for the tasks we all have to deal with, day in and day out.

In the Mesozoic era of computers, there were the big four software categories: word processor, spreadsheet, charting/graphics, and database. Graphics applications have become less important as a separate category, as mainstream word processors and spreadsheet programs now allow you to do sophisticated charting right inside your documents and worksheets. The same goes for databases. It used to be that if you wanted to keep something as simple as an address book, you would build one to suit your needs using a full-blown database application such as dBASE. Now specialty applications meet most database needs.

The most ubiquitous applications today are word processing, spreadsheets, email, general utilities, games, and software related to the Internet. You will learn about Internet connections in Chapter 17, "Making Internet Connections," and choosing the right viewer in Chapter 18, "Choosing Internet Applications." In addition, we cover games in Chapter 15, "Learning, Education, and Gaming." In this chapter you learn the common everyday applications that everyone needs.

Must-Have Software

Some applications are needed on everyone's computer. The most important are a good word processor and a spreadsheet application. Other essential applications include an email program and one or two utilities that we wouldn't want to be without. The good news is that chances are your computer came from the factory with these applications preinstalled.

It's true that not everyone may want or use email or some of the utilities we find indispensable. After all, so much is dependent on what you use your computer for, but word processing and spreadsheets are common to everyone, so we'll not only recommend what we think are the best of breed for these two categories, we'll give you our hard-won tips for getting them set up and running "out of the box."

Word Processor: Microsoft Word

The most commonly installed collection of applications is Microsoft Office. Office comes in several flavors, but even the most basic version of Office includes two of the applications that we have on our must-have list: Microsoft Word and Microsoft Excel. Microsoft Word is without a doubt the most powerful (and popular) word processor available on the PC for all-around use. (See Figure 14.1.)

Word can function in a variety of capacities:

- Plain vanilla "electronic typewriter"
- Standard business or home-use word processor
- Personalized business or home-use word processor (personalized using Word's powerful toolbar and template

customization features or Word's macro programming language, Visual Basic for Applications)

- Customized front-end publication engine with multi-tier client/server database connectivity

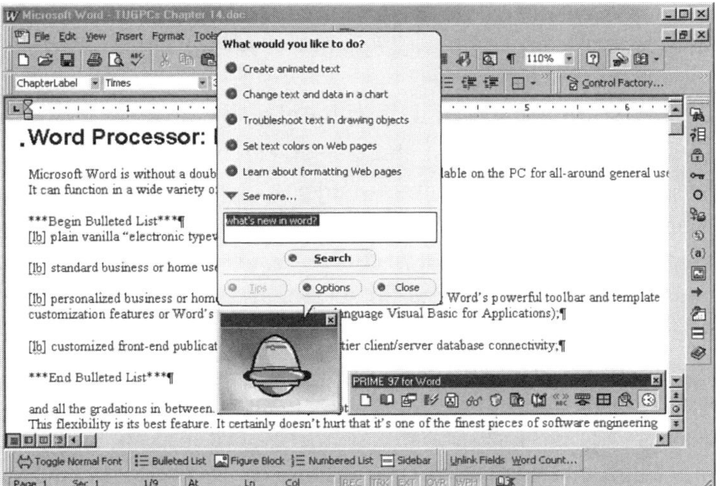

Figure 14.1
Microsoft Word in all its glory.

And Word covers all the gradations in between. Word can readily adapt itself as you use it, and it also allows *you* to easily adapt it. This flexibility is its best feature. It certainly doesn't hurt that it's one of the finest pieces of software engineering ever conceived in the history of mankind. In this section we'll cover the things you absolutely must do when you first start using Word.

Getting the Latest Version

Whether you own only Word or the entire Office suite, it's vitally important that you have the very latest version. Microsoft application maintenance releases are typically free to registered users. Free means you call a Microsoft toll-free number, answer some questions, and they ship out a new CD at no charge to you—not even charging shipping and handling. That's the easy part. The hard part is that Microsoft has a nasty tendency to post patches on its Web site and try to convince you that you really need the only patch, not the replacement CD. *Don't believe a word of it!*

Moneysaver
To order a maintenance release of any version of Microsoft Office, call 800-370-9272 in the U.S.

You absolutely and positively always want the replacement CD. Yes, this means you have to uninstall and reinstall the product in question, but because the patches and the patching process itself are often buggier than the unpatched version you're upgrading, the replacement CD is your best choice.

Customizing Where Your Documents Are Saved

The next most important change you can make is to tell Word precisely where you want your files to be saved. By default, Word (and its Office sibling applications) saves files to your My Documents folder. Earlier in this book, we recommended that you use a data folder hierarchy such as `D:\Data` followed by subfolders to segregate documents by their audience or purpose. If you adhere to that hierarchy, or even if you use your own, you'll be much better able to find documents after they've been saved, as long as you don't drop everything willy nilly into one single folder like My Documents. We recommend you set your default documents folder to `D:\Data\Winword\Docs` (see Figure 14.2).

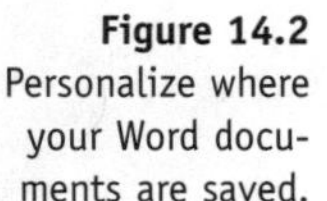

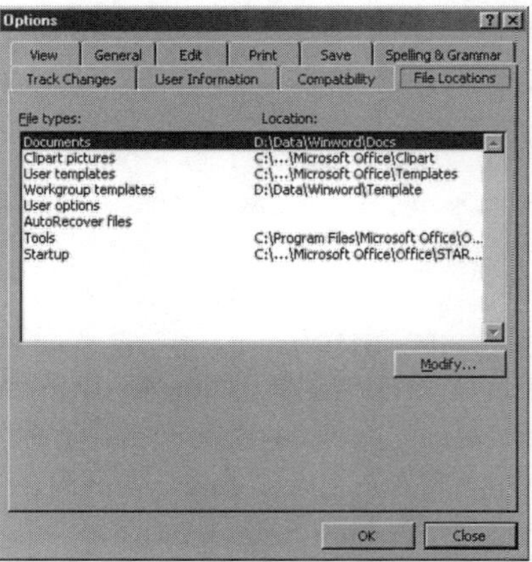

Figure 14.2
Personalize where your Word documents are saved.

You can have subfolders below Docs (for example, `Docs\Church`, `Docs\PTA`, `Docs\Clients`), and they're just a click away when you prepare to save a new file. Follow these steps:

1. In Word, select Tools, choose Options, and then click the File Locations tab.
2. Select the Documents item in the File Types list box, click the Modify button, navigate to the desired folder, click OK, and then click OK again to dismiss the dialog box.

Maximizing Word's Most Recently Used File List

Oddly, Word's designers aimed for the lowest common denominator here. As you open and save files, Word adds each file's filename to the Most Recently Used (MRU) file list. This convenient list is then quickly accessible at the bottom of the File menu; perform the following steps:

1. Press the Alt key.
2. Press the F key.
3. Press the number key associated with the file in the list (1 for the very last file you saved and closed, 2 for the second-to-last such file, and so on).

Word comes from the factory with the MRU limited to the last four files, but the maximum is nine. The fix here is easy; follow these steps:

1. Select Tools.
2. Choose Options.
3. Select the General tab.
4. Crank the Recently Used File List number up to 9.
5. Click OK (see Figure 14.3).

Personalizing Word's Master Template

When you create a new document by clicking the New icon at the far left edge of Word's main toolbar (it's officially called the Standard toolbar) Word effectively makes a copy of the file called Normal.dot and presents it to you as your new document. Normal.dot is Word's master template and is always open when Word is running.

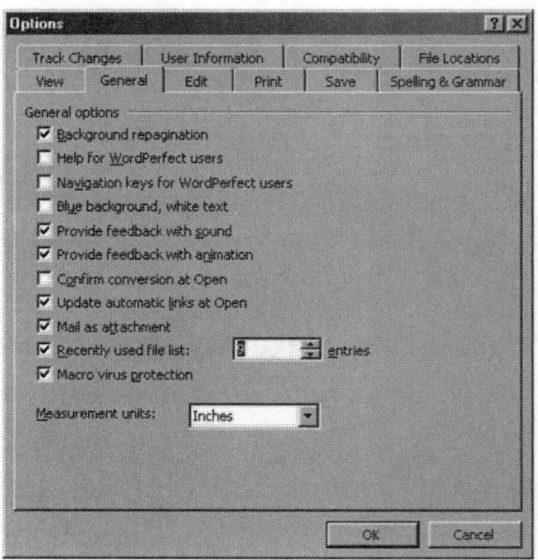

Figure 14.3 Maximize the number of documents Word stores on its Most Recently Used file list.

If you change something in Normal.dot, all new blank documents you create from that point forward reflect those changes. For example, to change your default font (the font Word automatically uses in new blank documents), the place to do it is inside Normal.dot. Ditto for page margin settings, heading styles, inter-paragraph spacing, headers and footers, and so on.

As an example of how you can make a change to Normal.dot and have it ripple through to all new blank documents, consider changing Word from its default Normal view to Page Layout view, which gives you a WYSIWYG (what you see is what you get) view of your document.

1. Click File, select Open, navigate to `C:\Program Files\Microsoft Office\Office\Templates`, and open Normal.dot.
2. Click View, and then Page Layout.
3. Click File, and then Close.
4. If you then exit Word and restart it, all your new documents come up in Page Layout view.

Using Smart Cut and Paste

Word's "smart" cut and paste feature is just one of dozens of what Microsoft calls IntelliSense features in Word and in Office. When smart cut and paste is turned on, Word intelligently closes in extra spaces left by a cut operation and adds spaces where appropriate when pasting. This feature is on by default (to change it, select Tools, Options, Edit, and click Use Smart Cut and Paste to deselect it).

Optimizing File Save Options

Word comes with a plethora of File Save preferences. The most important is Always Create Backup Copy. By selecting the former, you tell Word to make a backup copy of your file every time you save it. Each new backup copy replaces the previous copy. This backup file is given the name `Backup of [original filename here].wbk` and is stored in the same folder as the original. You may want to weed out some or all of these backup copies (for inactive files) at an interval of your choosing, as part of your ongoing system maintenance. To verify that this setting is on, follow these steps:

1. Select Tools.
2. Choose Options.
3. Select the Save tab.
4. Check the Always Create Backup Copy check box.
5. Click OK (see Figure 14.4).

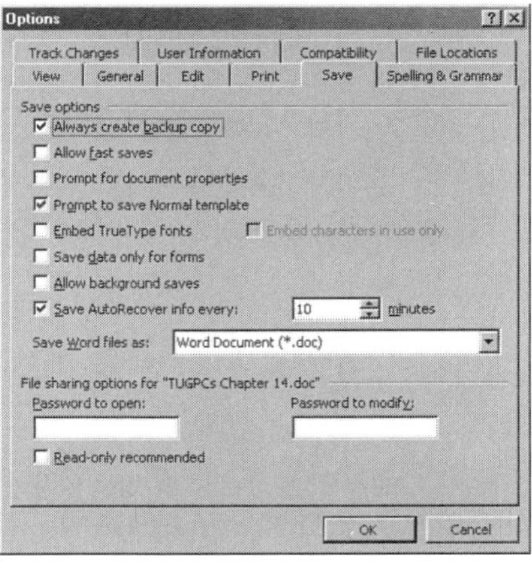

Figure 14.4
Get your file Save options just right.

Customizing Word's Toolbars

One of the most invigorating things you can do in any Office application is to customize its toolbars. A toolbar is a collection of buttons and menus in one place; when clicked, each one invokes a specific feature. Toolbars are new and improved versions of drop-down menus because you can get something useful to happen with one click instead of drilling down into multiple levels of menus and dialog boxes. You can easily customize toolbars in Word, Excel, PowerPoint, Access, and some versions of Outlook. Figure 14.5 shows Word's Customize dialog box. To get there, follow these steps:

1. Select Tools.
2. Choose Customize.
3. Select the Commands tab.
4. At this point you can press the F1 key to get help learning how to use the dialog box to customize your toolbars.
5. Click Close when done.

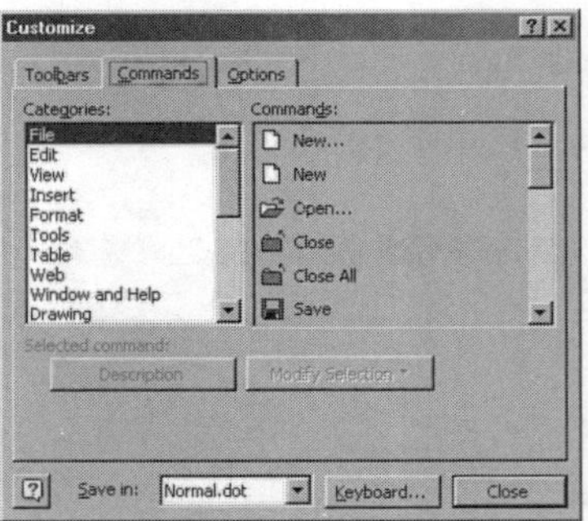

Figure 14.5 Word's powerful Customize dialog box.

From the factory, Word's toolbars are what we call the demoware versions. They're certainly not the working versions, and they must have been spawned to make for good road-trip demos by Microsoft sales reps. Changing toolbars to suit the way you work will dramatically increase your productivity. Saving a few clicks here and there may not seem like a good return on investment at first, but it makes a big difference over the long haul. Trust us.

The approach we suggest is to leave Word's built-in toolbars alone initially and create your own version(s) from scratch. By creating a new toolbar (rather than modifying a default toolbar) you can swap the new for the old and have a fully customized interface. If you ever want to revert to the default, just turn the custom toolbar off and the default toolbar on. Everyone has individual ideas about how best to customize Word's toolbars. The important thing is, as the saying goes, "Just do it." (Let Word's help system help you quickly create a new toolbar: ask the Office Assistant for `create a toolbar` and select the Create a Toolbar topic for step-by-step instructions.) The benefits are tremendous. You'll be amazed how quickly you come to love a Word environment refitted just the way you like it.

Bright Idea
Plenty of information on toolbars is available in Word's help system. Ask the Office Assistant for `toolbars` and navigate from there.

Changing Your User Preferences

All the Office applications share a semi-common dialog box called Options. (Outlook is the exception; it has an Options dialog box but the tabs are much different from those in Access, Excel, PowerPoint, and Word.) You get there by selecting Tools and then choosing Options. We have already described the most critical of these settings, but critical is a matter of degree. It's very important that you take the time to study each one of these tabs and its settings and get them just right for your work style. The tabs in Word's Options dialog box are titled as follows:

- View—Controls how documents appear onscreen and sets various Window objects such as the status bar, scrollbars, and so on.
- General—Sets a variety of critical multipurpose options ranging from background repagination to macro virus protection; essentially, this tab includes settings that didn't quite fit on any of the other tabs.
- Edit—Controls how Word behaves when you edit text and graphics.
- Print—Sets various printing preferences.
- Save—Specifies how you want Word to save documents.

- Spelling & Grammar—Controls automatic spell-checking features, the custom dictionary, and onscreen grammar notifications.
- Track Changes—Sets what Word does when you use its powerful revision-marking feature.
- User Information—Controls your personal information: name, initials, and postal mailing address.
- Compatibility—Determines how Word behaves when working with a document that originated with another word processor.
- File Locations—Sets the locations of key folders used by Word.

Bright Idea
Word's Help file lacks index entries on the Options dialog box's user preferences. However, you can get brief help (displayed in a small ToolTip-like pop-up window) for individual controls on each of the dialog box's tabs. To do this, use the What's This technique we described in Chapter 5, "Configuring Your New PC."

If you're a Word junkie who likes to fine-tune it until it really sings, you'll be interested in our series of Office add-ins. For Word, we have versions for Word 6, 95, 97, and 2000. We also have versions for Excel 5, 95, 97, and 2000. Each version of PRIME for Word includes several dozen features designed specifically to improve your productivity with Word. All PRIME add-ins are distributed as shareware, and each utility comes with a lifetime, 100%, no questions asked, money-back guarantee. PC World has selected PRIME 97 for Word 97 as a Top Ten Office Add-In! For more information go to `www.primeconsulting.com/software/index.html`.

Spreadsheet: Microsoft Excel

Excel is Microsoft's most venerable application. Like its younger sibling, Word, it too can function in a variety of capacities (see Figure 14.6). Its power also stems from the fact that a spreadsheet application—whether it's the progenitor VisiCalc or today's Excel—is a number-crunching engine with extensive programming capabilities. A formula is, after all, a small program. This programming power is subtly hidden from users who might ordinarily be a bit timid about doing some "programming" but who routinely and with relish, design complex, multilayered, what-if budgetary models.

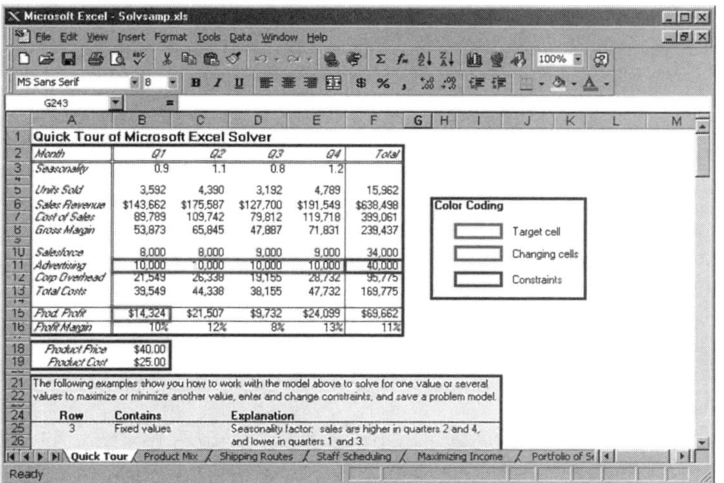

Figure 14.6
Microsoft Excel in all its glory.

Excel's capabilities fall into this range:

- Electronic ledger sheet with automatic subtotals and grand totals
- Flat-file database
- Statistical analysis platform (for example, cross-tabulation with PivotTables)
- Fully customized business management (personalized using Excel's macro programming language Visual Basic for Applications)
- Customized front-end calculation/graphing/charting engine with multi-tier client/server database connectivity

The following items define the most important actions you can take when you first begin working with any version of Excel:

- Getting the latest version—It's imperative that you install the very latest version. See our earlier instructions for how to contact Microsoft for a free replacement CD of any version of Excel that has been interim updated.
- Customizing where your workbooks are saved—As with Word, Excel saves files to your My Documents folder. For Excel, we recommend a home base of `D:\Data\Excel`.

Setting this preference is different in Excel than in Word; in Excel select Tools, Options, General, and then you must manually type in the default file location.

- Maximizing Excel's most recently used file list—You should crank Excel's MRU setting to the maximum of 9; the steps are the same as those described earlier for Word.
- Customizing Excel's toolbars—You'll want to replace Excel's demoware toolbars as quickly as you did Word's. See the section "Customizing Word's Toolbars."

Using AutoEntry

Excel enables you to set an option called AutoEntry that moves the active cell up, down, left, or right every time you press the Enter key. But we much prefer that the active cell *not* move when we press Enter, and we think you will too. To turn this feature off, select Tools, Options, Edit, and clear the Move Selection After Enter check box, and then click OK.

Always Create Backup

Excel and Word come with different file-saving options. Excel has no explicit user interface to match Word's fast save, background save, and AutoRecovery features (Excel does ship with an add-in called AutoSave that saves workbooks automatically at specified intervals, but it's not easy to find or activate for someone new to Excel). Excel does have a built-in Always Create Backup option that partly matches Word's Always Create Backup Copy feature, but it's buried beneath layers of user-interface muck. The steps in Excel are the following:

1. Open the workbook of interest.
2. Select File.
3. Choose Save As.
4. Click the Options button.
5. Check the Always Create Backup check box (see Figure 14.7).
6. Click OK, then click Save; when prompted whether you want to replace the file of the same name, select Yes.

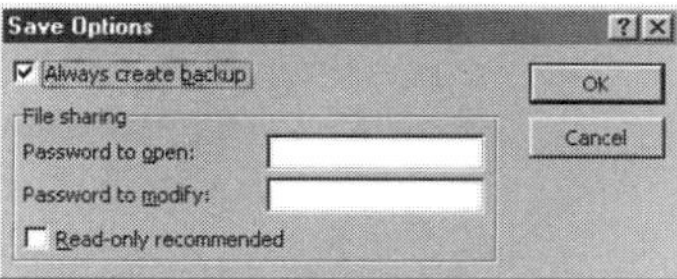

Figure 14.7
Excel's Always Create Backup option is confusingly different from Word's.

Changing Your User Preferences

As we mentioned earlier, Office applications share a semi-common dialog box called Options that's available by selecting Tools and then choosing Options. We have just described the most important of these settings for Excel. You should carefully study each one of these settings and get them just right for your work style. The tabs in Excel's Options dialog box are

- View—Controls how workbooks appear onscreen and sets various Window objects such as status bar, formula bar, scrollbars, gridlines, and so on.
- Calculation—Sets how workbooks are calculated.
- Edit—Controls how Excel behaves when you edit cells and other objects on a worksheet.
- General—Sets a variety of critical multipurpose options ranging from range reference style to macro virus protection; essentially, this tab includes settings that didn't quite fit on any of the other tabs.
- Transition—Controls whether (and how) Excel helps you make the transition from a different spreadsheet program—for example, from Lotus 1-2-3.
- Custom Lists—Allows you to edit Excel's built-in lists or define your own (used for AutoFill to create new cell values based on entering just one value; for example, typing `Monday` into a cell and populating the neighboring cells with the other days of the week).
- Chart—Sets a variety of chart-related options.
- Color—Enables you to customize your color palette.

Watch Out!
Excel's Always Create Backup preference must be set individually for each workbook you want to back up, whereas the setting in Word conveniently applies to all documents.

Page Breaks

Excel can show you where page boundaries fall inside the current worksheet. It does so using dashed lines. These boundaries are relative to a page defined by whatever your current print settings are. This helpful feature is off by default; to turn it on, follow these steps:

1. Select Tools.
2. Choose Options.
3. Select the View tab.
4. In the Window Options section, check the Page Breaks check box.
5. Click OK.

Email: Software Galore

If you don't plan to use email on your computer, you can skip this section. But if you plan to send and receive email, you're going to need an email application to handle the display and composing of your incoming and outgoing email traffic. No clear-cut consensus exists as to the "best" email program on the market (even among as small a group as the authors of this book), so a definitive recommendation is not possible. But we can point out the best bets.

The first consideration is the type of email package you use at work. If you use a given email package at the office, you might want to stick with that version on your home system as well. You're no doubt familiar with it and you'll have the most luck if you need to dial in and interact with your company's email system.

On the other hand, if you want an email application that doesn't need to connect up to a corporate email server, you have a variety of choices. Microsoft Outlook comes with the Microsoft Office suite and includes an address book, a calendar, a to-do list, task scheduling, journaling, and all the goodies found in a full-featured PIM (personal information manager) in addition to your email inbox. Lee and Jim are big proponents of Outlook and have co-authored a book on this very package (*Outlook Annoyances*, O'Reilly and Associates, ISBN: 1-56592-384-7). Dan, however, hates Outlook and favors the freeware package Pegasus Mail by David Harris (www.pegasus.usa.com), which does not try to deal with all the aspects of a PIM and instead, focuses on email. Another very popular shareware email package is Eudora by Qualcomm (www.eudora.com). You would not go far wrong with any of the email programs we mention in this section.

Microsoft has a free email-only program called Outlook Express (http://windowsupdate.microsoft.com/default.htm) that not only handles your email, but it doubles as a very nice Internet newsgroup reader.

If you favor Netscape for your browser, you can use their free, and very credible, email reader—Messenger (www.netscape.com/browsers/index.html).

Numerous other offerings are available—some free, some commercialware, some combined with PIMs or contact managers, and some standalone packages doing only email. We'll talk more about email programs in Chapter 18, "Choosing Internet Applications."

Mouse: Microsoft IntelliMouse and IntelliPoint

This is really a combination of hardware and software, both from Microsoft, but this mouse is so incredibly useful we think all users should have one on their systems. The mouse is called an IntelliMouse and its associated software is called IntelliPoint. Officially, IntelliMouse refers to the device and IntelliPoint refers to the software controlling the mouse.

The IntelliMouse looks just like the traditional Microsoft mouse, but with a wheel between the left and right buttons. The wheel can be rolled or pressed down (clicked). The idea is for you to roll the wheel up (forward) with your middle finger, which scrolls the current document (or whatever is displayed onscreen) up. Roll the wheel down and the document scrolls down. Extensive, clever extensions exist to this. Two quick examples are to click the wheel to enter a scroll-locked mode and to use the Ctrl key and the wheel to zoom within certain applications, such as Internet Explorer, Excel, or Word. The mouse and wheel are smartly calibrated to match the scroll speed on the screen to the speed with which you're maneuvering the device. Nice. Very nice. Get one. You may never use scrollbars again.

File Compression: Nico Mak's WinZip

It's impossible for us to envision using a PC for more than 10 minutes without needing to compress or uncompress a file. It's considered good manners to send any email attachments compressed in a format such as Zip or Uuencode; therefore, simply by reading your email you're likely to encounter a compressed file. If you have a batch of documents that you need to archive temporarily or permanently, zipping them is the perfect space-saving solution. If you download any freeware or shareware software, or if you need any new drivers, patches, maintenance releases, and the like from your existing vendors, you're bound to encounter zip files by the dozens.

Nico Mak's award-winning WinZip is far and away the best tool for file compression/decompression. It presents a familiar, easy-to-use but powerful graphical user interface shell around underlying compression/decompression algorithms. WinZip has a wizard-like interface for folks new to zip files, and it sports a Classic interface for more advanced users. The Classic interface melds right into Windows Explorer, allowing you to drag and drop files and showing options right on a file's right-click context menu. For example, you could right-click the file Autobiography.doc, and with one deft mouse move select the "Zip to Autobiography.zip" menu item—an instant zip file with the same root filename as the original.

Other neat features include virus-scanner interfacing, automatic handling of multidisk zips, a free Internet Browser Support add-on for a one-click download/open of zipped files on the Internet, the capability to zip/unzip with or without preserving the selected folder structure, password protection, the capability to view files from inside the zip container, and support for other popular Internet file formats (tar, gzip,

UUencode, BinHex, and MIME). Through external programs, ARJ, LZH, and ARC files are supported. Also included is an install/try/uninstall feature to assist with testing new programs; and more.

For more information or to download a shareware evaluation copy of WinZip, go to www.winzip.com.

Unofficially...
The term zip originated with a file compression product called PKZIP, developed by PKWARE, Inc. (PK are the initials of PKZIP's author Phillip Katz.)

Other Applications to Consider

We've found the applications mentioned in this section to be very useful given the type of work we do, and we recommend you seriously consider them. Don't discount an application such as Quick View or PaintShop Pro because they're shareware; this is becoming a mainstream way to market applications as computer users become more sophisticated and want to try an application before they purchase it.

Viewing Files: Quick View

Whether you realize it or not, you need a file viewer program. The good news is that Windows comes with one called Quick View. In Windows Explorer you can right-click a file and select Quick View from the pop-up menu. This handy little utility lets you view the contents of a files without having to open its parent application. For example, you can view a Word document in Quick View even if you don't have Word installed on your computer. Not only can you see the content, but you get a fully formatted view of how that file looks in its parent application.

Quick View was created for Microsoft to include in Windows by Inso (www.inso.com/qvp/qvpdwnld.htm). Inso also sells a more full-featured version of the utility called Quick View Plus ($59). The Plus version enables you to do things you cannot do in the version bundled with Windows, such as copying from the View window and printing documents without having the parent application on the local computer. This is a very neat and useful must-have utility.

Making Presentations: PowerPoint

If you need to do slide presentations, we recommend Microsoft PowerPoint. This application is bundled with Office Professional and is also available separately.

PowerPoint lends itself to many of the customization tips we mentioned earlier for Word and Excel, and it is quite versatile. You can create slide shows with a number of multimedia effects for sound and animation, as well as convert a slide show into a series of Web pages—all automatically.

Database: Microsoft Access

If you do actual database development, our recommendation is Microsoft Access. Access is bundled with the Professional and Premium versions of Office and is also available separately. Access data can be manipulated from either Word or Excel.

Access 2000 uses the Microsoft Data Engine (MDE), a replacement for the older JET database engine in Access 97. MDE uses stored procedures for developing server applications that use Access 2000 as their front-end and makes it easier to transparently upgrade to SQL Server 7 should your database demands grow.

Graphics: PaintShop Pro

PaintShop Pro is a low-cost application ($99 for a 30-day shareware trial version) that does what programs costing hundreds of dollars more offer. Create, retouch, and manage graphical images. You can even create animation in its Animation Shop companion program.

What we really like about PaintShop Pro is that a wealth of information about this popular program is floating around on the Internet that lets you create outstanding graphics, even if you don't know beans about graphics packages. The best site we've come across, with loads of step-by-step instructions for creating professional quality graphics, is Web Graphics on a Budget (`http://mardiweb.com/web/`).

Choosing and Evaluating Applications

You've seen our recommendations, but obviously we didn't cover every category of software. Fortunately, you can take advantage of a number of resources to find the right piece of software for the task at hand.

Most of the computer magazines (*PC Magazine*, *PC/Computing*, and *PC World*, to name just a few of our favorites) publish reviews of software. These reviews are "round-ups," in which they cover the top applications in a given category; they are a good source of information when you are looking to select a program for purchase. In addition, sites such as ReviewFinder collect links to various reviews and categorize them for easy searching. Here are the places we recommend you check when researching a product or software category to find an application that will suit your needs.

- PC Labs Software Reviews (`www.zdnet.com/pcmag/pclabs/sof/index.html`)—This is the Ziff-Davis (publisher of *PC Magazine*, *PC Week*, *PC/Computing*) review lab that covers hundreds of software products in every category you can imagine.
- PC World Top 400 (`www.pcworld.com/top400/0,1375,software,00.html`)—Access to the latest published reviews by category.
- ReviewFinder (`www.reviewfinder.com/0/0.htm`)—This site collects links to reviews on other sites around the Internet and categorizes them so you can zero in on the application you are interested in.
- The Naked PC (`www.thenakedpc.com`)—In our biweekly publication, *The Naked PC*, we routinely evaluate software packages, always with a sharp eye on best of breed. We also provide ongoing coverage on using and customizing the must-have applications listed in this chapter.
- Lockergnome (`www.lockergnome.com/issues/`)—Lockergnome is a daily electronic newsletter that has reviewed thousands of computer programs and has a searchable archive of past issues. The only trick here is that you'll have to know the name of the application because reviews are not categorized.

After you've decided on the software you want, check Bottom Dollar (`www.bottomdollar.com/software.html`), a search engine on the Internet that goes out and finds you the best deal available on a given piece of software from 15 vendors. Bottom Dollar makes finding the best price easy and lets you order the software right from their site.

Chapter Ending

- The must-have list of software no PC owner should be without: Microsoft Word and Microsoft Excel.
- Other applications we strongly recommend are: Nico Mak's WinZip, Inso Quick View, Microsoft PowerPoint, Microsoft Access, and PaintShop Pro.
- A plethora of Web resources are available to help you choose, evaluate, find, and buy applications, and we guide you through them.

Chapter 15

Learning, Education, and Gaming

IF YOU HAVE HAD A PC in your home for any length of time, you know that it can soon become the center of attention. With so many programs and games to choose from, you can easily purchase more software than you would ever have time to work your way through. In this chapter we talk about using your PC for education—both for the children and the adults. You learn where to look and how to evaluate learning software. We also look at games and show you how to keep them running without tearing your hair out.

Education for the Kids

Look around the shelves of any computer store and you will see many software titles claiming to be educational. Unfortunately, in today's market, educational often means that a program asks your child the ABCs or has them count to 10 once or twice. True educational programs actually teach their subject. Some of these are entertaining as well.

> "Putting a computer in front of a child and expecting it to teach him is like putting a book under his pillow, only more expensive.
> —Anon."

To get the most out of your educational software purchases, start by defining what you want. Decide exactly the kind of skill or information you want your child to learn. This may sound obvious, but it's a lot like grocery shopping. You know what you need before you go to the store but after you're there, your attention wanders to the pleasing sales displays and attractively packaged items. Sometimes you don't even make it home with what you set out to buy in the first place. So it is with software—except a lot more money is spent on the packaging.

With all the free information available on the Internet, would you still want to consider buying CD-ROM programs? In our opinion, the answer is yes. Consider the following advantages:

- Accessibility—Having your data on a CD-ROM makes it quick and easy to access. On the Internet you spend much of your time tracking down the data you want.
- Quality—With a CD-ROM program, you already know where to look, and you have an idea of the quality of the information provider before you start. On the Internet you don't always know the quality of the information you find.
- Speed—Downloading lots of large graphics files or movies can take time. A CD-ROM can contain as much as 650 megabytes of information. DVDs can hold 8 to 16 times that much. Downloading only 10 megabytes of video over the Internet can take as long as an hour over a standard modem connection.

You'll want to get reviews of any computer software prior to purchasing it. Look for software reviews in the following places:

Bright Idea
Try software before you buy. Many libraries have software you can check out. Your intended title may be available there. Be sure to virus-scan anything you check out prior to installation.

- Computer magazines usually have a column on software review. If the current issue doesn't have what you want, see if the magazine's Web site has back issues.
- SuperKids (`www.superkids.com`) keeps current reviews and price surveys of educational software titles.
- Ask your friends, neighbors, and coworkers if they have any experience with educational games.
- Demonstration copies of many programs are available from the manufacturer's Web site.

- Do a general search of the Internet for the title you are interested in.

Just a few short years ago, the Internet was largely composed of information from universities and colleges around the world. Much of this information still exists and is quite useful. The following is a quick list of some sites we routinely use to find educational resources on the Internet.

- Study Web (`www.studyweb.com`)—This site has lots of links pointing to resources on the Internet. They are broken down by the typical areas of study you'll be looking for.
- Microsoft in Education (`www.microsoft.com/education/`)—This site has resources for teachers and students. You'll find templates, tutorials, and other tools to help you use your computer for education.
- Schoolhouse (`encarta.msn.com/schoolhouse/`)—This site is an addition to Microsoft's Encarta program, with special emphasis on education.
- Ask an Expert (`njnie.dl.stevens-tech.edu/curriculum/aska.html`)—This site provides links to experts in many fields to whom you can email questions.
- Learn2.com: The Ability Utility (`www.learn2.com`)—This site has tutorials on many topics.

Many people are opting to educate their children at home. Whether or not you have chosen to do this, the homeschool community has resources you can use in locating educational material for your own children. You will find complete lesson plans, pointers to helpful software, and other useful information.

The following are a few Internet sites to get you started:

- Jon's Homeschool Resource Page (`www.midnightbeach.com/hs/`)—One of the longest-running homeschool resource centers on the Internet. You'll find plenty of jumping-off points here to keep you busy.

- Homeschool World (www.home-school.com)—Contains many articles about education.
- Home-Ed Magazine (www.midnightbeach.com/hs)—This site has back issues online and pointers to many resources, both online and off.

Education for the Adults

Adults will find many resources for education on the Internet and through CD-ROM programs available at your local software store. The same tips we gave you for evaluating children's CD-ROMs apply here as well. As always, the most important thing is to have a goal before you go searching for information. Without a goal, you will spend a lot of time chasing down dead ends instead of gaining the information you desire.

Some types of education are easier to present electronically than others. Many things require hands-on training to fully grasp the concept. Keep this in mind when evaluating educational resources for your PC.

Computer programming lends itself well to computer-based training (CBT). You'll find plenty of information related to the various programming languages, both on and off the Internet. Tracking down the data can be a daunting task. Later in this chapter, you'll learn our "Instant Expert" method of searching out resources on the Internet.

Bright Idea
Reading on the Internet can be tedious and tiring. If you have a lot of text to read, print it out first. If the page contains hyperlinks, consider writing the URLs next to the text to save time finding them later.

The Internet is being used effectively for distance learning. For some time, universities have offered courses via video, correspondence, radio, or television. Classes taught over the Internet are either live or in recorded sessions. For live classes, various software packages are used to communicate among the students and the class. Before you decide to take a course over the Internet, make sure you are prepared to spend the time needed to complete the material. Audio and video technologies are still not all they can be.

Here are some distance-learning resources you can access on the Internet:

- The Mining Co. Guide to Distance Learning (distancelearn.miningco.com) is a good guide to the distance learning options available. You'll find several articles and links to many courses being offered.

- ZD Net University (www.zdu.com) offers $5 courses that give you a quick overview of technical topics (see Figure 15.1). You probably won't become an expert, but you will know if this is a topic you want to pursue further. You may also be able to pick up enough knowledge to get you through the task at hand.

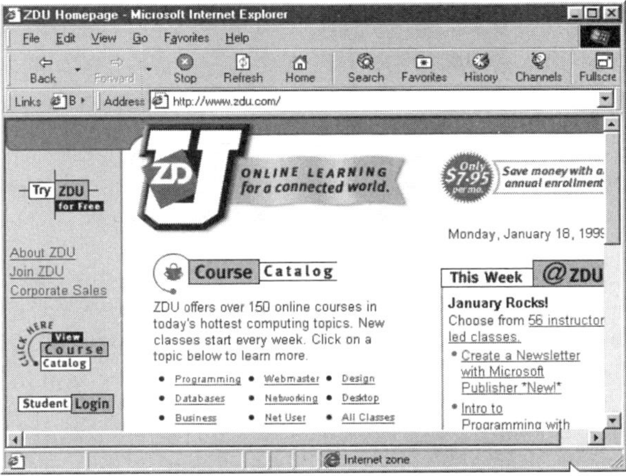

Figure 15.1
ZD University lets you take computer courses online.

- New Promise Online Education (www.newpromise.com) has a searchable catalog of 3,700 distance-learning courses across multiple accredited schools.
- The Learning Web (www.learning-web.com) breaks Internet-based courses down by category. Some courses are free.
- The World Lecture Hall (www.utexas.edu/world/lecture/) lists Internet-based courses from around the world.
- Sarah's Distance Learning Page (www.geocities.com/Athens/7519/) provides information from the viewpoint of student and teacher. Her link list is very thorough and gives you plenty of jumping-off points.

The Instant Expert Method

With all the information available on the Internet, how do you condense and digest it into a usable form? Further, how do you separate the wheat from the chaff? These two tasks can be daunting indeed. In Chapter 18, "Choosing Internet Applications," we'll talk about search engines and some tools that can help you cut down your searching time considerably.

What we want to discuss now is our "Instant Expert" method of Internet research. Generally this will work on any topic and will enable you to get up to speed very quickly on the concepts, lingo, and resources available. Although we cannot guarantee that you will succeed in any undertaking, this method will at least give you a big head start. In Chapter 20, "Taming Technical Support," we will discuss how to quickly search out answers to specific technical questions.

As always, the most important thing to do is define what information you are looking for before setting out on a search. What is the topic of your inquiry? What information do you already know? What information do you know you need to know? Write these answers down and you'll be off to a great start.

Read the Frequently Asked Questions (FAQ) for Your Selected Topic

Start at `www.faqs.org`, where the FAQs for all the Usenet newsgroups are archived, as shown in Figure 15.2. Be careful with the information and don't just accept it as true. Generally, the more technical the subject, the better the quality of the FAQ. The FAQ will be just what it says—a list of the questions most frequently asked to members of the newsgroup. Usually you will also find pointers to Web sites, books, mailing lists, and other helpful information. Use this as your jumping-off point and you will already have the answers to the questions that will occur to you as you continue your research. Following all the leads in a good FAQ can take quite some time and may supply all the information you need on some topics.

Figure 15.2
Faqs.org categorizes all the FAQs for you.

Browse Through Newsgroups Associated with This Topic

Start at DejaNews (`www.dejanews.com`) where you can look through all the postings to any particular group. You will have the names of the groups to look for from the FAQ information.

Unofficially...
When you look for information in Usenet newsgroups, try to find a group that isn't in the "alt." hierarchy. The quality of information goes up dramatically and is more targeted in other groups.

When you look through the newsgroup postings, you want to pay attention to the following things:

- Remember who answers questions thoroughly and consistently.
- See which topics come up consistently because those are probably some of the questions you'll be having soon. A combination of these topics and the FAQ will answer 80 percent of the questions you'll have.
- Check the home pages of people who put a link in their posts. Often, the home pages will contain a good list of links relevant to your topic.
- Start learning the lingo of the group. The more familiar you are with the language used on a topic, the more you'll be able to glean information as you read.
- Learn the personality of the newsgroup. Some groups have a certain "personality" in which the members are able to joke with one another, or they may even appear to be

Bright Idea
Start your own glossary when you are becoming the "Instant Expert." Make notes of acronyms, inside terms, and phrases that you don't understand. Your personal glossary will keep your time expenditures to a minimum.

rude. Learn what is going on before you join in the group so you won't be surprised by the answers.

Use the Internet Directories

If you've followed the steps so far, you should have a good idea of what you can expect from the Internet as a source of information on your chosen topic. You should also have a good idea of what resources are available outside the Internet in bookstores, software, magazines, and newsletters. The next step is to go to the Internet directories Yahoo! (`www.yahoo.com`) and The Mining Co. (`www.miningco.com`). Note that Internet directories are different from search engines because they have already categorized Web sites for you.

Many people make the Internet directories their first stop. We prefer to put it in the middle, after the FAQ and general newsgroup search. Because you did some research before coming to the directory, you'll find it easy to work through the mass of information provided there. You'll already have been to some of the sites and be familiar with what types of information to expect. You will not be as easily impressed by a slick-looking site that has questionable information. Your personal glossary will keep you from getting lost in the lingo. In short, you have already laid the groundwork for making quick work of the sites you find here.

Browse Discussion Boards

Your next stop should be to the various discussion boards around the Internet that pertain to your topic. An example of this sort of board is our own The Annoyance Board (`www.PRIMEConsulting.com/cgi-local/annoy.pl`), which deals with technical computer issues. Many of these boards exist and they are sometimes more personal and less congested than Usenet newsgroups. Finding these boards is another matter altogether. Here is an easy way to track down discussion boards. First, most discussion boards on run on two software programs: wwwboard and webbbs. These boards post their name at the bottom of the page. So searching for your topic and one of these names will turn up many discussion boards for you to choose from. As an example, if we were searching for discussion boards on juggling at the AltaVista search engine (www.altavista.com), we would type in either

```
+"juggle" +wwwboard
```

or

```
+"juggle" +webbbs
```

These searches will return a large number of hits. Do not feel overwhelmed, but realize that each message on the discussion board shows up as a separate hit. Look at the URLs that the search returned, and you quickly whittle this list down to size.

Search for Discussion Boards on the Internet

Spend some time familiarizing yourself with the different discussion boards. Bookmark the ones that are useful to you. Follow some of the same suggestions we made earlier for newsgroups in picking out the more knowledgeable and helpful members of the group, visiting their Web sites, and generally getting more familiar with the entire topic. Discussion boards can be more personal than Usenet newsgroups and often have far fewer daily messages to wade through.

Books

The Internet has many free books available. The trick is knowing where to look. Following are some sites that offer complete books on many topics. Companies that put current books online are betting that if a book is helpful and contains good information, it will be more valuable to you on your desk than on your screen. In addition to current books, many books from the past have full-text versions online.

- The Online Books Page (www.cs.cmu.edu/books.html) has pointers to more than 8,000 complete books online.
- The WWW Virtual Library (vlib.stanford.edu/Overview.html) keeps a good categorized list of pointers on the Internet broken down by topic.

Bright Idea
Don't ignore online books that you already own. You can download electronic books to your local hard drive and search their contents using the Windows Find Files utility. Often this is faster than trying to find information in the printed copy.

- Project Gutenburg (`www.promo.net/pg/index.html`) is a long-running Internet attempt at putting books online. Many of these books are classics or older works. The Other Links section of the site will point you to other online book depositories.
- ZD Net Help Channel (`www.zdnet.com/zdhelp`) has sample chapters from computer technology books available for reading online.
- Macmillan Personal Bookshelf (`www.mcp.com/personal`) allows you to read the full text of many computer books online.

Gaming

For many people, the central focus of their computer is playing games. It seems that games are often the first programs to push the hardware and use all the fancy new gizmos available. Staying on the cutting edge of computer gaming also means staying on the cutting edge of computer hardware. If you plan on playing lots of games, be prepared to change your computers configuration often to match each game you are playing.

Moneysaver
Staying at the top of the technology curve can be expensive. Keep your costs down by finding someone who likes to stay just behind the curve to buy your old hardware from you.

In Chapter 1, "Decisions on the Basic System Components," we discussed 3D video cards and DVD drives. Many games require this hardware just to run. The DVD drive carries great promise. Presently, games are coming on multiple CD-ROMS that must be switched in and out as you play. DVD has enough space on a disk to hold many CD-ROMS, thus eliminating the need for this switching.

Before you buy any game, be sure to check the hardware requirements printed on the side of the box. You will usually find a minimum and a recommended requirement listed. The minimum configuration will give you less-than-satisfactory performance. Think of the recommended configuration as your reference point. If your system meets the recommended configuration, the program usually performs well. The requirement you should be most concerned about is the amount of RAM required. For good game performance, you should have

8MB to 12MB more RAM than the recommended configuration calls for. Don't buy the game unless you have plenty of hardware to drive it.

To keep up with the latest information on gaming, the Internet is the way to go. With information being broadcast almost instantly, the Internet will be weeks or months ahead of print magazines. The following are a couple of jumping-off points to keep current with games:

- Intelligamer (`www.intelligamer.com`) offers reviews broken down by category, interviews with game developers, and strategy guides. In addition, you will find jumping-off points to other gaming sites.
- CNET Gamecenter (`www.gamecenter.com`) features hardware and software reviews, sneak peeks, tips, and discussion boards.
- Gamezone (`www.gamezone.com`) features demo versions of many games in addition to reviews and tips.

Chapter Ending

- Set learning objectives before purchasing educational software.
- Find reviews of the software you are interested in.
- Decide whether a CD-ROM or gathering information directly from the Internet is best for the data you are seeking.
- Use the "Instant Expert" method to familiarize yourself with new topics.
- Check the hardware requirements for games.

Chapter 16

Managing Devices and Device Drivers

IN THIS CHAPTER WE DISCUSS the issues surrounding the addition of system components that extend the capabilities of your computer. Trackballs, mice, monitors, modems, joysticks, imaging devices that include printers and scanners, telephones, hardware for video editing—you name it and something is sure to be available that you can plug into your computer to help you do even more.

It's important that you know how these peripherals and devices can be connected to your system and what you have to be aware of to keep your computer stable and running smoothly. Different technologies are at work here, along with some surprising limitations that you can slam into headfirst, if you're not careful.

Generally, a piece of equipment is referred to as a device if it goes inside your computer's chassis (sound and video cards, for example), whereas a peripheral is connected to your computer but is physically external to your system (such as your monitor or printer). But this set of definitions is strained a bit when you consider that a number of devices (such as modems and hard drives) can be either internal or external.

What IRQs Mean to You

The technology in today's computers keeps getting better. Processors are faster and memory is now measured in megabytes instead of kilobytes. Hard disks keep getting bigger and faster. Everything is improving so fast that it might surprise you how many limitations you can run into when adding devices and peripherals to your system.

Nothing drives this point home better than interrupt requests (IRQs). Each device attached to your computer uses its assigned IRQ to get the computer's attention. You've only got so many IRQs, and after you run out, you might not be able to hook that new gizmo you just bought to your computer.

To see how the IRQs are allocated to devices on your system, do the following:

1. Right-click the My Computer icon and choose Properties from the pop-up menu.
2. Click the Device Manager tab.
3. Make sure Computer is selected (this is the first entry in the hierarchy).
4. Click the Properties button.
5. Select the View Resources tab and check the Interrupt request (IRQ) option button.

This lists all the IRQs on your system (see Figure 16.1).

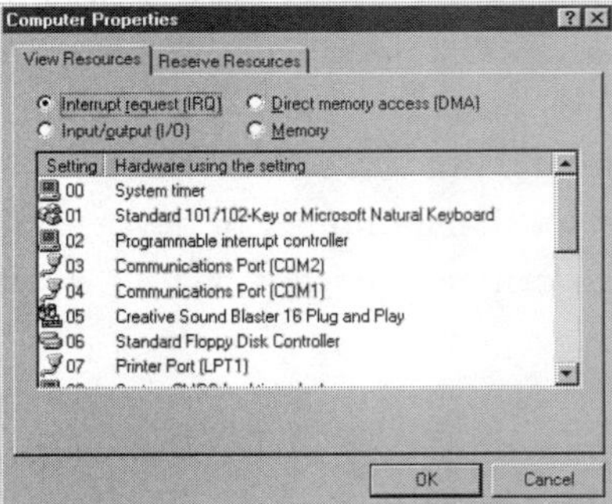

Figure 16.1
Getting a list of IRQ assignments.

Several IRQs used by the system itself are not available for you to use when adding devices. These are 0 (zero) for the system timer, 1 for the keyboard, 3 and 4, which are reserved for communication ports, and so on. At most, you'll have perhaps 7 of the possible 16 IRQs available for adding new components to your system. The basic things every computer needs—a video card, a printer port, a hard drive controller, and the like—use some of these discretionary IRQs, further reducing the number available.

Although you may think you can hook up any number of peripheral goodies that catch your eye, after you are out of IRQs, you may be out of luck. You can wind up having to uninstall and remove one peripheral before you can add a new one. This is especially true if you are using older hardware that does not support new bus technology such as Firewire or the new Universal Serial Bus ports, which we cover later in this chapter.

Bright Idea
Get a printout of your system's IRQ assignments by calling up the Device Manager, selecting Computer, and then clicking the Print button. Select System summary and you'll get a printed listing of key system information, including assigned IRQs.

If more than one device tries to access a given IRQ, you run the risk of crashing your system. Although computers now sport four communications ports (COM1 through COM4), they have to share the two available communication IRQs, IRQ3 and IRQ4, with no more than one device at a time actually using the IRQ. To make matters worse, some devices are happy only if they can have a specific IRQ. Most sound cards want IRQ5, for example, which was originally slated to be the LPT2 port. Because few users actually use the two LPT (line printer) ports that computers are configured for, this is usually not a problem unless your network card also wants IRQ5.

In Chapter 4, "When and When Not to Assemble Your PC," we talked about how the System Properties dialog box's Device Manager tab flags any devices that have a problem with an exclamation mark inside a yellow circle. For example, if two devices are in conflict over a given IRQ or if a device can't find an available IRQ to use, you'll get the exclamation mark warning sign on that item in Device Manager. By selecting the device and then clicking the Properties button, you can determine exactly what the conflict is (see Figure 16.2).

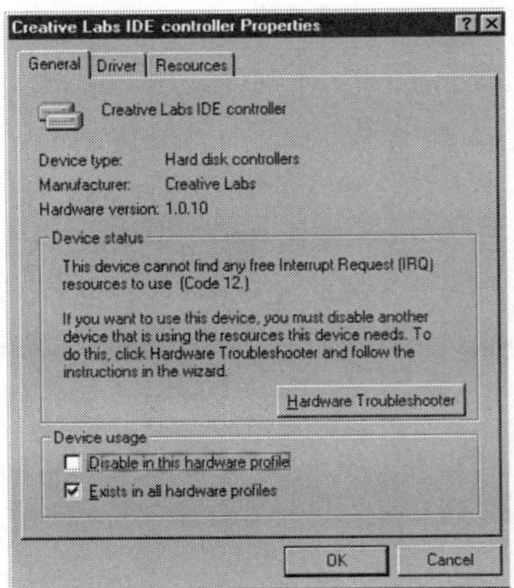

Figure 16.2
Checking the Device status section to determine where a conflict is occurring.

Watch Out!
On a lab computer with no available IRQs, we replaced a dead serial mouse with a new PS/2 mouse. The serial mouse used COM2 (IRQ3), but when we installed the new mouse in the PS/2 port, it grabbed IRQ5 and Windows played a quick game of musical IRQs. When the music stopped, the sound card was left without an IRQ and without warning, it suddenly stopped working. Beware when adding new hardware; Windows may reassign your IRQs for you and cause devices to stop working.

In this example, the device cannot find "any free Interrupt Request (IRQ) resources." When this occurs, you have to make some hard choices about what devices you have to keep operational and which you can disable or uninstall.

Another issue you may run into is I/O usage. Each device requires a block (sometimes more than one block) of system memory to call its own. And often, only so many contiguous blocks of memory are available to go around, resulting in another potential source of conflict. The good news is that Windows does a fairly good job of managing both IRQs and memory (especially with the newer plug-and-play devices), so you don't usually have a problem unless you load up your system with devices and start to run out of IRQs.

When you do have a conflict, you can open that item's Properties dialog box in Device Manager, select the Resources tab and uncheck the Use Automatic Settings check box, and then select the Resource type that is in conflict (the IRQ or the I/O memory, for example). Click the Change Setting button and you can search for a setting that is not in conflict with other devices (see Figure 16.3).

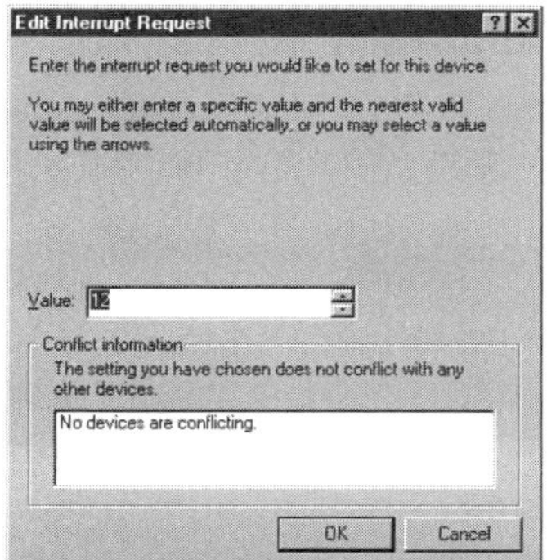

Figure 16.3 Resetting the IRQ for a device to eliminate a conflict.

Peripherals and Switchboxes

One way to save on IRQs is to hook up similar devices up to a single port (using one IRQ) via a mechanical switchbox. Commonly called AB boxes or data switches, these boxes can be used to connect a number of comparable devices.

For example, several external devices and peripherals other than printers can be connected to a computer via the parallel port (usually LPT1 using IRQ7). Often they have a *pass-through* connector, which lets you connect the printer to the same cable as the other device being hooked up to the LPT port. The problem is that frequently this does not work as seamlessly as advertised, creating instability in one or both devices. You can eliminate these problems by connecting the computer's LPT port to a switchbox and using the box to select between the different devices to ensure that only one device is connected to the port at a time.

Moneysaver
If you have more than one computer but do not have them networked, you can also use switchboxes to share parallel and serial devices between your computers.

We use switchboxes that let us connect a single mouse, a monitor, and a keyboard to a number of computers. With a flip of the switch, we're working on a different computer without leaving our regular workstation. This not only saves having to outfit each system with a keyboard, a monitor, and a mouse, but cuts down on the amount of desk space that these items would consume.

Monitors—The Essential Peripheral

Most people hook up the monitor when they set up the computer, and as long as it keeps working, they never give it another thought—except maybe to wish for a larger monitor. But a couple of things are important to keep in mind about monitors, the one peripheral that no computer is ever without.

Monitor Position

Probably the most important factor is positioning. In previous chapters we discussed how you should avoid putting your monitor where direct sunlight hits it, but where you position it in relation to where you sit is also a major consideration. Set up the monitor so you look slightly down at it to avoid neck strain. You want to be able to look at the monitor and the keyboard without a significant raising or lowering of the head. It's common to try to set the monitor so that it's at eye-level or even higher, but from experience, we've found this configuration very fatiguing over time.

Multiple Monitors

We talked about using switchboxes in a preceding section of this chapter and discussed using a simple switchbox to run several PCs from a single keyboard/mouse/monitor setup. But Windows 98 also supports running two monitors from a single PC, which expands your desktop and lets you run different applications on each screen. To do this, you need two video cards (PCI or AGP). One of the two monitors is designated as your primary monitor, and it displays all your desktop items when you start your computer.

Bright Idea
Run each of your two monitors at different screen and color resolutions; that way, you can develop Web pages or graphics and see how they'll look at 800×600 on one screen and at 1,024×768 on the other.

Drag icons from one computer screen to the other with your mouse. This can be a very useful and practical setup, enabling you to review a pertinent email message or spreadsheet, on one screen, while working on the report it relates to in your word processor, running on the other screen. Our favorite is developing Web pages in an HTML editor as the adjacent screen displays the page on a browser. Some users may find this much more useful than a single 19-inch or 21-inch monitor.

Printers

Traditional printers connect to your parallel port as either LPT1 (IRQ7) or LPT2 (IRQ5). You'll use at least one IRQ for your printer port even if you are printing to a network printer that is not physically connected to your computer.

Printers could easily take up an entire book of their own, and we only mention printers here because, like monitors, it's a peripheral that almost everyone has. It's important to keep your printer clean and as dust free as possible. That goes for your paper supply, too. Don't store your blank paper unwrapped where it can collect dust and be subjected to humidity or other environmental hazards—it can cause problems such as curling or increase the likelihood of paper jams.

Moneysaver
Spend some time with your printer's manual and learn how to perform routine cleaning maintenance. Perform this as part of your regular system maintenance. A clean printer has fewer problems, and this chore might save you a service call in the future.

If you have a black-and-white laser printer, always keep two toner cartridges—one in the printer and a replacement in your supply closet. Whenever you change the toner, order or buy a new one, thereby always having two on hand. Murphy's Law of Printing states that if you only have one cartridge, it will run out just before midnight on a Sunday when you have to get a major report printed for a 7:30 a.m. meeting on Monday.

Faster Peripheral Ports

Given the very real limitation in the number of IRQs and the relatively slow speeds at which the computer can drive most peripherals, a need exists to find a better, faster way to connect peripherals to your computer. Two technologies are starting to appear that do just that: Firewire and Universal Serial Ports.

What makes these technologies so exciting is that you can connect many devices to a single port, completely avoiding the problem of running out of the precious IRQs. They also support the *hot swapping* of peripherals; you just plug in a new peripheral and start using it—no installation, no fuss.

Improvements have also been made to the standard parallel printer port found on computers. Enhanced parallel ports, such as the Enhanced Capabilities Port and the Extended Capabilities Port, both increase the speed by which printers can communicate with computers.

Watch Out!
Firewire and USB support tree structures in which one device can serve as a "hub" for connecting other devices, but not all peripherals support this by providing the necessary connectors. To work around this, you can get *hubs* to let you connect multiple devices to a single port.

High Performance Serial Bus—Firewire

Firewire is a high-speed communications hardware standard that has been around since 1995, and it keeps threatening to become the "next big thing" any day now. It lets the PC transfer data between the CPU and connected peripherals at between 100 and 400 megabits per second (Mbps). This is fast, and it makes a standard serial connection snail-like by comparison at a pokey 115Kbps. What's more, you can connect up to 63 peripherals in a tree structure, in contrast to a linear A into B into C into D that is necessary in the current SCSI connection scheme.

Firewire also lets peripherals talk peer-to-peer, so your scanner could communicate with your printer, bypassing the computer entirely and not using any system resources.

You can find more expensive computer systems that come equipped with a Firewire serial port, which is becoming more commonplace. Devices that can take advantage of this technology are limited to digital video recorders and cameras at present, but this should change as more computers support Firewire.

Unofficially...
Technically, Firewire is the former name of this technology. Its official handle is IEEE 1394 or High Performance Serial Bus, so you may see it referred to as any of these terms. A Web site (`www.p1394pm.org/links.htm`) is available where you can get more information on the companies supporting this technology.

USB Ports

We mentioned the Universal Serial Bus (USB) briefly in Chapter 1, "Decisions on the Basic System Components." This technology is designed to make the "plug and play" of peripherals a reality. Simply plug a device into the USB port, and the computer automatically configures the device without the need to install cards in the computer, to reconfigure, or even to reboot the system.

USB runs at 12Mbps, and like Firewire, you can connect peripherals to other peripherals in a tree structure—up to 127 devices. However, USB is an order of magnitude slower than Firewire's 100Mbps–400Mbps range, so it is not a good candidate for faster devices such as hard disks or high-speed CD-ROMs, which would be better off on Firewire, when it becomes widely available, or the existing SCSI or ATA/IDE interfaces.

USB devices include peripherals such as modems, mice, monitors, joysticks, keyboards, CD-ROM drives (only up to 4x or 6x speeds), floppy or zip disk drives, printers, and scanners. You plug something in and start using it. This is very neat, saving time and effort.

Unofficially...
The outlets for the Universal Serial Bus ports on the back of your system are very different from either a standard serial port or a parallel port, so no danger exists of plugging a cable into the wrong port.

Windows 98 supports the USB and enables your PC to recognize USB peripherals. That's right—USB peripherals. To use USB, you need new devices (modems, mice, and so on) designed around this new bus technology. Because many of these devices don't exist yet, or didn't when Windows support for USB was coded, you still may need to install drivers for a given USB peripheral. Eventually, all this will work seamlessly (well, as seamlessly as these things ever work), and you will just plug in your peripheral and get started. Until the technology catches up with itself, however, some glitches will occur, such as having to manually install USB drivers.

Bright Idea
One of the best ways to find USB products is on the USB Org Web site (`www.usb.org`), which maintains a database of USB products that are available from various manufacturers.

Today, most new PCs come with USB ports, but finding peripherals to plug into them can be a bit of a challenge. Iomega has a USB Zip drive, and we've seen scanners, digital cameras, speakers, mice, and keyboards; therefore, USB products are starting to become widely available.

Converters are available, such as USB-to-parallel adapters, that enable you to connect a standard (non-USB) parallel printer to a USB port. USB-to-serial adapters are also available. Converters help by enabling you to utilize older, non-USB peripherals. As you replace older peripherals with newer equipment, these converters becomes less of an issue.

Enhanced Parallel Ports

The Enhanced Parallel Port (EPP) protocol was developed originally by a consortium of Intel, Xircom, and Zenith Data Systems to improve the performance of the standard parallel port while maintaining backward compatibility.

EPP was subsequently superseded by the IEEE 1284 bidirectional parallel port specification also known as the Enhanced Capabilities Port (ECP).

Both EPP and ECP are intended to increase the amount of data that can be pushed through the parallel port to get information to the printer faster. For this to happen, you have to first have a computer that is equipped with one of these newer ports. Second, the driver for the attached peripheral has to be written to take advantage of the specification. Third, the peripheral has to be designed to work with the faster data stream.

Bright Idea
You can find compliant products on the IEEE 1284 EPP/ECP Compatible Product List page (www.fapo.com/1284prod.htm).

Windows 95 and 98 both have built-in support for ECP. Although we think that USB or Firewire is a better way to go, if your existing equipment is ECP compliant, you should be taking advantage of it.

Networking to Share Peripherals

Sharing a monitor and keyboard between two PCs is easily done with a switchbox, as we've discussed, but more often you'll want to share peripherals such as printers and scanners (as well as actual data) among more than two computers.

The easiest way to do this is via some type of network. Windows makes this easy by supporting peer-to-peer networks, where each computer can share things, such as attached printers and hard disks, on an item-by-item basis with other computers. All you need is a network card in each computer and cabling to physically connect the machines together. The type of cabling, generally coaxial or twisted pair, is determined by the type of network cards you install (or that come installed) on your system. Although a complete tutorial on networking is beyond the scope of this book, we'll touch on the main points you have to consider when networking to share peripherals.

Windows 98 makes setting up a peer-to-peer network easy. You name each computer and assign them all to the same group. Right-click Network Neighborhood, and then select Properties. In the Network dialog box's Identification panel, you can set your computer and group names, as shown in Figure 16.4.

On the Configuration tab, you set up your networking protocols and determine whether you want to share print services and/or data files with others.

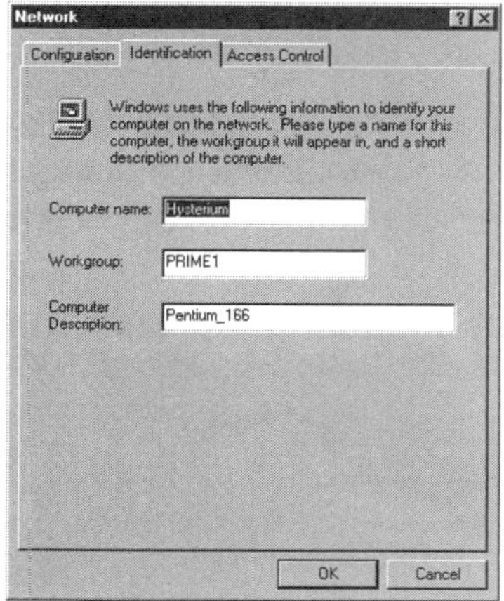

Figure 16.4
Each computer on a peer-to-peer network has a name and belongs to a group.

After you have set up your network and the computers can "see" each other, you can share drives and partitions by right-clicking them in Windows Explorer and selecting Sharing from the pop-up menu. You do the same thing with printers. Open up the My Computer window, double-click the Printers folder, and then right-click your attached printer and choose Sharing.

One of the biggest problems in sharing peripherals via a network is stringing the cable between your computers, especially if you are doing this at home. If all your PCs are in the same room, it's not so bad, but if you want to share the color printer in your den with the computer you installed for the kids in the playroom, you might have a cabling problem. Some alternatives exist to stringing wire down the hall and up the stairs.

The PassPort Plug-In Network from Intelogis is one such alternative. It uses the electrical wiring in your house to send signals between your computers and your printer. That's right, electrical wiring—as in the 110v electrical outlets that you have in each room. Admittedly it is a very scary concept, especially given all the warnings issued in this book about electrical spikes damaging your equipment. But the PassPort modules, according to Intelogis, provide adequate spike protection and are completely safe. Although we've used them ourselves, it wasn't during an electrical storm; you'll have to decide the risks given the electrical environment in which you work.

A PassPort Plug-In Network comes with two PC modules and one module for your printer. The modules plug directly into electrical wall outlets and connect to your PCs' parallel ports. A printer shared using this technology is not connected directly to a PC at all, but is just "plugged" into the wall outlet (see Figure 16.5).

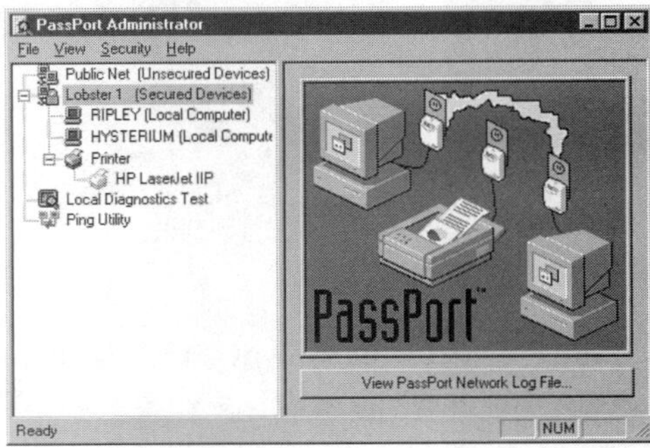

Figure 16.5 PassPort Administrator software manages both PCs and printers.

Module installation takes mere minutes and once connected, the modules recognize each other automatically. Setup is a snap using PassPort Administrator software that lists all the devices connected to the PassPort modules. Network cards are not required, and where the Administrator software is concerned, the emphasis is on ease of use. As an added benefit, PassPort comes with a version of Winproxy by Ositis Software that lets you share a single Internet connection between your networked computers.

Chapter Ending

- The number of available IRQs restricts the number of peripherals that can be connected to your system.
- Switchboxes can help manage peripherals.
- High-speed ports are making it easier to connect devices to your computer and increasing the speed at which they operate.
- Devices on a network can be easily shared.

PART V

Using the Internet

Chapter 17

Making Internet Connections

THIS CHAPTER COVERS HOW to get connected to the Internet. We'll give you tips to help you locate reliable Internet service. You'll learn all the right questions to ask to ensure that you get the Internet services you need and the reliability you deserve. We'll look at individual applications to use on the Internet in Chapter 18, "Choosing Internet Applications."

It used to be that you could get several types of connections to the Internet—SLIP, CSLIP, and PPP were the most common. Some required special scripts and software to get them running. Now all the networking software is built into Windows, and most Internet connections are done through a PPP (Point to Point Protocol) connection. Also gone are all the special scripting used to get connected. You will still run into this, but you won't have to figure it out on your own. The company requiring the scripting will supply it to you.

Choosing an ISP

Choosing an Internet Service Provider (ISP) is the most important part of the getting-connected equation. The quality of service and options offered vary greatly from one ISP to the next. The key to finding a good ISP is to know what you are

Unofficially... Don't get confused by all the acronyms you see being thrown around. IP, PPP, SLIP, SMTP, POP, and the rest all refer to protocols. A good rule of thumb is that when the acronym ends with a P, it is probably a protocol. Computer protocols define how two computers can exchange data and communicate with each other.

looking for. Unfortunately, this is often easier said than done. Most towns have a free computer newsletter such as *Computer Currents*, `www.currents.net`, which will have lots of ads by local ISPs. Visit the home pages of the ISPs and get a feel for the kinds of services that are available in your local area. We'll spend the rest of this chapter showing you how to narrow your choices and find a good ISP for your needs.

If you don't currently have an ISP, you'll want to find a way to access the Internet for researching ISP's. You may have access through your office or a friend's computer. Many public libraries have Internet access as well.

Types of ISPs

Several types of ISPs are available to choose from. We'll list each type and what you can expect from them along with the going rates at the time this was written. We'll talk about how you access the Internet later in this chapter. In some cases, such as cable Internet service, the access method and service provider are the same. Weigh your Internet needs carefully and don't pay for services you don't need. At the same time, you want the flexibility of expanding your services later without having to change your service completely.

- Proprietary national services—Examples of these are America Online (AOL), Microsoft Network (MSN), and CompuServe. Some force you to use their proprietary software instead of giving you a choice. You'll find several of these services in the Online Services folder on your desktop (see Figure 17.1). One advantage a service such as America Online offers is dial-up numbers in cities around the world. This can be useful if you travel a lot. Prices are around $19.95 per month, with additional charges for some services.

- Telephone companies—Most local and long distance telephone companies now offer Internet service. An advantage here is that you can be billed as part of your monthly phone statement. The disadvantage to these services is that you get telephone company customer service. If you like the customer service you get from your phone company, you might want to consider getting your Internet connection through them. Prices generally start at $19.95 per month and go up based on the services you purchase.

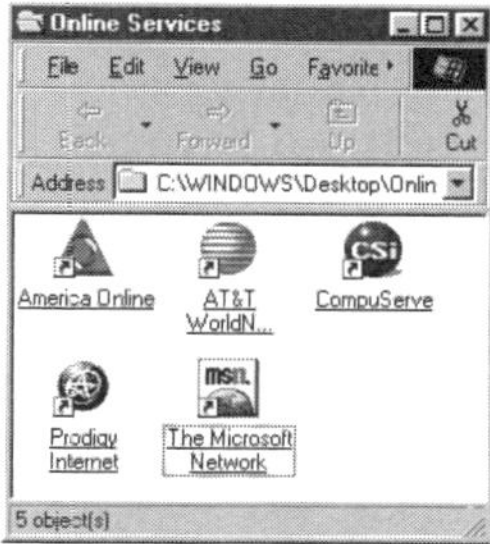

Figure 17.1
Look in the Online Services folder for proprietary Online Services.

- Local service providers—These are often small providers that service a small region and some local businesses. If you are careful and do your homework, you can find a very good ISP this way, and you'll be supporting a business in your local community. Prices range from $9.95 to $19.95 per month for unlimited usage. You can usually get a discount by paying for several months or a year in advance.
- Cable companies—A really good way to get lightning-fast access to the Internet. If you already have cable television, ask about cable Internet services. The cost is a little higher, but you gain that back in speed. The same caveat about customer service from the phone companies applies here. Also keep in mind that cable access is a shared pool. The line speed is divvied up among all the subscribers in a given area. Prices run about $50 per month.
- One size fits all—These providers offer you full service for a year at $99 or so. The price is low and the service can fluctuate depending on how much advertising they do in a given period of time. Some of these services can be a good value if you check them out thoroughly. We'll show you how to do that in this chapter.

Watch Out!
Some cable Internet providers don't allow certain protocols such as telnet to operate efficiently over their connection. If you have to use one of these protocols often, you might be better off with traditional Internet service.

The first important consideration is support. Who do you call when you have a problem, and what kinds of solutions will they offer? When you talk with people about their ISP, always ask about their experience with the company's technical support. The following are some things to watch for when evaluating an ISP's level of support:

- Who do you call when you have a problem, and what kinds of solutions will they offer?
- How do you contact technical support? Find out if they use the telephone, a pager, an answering service, email, or some other method.
- What hours is technical support available? Some places offer 24-hour-a-day, 7-day-a-week technical support. If this is important to you, be sure to choose a service that offers it.

ISP Features

You'll want to make a note of the features this ISP offers. The following are some common features you'll want to know about.

- Software—A common feature is free software for use with the service. In many cases, this is publicly available free software, meaning *nobody* pays for it. In other cases, you receive free copies of commercial software on the Internet. We'll cover Internet software in Chapter 18, "Choosing Internet Applications." Keep free software at the bottom of the list for consideration. Quality of service is much more important. Still, many times the free software an ISP supplies is preconfigured to work with their system. This can be a time-saver for you and cuts down on any tweaking you'll need to do to get up and running.
- Reliability—It doesn't matter how good the Internet connection you have is if you can't get connected because of busy signals. Even worse, busy signals seem to pop up when you are most anxious to look something up on the Internet. Some ISPs such as ImagiNet Communications (`www.imagin.net`) offer a "no busy signal" guarantee. If you

get a busy signal while dialing their service, you get a refund for the day. This is a great feature to have but very few ISPs offer it. Later in the chapter we'll talk about how you can check the busy signal ratio of an ISP before you sign up.

- Time limits—It used to be that only the proprietary services such as AOL and CompuServe charged you by the hour. Now some ISPs such as GTE (`www.gte.net`) are moving to a cost per hour model. You get a certain number of hours with your monthly service, and after that you are charged by the hour for usage. Try to avoid choosing a service that limits the amount of time you can spend online. You never know when you'll go over the limit, and keeping track of how many hours you have used can be a real chore. Make sure your ISP gives you unlimited access to the Internet for a fixed fee.
- Proxy servers—Another thing to ask about is whether the ISP uses proxy servers. A proxy server does just what it sounds like it would do—acts in your place when retrieving Web pages. An ISP will use a proxy server for two main reasons: First, if the ISP filters traffic based on content, then the proxy is their way of determining what you are requesting. Integrity Online at `www.integrityonline.com` is an example of this type of ISP. Second, it can help cut down on Web traffic overall. If you request the same page the person just before you requested, then the proxy can give you the same copy without retrieving it over the Web again. AOL and other large providers use proxy servers for this purpose. Chances are the company you work for uses a proxy server to access the Internet. Think about how often a popular page like Yahoo! is accessed, and you can see how this can add up quickly. Although this second reason may at first seem like a limitation, it may actually be a plus when a popular page is slow to respond due to Internet congestion. The proxy version of the page will come right down the wire.

Unofficially... Some ISPs filter Internet content for their customers. This can be a good idea if that's what your customers want. In our case, one such service would not display the main graphic on our innocuous *The Naked PC* newsletter site because we had named the graphic naked1.gif. Removing the word naked solved the problem.

- Shell accounts—Another feature many ISPs offer is a shell account. This enables you to use telnet to access the Internet from your account remotely. For example, if you were on vacation, you could use another computer to check your email without downloading the mail to the local machine. This is very handy and a feature that we value highly.
- Guarantee—With any ISP you are considering, be sure to ask if they have a money-back-guarantee period. Most reputable ISPs will offer you a full refund within the first 30 days if you aren't satisfied. This can add some peace of mind when you are starting with a new service.

Make a list of the features that appeal to you. In the next section, we'll discuss email and all the features you should look for related to sending and receiving email.

Email

The next major point of concern for you is the email capabilities that your prospective ISP offers. Ask about the following points:

- How many email addresses do you receive? You'll want to know whether these are separate email boxes or email aliases. Aliases are different addresses that arrive in the same email box. Separate email boxes will need to be downloaded separately. Find out how much it costs to add aliases or mailboxes later if you need them.
- Will your new email service be proprietary or standard? A proprietary email system dictates which email client (the program you use to read your email) you use. We'll talk about email clients in Chapter 18. Our preference is that your ISP allows you to use the email client of your choice.
- Do you have to be logged in to your ISP to retrieve your email? Most ISPs allow you to retrieve your mail regardless of where you are connected to the Internet. If you have to be logged in to your ISP to retrieve the mail, this can limit your ability to check your mail when your ISP's dial-in

access is down. Make sure you can access your email account from anywhere.

- Which protocols does your ISP support? The main protocols are POP (Post Office Protocol) and IMAP (Internet Messaging Access Protocol). POP downloads the mail from your ISP to your local machine. IMAP allows you to read the mail directly off the server. IMAP is useful if you'll be accessing your mail from multiple locations, such as work and home. However, using IMAP limits your choice of email clients.
- Will you be able to address your mail as being from a different service? We address our mail as being from PRIMEConsulting.com even though we use local ISPs. Some ISPs will not allow you to use anything other than your default email address. Avoid these if possible.
- Can you download your email without deleting it on the server? Normally your email is deleted after it is successfully downloaded. At times, however, you may want to leave the mail on the server. A good example of this is if you need to check the mail using a friend's ISP.
- Does the ISP offer a spam-filtering service? If you aren't getting spam now (unsolicited commercial email or UCE), you soon will be. Save yourself the trouble and find an ISP that filters it out for you. This is a very useful feature that you'll most appreciate when you have to use it.
- What are the limitations on the maximum size of an email message you can send or receive? Also, what is the limit of your email box? Although you may clear out your email frequently, that doesn't help you when you have to be away for a while unexpectedly. You don't want people who send you mail to get messages back saying that your mailbox is full.
- What limitations do you have on sending mail? Some ISPs limit the amount of outgoing traffic to discourage spamming. You'll want to know at what point your email will be

Bright Idea
If you can't connect to your ISP, you can often still retrieve your mail from a different ISP, such as a friend's. All you need to do is supply your standard email configuration to the email client on your friend's machine. This is the same information your ISP supplies you with when you sign up.

Bright Idea
If you are going on vacation and want an easy way to check your email, set up one of the free email accounts at a service such as Hotmail (`www.hotmail.com`). Hotmail will let you check your regular POP email box. This makes checking your email as easy as finding a computer hooked to the Internet.

considered troublesome and decide if you can live within that limit. You never know when you'll have an announcement to send to hundreds of people at once.

- Are you able to set automatic forwarding of your email? If you ever switch ISPs, you'll want to forward your mail from the old ISP to the new ISP until all your contacts have the new address. Some ISPs allow you to set this yourself. Others charge you for the privilege. Related to this is the capability to set up a vacation message to be sent to correspondents when you are on vacation. This feature should be provided for free and be within your control.

Reliability

Now that you have an idea what services you are looking for in an ISP, it's time to check up on their reliability. Don't just take the ISP's word for it—check with their customers. Most ISPs have a page of links to their customers' home pages. Go by these pages and look for email addresses. Write to each of these people and ask them about the reliability of the service. Be sure to ask how long the person has used this ISP, which other ISPs they have used, any problems they have had, and most importantly—would they recommend this ISP. Compile any feedback you get and make a list of questions it raises. You'll ask about these issues when you phone the ISP.

While you are waiting for the ISP's customer to write you back, you'll want to do some digging on your own. Go by Deja News (`www.dejanews.com`) and search for messages relating to the ISP. Just use the ISP's name as the search term. You're looking for feedback here, so take good notes. After you finish with Deja News, go by a search engine such as Infoseek and try to find information relating to the ISP. You probably won't find much from either of these two sources unless the ISP gives particularly bad service. That's okay because you're trying to avoid ISPs that give bad service!

After you get some feedback from the customers and have searched the Web for dissenting opinions, it's time to call the ISP. Run through your list of desired features and write down the answers you receive. Next, query the ISP about any questions you've uncovered in your research regarding their service. Make sure the questions are answered to your satisfaction. Ask how many dial-in access numbers they support. If at any time the person on the phone starts using technical terms you don't recognize, ask for clarification. Even though this is a sales person, it is usually indicative of the type of service you'll be getting in the future. Ask if you can call their technical support to verify some things. If so, call and describe your modem and other hardware and ask if they have any known conflicts with their system. Ask about any known problems with connecting to their service from your area. Also, try to call technical support during the busiest times—6:00 p.m. is a good time. Many people sign on just after work. Friday and Saturday evenings are some of the busiest times for ISPs as well. See how quickly you get help and how you are treated.

Try to get the access number for dialing into the ISP. By itself the access number is useless without a valid username and password. With the access number in hand, try dialing at some of the peak hours of the day that we mentioned previously. Do you get busy signals? Repeatedly? Do you get a clear line, or can you hear static and popping noises? These are just a few of the things you can check by having the phone number before signing up with a service. Usually the sales or technical support representative will let you have it after they understand that you are just evaluating the service.

Watch Out!
Don't ask one of the ISP's existing customers for the access number unless they are a personal friend of yours. This could lead to you being reported to the ISP as someone trying to break in. Not the sort of first impression you are wanting to make.

Finally, be sure to read any ISP's service level agreement and Acceptable Use Policy. Make sure that you can abide by the Acceptable Use Policy before agreeing to service from any ISP. Most will have these posted on their Web sites.

It may seem like an overwhelming task to choose an ISP. Remember, the above guidelines have proven useful to us and our professional and personal associates in the past. Each situation is different. Be sure to ask your friends and coworkers who they use for an ISP as well. Doing some basic research beforehand can save you lots of frustration down the road. Even if you pick an outstanding ISP today, there is no guarantee that their service will still be outstanding six months from now after they change owners or move offices. Make the best choice you can and don't settle for poor service.

Choosing a Modem

Before you expend a lot of effort choosing a modem, check to see whether your system already has one. Check your documentation to determine whether you have a modem, and if so, what the specifications are for the modem. If your system doesn't have a modem installed, you'll need to choose one.

Choosing a modem can be a daunting task indeed. Many protocols and numbers exist to look at and choose from. Our recommendation is to choose your modem and your Internet provider at the same time. What you are trying to avoid is buying a modem that supports one protocol, and then getting an ISP that doesn't support that protocol.

Unofficially... You never know what causes bad telephone lines. One time, the phone company came out to check our lines and pulled an eight inch diameter wasp nest out of the housing on the pole. Our phone service cleared up immediately after.

If you are purchasing a new modem and already have an ISP, call their technical support and ask which modems give good results with their service. Also ask which modems give bad results. They should be able to give you some specific brand names with realistic expectations of how they will perform with their service.

Even after getting the correct modem and a good ISP, you might still get bad connections to the Internet. This can be the fault of any of the phone lines and equipment between you and the ISP. Your ISP's technical support should be able to tell you which areas of your community have troublesome connections. One of us lives in an older community with terrible phone lines. When we had a second phone line installed in the house, the phone company ended up running new phone lines for about five miles just to get the connection working. As a result, our modem line is very clear but our phone line still crackles and gives poor service. Moral of the story—don't be too quick to blame the ISP for troubles. The phone company can come out and test your phone lines for you. Whether you can get them to do anything about it is another matter altogether.

The most common methods of attaching to the Internet are the following:

- Cable—Works through your local cable television company. Data is transferred to and from the Internet at speeds up to 30Mbps. Unfortunately, you have to share the bandwidth with the other people in the neighborhood. In heavy usage areas, actual speeds are being reported at 1.5Mbps for download and 300Kbps for upload. Even with the sharing, you are still ahead of the game. Cable connections do not require an additional ISP connection. Prices run about $50 a month.
- Modem—The most common way to connect to the Internet. The current standard here is 56k v.90. You really won't be able to receive data at greater than 53k because of regulatory restrictions. Connection speeds in the 44Kbps–48Kbps range are common according to the modem manufacturers.
- ISDN (Integrated Services Digital Network)—A fast digital phone line. Comes in two speeds: 64k or 128k. This technology has been around a while and is quite stable. Basically, ISDN consists of two lines that can handle 64k of data each. If you use both lines for data, you operate at 128k. Use one line for data and one line for your phone, and you'll be pulling data at 64k. Your ISP probably charges a different rate for each of these scenarios.
- Satellite—Uses a small satellite dish to transfer data to your computer from the Internet at speeds up to 400Kbps. You'll still need a traditional modem and ISP connection for sending data to the Internet.
- ADSL (Asymmetric Digital Subscriber Line)—High-speed phone line service. Download speed as high as 9Mbps can be achieved. Requires special equipment from the ISP. Not currently available in all areas.

What You'll Need to Know

After you have your new account, you'll want to write down the following crucial information in your system journal and store it in your NEAT box.

- All the dial-up access numbers your ISP offers.
- The username and password you use to access your account.
- If you have a static IP address—one that never changes—you'll need to know that. Most ISPs use a dynamic IP address that is randomly assigned each time you dial. You'll need to know which of these you have.
- If your ISP uses a proxy server, you'll need to know its name before you can do any Web browsing.
- The name of the server you download your mail from and whether it uses POP or IMAP for its protocol.
- The name of the server you send outgoing mail through, usually called the SMTP server. Many times this is the same as the server you download mail from. If so, be sure to make a note of that so you don't think you are missing an entry.
- The email addresses you receive mail from.
- Whether your DNS is assigned dynamically or statically. If the DNS is static, you'll need to know the name and address of the DNS server.

Be sure to list the information for each account you have. Having the information handy will enable you to quickly reestablish your connection in the event of a disk failure or other problem.

Connection Type

We'll briefly cover how to set up a new Dial-Up Networking connection inside Windows 98. Make sure you have your list of necessary information from the previous section. If you have a cable, a satellite, or an ISDN connection, you'll have a special set of instructions on how to get connected. The following steps cover setting up a standard modem connection through an ISP.

1. Open Windows Explorer and click the Dial-Up Networking folder to make it active.
2. Double-click the Make New Connection item.
3. The name you type in the first box is what will be used for your Dial-Up Networking Connection. Your modem should already be selected (see Figure 17.2). Click Next.

Bright Idea
Stop by The Naked PC Web site regularly and let us keep you current on crucial updates and helpful tips for keeping your Internet connection running smoothly.

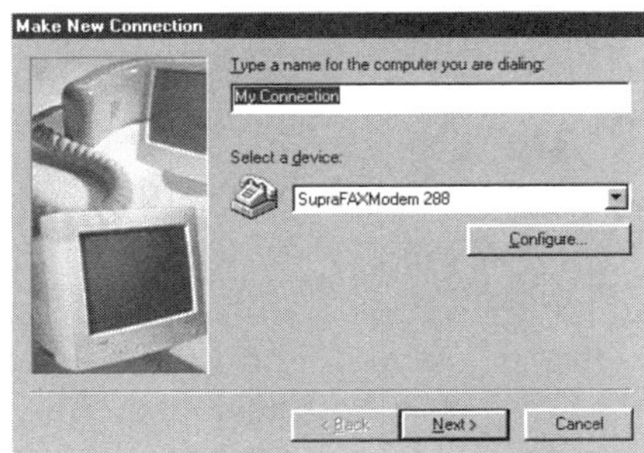

Figure 17.2
Fill in the blanks to create a new Dial-Up Networking connection.

4. Enter the phone number of your ISP, including the area code. Select the country you are dialing from. Click Next.
5. Click Finish to create your new Dial-Up Networking connection.
6. Repeat the above steps for each phone number your ISP has given you.

If your ISP has supplied you with specific Domain Name Server (DNS) or IP addresses, you'll need to add those now.

1. Right-click your new connection and choose Properties.
2. Select the Server Types tab.
3. Click the TCP/IP Settings button near the bottom of the dialog box.
4. Put your static IP address in the top section. Skip this if you don't have an assigned IP address (see Figure 17.3).

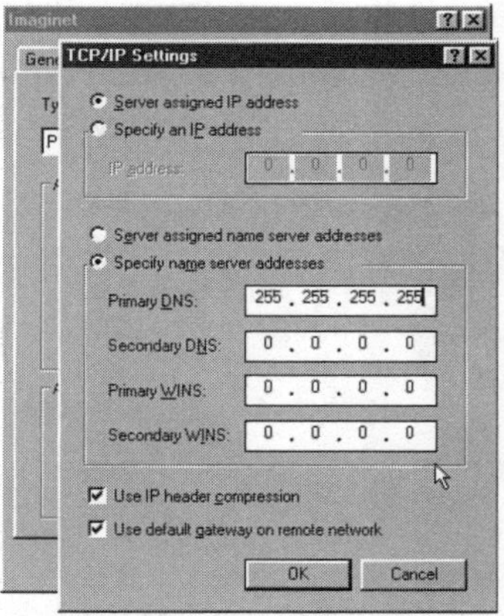

Figure 17.3 Configure your DNS servers and IP addresses here.

5. Put your DNS numbers in the lower section. Skip this if you don't have assigned DNS numbers.
6. Click OK, and click OK again to finish.

If you ever have trouble with your Internet connection and can't seem to resolve it, try this: Instead of messing with the settings of your previously working Dial-Up Networking connection, set up a brand-new connection with the settings your ISP gave you originally. It's rare that the settings get changed on your local machine. You don't want to mess up a good connection trying to troubleshoot when the problem is at the phone company or your ISP.

Chapter Ending

- Choose the type of ISP you need.
- Get the features you need from your ISP.
- Choose the right modem.
- Make a list of all your important connection information.
- Create Dial-up Networking connections.

Chapter 18

Choosing Internet Applications

IN THE PRECEDING CHAPTER, we talked about how to get connected to the Internet. In this chapter we'll cover which applications you need to use the Internet to your best advantage. The good news is that most of the better Internet applications are free. The bad news is that they also seem to be in a perpetual beta cycle (as we discussed back in Chapter 8, "Staying Ahead of the Game") with lots of buggy behavior.

The main applications you'll need to enjoy the Internet are a Web browser and an email client. You'll spend the majority of your time in these two applications, so we cover those in some detail. Then we touch on some other applications you'll find useful, some enhancements to your Web browser and email clients, and some applications for putting your own corner of the Web together. In this chapter, we cover your choices and help you decide which are best for you. One thing to keep in mind when you think of Internet applications is that not all applications have to reside on your computer. An Internet search engine is an application that runs on a remote computer but displays its results on your computer. We discuss both types of applications in this chapter, along with several that work both locally and remotely to bring you the data you are seeking.

Practical Email

Email is an interesting thing. At first it is merely convenient, then it becomes necessary, and suddenly, you can find yourself overwhelmed by it all. Your choice of clients makes a big difference in how pleasant your time spent managing your online correspondence is. We'll briefly cover the major email clients using the following criteria:

- Protocols—Which protocols can the client "speak?" In Chapter 17, "Making Internet Connections," we talked about the different protocols for email. The basic protocols are POP3 and IMAP for receiving mail and SMTP for sending mail. You'll want to make sure that your email client speaks the same language as your email server. Lightweight Directory Access Protocol (LDAP) is a directory protocol used for looking up names and email addresses. If your mail client supports this, you can do lookups in Internet directories such as Bigfoot (`www.bigfoot.com`), directly from your email client. Network News Transport Protocol (NNTP) is used to read Usenet newsgroup postings.
- Cost—A good email client doesn't have to be expensive. Find the features you need and then compare the cost. Only two of the clients we look at have a price tag: Outlook and Eudora Pro. One client, Eudora Light, is postcard ware. Just send in a postcard as payment for the program. All the rest are free.
- Filtering capability—The capability to automate your email handling and filing can be a tremendous time saver. If you are subscribed to a mailing list, a filter can automatically move all messages sent to the list into a folder you create for the list. Or if you are receiving unwanted mail even after asking the sender to stop, you can set a filter to automatically delete those messages. You'll want filtering that is powerful enough to grow into as your needs change. Three of these email clients offer advanced filtering—the capability to apply more than one filter to a given message. With an advanced filter, you can move a message

to a folder, add the message sender to your address book, and send a prewritten reply to the sender.

- Multiple accounts—The capability for your email client to handle multiple email accounts for one user. These accounts can exist on different mail servers with different login names and passwords. If you have more than one email account but want to receive all the mail into one email box, multiple accounts or identities will be an important feature for you.
- Multiple profiles—The capability for your email client to handle multiple users with separate email accounts. Each profile contains one user's email and address book. To access the email in another profile, you'll need to restart the email client. If more than one person reads email on the same computer but you don't want the messages mixed together, you'll want this feature.
- Add-ons—Are add-ons readily available for added functionality, such as encryption? The most popular encryption package is PGP (Pretty Good Privacy) from Network Associates/McAfee Software. We talked about PGP in Chapter 13, "Security at Work and at Home," and our concern here is how well it plugs in to the different email clients.
- Formatted email—All the clients we review are able to read and send formatted email. The formatting is HyperText Markup Language (HTML)—the same formatting used for Internet Web pages.

Unofficially...
Retrieve your email from anywhere. You don't need to be dialed in to your ISP to retrieve your email. All you need is a connection to the Internet. Your email client will still be able to contact your ISP's mail server and send and retrieve your email.

With these criteria in mind, we'll look at the big players in the email client category.

Microsoft Outlook Express

This email client comes standard with Windows 98 or Internet Explorer 4 (which means it's free and almost certainly already installed on your computer). It can handle multiple accounts and is easy to use. The filtering rules are simple to use but are limited in the logic you put in any one rule. For example, you can't set a rule to take all mail with a specific subject line and add or remove the sender's address to a distribution list.

If you installed PGP as discussed in Chapter 13, it adds itself as a menu item and puts a new icon on the toolbar for quick access. Outlook Express can speak LDAP, IMAP, POP3, and NNTP. Outlook Express is one of only two clients in our list that can read Usenet posts. Overall, Outlook Express is a good email client if you have one or more email accounts, use filtering to file your mail in different folders, and want an easy-to-use client. It works well with small or large volumes of email. Outlook Express has a tendency to send formatted email unless you explicitly tell it not to. For more information on Outlook Express, visit Microsoft's site (`www.microsoft.com/ie/ie40/oe/`).

Microsoft Outlook

If you were judging by names, it would seem that Outlook and Outlook Express are related. In reality this is not the case, and they are two separate clients with two separate ways of handling things. Outlook's filters are very powerful, and the feature set is very rich. PGP plugs in seamlessly by adding a menu for its services (see Figure 18.1). Outlook can speak LDAP, IMAP, POP3, and Microsoft Exchange. You will be able to use multiple accounts and multiple profiles to access your email.

Outlook also contains a full calendar and contact module. If it's important to you to have your calendar and contacts integrated with your email, be sure to give Outlook a look. On the other hand, the client is very large and puts heavy demands on your system. It is also full of inconsistencies. T. J. Lee and Lee Hudspeth have written a book on Outlook, *Outlook Annoyances* (O'Reilly & Associates) ISBN: 1-56592-384-7, that discusses this application in detail.

Outlook is the way to go if you need to have your email integrated with your calendar and task manager, especially if you are already running Microsoft Office and have Outlook as part of that software suite.

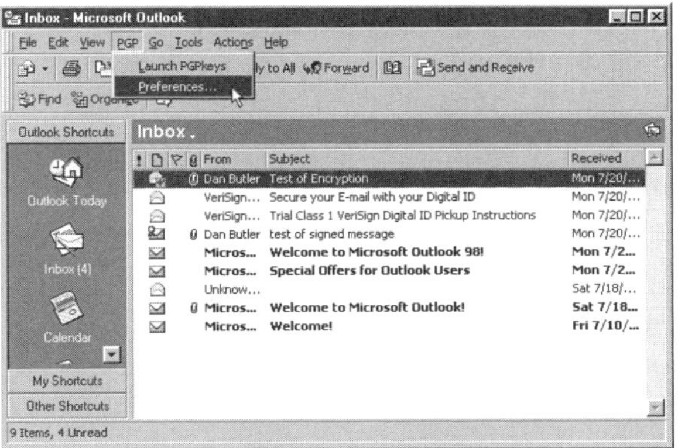

Figure 18.1
PGP adds itself to Outlook's menu.

Netscape Messenger

Built into the Netscape Communicator suite, Netscape Messenger is an easy–to-use mail client that supports POP3, SMTP, IMAP, and LDAP. The interface is pleasing and functional, but the filters aren't useful beyond simply filing and deleting messages as they arrive.

Messenger is more closely tied to the Netscape Web browser than either of the Outlook offerings are with Internet Explorer. When you are composing mail, you are actually in an HTML editor. Messenger has special menu items to help you maintain your account if you connect to a Netscape mail server. Find more information on Messenger at Netscape's Home Page (`home.netscape.com`).

If you are a Navigator user and the basic feature set offered by Messenger meets your needs, this email client may be all you'll ever need. Messenger supports multiple profiles.

Eudora Light and Eudora Pro

Eudora has been around for a long time and offers both a free version, Eudora Light, and a commercial version, Eudora Pro. Both of these clients offer mail filtering. Eudora Light's filters are basic and good for moving messages into folders. Eudora Pro has very powerful rules capabilities.

Eudora is one of the easier products to set up. During installation it asks you three questions, and you are off and running. The Pro version lets you assume multiple identities with a click of the mouse, retrieve email from multiple email accounts, color code your mail, and much more.

Eudora light supports the POP3 and SMTP protocols. Eudora Pro adds LDAP and IMAP. If you are looking for an easy–to-use yet powerful email client, have a look at Eudora. Download your free version of Eudora Light or a 30-day demo of Eudora Pro at `www.eudora.com`.

Pegasus Mail

One of the most powerful email clients available for Windows, Pegasus, is completely free. You are encouraged to buy a manual, but it isn't necessary. About the only restriction to the use of Pegasus is an anti-spam clause in the license. Pegasus offers an outstanding array of filters, color-coded email, multiple accounts, multiple profiles, and many other features. The power comes at a price, though. Getting all the filters and other items working together carries a slight learning curve. Pegasus currently supports POP3, NDS, SMTP, LDAP, and IMAP. If you don't need an integrated calendar and contact manager, Pegasus offers all the features you're likely to need. Find more information on Pegasus Mail at `www.pegasus.usa.com`.

Email Client Features at a Glance

The previous descriptions were brief overviews of each of the mail clients. Table 18.1 shows you the features we discussed at a glance. Visit the Web sites and read up on the email clients that interest you. Our best suggestion is for you to actually try each of the clients and find out which one is the most comfortable for your needs.

TABLE 18.1: EMAIL CLIENT FEATURES COMPARED

	Protocols						
	POP3	**IMAP**	**LDAP**	**NNTP**	**Cost**	**Filtering**	**Multiple Accounts/ Profiles**
Outlook Express	Yes	Yes	Yes	Yes	Free	Basic	Yes/No
Outlook	Yes	Yes	Yes	No	$99	Advanced	Yes/Yes
Messenger	Yes	Yes	Yes	Yes	Free	Basic	Yes/Yes 4.5
Eudora Light	Yes	No	No	No	Free	Basic	No/No
Eudora Pro	Yes	Yes	Yes	No	$39	Advanced	Yes/No
Pegasus	Yes	No	Yes	No	Free	Advanced	Yes/Yes

Email Netiquette

No matter which email client you choose to use, you'll want to take a moment and learn some simple rules of email "Netiquette." You want to be considerate of the recipients of your email. Don't make them jump through hoops to read your message, and don't waste their time chasing down things they don't need. Most of these rules are common sense, but they are still worth reviewing:

- Don't put any fancy formatting, such as bold text or fancy background graphics, into your email unless you know your recipient desires to receive mail with formatting in it. All the email clients have the capability to turn formatting off prior to sending a message. This should be your default mode of sending.
- Don't send large attachments without prior permission.
- Don't forward any email that says "Forward this to everyone you know!" to 200 of your closest friends, especially if it is warning of an email virus. Always check the validity of email virus alerts at Rob Rosenburg's Computer Virus Myths Page (`www.kumite.com/myths`) prior to forwarding.
- If your email has URLs pointing to Internet resources, include some explanation of what the link points to.

- Be cautious of what you send to a person's place of employment. Mail has been deemed the property of the employer and can legally be looked at. So be careful with the off-color and questionable jokes.

Browsing

After email, you'll probably spend the majority of your time surfing the Net. To do this, of course, you use a Web browser. We assume that most of you reading this book already use a Web browser or have in the past. You probably already have some preferences in that regard as well. In addition to the two major browsers, Netscape Navigator and Microsoft Internet Explorer, we'll discuss a couple of other browsers that you might have overlooked.

Netscape Navigator hails back to the old days of the Internet when Mosaic ruled the roost. Netscape introduced advanced features such as the capability to put information into tables and various ways to color your Web pages—revolutionary features that are now taken for granted. Prior to Netscape, every page had a gray background and black text. Microsoft began Internet Explorer by building on the Mosaic code base. Today the browser wars continue, with Netscape and Microsoft releasing new browsers every six months or so. They are always buggy through their first few maintenance releases, and it never seems as though the technology has time to slow down long enough to get the bugs worked out.

Netscape has a nifty feature called User Profiles that sets it apart from Microsoft's browser (see Figure 18.2). Each person using Netscape can have his or her own Profile with its own set of Bookmarks, Address Books, and Preferences. This way, every member of the family can customize the browser to their way of working, even though they're all using the same computer.

Internet Explorer, on the other hand, offers more features in the user interface with toolbars and other enhancements that can be docked on any side of your screen as needed, giving you quick access to the tools you are using (see Figure 18.3).

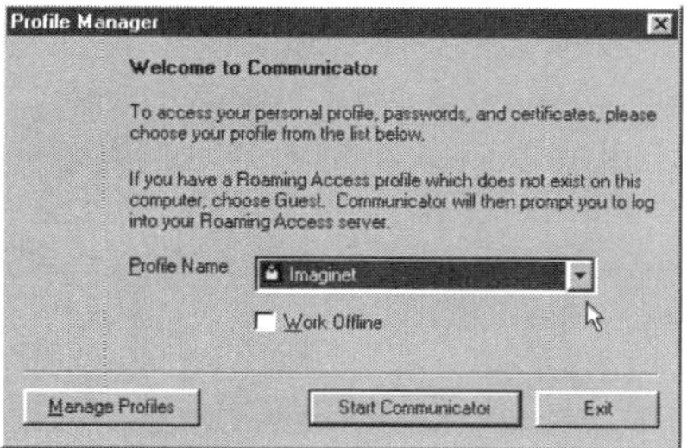

Figure 18.2
Netscape can manage multiple user profiles.

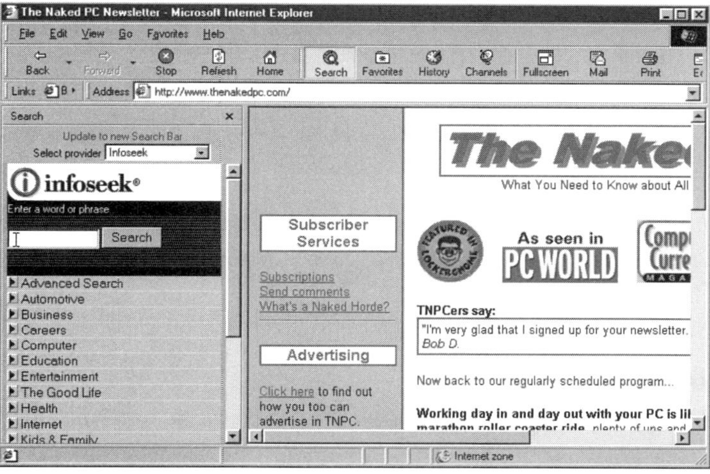

Figure 18.3
Internet Explorer puts special tool windows on the browser.

Bright Idea
If you find yourself using both Internet Explorer and Netscape, you may want to go to PRIME Consulting Group, Inc.'s Web site (`www.PRIMEConsulting.com/pdf/bookmarks.pdf`) and read the article on how to keep your Netscape Bookmarks and Internet Explorer Favorites straight and accessible from either program.

Which Web browser should you use? Try both of them and see which one feels the most comfortable to you, or as we do, you can keep both installed on your computer. You may find that you use different browsers for different tasks—or for viewing different sites—because many sites are optimized for one browser or the other.

Switching Web browsers is far less painful than switching email clients. With a Web browser, generally all you need to update is your saved Bookmarks or Favorites. With email you have stored messages, address books, and login information, among other things. You may find yourself alternating between Netscape Navigator and Microsoft Internet Explorer as the new releases leapfrog each other. To make your surfing as productive as possible, use keyboard shortcuts. Amazingly, nine keyboard shortcuts are the same in both browsers, as shown in Table 18.2. Keyboard shortcuts can be a real time-saver for tasks you perform often.

TABLE 18.2: COMMON BROWSER KEYBOARD SHORTCUTS

Keyboard Shortcut	Description
Alt+Left arrow	Equivalent to clicking the Back button. If both hands are on the keyboard, this is much faster than reaching for the mouse and scrolling up to the toolbar.
Alt+Right arrow	Equivalent to clicking the Forward button.
Ctrl+A	Selects the entire page (or frame).
Ctrl+D	Instantly adds the current page to your bookmarks list.
Ctrl+B	Displays the Favorites/Bookmarks window.
Ctrl+N	Calls up another browser window.
Ctrl+F	Pops up the Find dialog box.
Esc	Stops a page from further downloading.
Spacebar	Causes a page-down on the currently displayed Web page.

Other Browsers

Most people limit themselves to either Netscape Navigator, Internet Explorer, or both. However, other browsers, some of which are free, are available on the market and have specialized features that can help you in certain circumstances. We'll cover three such browsers:

Opera

Out of Norway comes the shareware browser Opera. Opera's strengths lie in its snappy performance and unique browsing features. One of these features enables you to view multiple Web sites at one time in the same browser (see Figure 18.4). Granted, each Web site has a small window, but often that is all you need to keep up with multiple sources of information. You can find Opera at `www.operasoftware.com`.

Opera's key features are speed, a low disk space requirement, and the capability to display more than one Web site at a time in the same window. The small footprint makes it a good secondary browser or one to use where disk space might be scarce. If you are looking for a faster way to browse the Web, give Opera a try.

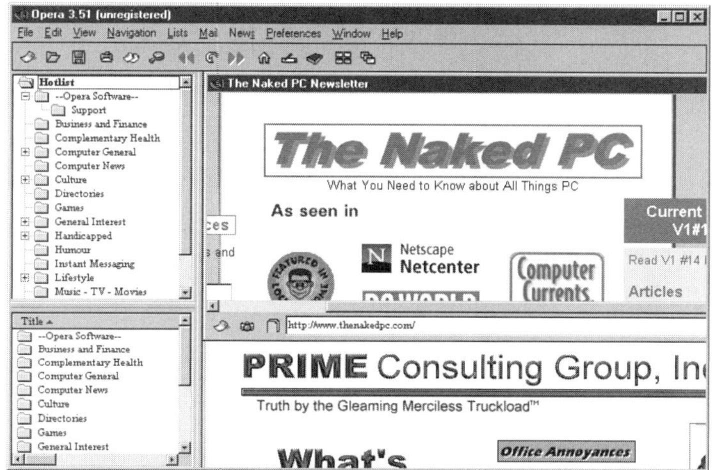

Figure 18.4
Opera displays multiple windows as you browse.

Lynx

Lynx is an extremely fast browser that is also free. It achieves its high speeds by being completely text based and by not displaying pictures at all (see Figure 18.5). Because it can't display the pictures, it doesn't even bother to download them. Earlier in this chapter we mentioned using different browsers for different tasks. We routinely use Lynx to browse busy message boards and other sites with a lot of text to read.

The main benefit of Lynx is its extreme speed. If you keep up with a lot of text-based information on the Internet, give Lynx a try. You can download Lynx at `www.crl.com/~subir/lynx/binaries.html`.

Unofficially...
Lynx is frequently used by people with disabilities. Its text-based interface allows screen readers—devices that read the text on the screen—to work efficiently. Unfortunately, many Web designers don't take this into account and build Web sites that are inaccessible to people who need to use these devices.

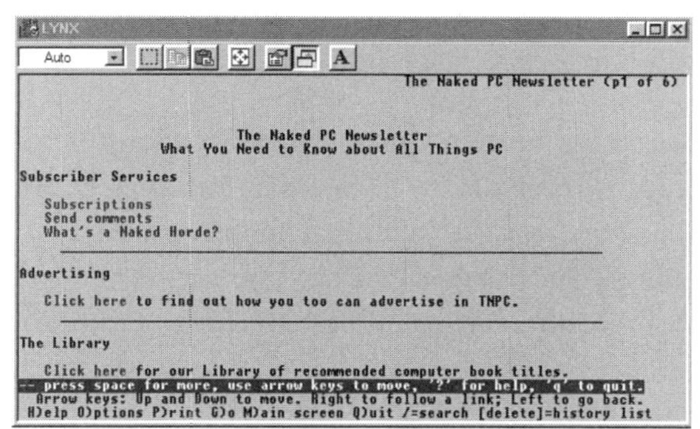

Figure 18.5
Lynx browses the Web quickly without graphics.

Neoplanet

Finally we have Neoplanet, which is not in and of itself a Web browser but instead is built on top of Microsoft's Internet Explorer. Its unique approach to browsing makes it worthy of mention here. Billing itself as bringing you "The best of the Web in 3 clicks or less," it does come close.

What it gives Internet Explorer is a different set of menus, toolbar buttons, and features (see Figure 18.6). Whether you like this interface is a matter of personal preference. The importance of this is that you aren't limited to the interface supplied by Microsoft. An advantage is that Neoplanet takes up very little disk space.

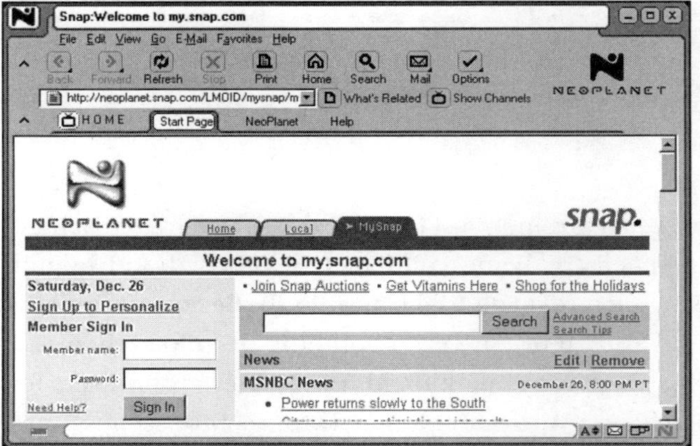

Figure 18.6 Neoplanet puts a different face on Internet Explorer.

Neoplanet's strengths are an enhanced search interface and an excellent start page. If you are a beginning user running Internet Explorer and you want help locating Internet content or just want more control over how your browser behaves, give Neoplanet a try. Neoplanet is free and can be downloaded from `www.neoplanet.com`.

Do-It-Yourself, Agents, and Offline Browsing

In addition to email and Web browsers, another class of Internet applications can gather information for you. This type of information includes subscriptions to newsletters and Web sites, agents, and Web browsing helpers. It's easy to find information on the Internet; the problem is the quantity of that information. It can take a long time to search for what you want and to sift the information you find, eliminate duplicates, and separate the wheat from the chaff.

An agent program gathers information unattended from the Internet and puts it on your local computer where you can work through it at your leisure. Newsletters on any topic can be sent directly to your inbox. Snakes can download entire Web sites to your local hard drive for browsing without the delays of the Internet. Stock tickers can keep themselves updated throughout the day and even present the information in place of your screen saver.

Bright Idea
An easy way to keep up with Web applications and tips is to subscribe to the Neat Net Tricks newsletter (www.neatnettricks.com). This biweekly newsletter will save you the time and trouble of searching out the best tips and tricks yourself. The down-to-earth style makes it an easy read, as well.

Subscriptions

Subscriptions are just what they sound like—you subscribe to information sources and they deliver the information to you. The most common type of subscriptions are newsletters you subscribe to via email that are delivered directly to your email box for free. Our own *The Naked PC* newsletter (www.TheNakedPC.com) is an example of this sort of subscription. After you are subscribed, the newsletter dutifully arrives every other week without any additional effort on your part. The Internet has thousands of newsletters on every conceivable topic. To locate newsletter and mailing lists, browse through the Liszt index (www.liszt.com). Subscribe to several in your areas of interest, and then weed out the letters that aren't useful and keep the ones that help you stay informed.

Agent Applications

Agents are programs that go out on the Internet unattended and retrieve the information that you seek. Some programs, such as WebSnake by eSynch, gather whole Web sites for later viewing offline. What this means for you is no more waiting for a Web site that you regularly frequent to download just to read the contents. You can save considerable time this way. WebSnake is shareware, and you can download it at www.imarkmall.com/websnake.html.

Do you get your news online? If so, try using PointCast to deliver your news to you at predefined times. You can set PointCast to gather the daily headlines, weather, and company information while you are getting ready to start your day (see Figure 18.7). Now when you sit at your computer, all the information is waiting for you or displaying in place of your screen saver. PointCast is free, and you can download a copy at `www.pointcast.com`.

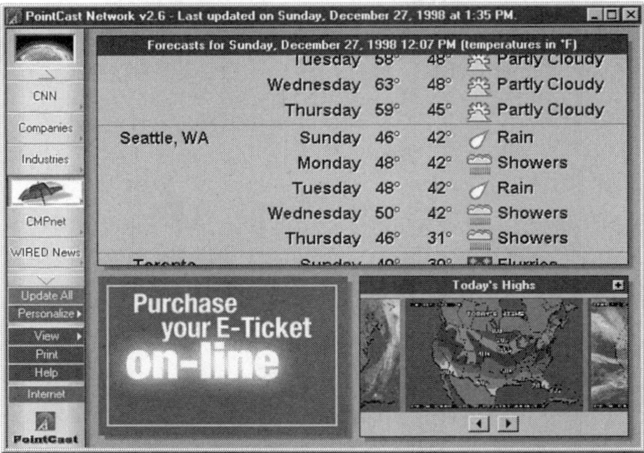

Figure 18.7 PointCast delivers weather and news to your desktop.

Another example of an agent is Oil Change by CyberMedia, which we discussed in Chapter 8, "Staying Ahead of the Game." Oil Change is an agent that searches the Internet looking for updates to the programs you have installed. This is a good example of an agent that does your searching for you, saving you considerable time that you would otherwise spend ferreting out the information for yourself.

> "In matters of truth the fact that you don't want to publish something is, nine times out of ten, a proof that you ought to publish it."
> —G. K. Chesterton (1874–1936), British author. "The Nameless Man." *A Miscellany of Men,* 1912.

Web Publishing and Development

The time will come when you want to put some information on a Web page of your own. Two steps are required to get this done. First, you need to have some space on a Web server; second, you need to create the Web pages themselves. Your ISP probably supplies you with space on which to put your Web pages. If not, you can get a free Web site at a service such as Geocities (`www.geocities.com`), Angelfire (`www.angelfire.com`), or Tripod (`www.tripod.com`).

Now you are ready to generate your own HTML documents. Before you run out to buy an HTML editor, have a look at what is already on your system. Windows 98 comes with a good basic HTML editor called Front Page Express. You'll find it at Start, Programs, Internet Explorer, FrontPage Express. If your material is mostly text, consider using Microsoft Word to generate your HTML pages. If you have tables of numbers and graphs, consider Excel. Slide shows can be generated easily with PowerPoint. To see the Web templates and capabilities of Microsoft Office, choose Start, New Office Document (see Figure 18.8). Now switch to the Web Pages tab and you'll see all the prebuilt templates and tools that Office provides.

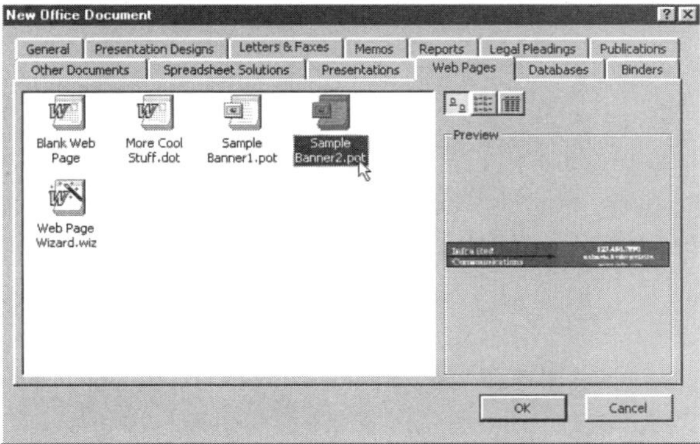

Figure 18.8
Use Office 97's templates to start Web pages.

When you are ready for more information on how to build HTML pages, start by looking on the Internet. Many tutorials are available, covering every technique you may want to use. A good starting point for tutorials is Yahoo!'s listing of Tutorials, Demos, and Talks at `dir.yahoo.com/Computers_and_Internet/Internet/World_Wide_Web/Information_and_Documentation/Tutorials__Demos__Talks/`. You will also find newsletters such as Poor Richard's Web Site News to be an excellent ongoing resource for your Web development efforts. You'll find Poor Richard's Web Site News at `www.poorrichard.com`.

Watch Out!
Save yourself some aggravation when you create Web documents. You'll be much happier with your results if you create new Web documents from scratch rather than trying to convert existing documents to HTML later. Converted documents tend to lose their formatting.

Must-Have Browser Add-ins and Plug-ins

As you navigate through the World Wide Web, you'll come across many types of files. Many of the files require special plug-ins in order for your browser to display them. In this section, we talk about the major plug-ins you'll need to view the majority of the content you'll come across online. You'll probably already have most of these plug-ins installed on your system. These applications are called plug-ins because they work in conjunction with your Web browser. Most of the plug-ins open directly inside your browser, eliminating the need for you to switch applications just to view the content.

In Netscape you can see which plug-ins you have installed by clicking Help, About Plug-ins. Unfortunately, Internet Explorer has no easy way to determine which plug-ins are installed. The plug-ins we find essential to viewing the information we find on the Internet are discussed next.

Adobe Acrobat

Many complex documents are published in Adobe Portable Document Format (PDF), which requires the Adobe Acrobat Reader. PDF retains all the original formatting and makes for very clean printouts (see Figure 18.9). The Acrobat Reader is free and can be obtained directly from Adobe at www.adobe.com. A good example of the use of PDF documents is the Internal Revenue Service Web site, which makes all the U.S. tax forms available as PDF documents at www.irs.gov.

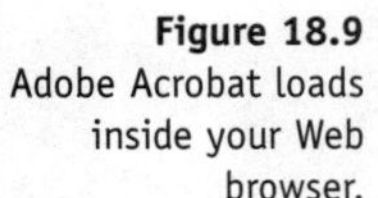

Figure 18.9
Adobe Acrobat loads inside your Web browser.

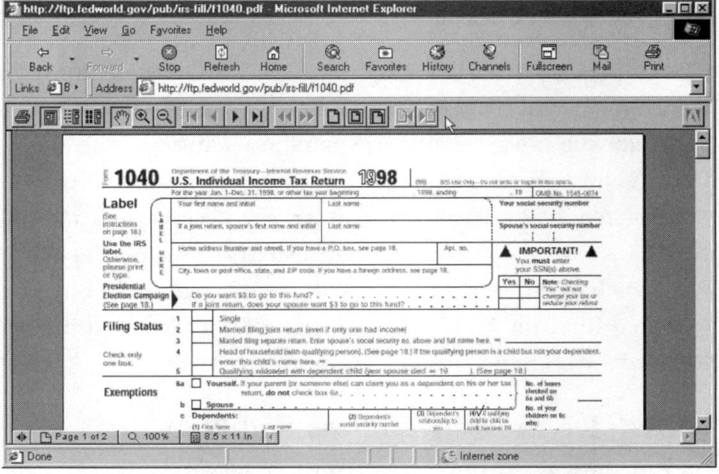

QuickTime by Apple

QuickTime is used to present video embedded in Web sites. You can get the player at www.quicktime.com.

Shockwave and Flash by Macromedia

Both Shockwave and Flash are technologies from Macromedia that bring animation and interactivity to your Web browser. You can get the plug-ins for both of these at www.macromedia.com/software/downloads/.

RealAudio and RealVideo

Many radio and television stations broadcast in RealAudio or RealVideo. You can get the player for free by going to www.real.com. Then stop by www.real.com/realguide and www.audionet.com to see a sampling of what the Web has to offer in both audio and video.

This is by no means an exhaustive list, but it covers 90 percent or more of the sites you are likely to run across. When you encounter a site that needs a plug-in you don't have, you'll usually be prompted to download and install it. Take a moment and decide if you really need the plug-in, because you can wind up with dozens of these add-ins that you may rarely need. If so, go ahead and download the file, install it, and be sure to record the details in your system journal.

Watch Out!
Don't just download every plug-in you come across. Over time, having too many that you never use may cause problems with your system. Avoid these problems by keeping your browser unencumbered with extraneous plug-ins.

Searching the Web

The World Wide Web (WWW) is a big place that is dynamic in nature. What's here today is gone tomorrow, with more new information in its place. Fortunately, searching applications are available that you can access online via your browser to make finding things on the WWW easier. Because these search services run in your browser, there is nothing to download or install on your local system. Search services fall into two categories: search engines and directory listings.

It is important to know the difference between a search engine and a directory. Search engines look through indexes of files on the WWW and return pointers to pages based on the search criteria you supplied. Directories are precompiled listings of sites grouped into categories. The search engines often have more current data than the directories, but you'll also find a lot of fluff popping up in your searches. What we've found to be an effective strategy for ferreting information from the Web is to start in the directories and branch out from there. After looking at several pages on your current topic, you'll begin to find links to other sites. These will often be better than where you started. You'll also start to notice the keywords you'll need to use to get a reasonable return from the search engines. The following list covers the major search engines and directories you'll want to use on the WWW.

Directories

Yahoo! and The Mining Co. are the two most popular directories you'll find on the Internet. Both break down Web sites by topic and let you quickly find the types of sites you are looking for. Find Yahoo! at `www.yahoo.com` and The Mining Co. at `www.miningco.com`.

Search Engines

When you are searching the Web, you'll find yourself using certain search engines more often than others. Usually, one engine is easier for you to use than another and just feels more comfortable. The following list contains the major search engines, along with a few that you might miss that we use all the time.

- AltaVista (`www.altavista.com`)—Easy to use and can translate documents to and from different languages on-the-fly.
- InfoSeek (`www.infoseek.com`)—Fast, and it groups results by Web site.
- HotBot (`www.hotbot.com`)—Very thorough and fast.
- Lycos (`www.lycos.com`)—One of the older search engines on the Web. Still useful.
- Excite (`www.excite.com`)—Large service with lots of options.

- WebCrawler (`www.webcrawler.com`)—Combination search engine and directory.
- DejaNews (`www.dejanews.com`)—Searches the tens of thousands of Usenet newsgroups and private company support newsgroups.
- Mamma (`www.mamma.com`)—Searches all the major search engines at one time.
- Ask Jeeves (`www.askjeeves.com`)—Search by typing a normal question in plain English to Jeeves.
- Sherlock@ (`www.intermediacy.com/sherlock/`)—Lots of information and pointers on how to find information on the Internet.
- The Web Search Cheat Sheet (`www.colosys.net/search`)—Contains all the syntax tips for searching the major search engines.
- Dogpile (`www.dogpile.com`)—Searches multiple sources for Web pages, weather, stock quotes, and more.
- SearchKing (`www.searchking.com`)—Lets you add your telephone area code to limit your search for Web sites dealing with your local area.

We'll finish up this section on search engines by pointing you to a resource to help you keep track of what you are searching for. Copernic is an Internet agent that searches multiple search engines, sums up the results, and keeps track of which sites have changed since you last visited (see Figure 18.10). The application itself works with your Web browser to help you navigate through your found results. One way Copernic saves you time is by summing up your search results. For example, if your search turns up the same page in HotBot, AltaVista, and Excite, Copernic lists it only one time and tells you where it found it. A second time-saver comes when you repeat your search at a later date. Copernic can show you which pages are new or updated since the last time you ran the search. No more going from page to page just to find which pages have changed. Find Copernic at `www.copernic.com`.

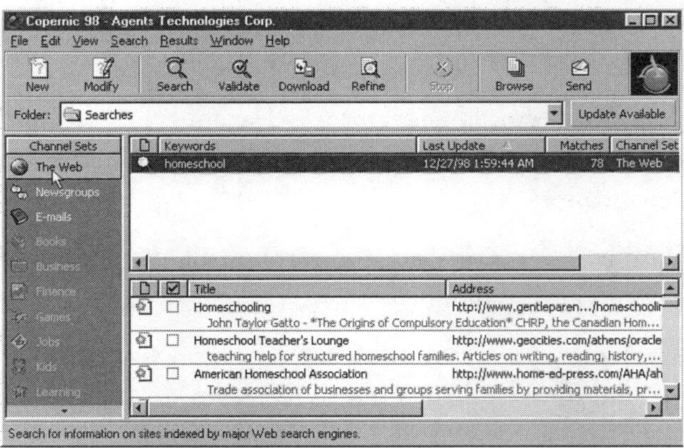

Figure 18.10
Copernic searches multiple sources at one time.

Chapter Ending

- Choose your email client based on your needs.
- Use different Web browsers for different tasks.
- Install the plug-ins you need.
- Use agents to do your work for you.
- Build Web pages with the tools you have.
- Use search engines to find what you need.

PART VI

Recovering from Disaster

Chapter 19

Recovering from a PC Disaster

IN CHAPTER 9, "PREPARING FOR DISASTER," we discussed at length the things you should do to be ready for a serious problem before it happens. In this chapter, we talk about the steps you can take after you find yourself in trouble.

Problems generally fall into one of three areas: a piece of software goes haywire and causes itself and/or other applications to behave in some undesirable manner, some hardware component breaks down, or you have a problem with a dynamic link library (DLL) or a driver. Although technically DLLs and drivers are software, they are not applications per se, so we'll talk about them separately.

Software Problems

You generally think of a software problem as something that causes your application to stop working correctly (always at the worst possible moment). But your operating system is also a piece of software, and when it gives you a problem, you quite often find that you cannot access *any* of your other applications.

One of the most intriguing aspects of software failures is their seemingly capricious nature. Your favorite application works fine one day, but the next day it starts giving you errors. Nothing new was installed, nothing was done to the system, yet you get these errors which just as suddenly go away and never crop up again. It's enough to make you scream.

You install application A, and the next time you use application B, it starts generating errors or refuses to run. What's the connection? It's very maddening and difficult to troubleshoot errors these days because of the design direction Windows has taken with shared DLLs and the registry.

A DLL is a collection of procedures (functions and subroutines) that can be called by different programs. Rather than have every application reinvent the wheel and include duplicate functions that Windows already provides in its DLLs, the idea of a shared DLL came about. A single DLL is in a central Windows folder, and every program in need of a specific routine can call that DLL. This gets tricky when a DLL is updated. Application A may install the latest new and improved version of a shared DLL only to cause application B to balk because it needs the older version to run properly. Or a poorly designed install routine might cause a newer DLL to be overwritten with an older DLL, causing grief to programs expecting the newer file.

The Windows Registry is also a focal point for software failures. The registry is where applications are supposed to store initialization and setting values. If one program changes a setting used by another program, problems arise.

Watch Out!
Before the advent of the registry, program information was stored within plain text .ini files. Windows still uses the Windows.ini and the System.ini files, and if they are damaged or deleted, your system can misbehave.

In this section we'll look at the types of errors you can run into and the steps needed to troubleshoot the problem.

General Protection Faults

A General Protection Fault or GPF is an application's way of letting you know things are amiss. How amiss can vary widely, as can the type of error or the way it's presented.

You might get a system error telling you that the current application is in trouble, recommending that you save any unsaved data, and giving you an option to Ignore the warning or to Close the application in question. Sometimes Ignore works, putting you back in the application and giving you the opportunity to save any data. Often however, the Ignore button only causes the message to be redisplayed until you click the Close button. Any unsaved data is usually lost.

The typical GPF error message simply tells you that your program has performed an illegal operation and will be shut down. A cryptic error code may be displayed, such as "0x03F7," which does not tell you much (later in this chapter we'll discuss a utility that provides a listing of all these error codes). You can click the Details button for a look at the memory registers when the failure occurred, but that's about it (see Figure 19.1). The application has died and any unsaved data is lost.

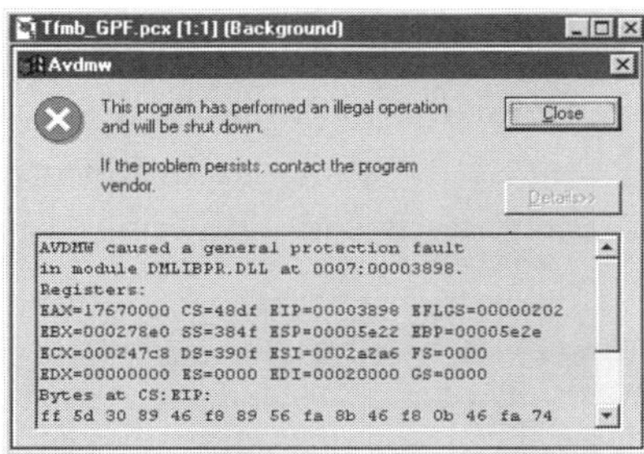

Figure 19.1
Click the error's Details button to see the memory register information.

Just as vexing is the "application has stopped responding to the system" error message that gives you the option either to wait and see if the program will "wake up" or force Windows to shut it down. Again, any unsaved data is lost.

When things really get fouled up, you can experience what's been called the "blue screen of death." When this happens, your Windows screen is replaced with a blue screen with white text that tells you something like "Fatal exception 0E at 015F:BFF9DBA7," indicating the memory address where the problem occurred. Pressing a key can return you to Windows, which gives you an opportunity to save any unsaved data. But often you are caught in an endless loop of fatal exception errors, leaving you with the only choice of hitting Ctrl+Alt+Delete and restarting your system.

Unofficially...
When an application dies with a GPF, unsaved data is usually lost. But if you're lucky, you can recover some or all of what was lost from any temporary file the application may have created. Look for files with a .tmp extension in both the Windows Temp folder (usually `C:\Windows\Temp`) and in the application's main folder.

There are several possible causes and courses of action you can take when you encounter these types of errors. Often a problem occurs once due to some transient problem and further action is not required, but sometimes a problem recurs, and some action is required on your part to correct the problem.

The Restart Option

If the problem is one where you had too many applications running at one time, system resources were too low, the swap file grew too large, the disk drive dropped precariously low on free space, or any of the things that can go wrong on a one-time basis, you may be able to correct things by carefully closing all your applications and shutting down your system.

Close the application that caused the problem, and assuming you can access Windows and your other running applications, close all open programs, saving any unsaved data. Restart Windows and see if your system stabilizes. If you ran into a blue screen of death, you might want to consider a full shutdown (powering down the system) and cold booting it to fully flush the system.

Verify and Replace Option

If a DLL has been corrupted, you will have to reinstall the file in question. This may require a reinstall of an entire individual program. How much of a hassle this is depends on the program.

Unofficially... If you're using Windows 95, you can rerun setup and you'll get an option to Restore Windows Files That Are Changed or Corrupted. This restores any corrupted DLLs but may also restore an earlier version of a file that you have updated since installing Windows 95.

For example, Microsoft Office 97 has a Reinstall option on its setup screen that will repeat the last installation (same programs and optional features installed) to restore any missing or corrupted files. If a missing or corrupted system file causes the problem, Windows 98 provides a utility—the System File Checker—that can help.

The System File Checker (SFC) is a utility of the System Information program in Windows 98. First, start the System Information program:

1. Click the Start button and then select Programs.
2. On the cascading menu, select Accessories, and then System Tools.
3. Click the System Information option.
4. Pull down the Tools menu and click System File Checker.

If you know that a specific file needs to be restored, select the lower option button and provide the filename. If you want to verify all your system files, select the first option button and click Start, as shown in Figure 19.2.

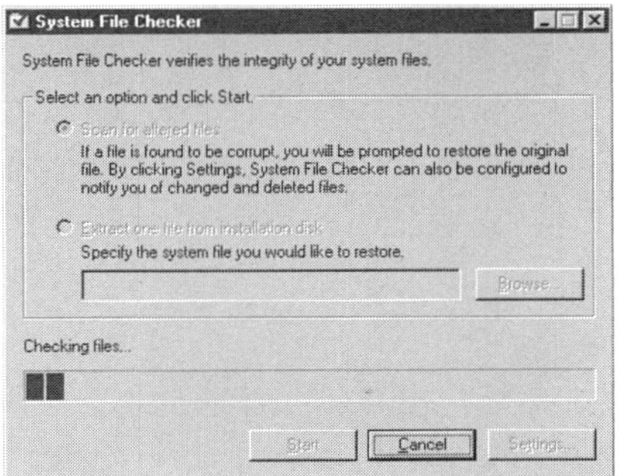

Figure 19.2
The System File Checker will verify all your system files.

If Windows finds a file that might be corrupted, it displays the filename and its location and gives you three options. First, you can choose to update the file information. This tells SFC that the current installed version is not corrupt, should not be replaced, and should not be considered bad the next time SFC runs. Second, you can choose to restore the file from the Windows 98 CD-ROM. This replaces the currently installed version with the original Win98 version. Finally, you can have SFC ignore this file this time. If you rerun SFC, the file will again be deemed bad, and you'll be presented with the same three options (see Figure 19.3).

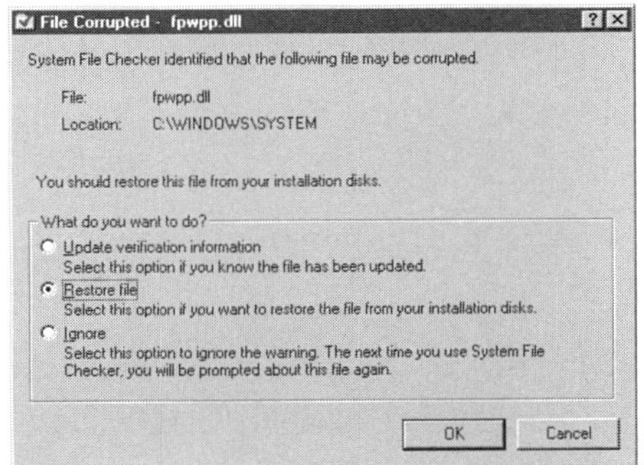

Figure 19.3
Choosing how the suspect system file will be handled.

By default, if you choose to restore a file from the Windows 98 CD-ROM, you'll have an opportunity to save the file to another folder. This makes it possible to undo the system file update if necessary (see Figure 19.4).

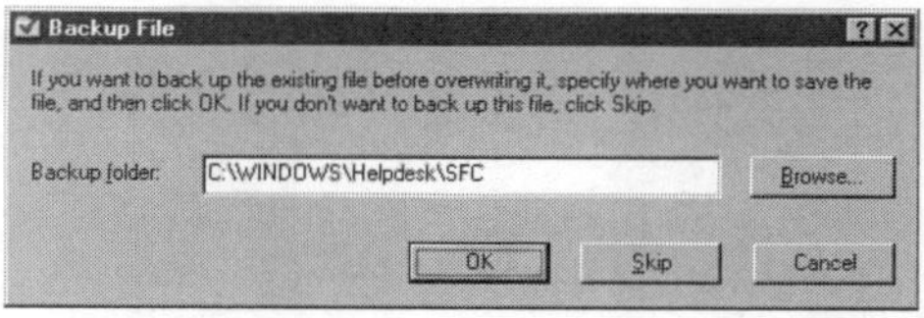

Figure 19.4 Keep backups of replaced files in case you want to undo the update.

Roll Back the Registry

Bright Idea Take this advice to heart; you must have a copy of your registry before you install anything on your computer so you can undo the effects of a bad install, if necessary. You need to copy both the User.dat and System.dat files, which reside in the `C:\Windows` folder. Save these to a disk that you keep in a safe place.

Many problems with applications running under Windows stem from something going wrong in the registry. We could fill an entire chapter with bizarre stories about strange application and system crashes that were the result of installing a device or application and having the registry get fouled up.

Fortunately, another System Information utility can fix problems with the registry and even restore a previous version of the registry. We touched on this utility back in Chapter 9. It's such a lifesaver of a utility that a repeat visit is warranted.

Registry Checker automatically scans your registry every time you start your computer. If Registry Checker notices a problem, it automatically replaces the registry with the backup copy that it has made (it makes a new copy once a day). You can manually run the Registry Checker from the Tools menu on the System Information program to make a backup copy.

To manually restore your registry, follow these steps:

1. Select Start, Shut Down, Restart in MS-DOS mode, and click OK.
2. From the MS-DOS command prompt, type `scanreg/restore`.
3. You'll see a list of the previous five backups (named Rb*nnn*.cab where *nnn* starts at 000) along with their date/time stamps; pick the latest known-good backup. The screen also indicates either Started or Not Started for each

backup file, meaning that the particular copy of the registry has successfully started your system or it hasn't, respectively. Pick the backup file you want to restore.

4. Choose Restore. If the restore is successful, Registry Checker tells you so. Likewise, if a problem occurred in restoring the CAB file, an error message appears. In this case, try restoring the next-oldest CAB.

Unofficially...
By default, the Registry Checker keeps five complete copies of your system's registry backed up. This gives you a five-day incremental history to restore from, if necessary (unless you manually back up the registry more often).

The Scanreg.ini file controls many of the Registry Checker's functions and settings. You'll find this file in your C:\Windows folder. This file can be edited in Notepad and you could, for example, increase the number of backups the checker maintains by changing the MaxBackupCopies settings. For example:

```
MaxBackupCopies=10
```

This increases the number of copies maintained, giving you a 10-day history of your registry files. Be careful editing this .ini file because the Registry Checker is a very important part of your disaster-recovery arsenal.

Operating System Problems

We talked about booting Windows into Safe mode back in Chapter 10, "Good Habits for a Trouble-Free System." When you power up your computer and Windows itself has a problem, Safe mode may be the only way you can correct the problem. The system may boot up into Safe mode (assuming Windows is functioning well enough to determine it has a problem), or you may have to force your system to come up in Safe mode. Hold down the Ctrl key as your system boots up and select one of the Safe mode options from the Start menu. On some systems, hold down the Shift key or press the F8 function key to get the Start menu. As previously discussed, in Safe mode you get a bare-bones version of Windows, generic VGA at 16 colors, very few drivers loaded, and so on, to give you a chance to uninstall, remove, install, or otherwise fix Windows.

Watch Out!
Sometimes nothing short of a Windows reinstall will fix the problem. Be sure to keep your Windows CD-ROM and any updates in your NEAT box, as discussed in Chapter 8, "Staying Ahead of the Game."

Not all problems require Safe mode; things such as shutdown problems or sound card issues can often be resolved without resorting to Safe mode. Microsoft provides various wizards that can help you resolve these types of problems.

Installation and Settings Issues

We mentioned the classic problem where you install a new video driver and you can no longer see anything when Windows boots up. Going into Safe mode with its generic graphics gives you a chance to change the driver or its settings to something that works for Windows. But you can run into trouble with other applications as well. Many applications want to restart Windows at some point during their installation, and if something has gone wrong, your system may not come back up properly. Safe mode can give you a way to get Windows working to the extent where you can go into Control Panel and uninstall the errant application.

Troubleshooting Wizards

Assuming you can get online, Microsoft provides troubleshooting wizards on its Web site, including an extensive help section for Windows 98 problems. Fire up your browser and surf to the MS Technical Support Troubleshooting Wizards (`http://support.microsoft.com/support/tshoot/`). Select Windows 98 in the drop-down list and click the Go button.

Topics, such as the following, have troubleshooting wizards associated with them:

- My computer does not start or shut down properly.
- I have problems using Advanced Power Management features or Standby mode on my computer.
- I have problems printing.
- I have problems with my modem.
- I'm having problems using the Active Desktop or Channel bar.
- Sounds are not played properly.
- I am having problems with DriveSpace.

- I need to fix a hardware conflict.
- I need help with networking.
- I receive memory-related error messages in Windows.
- My MS-DOS–based program does not work properly.
- I am having problems with PC Cards (PCMCIA).
- I need help with my display or with using multiple monitors.
- I'm having problems with DirectX.

A wizard asks you a series of questions, working you toward a specific solution (see Figure 19.5).

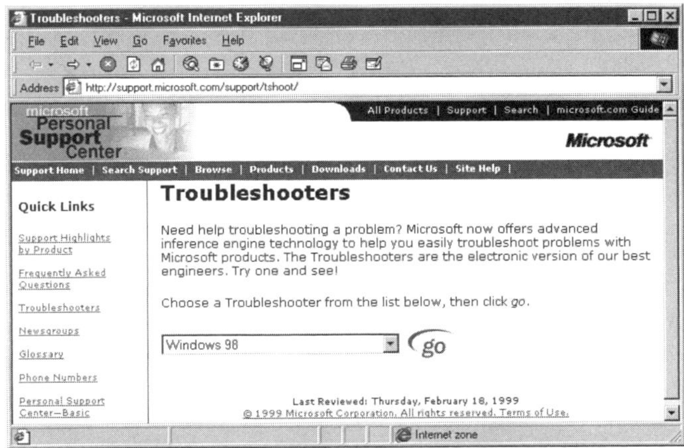

Figure 19.5
Using the Microsoft Troubleshooting Wizard over the Web.

Of course, the problem with wizards is that your problem has to be listed, and it has to ask you questions you can recognize and relate to or you may take a wrong turn. You can also search the Windows Help file index (click Start, Help) for `troubleshooting` and access several Help-file-based wizards. In Chapter 20, "Taming Technical Support," we talk about getting a real person to help you with your problem.

Unwanted Applications at Startup

Although not a critical problem by any means, having applications start by themselves can be very annoying. Examples range from the AOL Instant Messenger (this program installs itself with Netscape Communicator and runs whenever you start Windows, whether you want it to or not), to applications that start a dial-up networking connection with your ISP without your permission.

When you install the RealAudio Player G-2, it sets itself up to load whenever you start Windows. Then it proceeds to cause your computer to dial into the Internet every 10 minutes or thereabouts so it can see if a newer version of Real Audio is available that you should download.

Things used to be relatively straightforward when applications dropped a shortcut or executable into the `C:\Windows\Start Menu\Programs\StartUp` folder. You could look in the folder and delete or move anything in there that you don't want to have running whenever Windows starts. But application developers started getting sneaky about it. Some use the old Win.ini file's (yes, it's still a part of Windows 98) Load and Run settings to start themselves.

But the really clever applications use the Windows Registry to work their start-every-time magic. Several keys in the registry can be used to start applications:

- `HKEY_LOCAL_MACHINE\SOFTWARE\Microsoft\Windows\CurrentVersion\Run`
- `HKEY_LOCAL_MACHINE\SOFTWARE\Microsoft\Windows\CurrentVersion\RunServices`
- `HKEY_CURRENT_USER\SOFTWARE\Microsoft\Windows\CurrentVersion\Run`

Windows 98 provides the System Configuration Utility that you can use to ferret out these autoloading applications. To run the System Configuration Utility, click the Start button and then click Run. Type `MSConfig` and click the OK button. Various startup properties can be set with this utility on the General tab. The Startup tab gives you full control over which applications are started when Windows 98 fires up, and you can disable an application from doing so with a single click, unchecking the box next to that application (see Figure 19.6).

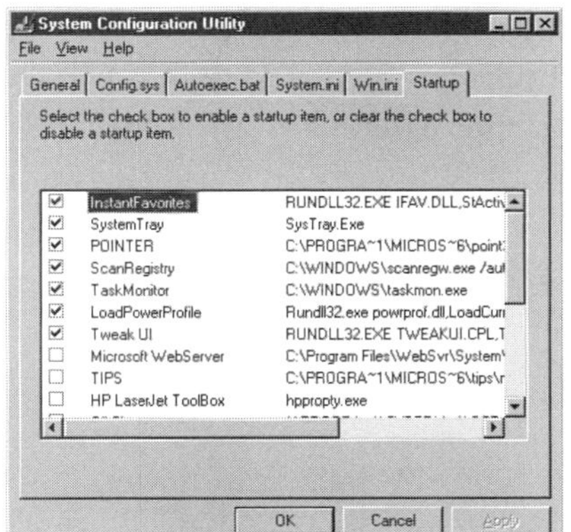

Figure 19.6
The StartUp panel gives you full control over applications running when Windows 98 starts.

Recovering from a Virus

Chapter 9, "Preparing for Disaster," spoke at length about getting and using a serious virus-protection software package. There's not much to add here except to remind you to keep your virus-detection and prevention software current by downloading the latest updates.

If you experience a virus outbreak, try to remain calm and use the tools the virus package provides, such as your virus emergency-boot disk. Start your PC with this disk and run your antivirus software. Be sure to scan any floppies that may have been used on the infected computer as well.

Bright Idea
It's a good idea to stay on top of the latest virus myths and rumors that float around the Internet. The best place for this is Rob Rosenberger's site (`www.kumite.com/myths/`), where you'll be able to separate fact from fiction.

Macro viruses are notorious for fast replication. Warn anyone you may have sent an infected file to immediately. Should you—or someone whose computer you may have infected—not have current antivirus software, you can download a trial version of the latest software from several of the major antivirus vendors on the Internet. The following are just a few:

- McAfee (`www.mcafee.com`)
- Symantec's Norton AntiVirus (`www.symantec.com`)
- Datafellows (F-Prot) (`www.datafellows.com`)

Hardware Problems

The good news is that most computer hardware is very reliable after you're past the early burn-in stage. Solid-state circuitry and few moving parts, combined with some common sense about setup, ventilation, heat, and power management, generally keeps a computer running much longer than its technical use. In other words, the computer will be running long after it's obsolete.

But problems still occur with hardware (most notably the hard disk) that qualify as a flat-out disaster.

Steps to Take

Some hardware problems such as a shorted motherboard or a burned-out power supply usually require major system surgery (and maybe the help of a skilled technician) to resolve. But you might be able to resolve other, more commonly encountered problems without even having to open up the system chassis.

Chronic hard disk problems can sometimes be traced to erratic power fluctuations. We touched on this in Chapter 1, "Deciding on the Basic System Components," and if you suspect a power problem, you should have your line voltage checked. An uninterruptible power supply might be the solution.

Don't overlook the obvious, either. In our consulting practice, we can tally the number of times we rushed out to a client who was having some catastrophic hardware problem only to discover that someone had knocked loose a cable. Before you panic when some peripheral stops working, you'll want to power everything down, disconnect all the cables from the device in question, clean the connectors of dust and debris, reconnect everything, and then power the system back up and see if any improvement occurred in the situation.

Review your system journal and see whether some logical suspect might exist. If you recently installed a piece of software or a new peripheral and then you started experiencing problems, this could give you a logical starting point in your troubleshooting efforts.

If you finally decide you need to call technical support or look beyond your NEAT box for help, check out our recommendations on getting technical support in Chapter 20, "Taming Technical Support."

Printer Won't Print

We've run into this problem more often than you might expect. The printer works fine, and then one day it won't print and your software is complaining that your disk is full. You scratch your head and wonder if the two are related. They are.

What's probably happening is that your application is trying to spool the print job to a temporary file in a temporary folder and no room is available on the disk for the file (which can be quite large, depending on what you're printing). This folder is normally the `C:\Windows\Temp` folder, unless you've defined a specific temp folder location in your Autoexec.bat file (look for a line that reads something like this: `TEMP=D:\Temp`).

The solution is to free up some disk space. Keep your Temp folder on the drive or partition with the most available space and periodically check this folder; files have a way of accumulating here. Delete anything with a file date older than the current day's date.

If the printer is physically connected to your computer (in contrast to printing over a network) you can tell Windows to print directly to the printer and avoid the Temp folder. Follow these steps:

1. Click the Start button.
2. Select Settings, and then click Printers on the cascading menu.
3. Right-click the printer you want and select Properties from the pop-up menu.
4. Click the Details tab and then click Spool Settings.
5. Select the Print Directly to the Printer option button and then click OK.

Hard Disk Crashes

Hard disk manufacturers used to talk about *mean time between failures* (MTBF) and quote the MTBF in hours to show how much more reliable their disk was as compared to their competition's. This is the *average* number of hours a disk ran before it stopped running—that is, crashed. You don't hear much about MTBF anymore (the word *failure* being a bad thing in advertising circles, in addition to the fact that modern drives often have proven MTBF ratings in the hundreds of thousands of hours range), but the fact remains that at some point your hard disk is going to crash. You may get an indication that a problem is starting to develop before you start losing data, or it may just up and die without so much as a whimper. Note that in this section, we're focusing on your hard or fixed disk; when we refer to a disk or a drive, we're talking about your hard drive.

Hopefully, you have a recent backup (see Chapter 11, "Backing Up") and have to worry only about data that you've generated since your last backup. If you've been working without a net, well, a disk crash is a traumatic event even if you have a current backup. Maybe you're backed up, maybe you're not.

The Big Question is what to do at that point.

Indications of Trouble, But Drive Is Operational

Sometimes you'll get a warning that your drive is about to join its ancestors. Several times our first indication that something was amiss was an odd noise emanating from the hard drive. You might start getting error messages when you try to open or save a file to disk. These are warning signs that indicate you may soon experience a drive failure.

Watch Out!
Never attempt to fix a hard disk problem until you've done everything you can to get a copy of your data off the drive. Anything you do to try to fix the problem can actually make things worse and render your data irretrievable.

If the drive is acting suspiciously but you can access your files, *do not reboot or turn off the computer.* Don't try to run ScanDisk or any other diagnostic or fix-it tools on the disk as long as you can access any of the files. Immediately get your backup current. Start with your most critical files, then your next most critical files, working your way to your least-valuable data files.

Only after you have copied all the data you need from the potentially failing drive should you run diagnostics on the drive or try to fix it. We talked about various diagnostic tools in Chapter 5, "Configuring Your New PC," such as ScanDisk, which comes with Windows, or a third-party diagnostic/repair utility such as the Norton Utilities from Symantec.

File problems can come from cross-linked files, foul-ups with the file allocation table (FAT), lost clusters, and so on, and you might get lucky and find that ScanDisk or Norton Disk Doctor can solve the problem. But if every scan seems to find new and more numerous errors, or if it looks like everything is fixed only to have more problems the next day, it's a good indication that the drive is heading for a major failure.

We've had drives that sounded a lot like when you drop a spoon down a running garbage disposal. After a call to the manufacturer (the drives in question were under warranty), a replacement disk was sent out. The way most drive makers work a replacement scenario is that you send them your drive and they send you a replacement. That system is not so good if the drive is still operational; who can go without their drive while they wait for UPS to show up? What we've wound up doing is giving the manufacturer a credit card number, which they charge for the replacement drive. They ship the replacement out overnight, and when they get the suspect drive back, they issue a credit on our card number.

Drive Fails to Boot

No worse way exists to start your computing day than hitting the switch and getting a DOS screen telling you that your SCSI or IDE device cannot be found and that you should "insert bootable media into appropriate drive."

First, you can try rebooting and see if the drive comes back up. If it does, you should start thinking backup and get your data backups up-to-date. We've seen systems that—for whatever reason—failed to boot up, but on retry they came up fine and never caused any further trouble. But don't count on it, and keep your critical files backed up.

If restarting your system does not help and you've used a third-party utility such as Norton's to create a Rescue disk, this is a good time to try that. Rescue disks are bootable and contain copies of your system's CMOS settings, the hard disk partition table, and its file allocation table. It tries to repair these things if need be, which might bring your disk back to life.

Watch Out!
Keep in mind that any attempts to fix a crashing disk can make the situation worse. The Norton Rescue disk has a nifty undo feature that lets you attempt to repair your disk but that can roll back those attempts, putting you back where you started.

Another thing you can try is to boot your system from your emergency boot disk that we discussed back in Chapter 9, "Preparing for Disaster," to see if you can access the hard disk at all after the system is booted. If you find that this works, copy your critical data off the hard disk as quickly as you can.

When All Else, Including Your Drive, Fails

It's time to check the hard disk controller. SCSI controllers usually have their own diagnostic software, and you should give that a shot to verify that the controller is working correctly. Check the CMOS to see that the drive information is correct, and as a final resort, open up the chassis and reseat the controller card (unless it's integrated into the motherboard itself) and all the drive cables. Then reboot your system.

At some point, you may simply have to pronounce your drive dead. In that case, your options—as far as getting the physical aspects of your system working again—are as follows:

- If you're running a dual-drive system as discussed in Chapter 11, follow the guidelines in that chapter to make your backup drive the bootable primary hard disk, and then proceed to install a new backup drive.
- If the failed drive is still under warranty, contact the manufacturer and arrange for a replacement drive.
- Buy a new replacement drive for the failed, out-of-warranty drive.

If you decide to install the replacement drive yourself, you'll find a major source of hard-drive information at The Tech Page (`www.blue-planet.com/tech/`). This site lists drives by manufacturer and includes setting information, complete with diagrams and jumper settings; it'll even show you the correct cable position (which side of the connector the red edge of the cable goes on). The Tech Page also has a collection of hard disk utilities that can be quite useful. Like so many things in life, a little advance research and preparation can go a long way to make a disk installation go more smoothly.

If you were not able to get your critical data off your failed drive, one last venue of hope still exists. Several companies specialize in recovering data from crashed disks. Using sophisticated software and even resorting to opening the drive and removing the platters under clean-room conditions, these firms can often recover data given up as irretrievably lost. Disks that have accidentally been reformatted can often be restored. The catch is the rather hefty cost involved.

Moneysaver
Try to find a firm that lets you detail the absolutely most-critical lost data, the data you must recover to make the salvage operation worthwhile, and that agrees that if this data turns out to be unrecoverable, they won't charge you or they'll charge you only a flat diagnostic fee.

Because circumstances vary, recovery companies won't quote a ballpark figure, but don't be surprised if you could buy yourself a nice new system for what it'll cost to get your drive recovered. In addition, although these companies can do amazing things when it comes to recovering your data, if the physical disk surface is damaged, nothing may be left to recover. Some firms we've encountered, such as MDS (`www.mdsdiskservice.com`), will perform a free evaluation on your drive so that you can determine if recovery is worthwhile at all. Usually, you get your recovered data back on a CD-ROM.

DLL/Driver Problems

In Chapter 16, "Managing Devices and Device Drivers," we discussed device drivers and IRQ conflicts and how to go about troubleshooting them, so we won't rehash that here. We will, however, give you a checklist and some other resources you can turn to for help when trying to fix these types of problems.

Driver Conflict Checklist

1. Boot Windows in Safe mode (see Chapter 10, "Good Habits for a Trouble-Free System").
2. Right-click My Computer and choose Properties.
3. Select the Device Manager tab.
4. Expand the category where the problem device is.
5. Select the errant device and then click the Properties button.

An error code will be displayed on the General tab panel. In Windows 98, some error codes cause a Solutions button to appear (notice in Figure 19.7 that the Hardware Troubleshooter button is displayed).

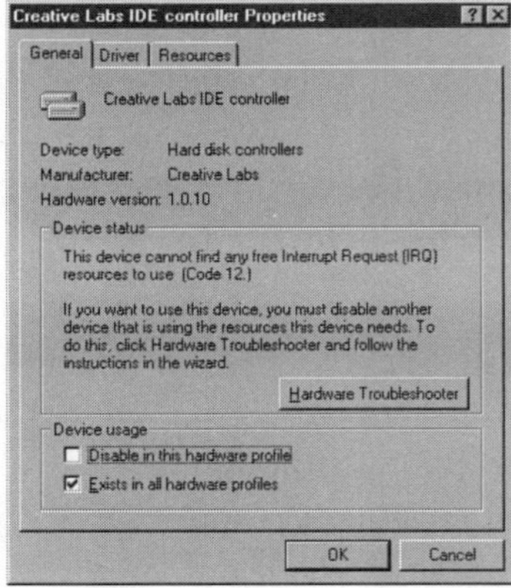

Figure 19.7 Displaying the error code for a device conflict.

Bright Idea The Hardware Troubleshooting Wizard will try to walk you through your problem and suggest solutions. You can start this wizard from the Windows 98 Help file; see the Troubleshooting Conflicting Hardware topic.

Troubleshooting DLL Problems

We've found a shareware program called DLL Show (`www.execpc.com/~sbd/DLLShow.html`) to be very useful for trying to resolve DLL problems; as a side benefit, it comes with a complete listing of all the error codes, with explanations. This utility displays all the processes currently running on your system. Select a running application and you get a list of all the DLLs on which that application is dependent (see Figure 19.8). This list can be printed out, which is very handy. Use this utility if you need to see whether a DLL is the latest version or to find out where it's located on your hard drive.

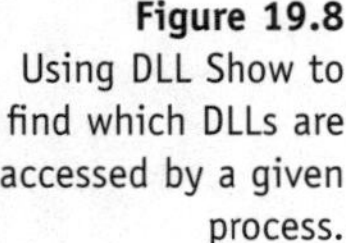

Figure 19.8 Using DLL Show to find which DLLs are accessed by a given process.

DLL Show

File View Tools Windows Help

Processes: 30	PID	Priority	Threads	Date	Version	Company
DLLSHOW.EXE	0xFFC7ED91	Normal (8)	1	Dec 17, 1998	Version 4.0	Software Design
EXPLORER.EXE	0xFFFFC169	Normal (8)	10	May 11, 1998	4.72.3110.1	Microsoft Corporation
HH.EXE	0xFFF8932D	Normal (8)	4	May 11, 1998	4.72.7322	Microsoft Corporation
KERNEL32.DLL	0xFFCFBD1D	High (13)	8	May 11, 1998	4.10.1998	Microsoft Corporation
MAPISP32.EXE	0xFFFBFA05	Normal (8)	4	Mar 26, 1998	5.5.2174.0	Microsoft Corporation
MDM.EXE	0xFFF91971	Normal (8)	2	Nov 11, 1997	1.00.7234	Microsoft Corporation
MMTASK.TSK	0xFFFFC8DD	Normal (8)	1	May 11, 1998	4.03.1998	Microsoft Corporation
MPREXE.EXE	0xFFFFEF01	Normal (8)	1	May 11, 1998	4.10.1998	Microsoft Corporation
MSGSRV32.EXE	0xFFFFFD91	Normal (8)	1	May 11, 1998	4.10.1998	Microsoft Corporation

Modules: 19	MID	Refs	Total	Size	Date	Version	Company
ADVAPI32.DLL	0x7EA73F0F	16	30	65536	May 11, 1998	4.80.1675	Microsoft Corporation
COMCTL32.DLL	0x7EA73F03	4	24	454656	May 11, 1998	4.72.3110.1	Microsoft Corporation
COMDLG32.DLL	0x7EA73F13	2	15	184320	May 11, 1998	4.72.3110.2	Microsoft Corporation
DLLSHOW.EXE	0x7EA73F91	1	1	278528	Dec 17, 1998	Version 4.0	Software Design
GDI32.DLL	0x7EA73F0C	12	30	155648	May 11, 1998	4.10.1998	Microsoft Corporation
IFAV.DLL	0x7EA73F27	1	14	204800	May 20, 1998	3, 0, 0, 387	Sergei O. Ivanov
KERNEL32.DLL	0x7EA73F0D	20	31	471040	May 11, 1998	4.10.1998	Microsoft Corporation
MSH_ZWF.DLL	0x7EA73F32	1	21	61440	Mar 23, 1998	N/A	N/A
OLE32.DLL	0x7EA73F1E	4	18	786432	May 11, 1998	4.71.1719	Microsoft Corporation

Open the application help window

Double-click a DLL in the lower window and the properties for that file are displayed, including the name, the product version, the authoring company, and so on.

Pull down the Windows menu and select Error Codes. DLL Show displays a complete listing of the documented Windows error codes (see Figure 19.9).

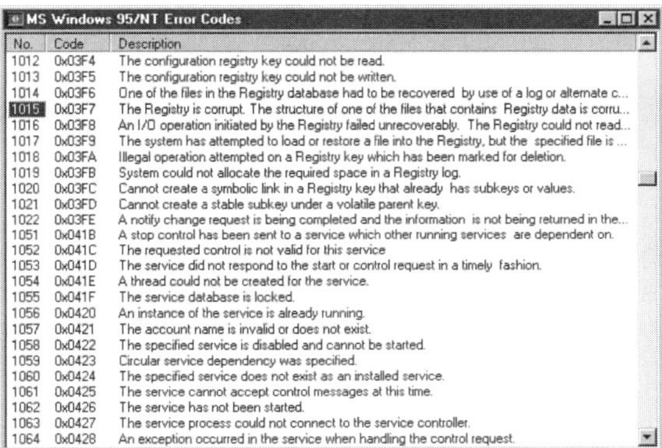

Figure 19.9
Tracking down the meaning of cryptic error codes.

This is useful when you run into a GPF that provides an error code and a lot of memory registry information, and you want to try to make some sense of what's going on with your system.

When you install Windows 98 (or reinstall it) you may find you suddenly have DLL problems in some of your applications. That's because Windows 98 thinks nothing of replacing a newer DLL with an older or different version if it thinks it will make the Windows operating system run in a more stable manner. As you might expect, this can have some serious consequences.

Windows provides a utility that can show you which DLLs it has replaced (Windows stores these replaced files so you can restore them if necessary). This is another of the System Information utilities (discussed earlier in this chapter). Run System Information and then select Version Conflict Manager (VCM) from the Tools menu (see Figure 19.10).

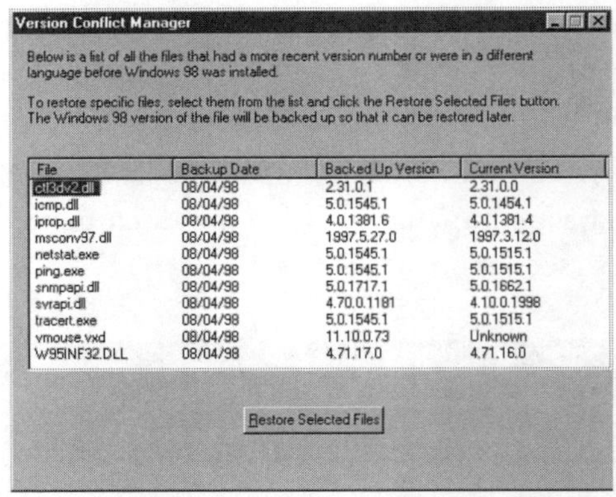

Figure 19.10 The Version Conflict Manager tracks which DLLs Windows 98 replaced during the install process.

VCM shows you the date the DLL was backed up, the version that was backed up, and the current version that is installed. By selecting a listed file, you can restore it if you determine that an application requires the more recent DLL and that its use won't crash Windows 98.

Chapter Ending

- Determine if a GPF is a random occurrence or the start of an ongoing problem.
- Restore a prior version of the registry.
- Stop unwanted programs from starting when Windows is started.
- Recover from a virus.
- Recover from a hard disk crash.
- Troubleshoot a driver or DLL conflict.

Chapter 20

Taming Technical Support

As we've discussed in previous chapters, you may find you need technical support from a variety of providers. It could be your PC's manufacturer, a software manufacturer, a device or peripheral manufacturer, a Webmaster, or your ISP. Technical support is a significant part of any computer-related service or product you buy. But only rarely do instructions come in writing about how to get support, so this chapter is dedicated to the gamut of technical support: the various ways you can get support, checklists on how to get the best support, and some online alternatives to the more traditional support channels.

Contacting Your PC's Manufacturer to Get Help

In Chapter 1, "Deciding on the Basic System Components," we describe the various service options and plans you're likely to encounter when buying a new PC. If you have a problem with your PC, the best place to start is with your manufacturer's technical support group. Your best bet for a disaster scenario is to get support by phone because warranty implications may exist.

When we have a catastrophic Windows 98 problem that falls outside the PC manufacturer's domain, here's the checklist we live by. Catastrophic means a problem that immediately crashes an application or the operating system or, if left unchecked, will shortly cause a system crash.

1. Earlier in this book, we advised that you store your data on a separate drive (or partition) away from your operating system and applications. By doing so you can quickly reinstall your operating system and applications while your data is safely preserved in another physical location.
2. Use Windows 98's built-in troubleshooting tools to research the problem. (See Chapter 5, "Configuring Your New PC," for more information.)
3. Study related topics in the *Windows 98 Resource Kit,* as discussed in Chapter 5.
4. Investigate the problem with Microsoft's Online Support. From any Microsoft product, the Help menu has a direct link there. For example, in Microsoft Word choose Help, Microsoft on the Web, and Online Support.
5. Get advice from the newsgroup or discussion group of your choice.
6. Call Microsoft Technical Support.
7. Call your friends and associates who might have an answer.
8. Perform steps 5, 6, and 7 at the same time to the extent possible. While you're waiting for a reply from one of the sources, the answer you're looking for may arrive from another.

When you call a help center by phone, you may be in for significant hold times depending on what day and time you call, but when you have a disaster on your hands, it's still better to deal with a real human being in real time. For less severe or mere informational inquiries, use any of your manufacturer's provided non-telephone support channels at your discretion.

The following is a list of the various contact channels to look for, in roughly descending order of the probability of getting a quick response:

- Telephone

- Email
- Web site
- Fax
- USPS

To find the contact numbers or addresses for these channels, open your NEAT box and look in your User's Guide, or see our separate list of Web-based contact resources (to follow). You can also check a company's home page (start with its simplified URL, such as `www.microsoft.com`) and look along the bottom of the page for text-based links labeled like these, or some variation thereof (shown here alphabetically):

- Contact
- Contact Info
- Contact Us (or Contact <*company name goes here*>)
- Customer Service
- Feedback
- For More Information
- Help
- Help Desk
- Press Room
- Send Email (or, Send Us Email)
- Support
- Technical Support (frequently shortened to Tech Support)
- Webmaster

Clickable buttons with similar labels may also be present.

In addition, the following is a list of the best places to go on the Web when you need to find a PC or other hardware manufacturer's contact phone numbers, email addresses, Web addresses, and so on.

- Microsoft Library Computer Company Information Center—http://library.microsoft.com/compcos.htm (mentioned in Chapter 8, "Staying Ahead of the Game").
- The Guide to Computer Vendors Search Engine—http://guide.sbanetweb.com/SBA_search.html. Enter the name (or keywords) for categorical searches for hardware vendors, software vendors, and value-added resellers.
- WinDrivers.com—www.windrivers.com (mentioned in Chapter 8).
- WinFiles.com—www.winfiles.com (mentioned in Chapter 8).
- PC Drivers HeadQuarters—www.drivershq.com (mentioned in Chapter 8).
- Win95/98 Drivers HeadQuarters—www.win98-drivers.com. Provides links to hardware and software manufacturers' Web sites or BBS phone numbers.
- comp.sys.ibm.pc.hardware.* FAQ—www.faqs.org/faqs/pc-hardware-faq/part5/ (mentioned in Chapter 8).
- OCL List of PC Software and Hardware Support—www.eurekanet.com/~ocl/support.html. Extensive listing of hardware and software manufacturers' Web addresses.
- Support Links Modem Companies—www.modemhelp.com/links/Modem_Companies/.
- Hoover's Online: The Ultimate Source for Company Information—www.hoovers.com.

Because so many of us use Microsoft operating systems and software, the following is a list of where to get help from this particular company.

- Telephone—800-936-3500.
- FastTips—A free automated support system, available 24×7 (Business Systems Products 800-936-4400; Development Products 800-936-4300; Desktop Systems 800-936-4200; Desktop Applications 800-936-4100).

- Priority pay-for-incident support—800-936-3500. Bill to a credit card; flat fee per incident (fee varies depending on OS/product); available 24×7 (except for a few holidays).
- Online Support—`http://support.microsoft.com/support/`. Free support via the Web; includes FAQs; drivers, patches, and other downloads; Support News Watch; access to newsgroups; Web Response; available 24×7.
- Knowledge Base (online)—`http://support.microsoft.com/support/` (part of Online Support, see above). More than 83,000 FAQs—and growing daily—are available on Microsoft's Web site; available 24×7.
- Knowledge Base (CD)—`www.microsoft.com/technet/` (for subscription and other information). The monthly subscription-based TechNet CD includes the entire Microsoft Knowledge Base, all Microsoft Resource Kits, numerous technical notes, tips, and techniques; drivers and patches; service packs; case studies; white papers; evaluation and reviewers' guides; training materials; and more; along with an excellent search interface.
- FAQs—`http://support.microsoft.com/support/default-faq.asp`. Organized by product.
- Newsgroups—`http://support.microsoft.com/support/news/default.asp` for information.
- Microsoft AnswerPoint Consulting Line—800-936-5200 at $190/hour; 6 a.m. to 6 p.m. PST Monday through Friday.
- Find out how to have Knowledge Base articles faxed or emailed to you—`http://support.microsoft.com/support/kb/articles/q162/3/87.asp`.

Unofficially...
A TechNet CD subscription, which gives you the entire Microsoft Knowledge Base on a CD-ROM, has been in our firm's consulting and technical writing arsenals since it first became available. We strongly recommend it for moderate to heavy-duty Microsoft users.

Moneysaver
The TechNet CD subscription is $299 for a single-user license and $699 for a server license. If you have three or more people on your staff who need the CD, buy the server license. The time you save by accessing this information from the CD, in contrast to over the Internet or by calling Microsoft directly, makes this a very cost-effective resource.

Using Knowledge Bases to Get Help

No single "be all and end all" knowledge base exists that you can go to on the Web to find the answer to any question. Instead, you need to create your own virtual knowledge base by doing a search on the Web or hoofing it down to your local

Unofficially...
The server for Microsoft's newsgroups is msnews.microsoft.com. See microsoft.public.win98.gen_discussion or any of the dozens of other microsoft.public.win98.* groups for information on Windows 98.

library. If you choose the former, use the following checklist for effective Web searching:

1. Write your query down in several ways. This helps get your creative juices flowing.
2. Check your spelling. Misspellings waste your time by producing bogus hits. (Hit is a synonym for one item in a search results list. Citation is another such synonym.)
3. Put quotation marks around phrases. A phrase is a set of words that must appear exactly as shown, such as "knowledge base." Using phrases greatly increases the likelihood of good hits.
4. Write down relevant synonyms for each word in your query. Synonyms are an easy way to improve the quality of search results.
5. Browse through Yahoo!'s categories. Yahoo!'s diligently and professionally categorized structure makes it ideal for organizing your thoughts.
6. Start with your favorite search engine and do one search to see if you quickly luck onto a good hit or two.
7. Get to know your favorite search engine's syntax. Although advanced search syntax can be tedious (and annoyingly dissimilar from one search service to another), it's one of the best ways to improve the quality of the search results list.
8. If you keep getting dreadful hits from your favorite three search engines, submit a shortened query to flush out more synonyms.
9. Use wildcard characters sparingly. Too many wildcards tend to produce off-target search results.
10. Use research service providers such as knowledge brokers, knowledge consultants, and information brokers.
11. Use fee-based Internet services such as the Electronic Library (www.elibrary.com).

12. Know when to quit a dead end.

13. When all else fails, search Usenet threads.

One very nice knowledge base we've found is Indiana University Support Center's Knowledge Base at `http://kb.indiana.edu`. It's a free, searchable index of 4,500 (and growing) well-written and current mini-FAQs about a wide variety of computing topics.

Bright Idea
Whether you're searching the Internet or the card catalog at your local library, if you work through a group of hits and the first few are relevant, don't stop reading until you reach at least two consecutive citations that are irrelevant. That way, you'll get the most targeted coverage of your subject and increase your chances of finding all the information you need. Don't assume that the first relevant citation contains *all* the information you might want on a given topic.

Using the Internet to Get Help

The Internet is quickly becoming a vast repository for help and support resources of all kinds. In this section we explore the most common types of help channels you'll find today on the Internet.

Communicating with a Manufacturer

The process of getting in touch with a software manufacturer is effectively the same as it is for contacting a hardware manufacturer. If the tips we provided earlier in the chapter don't pan out as you try to contact a company, try the following list of common email addresses (shown here alphabetically) where *domain* is the manufacturer's Internet domain name (which may or may not be the same as the company name):

- `feedback@domain.com`
- `info@domain.com`
- `sales@domain.com`
- `support@domain.com`
- `tech@domain.com`
- `webmaster@domain.com`
- *<product name>*`@domain.com` (for example, `magic@powerquest.com`)

Unofficially...
You can get a good listing of knowledge bases on various topics by searching Yahoo! for `"knowledge base"` (include the quotes).

Newsgroups

Some, but not all, hardware and software manufacturers provide technical support in a public electronic forum of some kind. The channels may be implemented either as newsgroups or as Web-based bulletin boards. In either case, check the company's Web site or printed documentation for access instructions.

Going Online to Find FAQs, Help, Support Centers, and Web-based Troubleshooting

A FAQ (Frequently Asked Question) is a document that covers frequently asked questions on a particular subject and provides answers and references for further research. Most Internet newsgroups maintain a primary FAQ describing the group's purpose, along with a summary of key facts. These primary FAQs are often large and very informative.

Although you can use DejaNews or AltaVista to search Usenet newsgroup messages, this shows what people have been posting in discussion threads but not the content of the associated FAQs. If you need carefully prepared and up-to-date FAQ material, skip reading busy newsgroups and go directly to MIT's FAQ listing.

MIT's vast FAQ listing arranges newsgroups in two ways. Browse to `ftp://rtfm.mit.edu/pub/` and locate the folders usenet-by-group and usenet-by-hierarchy. The usenet-by-group folder lists all newsgroups alphabetically by name. The usenet-by-hierarchy folder lists all the top-level hierarchy names. Many of these are esoteric, so go to `ftp://rtfm.mit.edu/pub/usenet-by-hierarchy/news/announce/newusers/How_to_find_the_right_place_to_post_%28FAQ%29` for a description of the common ones. If you scroll down this page (or search for `hierarchies` on the current page), you'll find the plain-English descriptions of the top-level hierarchy names.

Unofficially... If you want to avoid adult or pornographic content, a good rule of thumb is to avoid alt-prefixed newsgroups. (For what it's worth, the prefix alt is defined as "an anarchic collection of serious and silly subjects.") Use your own judgment here.

The following resources provide online help or serve as launching points for getting online help:

- Indiana University Support Center's Knowledge Base—`http://kb.indiana.edu`. Mentioned earlier in this chapter.
- John McDonnell's Researcher's Toolkit—`www.geocities.com/WallStreet/6100/index.htm`. John has prepared this neat site while surfing the Web in preparation for his *InfoAlert*

newsletter about online research; in particular, see his Computers and the Internet category.

- Yahoo!'s Beginner's Guides—`http://dir.yahoo.com/Computers_and_Internet/Internet/World_Wide_Web/Information_and_Documentation/Beginner_s_Guides/`.
- Yahoo!'s FAQs—`http://dir.yahoo.com/Computers_and_Internet/Internet/World_Wide_Web/FAQs/`.
- Yahoo!'s Web Directories—`http://dir.yahoo.com/Computers_and_Internet/Internet/World_Wide_Web/Information_and_Documentation/Web_Directories/`.

The following sites operate as online support centers:

- HelpTalk—`www.helptalk.com`. To quote their main page, "a free service providing personalized assistance in installing, using and trouble-shooting most Windows 95 [and 98] software and hardware."
- ModemHelp—`www.modemhelp.com/support.html`. Operates on a voluntary payment service plan whereby you're encouraged (but not required) to pay $10 if you're satisfied with the company's response to your query.
- Online Support Center—`www.onlinesupport.com`. Sports a bulletin board (The CorkBoard), where you can post and read threaded messages, and use HelpCrawler that's a front-end to search the Web for help on topics you specify.

Using the Phone to Get Help—A Checklist

When you contact any company's technical or customer support staff by phone, you need a strategy. The following is a checklist to use on such occasions. By following these steps, you'll minimize the amount of time it takes to get help, you'll get better quality help on the other end of the line, and you'll feel better (no yelling and screaming).

1. Have a pad of paper and pen handy because you'll be taking notes as you go.

Bright Idea
Use your system journal for taking notes if the call relates to your PC or any of its devices, peripherals, or software components.

Note-taking is the key. If later you can't remember what steps a representative suggested to follow, the replacement part number, or the Web site address for the updated driver, then you'll have to start all over again.

2. Get the representative's name and a direct call-back number (or direct extension) for follow-up calls.

   Ask for this information in a friendly way—especially the rep's name. Even though it's the rep's job to help folks like you, and it's probably a standard procedure for them to unhesitatingly provide a name or identification number when asked, respect them and set a good tone for the conversation.

3. Take copious notes of every conversation, including the date, time, and duration of the call.

   Every little conversational tidbit can be priceless later. We've found that it's best to write literally everything down, at least in shorthand. After you hang up the phone, go over your notes and fill in the details. The problem with not writing down everything is that Murphy's Law circles around, and eventually, the very tidbit you need (a replacement part number, for example) is the tidbit you didn't write down.

4. In the case of a relatively simple problem and if hold times aren't too long, call three times to get three opinions.

   If you get a solid correct answer on the first call, clearly you won't need to call back again. But if you don't understand what you were told on the first call, or if the solution doesn't work when you try it offline, you can get a better statistical sampling of help information by calling back and *not* asking for the same rep you spoke to before. Instead, get a different rep and pose your question again. If you keep getting bad or incomplete information, by the time you've called three times, you should have a much clearer picture of the situation. More on call-backs that run aground in step 6.

5. Get the provider's internal problem-tracking number (if they have one).

   Not every support organization uses problem-tracking numbers, but some do, and it pays to write it down for faster service should you need to call back.

6. If your second phone call doesn't resolve the problem (and you've elected to not try the "call three times for a good sampling of help" technique), no matter how nice the rep you're talking to is, insist on speaking to a supervisor and start escalating from there.

   Your time is priceless, so you be the judge about when to draw the line when you're getting the runaround. When you decide to opt for the "give me your supervisor" approach, do so kindly but firmly, and don't take no for an answer. The majority of support organizations *require* their reps to hand you off to a supervisor if you ask.

7. An angry tone of voice works against you, so no matter how much furniture you're throwing around in the background, try to stay cool while escalating the issue.

   Sure, as you're reading this right now without any adrenaline coursing through your veins, it may sound like mere self-help psychology, but keeping your cool throughout the phone call is probably the biggest factor in getting good help.

8. When all else fails, try another provider of whatever product or service it is that's troubling you.

   Let the wayward provider know they've lost a customer and that you're going to tell all your friends. Grass roots works.

Chapter Ending

- Get to Your PC's Manufacturer.
- Knowledge Bases
- Get to Other Manufacturers.
- Newsgroups
- Online FAQs
- Online Help
- Online Support Centers
- Online Troubleshooting
- A Phone Etiquette Checklist for Calling Technical Support.

PART VII

Appendixes

Appendix A

Glossary

Access provider A company that provides access to the Internet for your home computer.

Active Desktop Integrates the Internet and your Windows Desktop. Lets you update news and other items from the Internet automatically and displays them on your desktop.

ADSL Asymmetric Digital Subscriber Line. A digital technology that supplies high-speed data transfer for accessing the Internet. Data can be transferred to your computer at up to 6 megabits per second.

AGP Accelerated Graphics Port video-processing chip set. A bus specification from Intel that gives graphics cards faster access to memory, which speeds up your video processing.

ATA/IDE Advanced Technology Attachment. A protocol for computer hardware to access the data on a hard disk. *See also* SCSI.

ATAPI Advanced Technology Attachment Packet Interface. A standard protocol for accessing CD-ROM drives.

Backup A copy of your files for use in case of an emergency. Can be a copy of your whole system or just selected important files.

Batch file A small program that runs system commands at the DOS level. Used for automating common tasks.

BIOS Basic Input/Output System. A little bootstrap program that jump-starts your PC into being able to deal with the peripherals attached to it as the computer boots up.

Boot disk A floppy disk with the necessary system files for starting your computer without using the hard drive. Also referred to as "start disk" and "emergency disk."

Boot up Describes the process of turning on your computer and initializing the operating system.

Browser An application used to view the World Wide Web. Internet Explorer and Netscape Navigator are the two most popular browsers today.

Bus A hardware component used to transfer data to and from the different components of the PC.

Bus Clock Speed The speed in megahertz that the system bus runs.

Byte The amount of memory used to store one character of data. *See also* Megabyte.

Caddy Used by some CD-ROM drives. The caddy is a removable holder for your CD-ROM disks and protects them as they are used. The CD-ROM disk is first placed in the caddy and the caddy is placed in the CD-ROM drive.

Cartridge drives Removable drives used for either backup or transportable data purposes. Think of them as removable hard drives ranging from 100 megabytes to 2 gigabytes.

CD-ROM Compact Disc–Read-Only Memory. A thin plastic disk that holds 650 megabytes of data. Drives are available for writing your own CD-ROMs as well.

Channel Internet content that is delivered from the Internet to your local computer via Internet Explorer. *See also* Subscription.

CMOS Complementary Metal-Oxide Semiconductor. An integrated circuit that stores vital settings about your PC that are used at boot up.

Context menu Windows menus accessible by right-clicking inside of an application or Windows itself. The contents of the menu changes according to the current context for the object being right-clicked.

CPU Central Processing Unit. The CPU controls the main calculations and processes of your PC. The CPU speed is measured in megahertz.

Desktop A special folder in your Windows system that displays when all running applications have been minimized. Can contain Web content.

Device Manager Located in the Windows Control Panel, this dialog box gives you information on all your hardware devices, including the drivers they are using. Can show you system conflicts between hardware as well.

Dialog box A box containing information or options for you to fill out. Most often used to customize applications and report system status messages.

DIMMs Dual Inline Memory Modules. A RAM module that adds memory to your computer. Has two rows of pins for faster performance. *See also* SIMMs and RAM.

Directory *See* Folder.

DOS Disk Operating System. A command processor that interacts with Windows and your disk system. Can be programmed using batch files.

Double-click Quickly clicking the left mouse button twice on the same object. Can be adjusted in the Control Panel/Mouse applet.

Download Transferring a file from a remote computer to your computer. Can be done with FTP or your Web browser. Sometimes called GET.

Drag Clicking an object and then moving it to another location without releasing the mouse button. Can use either the left or right mouse button.

Explorer An application for examining and working with the file system in Windows.

Explorer view A view of your Windows file system with two panes—one with folders, one with files. *See also* Folder view.

Favorites A special Windows folder used to categorize pointers to Web sites and other data files. Easily customized.

Folder A named space on a computer disk for storing files.

Folder view A view of your Windows file system in a single window showing both files and folders. *See also* Explorer view.

FTP File Transfer Protocol. A method for transferring files from one computer to another over the Internet.

Full backup A complete copy of all the files on your system for use in case of an emergency computer failure.

Gigabyte 1,000 megabytes of storage space.

HTML HyperText Markup Language. A markup system used to format Web pages for the Internet.

HTTP HyperText Transfer Protocol. A protocol used to transfer Web pages from one computer to another over the Internet.

Icon A small picture representing an object on your computer. Usually a file, a folder, or a program function.

IDE Integrated Drive Electronics. *See* ATA/IDE.

IMAP Internet Mail Access Protocol. An emerging standard for receiving and filing Internet email.

Incremental backup A backup consisting of only the files that have changed since the last full backup.

IRQ Interrupt Request. A number assigned to various devices on your system to identify them to the CPU. Conflicts arise when two devices try to use the same interrupt to communicate with the CPU.

ISDN Integrated Services Digital Network. A fast digital phone line. Can transfer data at speeds up to 128 kilobytes per second.

ISP Internet Service Provider. A company that links your computer to the Internet.

Knowledge Base A searchable index of problem-solving information. Most companies are making these available for free via the Internet.

Left-click Using your left mouse button to select an object.

Left-drag Dragging an object using your left mouse button.

Megabyte A measurement used to specify memory storage sizes. 1,000 kilobytes.

Megahertz Millions of cycles per second. A measurement of system processor speeds.

Memory Where a computer stores data. Can be either permanent (relative to what happens when you turn off power to the device) as in a hard drive or a CD-ROM, or temporary as in RAM.

MIDI Musical Instrument Digital Interface. A standard for connecting computers and musical instruments.

Motherboard The main circuit board of your computer. Everything plugs into it.

My Documents A Windows system folder used to store documents that you create.

Newsgroup An Internet gathering place for people with common interests to exchange messages. Usenet is a collection of more than 15,000 newsgroups.

NNTP Network News Transport Protocol. A protocol used to transmit Usenet news around the Internet.

OEM Original Equipment Manufacturer. Refers to the company that actually built the computer, which is not necessarily the same company that sold the computer.

POP Post Office Protocol. A protocol for receiving Internet email. *See also* IMAP and SMTP.

PPP Point to Point Protocol. A standard protocol for connecting personal computers to the Internet.

Program files A Windows system folder to which Windows installs new software.

Protocol A set of rules and conditions that perform a certain function. Usually used to have computers talk to each other. *See also* FTP, POP, IMAP, NNTP, SMTP, and TCP/IP.

RAM Random Access Memory. Refers to electronic memory. Any data stored in RAM is erased when the computer's power is turned off. *See also* SIMMs and DIMMs.

RAS Remote Access Server. A method used to connect one computer directly to another computer from a remote location.

Recent Documents A list on your Start menu of the last 15 documents opened on your system.

Right-click Using your right mouse button to select an object by clicking and releasing the right button.

Right-drag Dragging an object using your right mouse button.

ROM Read-Only Memory. Memory chips that are preprogrammed with data that cannot be written over.

SCSI Small Computer Systems Interface. A protocol for connecting computer devices such as hard drives and CD-ROMs in a chain.

SDRAM Synchronous Dynamic Random Access Memory. A high-speed RAM module.

SendTo A special Windows menu added to Explorer context menus to help you send or move data around on your system.

Shortcut An icon that points to a file, a folder, or a program on another part of your system.

SIMMs Single Inline Memory Modules or RAM. A RAM module for adding additional memory to your computer. *See also* DIMMs.

SMTP Simple Mail Transport Protocol. A protocol used for sending Internet mail.

Sockets Communication channels used by your computer to interact with the Internet.

Start Menu A hierarchical listing of programs available on your computer. Easily customizable by the user.

StartUp A Windows folder that contains programs that run every time you boot your computer. Can be bypassed by holding the Shift key down while Windows loads.

Subscription Means you are a member of an Internet mailing list. Often free. *See also* Channel.

System Folder A special folder used by the Windows operating system. *See also* Desktop, Favorites, SendTo, StartUp, Recent Documents, and My Documents.

System Tray The small area on the right end of the taskbar where system-level programs display their icons.

Taskbar Runs across the bottom of the Windows screen. Contains the Start menu, toolbars, running programs, the system tray, and optional toolbars.

TCP/IP Transmission Control Protocol/Internet Protocol. A standard set of networking protocols that tie the Internet together and allow computers to talk with each other.

Telnet A protocol that lets you log in to a computer across the Internet and execute commands.

Toolbar A row of icons that activate various commands in a program. Usually runs across the top of the host application.

Tray *See* System Tray.

Uninterruptible Power Supply *See* UPS.

Universal Serial Bus A computer port that supports high-speed transfers and multiple devices on one port. Used to connect printers and other devices to your computer.

Upgrades Newer releases of software and hardware. These often contain fixes to bugs, feature enhancements, and other benefits.

Upload Transferring a file from your computer to a remote computer. Usually done with FTP. Sometimes called PUT.

UPS A backup power system for your computer. Should the power go out, the UPS battery kicks in and gives you time to shut your system down gracefully.

URL Uniform Resource Locator. An addressing schema for Internet sites. Defines the protocol and the Internet address needed to reach a remote resource.

USB *See* Universal Serial Bus.

Usenet A series of many thousands of message boards on the Internet.

Virus A program or fragment of code that infects and causes damage to files, typically without your knowledge.

VRAM Video Random Access Memory. Special RAM designed for graphics cards to speed up graphics operations.

Windows key A keyboard key labeled with the Windows logo and located between the Control and the Alt keys. Performs various functions specific to the Windows operating system. Not all keyboards have these keys.

WRAM Windows Random Access Memory. RAM used in video adapters.

WSYIWYG What You See Is What You Get. A term meaning that what you see on the screen is what will come off of the printer.

WWW World Wide Web. The graphical part of the Internet accessed using a Web browser.

XCOPY DOS-based command for duplicating files.

Appendix B

Resource Directory

WHEN YOU HAVE a computer problem or if you need more information about a peripheral you're thinking of buying, where can you turn? In this guide we've tried to pull together the resources you'll need to keep your computer from making you crazy. We'll show you where to look first for software upgrades, hardware, virus and bug information, where to get support, and where to find utilities.

Computer Companies

Guide to Computer Vendors Search Engine

`http://guide.sbanetweb.com/SBA_search.html`

A searchable database of computer vendors where you can find equipment manufacturers and software vendors.

Hoover's Online

`http://www.hoovers.com`

Referring to itself as "the company that covers companies," Hoover's enables you to search for corporate and company information on a number of firms across several industries.

Microsoft Library—Computer Company Information Center

`http://library.microsoft.com/compcos.htm`

A listing maintained by Microsoft of more than 1,800 computer companies.

OCL List of Software and Hardware Support

http://www.eurekanet.com/~ocl/support.html

An extensive alphabetical listing of hardware and software manufacturers' Web addresses.

Education and Games

CNET Gamecenter

http://www.gamecenter.com

Features hardware and software reviews, sneak peeks, tips, and discussion boards.

Gamezone

http://www.gamezone.com

Provides demo versions of a number of popular games in addition to reviews and tips.

Home-Ed Magazine

http://www.home-ed-press.com/

This site has back issues of the magazine and a collection of links to educational resources that are on and off the Web.

Homeschool World

http://www.home-school.com

A collection of articles on homeschooling and on education on the Internet, with links to other home school organizations.

Intelligamer

http://www.intelligamer.com

Intelligamer offers reviews broken down by category, interviews with game developers, and strategy guides.

John McDonnell's Researcher's Toolkit

http://www.geocities.com/WallStreet/6100/index.htm

Pointers to online research sites around the Internet.

Jon's Homeschool Resource Page

http://www.midnightbeach.com/hs/

Jon's Homeschool Resource Page is one of the longest-running homeschool resource centers on the Internet.

Learn2.com—The Ability Utility

http://www.learn2.com

This site lists tutorials, discussion areas, and helpful advice on a dozen different subjects.

Macmillan Personal Bookshelf

http://www.mcp.com/personal

Macmillan Computer Publishing makes the full text of many computer books available for reading online.

Microsoft in Education

http://www.microsoft.com/education/

Here both teachers and students will find templates, tutorials, and other tools to help in using the computer more effectively for education.

New Promise Online Education

http://www.newpromise.com

A searchable catalog of 3,700 distance-learning courses across multiple accredited schools.

Project Gutenberg

http://www.promo.net/pg/index.html

A site dedicated to putting books online. Many of these books are classics or older works. The Other Links section of the site points you to other online book depositories.

Sarah's Distance Learning Page

http://www.geocities.com/Athens/7519/

Sarah, a teacher, presents information from the viewpoints of both student and teacher. This site includes a large number of links of interest to educators and links of interest to students.

Schoolhouse

http://encarta.msn.com/schoolhouse/

Schoolhouse is an addition to Microsoft's Encarta program, with special emphasis on education; it includes specific lessons that can be searched by subject, grade level, or keyword.

Study Web

http://www.studyweb.com

A collection of links to educational sites sorted by areas of study.

SuperKids Educational Software Review

http://www.superkids.com

Current reviews and price surveys of educational software titles.

The Learning Web

http://www.learning-web.com

Offers a number of online courses across several topics, including computers and technology. Most of the classes are fee based.

The World Lecture Hall

http://www.utexas.edu/world/lecture/

A comprehensive catalog of Internet-based courses offered from around the world.

ZDNet Help Channel

http://www.zdnet.com/zdhelp

The Books section makes sample chapters from computer technology books available for reading online.

ZDNet University

http://www.zdu.com

Ziff Davis offers $5 quick courses that give you an overview of more than 150 online courses covering a variety of technical topics.

Email

Microsoft Windows Update

http://windowsupdate.microsoft.com/default.htm

Microsoft's free email-only program, Outlook Express, not only handles your email but also doubles as a very nice Internet newsgroup reader.

Microsoft's Outlook Express Homepage

http://www.microsoft.com/ie/ie40/oe/

Information and download site for Microsoft's free email client.

Netscape Products

http://www.netscape.com/browsers/index.html

Netscape's browser includes a free and creditable email reader, Messenger.

Pegasus Mail by David Harris

http://www.pegasus.usa.com

Information and downloads for the popular (and free) Pegasus email client.

Qualcomm's Eudora Place

http://www.eudora.com

Information and downloads for Eudora and Eudora Light, popular email clients. The Light version is free.

Ergonomics and RSI

Paul Marxhausen's Computer Related Repetitive Strain Injury

http://engr-www.unl.edu/ee/eeshop/rsi.html

Paul provides a good introduction to RSI and its causes, along with numerous resources and information on this serious condition.

Possibility Outpost RSI Jump Station

`http://gateway.possibility.com/RsiJump.html`

A collection of links to sites on RSI, ergonomics, physiology, cause and prevention, products, and support groups.

RSI Help

`http://www.rsihelp.org`

A site created so people can find information about this disorder and share their experiences.

Stretching, Inc. Online

`http://www.stretching.com/html/stretches.htm`

Stretching exercises and other strain-relieving practices.

Hardware

The 3Dfx Files

`http://www.3dfx.com`

3Dfx company site with information, drivers, and technical information on this popular video card.

American Power Conversion

`http://www.apcc.com/english/power/index.cfm`

American Power Conversion produces relatively inexpensive and reliable Universal Power Supply devices; it also provides excellent customer service.

Anand Tech CPU Reviews

`http://www.anandtech.com/html/reviews.cfm?types=yes&TopicTypes=101`

Rates the various CPU microprocessors on the market and includes reviews and discussions.

The Better Business Bureau

`http://www.betterbusinessbureau.com`

Check out that corner clone vendor with the Better Business Bureau before you purchase a custom system.

CD-ROM and Audio Help Links

http://mptbbs.simplenet.com/ctech4.htm

A collection of links that cover everything you might need to know about CD-ROM drives and sound cards.

Creative Labs—Drivers and Patches

http://www.soundblaster.com/wwwnew/tech/ftp/ftpnew.html

Get the latest updated drivers for your Creative Labs sound card.

Crucial Technology's Memory Upgrade Configurator

http://www.crucial.com

Enter your system and find out for how much memory your computer can be configured. Order the proper memory upgrades directly from this site.

Dell Computers

http://www.dell.com/

Mail-order supplier of built-to-order computers.

Diamond Multimedia

http://www.diamondmm.com

Makers of video, sound, and home network cards, as well as a superior line of modems. Drivers and technical support are available on this site.

Drivers Headquarters

http://www.drivershq.com

Track down the device driver you need by category.

Gateway Computers

http://www.gateway.com/

Mail-order supplier of built-to-order computers.

Hewlett-Packard Customer Care

http://www.hp.com/cposupport/eschome.html

Download the latest printer drivers for Hewlett-Packard printers.

How to Check Hard Drive Configuration

http://service1.symantec.com/SUPPORT/nunt.nsf/docid/1996112575859

Symantec Corporation's excellent tutorial on determining a hard drive's configuration and troubleshooting configuration problems.

IEEE 1284 EPP/ECP Compatible Product List Page

http://www.fapo.com/1284prod.htm

A list of products that support one or more modes of the IEEE 1284 standard (parallel port specification).

Intel's iCOMP 2.0 Index Specifications

http://www.intel.com/procs/perf/icomp/index.htm

Intel's iComp index shows the approximate, relative performance of Intel microprocessors on 32-bit applications and benchmarks.

Iomega Corporate Home Page

http://www.iomega.com

The premiere manufacturer of removable media hard drives. Get the latest product information and technical support.

Links to 1394 Content

http://www.p1394pm.org/links.htm

Products and manufacturers that support the FireWire bus standard (IEEE 1394 aka High Performance Serial Bus).

Manageable Software Services, Inc.

http://www.manageable.com

Catch-UP is a free upgrade manager that checks your installed software and helps you download the latest version.

Micron Electronics

http://store.micronpc.com/

Mail-order supplier of built-to-order computers.

Microsoft DirectX Multimedia Expo

`http://www.microsoft.com/directx/default.asp`

Download the latest Direct X multimedia drivers for Windows from the Microsoft site.

Microsoft Technical Support Troubleshooting Wizards

`http://support.microsoft.com/support/tshoot/`

The main page for Microsoft's Troubleshooting Wizards.

The Tech Page Hard Drive Jumpers and Specs

`http://www.blue-planet.com/tech/`

This site lists drives by manufacturer and includes setting information complete with diagrams and jumper settings; also included is a handy collection of hard disk utilities.

Thomas Pabst's Intel Roadmap

`http://www2.tomshardware.com/irm298.html`

Nicely done, thorough, text-and-graphics time chart of the Intel Pentium processor family.

ViewSonic Display Technology Products

`http://www.viewsonic.com`

Manufacturer of one of the more reliable and popular lines of CRT monitors.

Win98 Drivers Headquarters

`http://www.win98-drivers.com`

Find the latest updated Windows device drivers on this site.

WinDrivers.com

`http://www.windrivers.com/`

Find the latest drivers by searching for a given device manufacturer.

WinFiles

`http://www.winfiles.com/drivers`

Searchable database of device manufacturers that enables you to find the latest device drivers for your hardware.

ZeroSurge, Inc.

`http://www.zerosurge.com/index.html`

ZeroSurge manufactures surge suppressors that do not rely on MOVs and therefore should not wear out over time.

Internet

AnyWho Directories

`http://www.anywho.com`

Search for phone numbers, addresses, and email addresses, and even do reverse phone lookups on this snooper site.

Apple QuickTime

`http://www.quicktime.com`

Apple's free Multimedia Browser plug-in enables you to view QuickTime videos over the Internet.

Audionet

`http://www.audionet.com`

Index of Multimedia broadcasts over the Internet, including news, music, videos, live broadcasts, and more.

The Federal Web Locator

`http://www.law.vill.edu/fed-agency/fedwebloc.html`

Find any branch of the vast federal bureaucracy fast with this locator site. From the National Bioethics Advisory Commission to the Internal Revenue Service, this site has it all.

Geocities

`http://www.geocities.com`

Geocities is a Web-hosting company that provides free, limited Web sites. Although you can't beat free, you have to put up with ads appearing on your site.

GTE

`http://www.gte.net`

Phone companies are popular Internet service providers. GTE is a regional provider that has a number of connection and ISP services.

ImagiNet Network

http://www.imagin.net

Internet service provider home page showing the typical services an ISP makes available to its subscribers.

Integrity Online

http://www.integrityonline.com

Integrity differentiates itself as an Internet service provider by filtering adult and questionable content before it ever gets to your browser.

The List—The Definite ISP Buyer's Guide

http://thelist.internet.com/

Helps you to find a provider that offers the access speed and computing services that satisfy your needs and budget. Search by area code or country code.

LYNX

http://www.crl.com/~subir/lynx/binaries.html

A pure text browser, Lynx is free and enables you to browse the Web without having to be distracted or delayed by graphics.

Macromedia

http://www.macromedia.com/software/downloads/

Macromedia's Shockwave and Flash plug-ins are used on a growing number of Web sites to provide animation and special effects. Download these free plug-ins to see Shockwave-enhanced pages in your browser.

Microsoft BackOffice Live

http://backoffice.microsoft.com

Microsoft's line of BackOffice products, including its proxy Web server.

Neoplanet

http://www.neoplanet.com

The Neoplanet Web browser lets you put a different "face" on Internet Explorer. Very interesting and worth a look if you use the Microsoft browser.

Netscape Products

http://home.netscape.com/download/index.html

Download the latest version of the Netscape Navigator browser and its components at this site.

Netscape Server Products

http://www.netscape.com/servers

Netscape's line of server products, including its proxy Web server.

Netscape Smart Update

http://home.netscape.com/download/index.html

Get the latest Netscape Navigator updates by using this automated service page.

Netscape's Home Page

http://home.netscape.com

Netscape makes Navigator, one of the top two browsers in use. This site has information on all the Navigator components, including Messenger, the email client built into Navigator.

Opera Software

http://www.operasoftware.com

Opera is an alternative browser offering several features not found in Navigator or Internet Explorer.

Real Guide

http://www.real.com/realguide

Real Networks directory of Internet broadcasts. Listen to streaming audio feeds from a number of interesting resources over the Internet.

Real Networks

http://www.real.com

The leader in Web audio, the Real Audio plug-in can be downloaded for free, or you can purchase a more advanced version.

Yahoo!'s Internet Blocking and Filtering Resources

http://dir.yahoo.com/Business_and_Economy/Companies/Computers/Software/Internet/Blocking_and_Filtering/

A listing of products that enable you to block or not block a certain application, a Web site, particular content, or a particular piece of data.

Yahoo!'s Internet Tutorials

http://dir.yahoo.com/Computers_and_Internet/Internet/World_Wide_Web/Information_and_Documentation/Tutorials__Demos__Talks

Tutorials and information on building Web pages, design concepts, adding audio, working with intranets, and more.

Miscellaneous

Amalgamated Binaries

http://www.ambin.com

Makers of amusing and entertaining software programs available as freeware.

Bottom Dollar

http://www.bottomdollar.com/software.html

This site is a search engine that finds the best deal available on a given piece of software among 15 vendors.

Company Sleuth

http://www.companysleuth.com/

An email service that tracks information on companies in which you hold stock. The information is delivered right to your email box.

Pricewatch

http://www.pricewatch.com

Find the best street price on a computer product by using Pricewatch. Search by category or by a given manufacturer.

ReviewFinder

http://www.reviewfinder.com

This site collects links to reviews on other sites around the Internet and categorizes them so you can focus on the application of interest.

Scott Pakin's Automatic Complaint-Letter Generator

http://www-csag.cs.uiuc.edu/individual/pakin/complaint

Make a few selections from drop-down menus and generate a hilarious complaint letter (never touched by human hands).

United States Internal Revenue Service

http://www.irs.gov

The IRS site is a great example of a Web site that utilizes Adobe Acrobat documents.

University of Michigan Documents Center—Government Resources on the Web

http://www.lib.umich.edu/libhome/Documents.center/govweb.html

A listing of government resources and Web sites, including a current list of congressional members' email addresses.

Newsletters and Publications

Computer Currents

http://www.currents.net

Computer Currents is a popular, free computer magazine. This site has news, reviews, and editorial comments on computers and the computer industry.

InfoWorld Electric

http://www.infoworld.com

IDG's online computer magazine. This site is a great resource for computer industry news.

Listz—The Mailing List Directory

http://www.liszt.com

Master index of Internet mailing lists. Find the lists that cover the topics that interest you.

Lockergnome

http://www.lockergnome.com/issues/

This daily electronic newsletter has reviewed thousands of computer programs and provides a searchable archive of past issues. (You'll have to know the name of the application, however, because reviews are not categorized.)

The Naked PC Newsletter

http://www.TheNakedPC.com

A free email newsletter on a wide variety of computer-related topics. It's like having a friendly computer consultant drop in on you every other week.

Neat Net Tricks

http://www.neatnettricks.com

Jack Teems's popular newsletter on Internet tips and tricks is delivered right to your email box.

PC Labs Software Reviews

http://www.zdnet.com/pcmag/pclabs/sof/index.html

This is the Ziff Davis (publisher of *PC Magazine, PC Week, PC/Computing*) review lab that covers hundreds of software products in every imaginable category.

PC Magazine Online—Readers' Choice Service and Reliability

http://www.zdnet.com/pcmag/special/reliability98/index.html

Annual review of service and reliability for computers, printers, and software.

PC World Top 400

http://www.pcworld.com/top400/0,1375,software,00.html

Access to PC World's latest published software reviews by category.

PCWeek Online

http://www.zdnet.com/pcweek/news/news.html

PCWeek magazine's online version, containing news, commentary, articles, and reviews.

Poor Richard's Web Site

http://www.poorrichard.com

Popular biweekly free newsletter on issues related to building and maintaining a Web site.

ZDNet

http://www.zdnet.com

The gateway site to a number of computer magazines' online Web sites (all published by Ziff Davis).

Searching the Web

Ask Jeeves

http://www.askjeeves.com

Ask Jeeves is a unique Internet search engine that lets you phrase your search query in plain English.

Bigfoot

http://www.bigfoot.com

Bigfoot is one of the major Internet address directory services. Bigfoot claims to include not only the most names, but also the most accurate list of names and addresses on the Internet.

Copernic Home Page

http://www.copernic.com

Copernic is a freeware Internet search application run on your local computer that enables you to consolidate search results.

Dogpile

http://www.dogpile.com

A meta search service, Dogpile enables you to search across multiple search engines at once.

Electronic Library

http://www.elibrary.com

Fee-based research databases.

Internet Search Engines

http://www.altavista.com
http://www.infoseek.com
http://www.hotbot.com
http://www.lycos.com
http://www.excite.com
http://www.webcrawler.com

The most popular search engines. Search engines find sites on the Internet and index their content, enabling you to search for sites by entering keywords and phrases.

Mamma

http://www.mamma.com

Mamma is a meta search service that enables you to search a number of Internet search engines at once.

The Mining Co.

http://www.miningco.com

An Internet directory search service divided into topics, with each topic the responsibility of a guide. Guides are people who maintain the site listings for that topic; they mediate any discussion boards and are available for questions via email.

The Mining Co. Guide to Distance Learning

http://distancelearn.miningco.com

On this site you'll find numerous articles and links to many courses offered online.

SearchKing

http://www.searchking.com

SearchKing claims to be the "next generation search engine" dedicated to having only "relevant" sites listed in their index. A unique feature enables you to search by area code to find companies and services on the Web that are local to a given location.

Sherlock—The Internet Consulting Detective

http://www.intermediacy.com/sherlock/

Sherlock offers information on how the various search services work and how you can search the Internet more effectively.

The Web Search Cheat Sheet

http://www.colosys.net/search

Find the search syntax for all the major search engines. Improve your searching ability by using the proper advanced syntax.

Yahoo!

http://www.yahoo.com

Yahoo! is an Internet directory search service (in contrast to a search engine). A directory service segregates Web sites into categories by topic.

Yahoo!'s Web Directories

http://dir.yahoo.com/Computers_and_Internet/Internet/World_Wide_Web/Information_and_Documentation/Web_Directories

Pointers to directories of Web sites other than Yahoo!

Software Utilities

Adobe

http://www.adobe.com

The free Adobe Acrobat Reader enables you to view PDF files, which are popular for distributing files for viewing over the Internet.

BCM Advanced Research, Inc.

http://www.bcmgvc.com

BCM Diagnostics is a shareware utility that enables you to run benchmarks and perform hardware stress testing on your system.

CheckIt 98

http://hotfiles.zdnet.com/cgi-bin/texis/swlib/hotfiles/info.html?fcode=000NTN

The ZDNet Software Library download page for CheckIt 98 has a solid collection of testing and troubleshooting utilities for Windows 98.

CyberMedia

`http://www.cybermedia.com/products/oilchange/`

Download CyberMedia's Oil Change program to automatically update your applications.

Dr. Hardware—PC Test and Benchmark

`http://ourworld.compuserve.com/homepages/pgsoft/`

Dr. Hardware is a shareware system analysis and reporting tool.

Free Quick View Plus Downloads

`http://www.inso.com/qvp/qvpdwnld.htm`

A limited version of Inso's Quick View is included for free in Microsoft Windows. Inso also sells a more full-featured version of the utility called Quick View Plus ($59). The Plus version enables you to do things you cannot do in the version bundled with Windows.

Microsoft Softlib

`ftp://ftp.microsoft.com/softlib/ then get softlib.exe and index.txt`

This text file contains a listing of the downloadable files on the Microsoft FTP server. It's a great way to avoid the sometimes less-than-helpful Windows Update and download the file you want directly.

Microsoft Windows PowerToys

`http://www.microsoft.com/windows95/downloads/contents/wutoys/w95pwrtoysset/default.asp?site=95`

Download the unsupported but very useful Windows 95 PowerToys from Microsoft.

Microsoft Windows Update

`http://windowsupdate.microsoft.com/default.htm`

Microsoft has automated the updating of Windows and key applications along with patches and service releases via the Web.

MMXTest

http://www.calsci.com/downloads/MMXtest.zip

MMXTest is utility that reports which family of processor you have and whether it supports MMX. It's free for the downloading.

Net Nanny Software, Ltd.

http://www.netnanny.com

A very useful tool for securing your PC and filtering the Internet content you'll allow to be displayed on your system; you can also control access to any application on your computer.

Ontrack Data International, Inc.

http://www.ontrack.com

Ontrack provides a number of products and utilities for hard disk data recovery.

PC Medic

http://hotfiles.zdnet.com/cgi-bin/texis/swlib/hotfiles/info.html?fcode=0000OP

The ZDNet Software Library download page for PC Medic. Network Associates' PC Medic is a diagnostic utility for Windows 95 systems.

Power Management Troubleshooter Tool

http://support.microsoft.com/support/kb/articles/Q185/9/49.asp

Download pmtshoot.exe, Microsoft's power management troubleshooter tool.

PRIME Consulting Group, Inc.—Software

http://www.primeconsulting.com/software/index.html

PRIME Consulting Group's indispensable series of Office add-ins: versions for Word 6, 95, 97, and 2000, in addition to versions for Excel 5, 95, 97, and 2000.

Software Design by Gregory Braun

http://www.execpc.com/~sbd/index.html

A number of useful Windows shareware utilities can be found here, including DLL Show for determining which running processes utilize various DLLs installed on your system.

Symantec—Norton Utilities

http://www.symantec.com/nu/fs_nu3-95.html

The Norton Utilities are the king of the hill for all-around Windows utilities. From problem diagnosis and repair to anti-virus protection, this is a great package.

Symantec Trialware

http://shop.symantec.com/trialware/

Here you can download trial versions of many of the Symantec products, such as Norton CrashGuard and Antivirus.

Tape-it by PGSoft, Inc.

http://www.pgsoft.com

Tape-it assigns your tape device a drive letter, and you can copy files to and from the tape just as you would a hard disk.

V Communications, Inc.

http://www.v-com.com

System Commander Deluxe can be used to run multiple boot configurations on the same hard disk partition.

Web Graphics on a Budget

http://mardiweb.com/web/

Step-by-step instructions for creating professional-quality graphics using JASC Paint Shop Pro.

Websnake

http://www.imarkmall.com/websnake.html

A leading software package for retrieving Web pages for offline browsing. A huge time saver if you frequent a number of Web sites regularly.

ZDNet Virtual Lab

`http://www.zdnet.com/vlabs/index.html`

ZDNet maintains an online laboratory that enables you to actually test components attached to your PC via your Web browser.

Support

alt.comp.virus FAQs

`http://webworlds.co.uk/dharley/`

A list of FAQs from the alt.comp.virus newsgroup.

Association of Personal Computer User Groups

`http://annarbor.apcug.org/`

The Association of Personal Computer User Groups (APCUG) is an international, platform-independent, volunteer-run non-profit body devoted to helping user groups to offer better services to their members.

Deja News—The Discussion Network

`http://www.dejanews.com`

On this site you can read, search, participate in, and subscribe to more than 80,000 discussion forums, including Usenet newsgroups.

Excel 97 Annoyances

`http://www.primeconsulting.com/annoyances/excelannoy.html`

Excel 97 Annoyances is a book that answers your questions about Excel's structure, capabilities, bad habits, and soul. This book, like its sibling on Word, provides the nitty gritty on all aspects of Excel and pays special attention to customizations.

FAQs for All Usenet Newsgroups

`http://www.faqs.org`

Contains lists of the questions most frequently asked Usenet newsgroups. Most FAQs include pointers to Web sites, books, mailing lists, and other helpful information for a given topic.

HelpTalk

http://www.helptalk.com

A free service providing personalized assistance in installing, using, and troubleshooting most Windows software and hardware.

Indiana University Support Center's Knowledge Base

http://kb.indiana.edu

Indiana University's free searchable database of more than 4,500 answers to questions about computing.

Microsoft FAQs

http://support.microsoft.com/support/default-faq.asp

Frequently asked questions put together by Microsoft Support Engineers.

Microsoft Knowledge Base by Email Service

http://support.microsoft.com/support/kb/articles/q162/3/87.asp

Microsoft has a program whereby you can have Knowledge Base articles emailed directly to you.

Microsoft Library—Computer Resources

http://library.microsoft.com/comp.htm

This site has general computer information, a listing of computer industry publications, a listing of standards-setting bodies, and other handy information.

Microsoft News

http://support.microsoft.com/support/news/default.asp

The latest company news from Microsoft.

Microsoft Office Developer Forum

http://www.microsoft.com/OfficeDev/

A resource site for those developing applications in Microsoft Office.

Microsoft Personal Computer Information

http://register.microsoft.com/regwiz/personalinfo.asp

Sign up with Microsoft and get notification via email of the latest articles added to Microsoft Knowledge.

Microsoft Product Support Services

http://www.microsoft.com/support

Use this main page to pick from a plethora of Microsoft support channels.

Microsoft Support

http://support.microsoft.com/support

Microsoft's Web-based Support Center. Search its extensive Knowledge Base online.

Microsoft TechNet

http://www.microsoft.com/technet

Microsoft TechNet is a resource that helps computer professionals navigate through the complex world of information technology using Microsoft products and technologies.

Microsoft's Home Page

http://www.microsoft.com

Main entry point for Microsoft's Web site.

MIT's Usenet FAQ archive

ftp://rtfm.mit.edu/pub/usenet-by-hierarchy/

Usenet FAQs broken down by category.

ModemHelp

http://www.modemhelp.com/support.html

Voluntary payment site for help with modem problems.

NSTL Online

http://www.nstl.com/html/nstl_y2k.html

The world's leading independent information technology testing organization. This page has links to the NSTL's Year 2000 testing tools and services.

The Online Support Center

http://www.onlinesupport.com

User-based resource for helping people with their computer and Internet-related problems.

Sound Card Information

comp.sys.ibm.pc.soundcard.advocacy
comp.sys.ibm.pc.soundcard.games
comp.sys.ibm.pc.soundcard.misc
comp.sys.ibm.pc.soundcard.music
comp.sys.ibm.pc.soundcard.tech

Newsgroups on the Internet with information on sound cards.

Word 97 Annoyances

http://www.primeconsulting.com/annoyances/wordannoy.html

Word 97 Annoyances is a book that takes you on a thorough tour of Word's mindset, features, habits, and quirks.

WUON—Using Bookmarks and Favorites Together

http://www.PRIMEConsulting.com/pdf/bookmarks.pdf

Article on how to keep Navigator Bookmarks in sync with Internet Explorer Favorites.

Yahoo!'s Beginner's Guides

http://dir.yahoo.com/Computers_and_Internet/Internet/World_Wide_Web/Information_and_Documentation/Beginner_s_Guides

Pointer to guides for Internet beginners on a variety of subjects.

Yahoo!'s Pointer to FAQs

http://dir.yahoo.com/Computers_and_Internet/Internet/World_Wide_Web/FAQs

A collection of links to Frequently Asked Question listings from a number of sources.

Virus, Bugs, and Security

AVP Virus Encyclopedia

http://www.avp.ch/avpve

A well-organized encyclopedia of more than 2,300 viruses.

Bug Net

http://www.bugnet.com

Stay up-to-date on the latest software bugs by checking Bug Net.

Computer Virus Myths

http://www.kumite.com/myths

Rob Rosenberger's site is an objective reality check in the midst of all the hoopla and media hype surrounding viruses.

Data Fellows

http://www.datafellows.com/vir-info/

The Data Fellows site (home of F-Prot and F-Secure antivirus software products) claims to have been the very first antivirus site on the Web.

IBM Antivirus Online

http://www.av.ibm.com/current/FrontPage/

Big Blue's virus information site.

McAfee Online

http://www.mcafee.com/

Get free, fully functional evaluation copies of McAfee's award-winning security, antivirus, and utility software.

NCSA Virus Lab

http://www.ncsa.com/services/consortia/anti-virus/lab.shtml

A multitude of links, news, alerts, surveys, information about hoaxes, virus descriptions, a wild list, and more.

Release 1.0—Privacy Protection

http://www.edventure.com/release1/0498.html

Esther Dyson's great article on privacy and the Internet.

Symantec Antivirus Research Center

http://www.symantec.com/avcenter/index.html

Information on the latest crop of viruses waiting to infect the unwary.

ThunderBYTE

`http://www.thunderbyte.com/`

Norman ThunderByte Virus Control for DOS, Windows 3.x, Windows 95, and Windows NT.

VIRUS-L/comp.virus Frequently Asked Questions (FAQ)

`http://www.cis.ohio-state.edu/hypertext/faq/usenet/computer-virus/faq/faq.html`

FAQs compiled by many of the Virus-L mailing list contributors and its Usenet news group.

Yahoo!'s Viruses Directory

`http://www.yahoo.com/Computers_and_Internet/Security_and_Encryption/Viruses/`

An excellent set of informative links to antivirus and related companies, virus specifics, legends, directories, and newsgroups.

Appendix C

Further Readings

HERE YOU'LL FIND a comprehensive listing of books that are related to the five parts of this book. You can use this list to locate books that may take you farther down a road less-traveled than this one.

Part I—Acquiring Your New PC

From dealing with sales people to developing effective habits to getting the best from a color printer, these books will help you prepare for your crusade to acquire the ideal new PC.

- Covey, Stephen R. *The Seven Habits of Highly Effective People: Restoring the Character Ethic.* G K Hall & Co., 1997. ISBN: 0783881150. www.amazon.com/exec/obidos/ASIN/0783881150/
- Gelernter, David Hillel. *Machine Beauty: Elegance and the Heart of Technology.* Basic Books, 1998. ISBN: 0465045162. www.amazon.com/exec/obidos/ASIN/0465045162/
- Johnson, Steven A. *Interface Culture: How New Technology Transforms the Way We Create and Communicate.* Harper San Francisco, 1997. ISBN: 0062514822. www.amazon.com/exec/obidos/ASIN/0062514822/
- Macaulay, David. *The New Way Things Work.* Houghton Mifflin Co., 1998. ISBN: 0395938473. www.amazon.com/exec/obidos/ASIN/0395938473/

- Norman, Donald A. *The Invisible Computer: Why Good Products Can Fail, the Personal Computer Is So Complex, and Information Appliances Are the Solution.* MIT Press, 1998. ISBN: 0262140659. www.amazon.com/exec/obidos/ASIN/0262140659/
- Stone, M. David. *The Underground Guide to Color Printers: Slightly Askew Advice on Getting the Best from Any Color Printer.* Addison-Wesley, 1996. ISBN: 0201483785. www.amazon.com/exec/obidos/ASIN/0201483785/
- White, Ron. *How Computers Work.* Que, 1998. ISBN: 078971728X. www.amazon.com/exec/obidos/ASIN/078971728X/

Part II—Making the PC Yours

These books wrestle Windows 95 and Windows 98 to the mat. They range from desktop references to detailed exposé.

- Bott, Ed, and Ron Person. *Special Edition Using Windows 98.* Que, 1998. ISBN: 0789714884. www.amazon.com/exec/obidos/ASIN/0789714884/
- Karp, David A. *Windows 98 Annoyances.* O'Reilly & Associates, 1998. ISBN: 1565924177. www.amazon.com/exec/obidos/ASIN/1565924177/
- Leonhard, Woody, and Barry Simon. *The Mother of All Windows 98 Books.* Addison-Wesley, 1998. ISBN: 0201433125. www.amazon.com/exec/obidos/ASIN/0201433125/
- *Microsoft Windows 95 Resource Kit: The Technical Guide to Planning for, Installing, Configuring, and Supporting Windows 95 in Your Organization.* Microsoft Press, 1995. ISBN: 1556156782. www.amazon.com/exec/obidos/ASIN/1556156782/
- *Microsoft Windows 98 Resource Kit.* Microsoft Press, 1998. ISBN: 1572316446. www.amazon.com/exec/obidos/ASIN/1572316446/
- O'Reilly, Tim, and Troy Mott. *Windows 95 in a Nutshell: A Desktop Quick Reference.* O'Reilly & Associates, 1998. ISBN: 1565923162. www.amazon.com/exec/obidos/ISBN%3D1565923162/

Part III—Avoiding Problems

Security issues are the focus in this section.

- Alexander, Michael. *The Underground Guide to Computer Security: Slightly Askew Advice on Protecting Your PC and What's on It.* Addison-Wesley, 1995. ISBN: 020148918X. www.amazon.com/exec/obidos/ASIN/020148918X/
- Cobb, Stephen. *The NCSA Guide to PC and LAN Security.* McGraw Hill Text, 1996. ISBN: 0079121683. www.amazon.com/exec/obidos/ASIN/0079121683/

Part IV—Choosing More Software

There's always more to learn and discover about software titles, design, and just plain having fun with it.

- Gralla, Preston. *Online Kids: A Young Surfer's Guide to Cyberspace.* John Wiley & Sons, 1996. ISBN: 0471135453. www.amazon.com/exec/obidos/ISBN%3D0471135453/
- Keizer, Gregg. *The Family PC Guide to Homework.* Hyperion, 1996. ISBN: 0786882069. www.amazon.com/exec/obidos/ISBN%3D0786882069/
- Leonhard, Woody, Lee Hudspeth, and T.J. Lee. *Office 97 Annoyances.* O'Reilly & Associates, 1997. ISBN: 1565923103. www.amazon.com/exec/obidos/ASIN/1565923103/
- Mead, Samuel. *The Family PC Guide to Cool PC Projects.* Hyperion, 1996. ISBN: 0786882077. www.amazon.com/exec/obidos/ISBN%3D0786882077/
- Tufte, Edward R. *The Visual Display of Quantitative Information.* Graphics Press, 1992. ISBN: 096139210X. www.amazon.com/exec/obidos/ASIN/096139210X/
- *The Windows Interface Guidelines for Software Design: An Application Design Guide.* Microsoft Press, 1995. ISBN: 1556156790. www.amazon.com/exec/obidos/ISBN%3D1556156790/

Part V—Using the Internet

If you want to delve deeply into the cyberjungle, any of these books can serve as your tour guide.

- Gralla, Preston, and Mina Reimer (Illustrator). *How the Internet Works: Special Edition.* Ziff Davis Press, 1997. ISBN: 1562765523. www.amazon.com/exec/obidos/ASIN/1562765523/
- Kent, Peter. *Poor Richard's Web Site: Geek-Free, Commonsense Advice on Building a Low-Cost Web Site.* Top Floor, 1998. ISBN: 0966103289. www.amazon.com/exec/obidos/ASIN/0966103289/
- Krol, Ed. *The Whole Internet User's Guide & Catalog.* 2d ed. O'Reilly & Associates, 1994. ISBN: 1565920635. www.amazon.com/exec/obidos/ASIN/1565920635/
- Shipley, Chris, Matt Fish, and Mina Reimer (Illustrator). *How the World Wide Web Works.* Ziff Davis Press, 1996. ISBN: 1562763695. www.amazon.com/exec/obidos/ASIN/1562763695/

Part VI—Recovering from Disaster

- Poor, Alfred E. *The Underground Guide to Troubleshooting PC Hardware: Slightly Askew Advice on Maintaining, Repairing, and Upgrading Your PC.* Addison-Wesley, 1996. ISBN: 020148997X. www.amazon.com/exec/obidos/ASIN/020148997X/

Appendix D

Important Documents

HERE YOU'LL FIND references to company white papers, documents, specifications and standards, all arranged categorically from "Application Help" to "World Wide Web."

Application Help

Description	Name	URL/Source
Backup software	Top Ten Backup Tools	www2.pcworld.com/news/daily/data/0598/980508160030.html
Email	Move from Exchange to Outlook with Ease	www.zdnet.com/products/content/pccg/1101/259422.html
Equation editor	Equation Editor and the Equation Field: Go Figure	www.primeconsulting.com/pdf/equation.pdf
Graphics	Build an Office Diagram That's Smart and Secure	http://205.181.113.83:31019/pccomp/oc/projects/1097p4/1097p4.html
Spreadsheets	Build the Perfect Time Tracker	http://205.181.113.83:31019/pccomp/oc/projects/1097covr/1097covr.html
Spreadsheets	Master Excel Spreadsheets	www.zdnet.com/products/content/pccg/1101/259421.html

continues

Application Help (CONTINUED)

Description	Name	URL/Source
Spreadsheets	Master Your Workday with PivotTables	http://205.181.113.83:31019/pccomp/oc/projects/1097p1/1097p1.html
Spreadsheets	SuperAutoEntry in Excel	http://search.zdnet.com/cgi-bin/texis/zdhelp/zdhelp/single.html?Ueid=909805
Various	Help! The Best Tips! Tricks!	www.zdnet.com/pccomp/features/excl1297/help/help.html
Various	Microsoft's Top 25 Office 97 Answers	www.zdnet.com/zdhelp/howto_help/office25/office25_01.html
Word processing	Make Word's Shortcut Menus Do What You Want	http://205.181.113.83:31019/pccomp/oc/projects/1097p2/1097p2.html
Word sequence fields	When Numbering in Word Gets Tough, the Tough Get SEQuenced	www.primeconsulting.com/pdf/seqfield.pdf
Year 2000	Tools for Testing Off-the-Shelf Apps	www.zdnet.com/pcmag/special/y2k/features/main/docs/348621.htm

Browsers

Description	Name	URL/Source
Microsoft Internet Explorer	Press Information	www.microsoft.com/windows/ie/press/
Netscape Communicator (Navigator)	FAQs	www.ufaq.org
Netscape Communicator (Navigator)	Press Information	http://home.netscape.com/company

Computers

Description	Name	URL/Source
Consulting	Essential Questions to Ask Your Computer Consulting Company	www.primeconsulting.com/faqs/faq2800.html
Software review	Chart Your Options	www4.zdnet.com/pccomp/features/fea0797/office/chart.html
Software review	Control Your Contacts	www4.zdnet.com/pccomp/features/fea0797/office/contact.html
Software review	Put Your Business on the Web	www4.zdnet.com/pccomp/features/fea0797/office/webpub.html
Software review	Stay on Schedule	www4.zdnet.com/pccomp/features/fea0797/office/sched.html
Technical jargon and acronyms	NetLingo	www.netlingo.com/
Technical jargon and acronyms	PC Webopaedia	http://webopedia.internet.com
Tips and tricks	Undocumented PC Secrets	www.zdnet.com/pccomp/features/excl0498/pcsecrets/

Hardware

Description	Name	URL/Source
CD-R information	The Rewritable Revolution	www.zdnet.com/products/stories/reviews/0,4161,318186,00.html
Hard drives	Hard Drive Configuration Simplified (Symantec Knowledge Base)	http://service1.symantec.com/SUPPORT/nunt.nsf/docid/1997125142832
IDE	IDE (Integrated Drive Electronics)	www.whatis.com/ide.htm

continues

Hardware (CONTINUED)

Description	Name	URL/Source
Removable storage	Big Capacity Sizzling Speed	www.zdnet.com/pcmag/features/storage/intro.html
SCSI	SCSI (Small Computer System Interface)	www.whatis.com/scsi.htm
UPS	Uninterruptible Power Source (UPS) FAQ	www.lib.ox.ac.uk/internet/news/faq/archive/ups-faq.html

World Wide Web

Description	Name	URL/Source
Digital Subscriber	DSL and xDSL Line	www.whatis.com/dsl.htm
File transfer	Save Files to and from the Internet Instantly	http://205.181.113.83:31019/pccomp/oc/projects/1097p3/1097p3.html
Internet history	Request for Comments	www.faqs.org/rfcs/
Internet tips and tricks	Amazing Free Stuff	www.zdnet.com/pccomp/features/excl0898/freestuff/welcome.html
Internet tips and tricks	Find Anything Fast	www.zdnet.com/pccomp/features/excl1198/netsecrets/find-intro.html
Internet tips and tricks	How to Get Ahead	www.zdnet.com/pccomp/features/excl1198/netsecrets/howto-intro.html
Internet tips and tricks	Steals and Deals	www.zdnet.com/pccomp/features/excl1198/netsecrets/steals-intro.html
Internet tips and tricks	Undocumented Internet Secrets	www.zdnet.com/pccomp/features/excl1197/undo/toc.html
Internet tips and tricks	Work the Web	www.zdnet.com/pccomp/features/excl1198/netsecrets/work-intro.html
Intranet	Build an Intranet in an Hour	www.zdnet.com/pccomp/oc/projects/0198covr/0198covr.html

Description	Name	URL/Source
Language translation	AltaVista Translation with SYSTRAN	http://babelfish.altavista.digital.com/cgi-bin/translate?
Networking	Personal Wide-Area Nets on the Web	www.primeconsulting.com/pdf/personalnets.pdf
Peer to peer	Peering Across the Internet	www.primeconsulting.com/pdf/peering.pdf
Search engine technology	Search Engine Watch: News, Tips, and More About Search Engines	www.searchenginewatch.com/facts/others.html
Site development	Put Your Business on the Web in 24 Hours or Less!	www4.zdnet.com/pccomp/features/fea0697/special/welcome.html

Index

Symbols

A

B

C

E

F

G-H

J-L

M

N

O

P

Q-R

S

T

V

W

X-Z